What Others Say

"I really must compliment you on an outstanding work. As I probably mentioned when we were together, I am not intuitively drawn to a lot of counseling and inner healing stuff that I have seen. Frankly, I don't like most of it.

Without a doubt yours is the best, and I could really think of nothing to add to improve it. If you knew how opinionated I am, the fact that I have nothing to say would really give you a frame of reference for how great I think this work is!

As a local church pastor who confesses to 'unenthusiasm' toward trendy, pop-culture Christian counseling methods that seem to dominate much of the evangelical Church, I am happy to have found your ministry."
Dr. Stephen R. Crosby, Pastor, Author, Professor, Wasilla, Alaska.

"Since I came to see you, my life has changed drastically. I feel like I was blind before that time and that God has opened up my eyes and now I can see. I lived the first 20 years of my walk with the Lord blaming everyone else for my unhappiness . . . Anyway, things are good here with the Rosenthals. Ron and I are able to work through things now and he continues to amaze me with his new ability to forgive and reconcile. WOW!"
Wisti Rosenthal, Emmett, Idaho.

"I asked, 'Why, Lord?' An answer came to my heart. 'When you feel rejected by others, you reject yourself. When you fail to accept and love yourself, in no time the bad fruit begins to take over.'

This is what I had been learning in Ed's teaching and now I could see it in myself. I quickly reread the relevant chapters of the book again. It all made such sense. For how many years had I been turning the slightest sense of rejection into rejection of myself? Oh so long! It had become a natural response. I certainly didn't need to think it through - the path down that track was well worn by 50 years of constant use. No matter how much I had filled my mind with the statements of truth about who I was in Christ, there was another louder message from my very own heart."
Marilyn Rowsome, Missionary to Papua New Guinea.

"I had been living my life actually believing when something b~~
when I sinned God disappeared and I was on my own . . . O^
glad He was there! He never leaves His children, and h~
before I knew He was. He showed me He was ther^
. . . I wanted you to rejoice with me and know hov
book."
C.C., Moscow, Idaho.

(See Appendix A for additional testim   .es)

I Will Give You Rest

How You Can Experience
The Peace Jesus Promised

Edward Kurath
Foreword by John L. Sandford

I Will Give You Rest
How You Can Experience The Peace Jesus Promised

Copyright © 2003 by Edward Kurath
Published by: Divinely Designed
P.O. Box 999   Post Falls, ID 83877
www. DivinelyDesigned.com

ISBN 0-9764551-0-2

Printed in the United States of America

Copyright Permission:

Foreword

by John L. Sandford,
Co-founder, Elijah House, Inc.

Ed Kurath has composed a most helpful workbook for Christian prayer therapists, for those receiving their ministry, and in fact for every Christian in their walk with the Lord. Clear concise definitions help to clear away possible confusions. Copious biblical quotes and references ground the entire field of inner healing in the biblical base in which it was birthed and to which it belongs, demolishing the confusions of some who may still have tried to maintain that this ministry is unbiblical. The format enables easy comprehension of sometimes-complex material, and the many diagrams add clarity - "one picture is worth a thousand words."

Ed's book is unique among the many I have recommended in that he includes many quotes and footnotes from theological and professional counseling sources. This gives the book a wider range and perspective than most.

Ed speaks of the "Treasure Inside," and of our need to love and treasure our hidden treasure. This is especially valuable because it introduces a positive note of transformation into what God intended us to be all along. So often, inner healing books focus so much upon discovering the hidden evil practices of our fallen nature (see Colossians 3:9-10) that counselors, following that lead, have sometimes tended to leave their clients feeling squashed and worthless. Ed's emphasis lifts both counselors and clients into the resurrection side of healing, and thus into hope that abides.

Thus, Ed lifts the ministry of prayer counseling beyond mere healing, or restoration to functionality, into God's eternal purposes of redeeming and transforming His children's character into the nature of Jesus, which is what the word "salvation" truly means. Many in the counseling field see their task as healing, i.e. fixing broken parts so they work. Ed places prayer ministry in its true context, the work of our Lord Jesus Christ not only to restore us but to use every incident of our lives to write into our character that blessed nature - His - that alone equips us for eternity.

The book is intended to be a practical guide for all Christians who are serious about their walk with the Lord, for those who want to be more successful in obeying Him than they have hitherto been able. Those who are willing to do the hard work required to walk in the new way will discover great rewards. The rewards will come from the Lord as you become the person He has always wanted you to be.

At the same time the book is not intended only for those who have serious emotional struggles, but rather for all of God's children. We all fall short, and the Lord wants us to be more successful.

To counselors I would also say, this book should become a most valued and active resource in the libraries of all those whom the Lord calls to minister to the depths of others' hearts and lives. I recommend you make it a daily workbook, especially urging clients to read it and put it to work as they proceed in prayer therapy, and beyond, in their daily lives.

Table of Contents

Section II: Fullness of Life

Section III: Appendices

Acknowledgments

This book is actually a team project. The foundation from which it grew is multifaceted. There is a saying that the most important thing a person brings to their counseling is themselves. Therefore, under the guiding hand of the Lord, all that has happened in my life, and all the people with whom I have had relationship, have contributed to my ministry and eventually to what I have written.

More directly, there were those who counseled me when I was in great need, and those who taught me about Inner Healing. All those I counseled deepened my understanding of God's ways. What I have written about would be simply a theory without their encounters with the Lord that changed their lives.

Then there has been my wife Kay, who is God's gift to me. But that is another whole story. And there has always been the Lord, who clearly has been in charge of my life and this project, from the very beginning.

Specifically, I would like to thank those who worked directly on the book. Several of them contributed a significant amount of their time and talents, and the final product is significantly improved because of their efforts: Charlie and Debra Finck, Ken and Donna Gift, Ron and Wisti Rosenthal, Marilyn Rowsome, Phyllis Brown, Darlene DeYoung, Mary Numme, Sanna Urvas, John Sandford, Mark Sandford, my wife Kay, and numerous clients who gave me their reaction to the earlier draft.

My understanding of the scriptural basis to the way to God's rest was made possible by my professors at Denver Seminary and by the writings of Rudolf Bultmann.[1]

Hopefully, what I have to say will be anointed by the Spirit of the Lord to richly bless you.

---

[1] **See Endnote A-1** for more on the contribution of Rudolf Bultmann

Introduction

This book is intended for all Christians who fall short of the glory of God - which is all of us!

But God doesn't want us stuck in that state. He wants to set us free, now, <u>in this life</u>. He sent Jesus to provide the way.

This is meant to be a practical book. In it I give detailed instructions as to <u>how</u> you can appropriate into your life what Jesus did for you. I then encourage you to act on what you learn, because the knowledge you gain will only be valuable to you if it changes your life.

First Look For The Big Picture

I have written the book on three levels. First, there is the main text, which is what I really want you to understand. Then there are footnotes with additional information to help authenticate what I have just said. Finally, there are endnotes which provide still further details. I would suggest that the first time you read the book that you ignore the Footnotes, the Endnotes, and the Appendices. In this way you will be most likely to see the big picture.

Some of what I say may be challenging and new to you. Allow yourself time to digest it.

Words

Words can be misleading. I have included a glossary so that you can more clearly understand what I am saying. In addition, there are some commonly used English words that are potentially loaded with misinformation for people in our culture.

For instance, *Though He was a Son, yet he learned obedience by the things which He suffered* (Hebrews 5:8). In our culture we automatically tend to jump to the conclusion that this is cognitive, intellectual learning. Yet the Greek text makes it clear this was experiential "learning." In order to avoid such misperceptions, I avoid (as much as possible) using English words that can easily lead

my reader to misunderstand what I am saying. Some of these words
I avoid using are "mind," "decide," "know," "learn," and "think."

Subjects I Have Omitted

This book is intended for every Christian, to provide a firm biblical
foundation for living their Christian life. Because this book is
intended for such a general audience, I have not attempted to
address every specific symptom or condition that exists. Examples
of what I have not addressed are things like generational sin,
Dissociative Identity Disorder, Satanic Ritual Abuse, in-utero
wounding, and spiritual strongholds.

Psychological Labels

I avoid the secular labels that psychology has used to describe
emotional symptoms. They use labels such as Borderline
Personality Disorder, Bipolar Disorder, and Obsessive-Compulsive
Disorder. I have avoided such labels because I have not found these
classifications of symptoms to be particularly useful in finding the
root cause of a problem and bringing about healing.

Others Have Been Healed

If your question is, "Does this really work?" the proof is changed
lives. In order to encourage you, I have included experiences and
testimonies of actual people in Appendix A.

Chapter 1

"I Will Give You Rest"
But How?

There is hope. There was a time when my life was falling apart, and I was in great emotional pain. Though I was a Christian, it didn't seem that my faith was effectual in helping me. In fact, the more seriously I sought to follow Jesus, the greater the strife and discord in my life. There seemed to be no answer. Everything I did seemed to make the situation worse. I was at my wits end.

Unexpectedly, through a very strange turn of events, the answers began to come. I met a Christian psychiatrist who knew about my pain and was confident that he could help me.

He was right! He was using prayer as the healing agent, and was following the path laid down by John and Paula Sandford of Elijah House. As the weeks went by, as we prayed in specific ways, relief began to come. God was healing me, step by step, bringing more and more peace.

It was a miracle!

That all began over twenty years ago. During those years I have been drawn to the Lord's ways like a fly is drawn to honey. The more He healed my heart, the better life became. God has radically changed my life. I have a degree of peace and fulfillment that I previously couldn't even imagine, and I know it is a gift from Jesus.

It is my prayer that you be blessed in a similar way. I know this is what the Lord wants for you, too. Jesus died to provide the way for you to experience the peace He promised, in this life. On my own journey I have discovered that what Jesus provided for the children of God is much more potent than I had previously known and believed. The Lord knew that I would initially underestimate what Jesus did for me, as the Apostle Paul wrote,

What eye has never seen, nor ear heard,
What never entered the mind of man,
God has prepared for those who love him.[2]

His provision is indeed much more magnificent than we can imagine.

Two Miraculous Gifts

Jesus did provide a way for us to get to heaven. Through His sacrifice on the cross He made it possible for us to actually become God's children. He gave us eternal life, and we will spend eternity with Him in heaven. This was a miracle.

He also provided for us in this life. This provision is also a miracle. He did not demand a high level of obedience from us and then leave it up to us to carry this load.

"Come to Me, all you who labor and are heavy laden, and I will
give you rest. Take My yoke upon you and learn from Me, for I
am gentle and lowly in heart, and you will find rest for your
souls. For My yoke is easy, and My burden is light" [3]

And yet it has tended to be our experience that our faith is a hard yoke and a heavy burden. Many of us have tried so very hard to live up to what God expects of us.

We have tried to love God.
We have tried to love other people.
We have tried to lay down our lives for the Gospel.
We have tried to keep our thoughts and actions pure.

---

[2] **1 Corinthians 2:9**, Schonfield.

[3] **Matthew 11:28-30.**

But instead of joy and success, we find misery, pain, failure, and condemnation. Our Christian life is not what we know it should be. The harder we try, the more we fail. We become exhausted and discouraged. We agree with Paul when he says:

> *For what I am doing, I do not understand. For what I will to do, that I do not practice; but what I hate, that I do.*
> *O wretched man that I am! Who will deliver me from this body of death?* [4]

I Tried And Failed

When I was a new Christian, I wanted to please God and draw closer to Him. I came up with a simple plan. I decided that every 15 minutes I would simply turn my thoughts towards Him, and say, "Hello God." At work there was a big clock on the wall right in front of me. That was the ideal setup for me to fulfill my plan.

Then I would get busy. I would look up at the clock and realize it had been two hours since I had last prayed. I would feel like a failure and renew my determination. Then I would fail again, and again, and again. I wasn't offering to go to China as a missionary, or to walk on a bed of hot coals. What I was intending to do was so simple, and yet I couldn't do that tiny little thing. O wretched man that I was!

We All Struggle

Not only do we ourselves try and fail, when we look around us it is hard to find other Christians who are not struggling similarly. We may feel like hypocrites, and unbelievers are quick to give us this label.

---

[4] **Romans 7:15 and 7:24 .**

This is hardly the picture presented in the Gospel (the "good news"). What is wrong?

The answer is so strange to our natural thinking that the solution to our struggle never crosses our mind. As I had discovered, truly, it has not entered into the mind of man what God has prepared for us.

We can't figure it out.

God has to reveal it to us.

He has revealed the answer in the Bible, but our understanding has been blocked. We have looked at the Word, but have not seen the solution revealed therein. Jesus said of Himself:

> *"The Spirit of the Lord is upon me, because he hath anointed me to preach the gospel to the poor; he hath sent me to heal the broken-hearted, to preach deliverance to the captives, and recovering of sight to the blind, to set at liberty them that are bruised"* [5]

You may be familiar with this promise, but how can it become a reality in your life?[6]

How?

The provision through Jesus exists, but you need <u>detailed instructions</u> as to <u>how</u> to lay hold of those promises.

Suppose I want to learn to play golf. An expert tells me, "You hit this little white ball with this club until it goes into that hole over there." This is true information, but it isn't enough. I need more detailed instructions

Those detailed instructions that you need are what I am going to give you in the following chapters.

Above all, apply the truth. Jesus' provision can redeem your life, but you need to act if you are to appropriate what He has provided.

---

[5] Luke 4:18, KJV.

[6] See **Endnote #1-1** for more on the fact that Jesus provided for this life also.

You will remember that you did not become a child of God until you professed His lordship. To become a child of God, you first needed to believe, but then you had to act by speaking:

That if you confess with your mouth the Lord Jesus and believe in your heart that God has raised Him from the dead, you will be saved. For with the heart one believes to righteousness, and with the mouth confession is made to salvation (Romans 10:9-10).

You need to do the same thing regarding Jesus' provision <u>in this life</u>. To be healed, you first need to <u>believe</u> (which is only possible if you understand His provision), but then you need to <u>act</u> by speaking (pray). Then you will begin to experience this second miracle in your life.

We Are All In The Same Boat

This is not a book on counseling. It is not a book written only to the sick few who are in dire need. It is intended for every Christian, because we all struggle and fall short of what we know God wants for us. Jesus did not come to save just a few. He came for all who would accept Him.

Let's Turn On The Lights!

Have you ever tried to find your glasses in the dark? Or have you ever tried to find the light switch in a strange dark room? They are present, but you just cannot see them. Because you cannot see them (your glasses, or the light switch), you cannot make use of them. However, if you can turn on a light, you can easily see them. So let's start turning on some lights!

Come with me as I share with you the great gift the Lord has given to those who love Him.

Chapter 2

Why You Are Stuck
God's Laws At Work

For what I am doing, I do not understand. For what I will to do, that I do not practice; but what I hate, that I do (Romans 7:15).

These words haunt all of us. This is the common experience of all those who are trying to please the Lord, who want to walk in His ways.

God knows that you continually fail, and He wants it to be different. He wants so much to set you free from this bondage that He sent Jesus to make it possible.

There is a clear and profound reason why we are all stuck doing what we don't want to do, and I will now go on to explain why.

The Reality God Created

When God created the universe, He created it to operate in an orderly way in accordance with unchangeable laws. There are three aspects, or realms, to the reality we experience:

1. **The physical**
2. **The spiritual**
3. **The psychological**[7]

---

[7] Some would call this the realm of the "soul." However, I have avoided using the word "soul" because it is loaded with meaning to many Christians. It is usually perceived as referring to something negative or sinful. But in the Bible "soul" has many meanings, some referring to something sinful, but often not. What I am referring to here is not "bad," but rather is simply an aspect of life which is based upon our own strengths and abilities and natural tendencies. As with the physical world, in and of itself the psychological realm carries no moral significance. It just exists.

The Physical Realm

We can all see the orderliness of the physical realm. The physical laws, such as those of physics, chemistry, and mathematics, are unchangeable. We may not fully understand them, and we may misapply them, but they still operate. Since the New York Trade Center Towers fell in the terrorist attack, there are studies going on to understand what was wrong with their design that allowed them to fall. These studies are being done in order to see if we can learn something that will prevent such collapses in buildings of the future. We can learn how to prevent it because the laws of physics are constant. There are no exceptions. Nobody thinks the Towers fell because something went wrong with the laws of physics.

If I were to go onto the roof of my house, convinced that I can fly, flap my arms really hard and step off the roof, I would make a discovery. I would then discover myself lying on the ground with a broken leg. It wouldn't matter whether I knew about the law of gravity or not. It wouldn't matter if I understood it, or whether I agreed with it, or whether I believed in it. It wouldn't matter how much faith I had that gravity didn't apply to me. My broken leg wouldn't mean God was angry with me. I didn't break God's law, all I did was demonstrate it. The law of gravity is constant. There are no exceptions.

The Spiritual Realm

The spiritual realm (another aspect of reality) is just as orderly as is the physical realm, and it always operates according to unchangeable laws and principles. God told us about these laws in the Bible. His commandments are simply a description of how the spiritual realm operates. When He said not to lie, He was saying, "Please don't lie; because if you do, something bad will happen to you." It is the same as God saying, "Please don't step off the roof, because something bad will happen if you do." In the physical realm, nobody ever defied the law of gravity. The spiritual realm is just as sure, and so nobody ever gets away with anything. There is always a consequence.   The law of God always operates.[8] Disobeying God's warning is what we call sin.   When we sin, we will <u>always</u> reap harmful consequences. The consequences are often less immediate and less easy to connect to our specific misdeed than when we are reaping from physical laws, but they are just as sure.

The Psychological Realm

The third aspect of reality is the psychological realm.   The psychological realm operates in accordance with our own powers and abilities. Habit patterns, our intellect, and our own willpower are aspects of the psychological realm.   Our willpower has been given to us as a tool to manage this psychological realm, and it has authority there. If I have a habit of brushing my teeth without flossing, and I decide

> **Disobeying God's warning is what we call "sin."**

to start flossing, I can generally succeed in doing so. I may forget from time to time, but eventually the new habit pattern will be established. I experience victory.

We Have Made A Huge Mistake

But we have made a huge mistake, because we have believed that our willpower has authority in the spiritual realm.   However, our willpower <u>only</u> has authority in the psychological realm. We cannot overcome or defy the physical laws or spiritual laws with our willpower.

Our willpower is impotent in defying the laws of the physical realm, and it was never given to us for this purpose. We cannot fly by flapping our arms. We cannot lift a 500 pound weight. We discover that no matter how much we want to lift it, we can't. We can will it, but we cannot perform it.

---

[8] What I am referring to as "God's laws" are the true ways that God set up the spiritual realm to operate. Man's additions do not have the same power. We may or may not accurately understand God's laws; but since they are true, they operate whether or not we know them or understand them.

Our willpower is equally impotent in the spiritual realm, and it was never given to us for this purpose. We discover this when we try to do a spiritually impossible task, like obeying the laws of God. We discover that no matter how hard we want to do the good that we ought to, we cannot. We can "will" it, but we cannot perform it. *O wretched man that I am* (Romans 7:24). Our failure to do the good that we want to do is not due to a lack of willpower, it is due to our misunderstanding about reality.

> **When we try to use our willpower to control the physical or spiritual realms, we fail.**

We are under the illusion that we ought to be able to "will" it and thus do it.

To imagine the relative power of our willpower and the operation of God's laws (the spiritual realm), picture an ant standing on a highway. A huge truck is coming his way at full speed, and the ant thinks he can stop the truck by standing up and blocking its movement with his body.

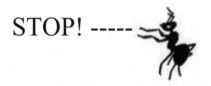

The ant's degree of failure is at the same level as our failure to stop the operation of God's laws with our own willpower! Yet we have been under the delusion that we can do so. And much worse, we think that God has expected us to be able to do so!

Unfortunately, we have often been led into striving by teachings that imply that we are supposed to be able to live up to the higher standards, as delineated in the Sermon on the Mount in Matthew, Chapter 5. However, this is not what Jesus is telling us to do. Rather, He is telling

> **Jesus did <u>not</u> say that you should "act" like Him, but that you should "be" like Him.**

us that we cannot possibly do it with our own willpower.

> *"For I say to you, that unless your righteousness exceeds the righteousness of the scribes and Pharisees, you will by no means enter the kingdom of heaven"* (Matthew 5:20).

What was the righteousness of the scribes and Pharisees? It was their willpower! And we need a righteousness that exceeds willpower. Jesus goes on to say that the only way we can truly keep the laws of God is to be changed into His image:

> *"Therefore you shall **be** perfect, just as your Father in heaven is perfect"* (Matthew 5:48 I added the bold).

Jesus did <u>not</u> say, "You shall <u>behave</u> perfectly," but rather He said, "You shall be perfect" (be like Me). We will have a new existence, a new nature. We will <u>be</u> like Him! "Being" like Jesus leads to, and results in, "behavior" like Jesus.[9]

The Illusion Of Our Willpower

One of the great tragedies in our Western culture is the elevation of our willpower and our intellect to the throne of our life. We think that the only things we can trust are these two faculties. The heart, and anything that we cannot consciously understand or control (such as our emotions) are seen as untrustworthy, or even perhaps as bad.

---

[9]   **See Endnote #2-1** for more on Matthew, Chapter 5.

We are stuck in this delusion. Our trust is so firmly entrenched in our willpower and intellect that whenever we are in need, without thinking we automatically rely on our willpower and intellect.

The bumper sticker that says "Just Say No" is a perfect example of this. If people who were hooked on drugs could "Just Say No," many would. Many try - and fail, over and over again. Their failure is the result of "trying hard" to quit - making a decision with their intellect and relying on their willpower to bring it to pass. They are <u>doomed to failure</u> because of

> **Our trust is so firmly entrenched in our willpower and intellect that whenever we are in need, without thinking we automatically grab those "tools."**

what we have just seen about God's laws. This misunderstanding is a big problem, and it is rampant in the Church.[10] The Bible makes very powerful statements regarding the illusion of our will.[11] It is a universal flaw in mankind to think we can manage our own life in our own strength. It is so automatic, insidious, and covert that we don't even realize what we are doing.[12]

We may now be tempted to say, "What's the use? If I can't stop the operation of God's laws which are impelling me to do what I

---

[10] In <u>The Bondage of the Will</u>, Martin Luther makes the point that our willpower has no authority in the spiritual realm. He says, "That is to say, man should realize that in regard to his money and possessions he has a right to use them, to do or to leave undone, according to his own 'free-will' - though that very 'free-will' is overruled by the free-will of God alone, according to His own pleasure. However, with regard to God and in all that bears on salvation or damnation, he has no 'free-will,' but is a captive, prisoner and bondslave, either to the will of God, or to the will of Satan" (p.107).

 Paul says that to try to keep the Law in our own power sets in motion a curse in the spiritual realm, and Jesus is the only one who can end that curse: *For as many as are of the works of the law are under the curse; for it is written, "Cursed is everyone who does not continue in all things which are written in the book of the law, to do them." But that no one is justified by the law in the sight of God is evident, for "The just shall live by faith." Yet the law is not of faith, but "The man who does them shall live by them." Christ has redeemed us from the curse of the law, having become a curse for us (for it is written, "Cursed is everyone who hangs on a tree.)"* (**Galatians 3:10-13**).

[11] Romans 7:7-25 makes an especially potent and clear statement regarding the futility of trying to use your willpower to keep the law.

 Also See Endnote #2-3 for a detailed discussion of Romans, Chapter 7.

[12] There is a popular teaching that God strengthens our will so that we can obey Him. There is no scriptural basis for this, and this view tends to set us into striving. The Lord wants us to be like Him, not to act like Him. **See Endnote #2-2** for more on this erroneous teaching.

don't want to do, I might as well give up." But there is a way to obey the Lord. We just need to understand the provision that Jesus has made for us and make use of it. Let me give another example.

Another huge truck is speeding down the highway. A traffic jam lies ahead, and the truck driver needs to stop the truck quickly. Does he open the door and drag his foot on the pavement to stop the truck? Of course not. He doesn't have within himself the power to stop the truck. What he does do is to <u>decide</u> to press the brake pedal, and then to <u>act</u> by actually pressing it. This activates a powerful brake system, which has been provided for just such a purpose, and the truck comes to a stop. The driver didn't stop the truck by his own power, but he did need to do the following:

1. <u>Recognize</u> the problem.
2. <u>Believe</u> in the brake system.
3. <u>Decide</u> to activate the system.
4. <u>Act</u> by physically pushing the brake pedal.

That was his job as the driver. If he didn't act, there would be a mess. In this same way, in spiritual matters, we have to:

1. <u>Recognize</u> the problem.
2. <u>Believe</u> in the powerful provision Jesus has given us to stop the operation of God's laws against us.
3. Use our willpower to <u>decide</u> to activate the provision.
4. <u>Act</u> by praying.

As you can see, our willpower does have a part to play in our being set free, but it is not the force or power that brings it about. I will elaborate on this process of being set free in the next few chapters.

God's Laws Bring "Good" or "Bad"

God has provided a system that has sufficient power to stop the operation of God's laws that are bringing destruction, frustration, and failure into our life. However, before we can activate it, we first need to understand more about how God's laws cause us to do the things that we hate.

When God created the spiritual realm, there were two possible ways for a person to exist. If we align our lives with what brings good things (we "obey the Law"), we receive good consequences (blessings). When Adam and Eve walked in the Garden of Eden in obedience to God, life was good.

On the other hand, if we align our lives with what brings bad things (we "disobey the Law"), we experience bad consequences (curses). When Adam and Eve disobeyed God and ate of the tree of the knowledge of good and evil, bad things resulted.

Blessings always flow when we are aligned with His laws. All of us are reaping blessings in certain areas of our life. For example, my son was having financial problems shortly after he graduated from college. He had recently made a decision to follow Jesus, and I spoke to him about tithing. He said, "Dad, how can I give ten percent off the top of my paycheck? I can't pay my bills as it is." But he believed what the Bible said and began to tithe. Immediately, and to my son's astonishment, his financial problems ended. He has continued to tithe, and the Lord has continued to bless his finances. A word of caution is in order. Having money is not always good, and not having money is not always bad. This will become clearer as you read more chapters.

We don't want the blessings to stop. We want more of them. As we align ourselves with the way the spiritual realm is constructed for blessings, we receive blessings. Therefore it is important for us to know how the spiritual realm works for blessing so that we can receive more good.

On the other hand, we also need to understand how the spiritual realm works against us when we sin, so that we can stop the bad things from continuing to happen.

When we sin, we set in motion God's laws against us. We will surely reap what we sow. We don't sow corn and reap cotton. We don't sow sin and reap blessings. We sow sin and reap bad consequences. There are, of course, many ways that we can sin, and they all have consequences.[13]

---

[13] **Galatians 5:19-21** gives a partial list of possible sins, *adultery, fornication, uncleanness, licentiousness, idolatry, sorcery, hatred, contentions, jealousies, outbursts of wrath, selfish ambitions, dissentions, heresies, envy, murders, drunkenness, revelries, and the like.*
Footnote Continued On Next Page

These consequences are the behaviors that we don't want to do. We are impelled to do them by the operation of God's law, and as a result, our willpower is completely unable to free us from this bondage.[14] Paul reveals the answer to our bondage to these consequences when he writes:

O wretched man that I am! Who will deliver me from this body of death? I thank God – through Jesus Christ our Lord! (Romans 7:24-25).[15]

The System That Has Enough Power

For us to have victory over the destruction, frustration, pain, and failure in our life, God had to provide a system that had sufficient power. In fact, for us to be set free requires a miracle![16]

Jesus was sent by the Father to provide a way out for us. He came to take away our sins. His blood is the only cure for sin, and sin is what is causing our problem. When we pray, as we repent[17] and are forgiven, Jesus pays off our debt and takes it upon Himself. The negative consequences resulting from the sin will continue into eternity, but Jesus will take over bearing the weight of that, and we are set free. For us, in regard to this particular sin, it is as though we

---

1 Corinthians 6:9-10 lists more sins: *Neither . . . homosexuals, nor sodomites, nor thieves, nor covetous . . . nor extortioners will inherit the kingdom of God.*

My purpose is not to try to give an exhaustive list of sins, but to give common examples.

[14] In fact, trying to stop the operation of God's laws in our life is not just foolish and ineffective, it is sin **Read Chapter 13 "The Bad Part"** and **See Endnote #3-2** for more on the fact that our own striving effort to keep the Law is sin.

[15] **See Endnote #2-3** for more discussion of the illusion of our willpower and Romans, Chapter 7.

[16] Then the question is, <u>how</u> do we <u>become</u> like Jesus? The answer is, it takes a *miracle*. "It means that free, ethical obedience can have its origin only in miracle, quite in keeping with the view that from the fetters of flesh and sin man must be freed to obedience by the deed of God" (Bultmann, <u>Theology of the New Testament</u>, Part II, p.337). We need a legal transaction to take place in the spiritual realm if we are to <u>be</u> like Jesus. So being saved into God's kingdom and being changed into His image are miracles. They are both things that no man can accomplish through his or her own strength and ability. Read Chapter 6, "God Is On Your Side," for more on this miracle.

See Endnote #2-4 regarding God's eternal plan and the Law

[17] To repent means, in part, "implying pious sorrow for unbelief and sin and a turning from them unto God and the gospel of Christ . . . Jesus draws a picture of the true penitent person. Such is assured of the forgiveness of the Father" (Zodhiates, p.969). See Glossary for more.

had never committed it. The bad thing going on in our life as a consequence of our sin ceases to happen.

The "Blood" And The "Cross"

I will often refer to Jesus' "blood" and His "cross." Some writers admonish us to "take it to the cross," or to "apply the blood." References to "blood" and "cross", either in combination or separately, are short hand ways of referring to the whole provision that God made for us, through the sacrifice of Jesus, to forgive us our sins and cleanse us from unrighteousness (1 John 1:9). The provision is God's way of setting us free from our own sin and its consequences which resulted from our following in the footsteps of Adam and Eve. This entire book is an attempt to make clear what this provision is, and to help make the "blood" and the "cross" effectual in your daily life. Also see "Blood of Jesus" and "Cross of Christ" in the Glossary.

Even though Jesus paid the penalty for our sin when He died on the cross 2000 years ago, we need to do something to bring the benefits of that provision into our lives.[18] He has offered to pay our debt for us, but we need to accept it in a specific circumstance. We need to apply this provision purposefully to a particular sin for it to have an effect in our heart. Only when we take specific action, (we pray

> **Since the thing causing our ongoing problem is sin, there is only one cure, and that is the blood and the cross of Jesus.**

to repent and are forgiven) do we benefit from the provision He has already made for forgiveness of our sins. In my previous example, the truck driver had to press the brake pedal to engage the powerful brake system built into the truck. I will write more about how to pray in the next few chapters.

---

[18] Please note that when I sin, this does not mean I am then going to hell. If that were the case, heaven would be empty, as we all sin and fall short of the glory of God (Romans 3:23). Our sin does have negative consequences, but we will still be saved (1 Corinthians 3:15). Also see **Endnote #4-6**.

Suppose some generous person placed $1,000 in my checking account. When I write a check, I benefit from the money. As long as I don't know about the money being there, or as long as I don't <u>believe</u> it is there, or as long as I don't <u>decide</u> to make a withdrawal and <u>act</u> by writing a check on that account, this money is of no benefit to me. It could remain unused in my account until the day I die. So it is with the gift God gave us in the sacrifice of Jesus. We need to know that the provision is there. We also need to know how to apply it to our real life struggles, and we need to act.

There Are <u>Two</u> Ways To Stop Bad Behavior

When we recognize undesirable behavior, we have probably thought there was only one way of stopping it. But it should now be clear that there are <u>two</u> ways, because there are <u>two</u> possible sources of the bad behavior, the <u>psychological</u> realm and the <u>spiritual</u> realm. To stop the undesirable behavior we need to use the "tool" that is effectual in that particular realm.

If we have "tried" to change our behavior by using our willpower (psychological realm), but the bad behavior (bad fruit) has continued, we have simply been using the wrong "tool." Since our willpower was ineffective, we now know we are dealing with a spiritual problem and we need to use the appropriate tool - the blood of Jesus. In the past we may have thought the only option available was our willpower.

Our willpower is not trash, nor is it useless. It has a job to do, but its area of authority is in the psychological realm, not the spiritual realm. Both a watchmaker's screwdriver and a sledgehammer have a purpose. One would not be very successful in splitting wood with a watchmaker's screwdriver, nor be very successful in repairing a watch with a sledgehammer. We need to use the right tool for the job at hand.

See the adjoining page for an illustration of the two alternatives you have at your disposal to stop undesirable behavior.

<u>Two Alternatives</u>
<u>For Changing Bad Behavior</u>

Recognize undesirable behavior

Consider two possible sources:

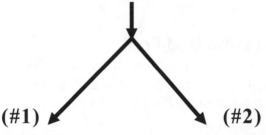

(#1)   **(#2)**

<u>Psychological Realm</u>	<u>Spiritual Realm</u>
Habit/impulse	**Sin (bad root)**
↓	↓
Undesirable behavior	**Undesirable behavior (bad fruit)**
↓	↓
Decide to do better	**Decide to do better**
↓	↓
Willpower	**Blood of Jesus (become like Him)**
↓	↓
Desirable behavior	**Desirable behavior (good fruit)**

Undesirable behaviors that have their source in the spiritual realm are rigid, compelling, and powerful, and they resist our efforts to overcome them. We are stuck, are at their mercy, and feel defeated. [19] These behaviors that are destructive (what I will call bad behavior, or bad fruit) can either be acts that hurt others, or they can be co-dependent behaviors that hurt us. See examples of these behaviors in the following footnote[20] and in Appendix B, "Codependence."

Bad Roots and Bad Fruit

When we sin and plant an area of wounding in our heart, the sin dwelling in that area can be called a "bad root." By their very nature, bad roots produce "bad fruit," whereas "good roots" produce "good fruit."

> *"Even so, every good tree bears good fruit, but a bad tree bears bad fruit. A good tree cannot bear bad fruit, nor can a bad tree bear good fruit. A good tree cannot bear bad fruit, nor can a bad tree bear good fruit. . . Therefore by their fruits you will know them."* (Matthew 7:17-18, 20).

---

[19]
John 8:34-36, *Most assuredly, I am saying to you, Everyone who habitually commits sin is a slave of sin. But the slave does not abide in the house forever. The Son abides forever. If therefore the Son make you free, you shall be free individuals in reality"* (Wuest). The verb "commit" is the Greek present participle form, which expresses continuous or repeated action. So when we are reaping from a bad root over and over, we are a slave to it - a slave has no choice but to obey his master. But Jesus can set us free from this bondage.

[20]
These rigid behaviors come in many forms, and I will list some to illustrate. Perhaps as you scan this list, you will find at least one that applies to you. Addictions are common examples of bad fruit, such as workaholism, gambling, television, computer games, overeating, alcohol, drugs, pornography, promiscuity, adultery. Some bad fruit is relational, such as compulsion to control or manipulate, verbal abuse, blaming others, always being the one that is at fault, lack of intimacy, romance problems, sexual problems, not being thoughtful, not spending time with loved ones, lack of empathy, lack of emotion, hard heartedness, people pleasing, being compelled to be "nice," anger or being passive, being obsessed with one's appearance or what other people will think, fear of meeting new people, lying. Other examples are compulsive behaviors, being greedy or miserly, financial problems or being overly thrifty, being driven by anxiety or fear, occult involvement. Bad fruit is compulsive, rigid, extreme, and beyond our conscious control.

The bad things happening in our lives, including bad behavior, are "bad fruit" from a "bad root." There is no bad fruit without a bad root being present. A bad root <u>always</u> produces bad fruit, and a good root <u>always</u> produces good fruit. The root produces fruit after its own kind. There are no exceptions. Bad behavior <u>never</u> comes from a good root, and good behavior <u>never</u> springs from a bad root.

Track Backward From-Fruit-To-Root

Once you realize that your willpower is impotent to stop the bad behavior, you can recognize that you are dealing with a spiritual problem in your life (bad fruit). Then you must find the source (the bad root). <u>You must track backward from the bad fruit to the bad root</u> (from the behavior to the cause).

The following story illustrates how a person's bad behavior is connected to sin. Mike had an angry father. When Mike was a little boy, his

> **Bad fruit <u>always</u> comes from a bad root.**

father sinned against Mike by abusing him verbally and physically. Mike hated the abuse and judged his father for it. Mike's father used to lose his temper and beat Mike, and much to his dismay, as an adult he found himself losing his temper and beating his own son, just like his father did to him. Mike hates the sinful behavior he is impelled to do, but he can't stop it, no matter how hard he tries. In truth, he is being impelled to do these sinful things by the operation of God's law. He has a bad root (the Bitter Root Judgment he made as a little boy) that is producing the bad

> **Steps for applying Jesus' provision**
> **1. Find the root**
> **2. Pray**

fruit[21] (the present sinful behavior that he hates).

---

[21] In **Hebrews 12:15** the Bible uses the term 'the root of bitterness' for something that can spring up and cause problems and affect many: *looking diligently lest anyone fall short of the grace of God; lest any root of bitterness springing up cause trouble, and by this many become defiled;*

Once You Identify The Bad Root, Then Pray

Once you identify the bad root, you need to pray about it. There is no other cure. Without prayer, (repenting and being forgiven) there is no forgiveness of sin. I will talk more about how to appropriate Jesus' provision in Chapter 5, "Forgiving Ends These Problems."

When the bad root is gone, a bad tree no longer is present to produce the bad fruit. An apple tree can illustrate this principle. An apple tree bears apples. If we pick the fruit off an apple tree, apples will grow back. The tree will not replace the apples we picked with peaches, but with more apples. When we see an apple, we know that it came from an apple tree, not a peach tree. When there is no more apple tree, there are no more apples produced.

When the bad root is gone, a bad tree no longer exists to produce the bad fruit.

Isn't Bad Fruit Sin?

I have been emphasizing healing bad roots, but bad fruit is also sin. Mike's bad root (judging his father) was sin. In addition, his bad fruit (abusing his own son) was also sin, and it needed to be forgiven by Jesus. We need to hate our bad fruit and want it to change. But it is important to understand the difference between the fruit and the root so that the bad behavior stops recurring. In my example, Mike does need to repent of his current abusive behavior (pick off the fruit); but if he stops there, it will simply happen again (grow back). The only way to stop this cycle he hates is to deal with his childhood judgment against his father (dig up the bad root). I will address this whole process in more detail in Chapters 4 and 5.

Since bad fruit <u>always</u> comes from a bad root, and good fruit <u>always</u> comes from a good root, the only way to stop the tree from bearing bad fruit is to remove the bad root and substitute the "good root" (Jesus).

> **To stop the bad cycle, the blood of Jesus needs to be applied, but to the <u>root</u> rather than to the fruit.**

In the Church we have primarily been fruit inspectors, and we have focused on picking off the bad fruit. This is important, since the bad fruit is sin. But we have failed to understand the necessity of removing the bad root, and so we have failed in our Christian walk, over and over again: *what I hate, that I do* (Romans 7:15). The provision that Jesus made for removing our sin must be applied to the <u>root</u> and not just to the fruit to be effectual in setting us free.

Please be aware that once our heart has been cleansed by Jesus, and the reaping in the spiritual realm has been stopped, there may still be some residual consequences in the world around us from our previous sins. For instance, Mike's own children will likely still be angry with him and will have judged him for his past abusive behavior towards them. They are therefore wounded and will need to be healed by Jesus. In addition, his past abusive behavior may have led his wife to divorce him. Then, even though he has been healed, his family may remain broken.

Summary

God created an orderly universe that operates in accordance with unchangeable laws. He originally intended for these laws to apply to humanity for our blessing. If we would live as God intended, and thus in accordance with the way the spiritual realm works, we would be blessed. But when Adam and Eve fell, the cursing side of His laws also began to apply to us. When we sin, we set in motion God's laws working against us. We do not have within ourselves the ability to stop the operation of God's laws, and so we have to pay the consequences of our sins. God knew how helpless we were, so Jesus came to rescue us from this impossible situation.

Chapter 3

Remove All The Bad Roots
It Is Possible

A subtle but profound misunderstanding of what we are like inside has made it difficult for many Christians to see how there can be sin inside us. There is a prevalent view that implies that inside we are like a jar, a container with a single compartment. Therefore, when we give our life to Jesus, He forgives our sins and the jar is now clean. Now that we are pure on the inside, we should be able to act pure on the outside.

The reason this view is erroneous is that, unfortunately, this is never the way it works. I know of no one, including myself, for whom life has been this way. And it was not that way for Paul when he wrote the book of Romans (specifically Chapter 7) for us.[22]

The truth is that inside we are more like a honeycomb than a honey jar. We have many compartments inside, not just one. Some of the compartments contain Jesus, and those are like the "good roots" referred to in Scripture, and which I referred to in the prior chapter. These good roots produce good fruit.

But the fruit of the Spirit is love, joy, peace, longsuffering, kindness, goodness (Galatians 5:22-23).

---

[22] **Romans 7:15-17,** *For what I am doing, I do not understand. For what I will to do, that I do not practice; but what I hate, that I do. If, then, I do what I will not to do, I agree with the law that it is good. But now, it is no longer I who do it, but sin that dwells in me.*

"Even so, every good tree bears good fruit, but a bad tree bears bad fruit. A good tree cannot bear bad fruit, nor can a bad tree bear good fruit. A good tree cannot bear bad fruit, nor can a bad tree bear good fruit. . . Therefore by their fruits you will know them." Matthew 7:17-18, 20.

However, some of the compartments still contain bad roots. These bad roots produce bad fruit, as I have previously mentioned, and they are still present and continue to produce bad fruit even after we become a Christian. These bad roots are shown as dark spots in the following honeycomb diagram.

Honeycomb   Honey Jar

We need to bring Jesus into <u>each</u> compartment of the "Honeycomb" that has darkness in it. This transformation is a process, not a one-time event.

This is the sanctification process which is addressed in so many places in the Bible. Bringing Jesus into each

> **This transformation is a process, and not a one-time event.**

compartment is the process of being changed into His image.

Once Jesus has taken up residence in that particular place in our "Honeycomb," He produces the good fruit automatically, because Jesus can do nothing but produce good fruit. It is His nature. As He takes over that part of our heart, <u>His nature actually becomes ours</u> in that area. This good root that now resides in that part of our "Honeycomb" then produces good fruit.

For instance, if we have struggled with lying, we have found that trying hard not to lie hasn't worked (trying implies use of our willpower). We find ourselves still lying. We need to find the bad root. Perhaps we realize that our father lied

> **Jesus' nature actually becomes ours in that particular area in us.**

to us, and we judged him for it (we sinned by judging him). This bad root is causing the bad fruit. When we deal with the bad root and replace it with the life of Jesus, we find we just don't lie anymore.[23] There is now good fruit, which is evidence of Jesus in that place in us. It is now so natural not to lie that we may not even be aware that we are different, because it is a new "us."[24] Does this sound too good to be true? Believe me, it <u>is</u> true. Better yet, believe Jesus when He said,

> *"Therefore you shall **be** perfect, just as your Father in heaven is perfect"* (Matthew 5:48, I added the bold).

When Jesus cleanses one compartment of the Honeycomb, it does not mean that all the compartments are clean. Other bad roots will undoubtedly remain, and they

> **We need to keep on being transformed as God shows us areas in our heart that need healing.**

---

[23]   In the next few chapters I will explain <u>how</u> to take out the bad root and replace it with a good one. Here I am simply showing the <u>necessity</u> for this change to happen.

[24]   God will change you inside, and thus cause you do what He does. **Ezekiel 36:27**: *I will put My Spirit within you and cause you to walk in My statutes, and you will keep my judgments and do them.* God will not coerce, compel, or require you to do it, because you can't. He knows He must do it in you. It is not a question of "if" He will do it. It is a question of **"how"** this can become reality in you, which is the purpose of this book.

   See Endnote #3-1 for more scriptures which promise this transformation under the New Covenant.

will be causing other bad fruit.   We need to continue being
transformed as God shows us areas in our heart that need healing.
This is what Paul meant when he said,

> work out your own salvation with fear and trembling; for it is
> God who works in you both to will and to do for His good
> pleasure (Philippians 2:12-13).

We will look more fully at the necessity to keep working on this
process in Chapter 17, "It Is A Journey."

Ripeness

All of us want to be <u>completely</u> healed and set free <u>right now</u>. Once
you discover that healing and relief from your pain and bad fruit is
possible, you don't want to wait. You may wonder why this process
has to take the rest of your life. Doesn't God want you healed?

You need to be patient. Jesus is directing your sanctification
process,[25] and He is proceeding as fast as possible. You are not
behind schedule. There are many possible reasons for any delay. If
He is going slowly, you can be
assured He is acting slowly for
a good reason. For instance, if
the bad root relates to a very
traumatic event, the memory of
the event may be deeply buried.
Your defenses buried it

> **Jesus is directing your sanctification process. If He is going slowly it is because that is what is best for you.**

specifically so you wouldn't have to relive it. To see it again before
you are prepared might cause you to be re-traumatized. Because
God loves you, He wants you healed, not wounded further. Before
revealing such a root to you, He spends time preparing you. He will
not let you see it until you will be able to see it without again being

---

[25]   **See Chapter 6**, "God Is On Your Side" for more about God's involvement in your life.

wounded. God's process will have made you ripe to deal with this root.

"Ripeness" is like picking apples. If you try to pick an apple before it is ripe, it is difficult to pull off the tree, and you are likely to damage the branch. However, ripe apples fall off easily in your hand. So the Lord ripens you so that when you pray (when you apply the blood of Jesus), it is easy. Then the process brings healing. But you can't rush your healing any more than you can speed the ripening of the apples on a tree.

Inside-Out!

"If you love Me, keep My commandments" (John 14:15).

When we read a scripture like this, <u>we tend to strive</u> to keep His commandments, because we want to please God. We want Him to know that we love Him, and it seems as though this scripture is telling us that the way we can prove our love for him is to keep His commandments. How can one reconcile this with what we have been discovering about our inability to keep His commandments in our own strength (that is, with our willpower)?

Fortunately, Jesus clearly explains what He meant in the context surrounding the above scripture. The explanation is in John 15:5, which is sandwiched between two scriptures that talk about keeping His commandments.

"He who has My commandments and keeps them, it is he who loves Me. And he who loves Me will be loved by My Father, and I will love him and manifest Myself to him" (John 14:21).

*" I am the vine, you are the branches. He who abides in Me, and I in him, bears much fruit; for **without Me you can do nothing"** (**John 15:5**, I added the bold).* [26]

"If you keep My commandments, you will abide in My love, just as I have kept My Father's commandments and abide in His love" (John 15:10).

What could be clearer than *"**without Me you can do nothing**?"* Keeping this in mind, then John 15:10 is saying something like, "If you keep My commandments this is <u>evidence</u> that you have been changed into My image, because on your own you could not do it. When you have My nature, you love the Father in exactly the same way that I do." Jesus loves the Father because that is His nature.

The reason that we can be thrown into striving to keep God's commandments is that we are confused about how we go about pleasing God. We focus on our <u>behavior</u> (keeping the commandments) rather than the <u>cause</u> of the behavior (our heart condition). We try to keep the

> **Our Christian life is meant to be lived from the inside-out, not from the outside-in.**

---

[26] John 15:1-10, *"I am the true vine, and My Father is the vinedresser. Every branch in Me that does not bear fruit He takes away; and every branch that bears fruit He prunes, that it may bear more fruit. You are already clean because of the word which I have spoken to you. Abide in Me, and I in you. As the branch cannot bear fruit of itself, unless it abides in the vine, neither can you, unless you abide in Me. I am the vine, you are the branches. He who abides in Me, and I in him, bears much fruit; for without Me you can do nothing. If anyone does not abide in Me, he is cast out as a branch and is withered; and they gather them and throw them into the fire, and they are burned. If you abide in Me, and My words abide in you, you will ask what you desire, and it shall be done for you. By this My Father is glorified, that you bear much fruit; so you will be My disciples. As the Father loved Me, I also have loved you; abide in My love. If you keep My commandments, you will abide in My love, just as I have kept My Father's commandments and abide in His love."*

commandments in order to prove that we love God.   That is backwards.

We can only please God by first being changed into the image of Jesus, and then we will keep the commandments because that is now our new nature.[27]   The heart has to change first, and then the behavior will change. Changing our behavior does not change our heart. [28] 1 John 4:19 says,

We love him because He first loved us.

This is the direction of the flow, from God to us, not the other way around.   If you are not clear on this, you can misread many scriptures.[29]   I would suggest that you read John 14:15 through 15:17 in your Bible to get the full flow of what Jesus is saying. [30]

Let me illustrate this with a parallel. Imagine that I break my leg.   It hurts, so I take a painkiller, and it hurts less (I manipulate the symptom).   But

> **God's commandments are a way of measuring whether we have a bad root inside.**

---

[27]   **John 15:10,** *"If you keep My commandments, you will abide in My love, just as I have kept My Father's commandments and abide in His love"* We will do it just like He did. Was the Father's love of Jesus conditioned on His behavior? No, it is clear that Jesus was filled with the Holy Spirit, and what He did was the result of the presence of God in Him. *"Most assuredly, I say to you, the Son can do nothing of Himself, but what He sees the Father do; for whatever He does, the Son also does in like manner"* (John 5:19).

In these scriptures in John in which God's love seems to be conditional, Jesus is actually saying that we will be keeping His commandments as a result of His presence (His love) abiding in us, because it will be an overflow of a heart that has been changed. Then John 15:10 would be saying something like, "He who keeps My commandments (the symptom or good fruit) must have My love abiding in him (the cause or the root), or he couldn't do it."

When Jesus says we should keep His commandments He is simply saying that is how we can tell whether there is a good or a bad root inside.

[28]   Our behavior is the evidence of our heart condition, and it actually expresses what is in our heart. But it is not the basis, of our heart condition. (Hulbert, Lesson 68).

[29]   **See Endnote #3-3** for more scriptures illustrating this confusion.

[30]   Trying hard to obey God in our own strength is sin because we are under the illusion that we can do God's job. We are subtly taking God's place. Hopefully you can now see that when we are reaping bad things in our life it is the consequence of sin. Jesus is the only One who can stop this. This tendency for us to try to keep the Law in our own strength is a subtle and deadly trap. For a more detailed discussion of why trying hard to keep the Law is sin, **See Endnotes #2-3 and 13-5. Also see Endnote #3-4.** for more on "symptom" (fruit) versus "cause" (root).

the leg is still broken (the cause). If I neglect the painkiller, it hurts a lot. If the doctor said that a healthy leg shouldn't hurt, I would agree. If mine weren't broken, it wouldn't hurt. But saying my broken leg shouldn't hurt doesn't keep it from hurting. The only way for my leg pain to go away (the symptom, or bad fruit) is for my broken leg (the cause, or bad root) to heal (be changed to a good root).

Similarly, when I sin, there is a wound in my heart. It causes emotional pain and I have bad fruit, so I try to act differently (I manipulate the symptom). But it doesn't work very well, because there is a bad root inside me (the cause). When Jesus says that I should keep His commandments, I would agree. If I didn't have the bad root in my heart, the bad things wouldn't happen. But saying I should keep His commandments does not make it possible as long as Jesus isn't abiding in that particular area of my heart (my heart is wounded). The only way I can keep the commandments (the symptom) is for my wounded heart (the cause, or bad root) to be healed and for Jesus to take up residence there (the bad root to be changed to a good root). The symptom is not the cause. We have had it backwards, and have focused on the symptom (the fruit outside) and not the cause (the root inside).

Keeping God's Commandments

When Jesus says that we should keep His commandments He is simply saying that is how we can tell whether there is a bad root inside us. Be careful not to be confused about this. The emphasis is <u>never</u> on the fruit, but is always upon the root. Focusing on the bad fruit can set us to striving to keep the commandments with our willpower - and thus doom us to failure. It is a subtle but deadly trap,[31] and we so easily stumble on this stumbling stone.[32]

There are many scriptures that can be misunderstood if we confuse the fruit with the root. The book of James has some significant examples of these kinds of scriptures, such as:

- *Thus also faith by itself, if it does not have works, is dead* (James 2:17).

- *You see then that a man is justified by works, and not by faith only* (James 2:24).

These scriptures are simply saying that if there are no "works" (no good fruit) this is evidence that there is no "faith" (no good root). They are not mandating "trying" with our willpower. Good fruit is all about outward evidence (our behavior), whereas good roots are all about the cause (conditions hidden inside us).

---

[31] **Read Endnote #3-2** and **Chapter 13, "The Bad Part"** for more details on this subtle and deadly trap.

[32] *But Israel, pursuing the law of righteousness, has not attained to the law of righteousness. Why? Because they did not seek it by faith, but as it were, by the works of the law. For they stumbled at that stumbling stone* (Romans 9:31-32).

When we find it difficult to obey a commandment of the Lord, we have three choices:

1. We can <u>ignore</u> the command.
2. We can <u>try</u> to obey the command in our own strength (our willpower) - - - The Downward Path below.
3. We can have the Lord deal with the bad root through the <u>blood of Jesus</u> - - - The Healing Path below.

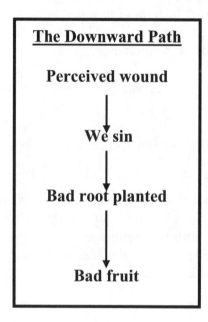 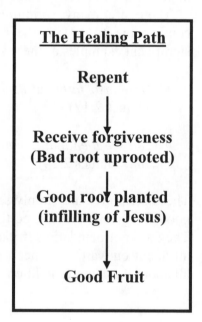

We Plant New Bad Roots

The healing path is to bring Jesus into each bad root in our "Honeycomb." Unfortunately we also frequently plant new bad roots inside.

There are many ways that we all sin and thus plant more bad roots in our "Honeycomb." However, the sin that produces most of the damage and destruction in our lives is the sin of <u>judging</u>. Jesus singled out this sin when He said,

"Judge not, that you be not judged. For with what judgment you judge, you will be judged; and with the same measure you use, it will be measured back to you" (Matthew 7:1-2).

When we judge another, we will surely reap bad consequences.[33] When we plant a bad root in our "Honeycomb" by judging, we can call the bad root a "bitter root" and the action of judging a "Bitter Root Judgment." [34] I will frequently use these terms in the rest of the book. In the next chapter it will become more clear why this particular sin of judging is so serious and so destructive.

Not Just For A Sick Few

Now that you understand the truth about bad fruit and bad roots, it should be clear that this process is not something for only a few Christians who are really sick emotionally. We all sin and fall short of the glory of God (Romans 3:23), and Jesus died to set all of us free from this bondage. This process of being changed into the image of Jesus, which is also called "Inner Healing" by some people, and referred to as "sanctification" in the Bible, is the normal walk for all Christians. In the Chapter 6, "God Is On Your Side" I will explore in detail how very important this process is to God. It is His gift to us.

---

[33] **Galatians 6:7**, *Do not be deceived, God is not mocked; for whatever a man sows, that he will also reap.*

Luke 6:37, *Judge not, and you shall not be judged. Condemn not, and you shall not be condemned. Forgive, and you will be forgiven"*

Read Chapter 4, "Judging Causes Problems" for more on this.

[34] **Hebrews 12:15:** *Lest any root of bitterness springing up cause trouble, and by this many become defiled.*

Summary

We have a tendency to sin often. When we do, we plant dark places in our "Honeycomb," and these prevent us from following God's laws in those particular areas of our life. These bad roots produce bad fruit. When we repent and bring Jesus into those dark areas of our "Honeycomb," one area at a time, we are changed into His image, step by step. As He takes up residence in those particular areas, the cursing side of the law stops. The good root of Jesus produces good fruit.

God's commandments are a way of measuring whether we have a bad root inside. If we misunderstand and thus try to keep them with our willpower, we will fail.

Even though we have the tendency to sin often, we have the living presence of Jesus, and He provides His blood to wash us clean every time. There is no shortage of the blood of Jesus. Through this provision, He has provided the way for us to be set free from the sins that beset us, by changing us into His image.

Now perhaps you can better understand why Matthew 11:28-30 and the title of this book so clearly describe your struggle.[35]

Come to Me, all you who labor and are heavy laden, and I will give you rest. Take My yoke upon you and learn from Me, for I am gentle and lowly in heart, and you will find rest for your souls. For My yoke is easy and My burden is light.

---

[35] **See Endnote #3-5** for a detailed description of Matthew 11:28-30.

Chapter 4

Judging Causes Problems
We All Sin Frequently By Judging

If I were to observe that my neighbor never mows his lawn and that his yard is always a mess, somebody may say to me, "Don't be so judgmental." When I observe this about my neighbor, am I judging? Am I sinning? It is certainly important for us to know the answer to these questions so that we can avoid sinning and thus creating problems for ourselves as a result. Of course there are other sins besides "judging," but this particular sin causes the most problems in our lives.

There I Both "Good" And "Bad" Judging

"Judging" is not always sin. The Bible talks about four types of judging, three types that are not sin (good judging), and one that is sin (bad judging). What is confusing is that the Bible uses the same Greek word to refer to all four types, and so one must rely on the <u>context</u> to discern which type is being referred to.

Good judging:
- The judging that <u>Jesus does</u>. Since He is the just and righteous Judge Who has been appointed to this position, He has a right to do this.[36]

- The <u>judicial authority</u> that is to be exercised corporately by the Church in regard to members of the Church. Judging in this context is appropriate and ordained by God.[37]

---

[36] **See Endnote #4-1** for the definition of the word "judge."

- An activity that we are supposed to engage in as individual Christians.   An English word that would perhaps be more appropriate for this function would be "discernment." We are to use wisdom and to exercise discernment.   It is not only permissible to see the negative in a situation or a person, we are encouraged to do so.[38]

Bad (sinful) judging

- The fourth type of judging is the type of judging that we are not supposed to do as individual Christians. This type of judging by us is sin. When we do this type of judging, we are seeing the negative in a situation or a person, but we are also setting ourselves up as the judge, jury, and hangman.[39]

The Sinful Judging Is Destructive

There are, of course, many ways we can sin. However, of all the sins that we commit, this "bad" judging is the sin that causes the most problems in our lives. When we find ourselves doing the things that we hate, the root that is causing this bad fruit is almost always a judgement.

---

[37]
1 Corinthians 5:12-13, *For what have I to do with judging those also who are outside? Do you not judge those who are inside? But those who are outside God judges. Therefore "put away from yourselves that wicked person."* The whole section, 1 Corinthians 5:1-6:9, concerns this issue.
   Also **See Endnote #4-2** for more detail on the judging we are to do.

[38]
   See Endnote #4-2 for more detail on the judging we are to do.

[39]
   Matthew 7:1-2, *Judge not, that you be not judged. For with what judgment you judge, you will be judged; and with the same measure you use, it will be measured back to you.*
   Luke 6:37, *Judge not, and you shall not be judged. Condemn not, and you shall not be condemned Forgive, and you will be forgiven.*
   Romans 14:4, *Who are you to judge another's servant? To his own master he stands or falls. Indeed, he will be made to stand, for God is able to make him stand.*
   James 4:11-12, *Do not speak evil of one another, brethren. He who speaks evil of a brother and judges his brother, speaks evil of the law and judges the law. But if you judge the law, you are not a doer of the law but a judge. There is one Lawgiver, who is able to save and to destroy. Who are you to judge another?*
   See Endnote #4-3 for more detail regarding judging we are not to do.

. . . lest any root of bitterness springing up cause trouble, and by this many become defiled (Hebrews 12:15).

Considering the size of the problem this sin causes, surely it must be a very serious issue.

The problem has its source in the Garden of Eden. When the serpent said, *"For God knows that in the day you eat of it your eyes will be opened, and you will be like God, knowing good and evil"* (Genesis 3:5). Adam and Eve took this bait because something inside of them wanted to be like God. Satan knew all about this sin, because this was also his big transgression.

Therefore, when we judge another we are <u>taking the place of Jesus</u>, and of course this is a very serious transgression. Jesus is the only one who has the right to judge.[40] So when we judge, we are usurping God's place.[41] When we do this, we are violating the first Great Commandment: *You shall love the Lord your God with all your heart, with all your soul, and with all your mind* (Matthew 22:37). There is only one God, and it isn't us! We are doing the judging because we do not trust God to take care of us and to hold others accountable when they trespass against us (and therefore wound us). We feel we must take the law into our own hands; because if we don't do it, we believe that nobody will.

All major problems in our human life have their roots in the Garden of Eden, and in the two great commandments of Jesus.[42] God has truly explained spiritual reality to us in such simple terms!

---

[40] **See Endnote #4-4** for more on the judging by Jesus.

[41] "But man misunderstands himself and puts himself in the place of God. And every man comes out of a history that is governed by this misunderstanding. He comes out of a lie; he is determined by the flesh whose power he cannot break. Were he to imagine that he could break it, he would assume that he does have himself in his own power after all and would thereby repeat the primal sin" (Bultmann, <u>Existence and Faith</u>, p.83).

[42] **Matthew 22:36-40,** *"Teacher, which is the great commandment in the law?" Jesus said to him, "You shall love the Lord your God with all your heart, with all your soul, and with all your mind. This is the first and great commandment. And the second is like it: You shall love your neighbor as yourself. On these two commandments hang all the Law and the Prophets."*

Our Weakness

Why do we all judge so quickly? It is a part of our fallen nature. When we perceive that we have been wounded, we <u>always</u> automatically react with bitterness, judgment, and blame.   For instance, picture yourself in your kitchen cutting up a carrot. The phone rings, and you lose your concentration and cut your finger instead of the carrot. What is your immediate response? Do you blame the carrot? Do you blame the dull knife? Do you blame your spouse for not sharpening the knife? Do you blame the person who called you? Or do you blame yourself, saying something like this, "You dummy. Why weren't you paying more attention to what you were doing?"

Blaming <u>myself</u> was always <u>my</u> typical response.

Stop for a minute and think about what your response would be.

Why couldn't the cut finger just be something that happened? Why did somebody or something have to be at fault? The answer is because it is our fallen nature to judge.

<u>This is the problem</u>. Daily we plant numerous roots of bitterness. Since life in this fallen world entails lots of wounding, we do a lot of judging. It is automatic, and we have done it before we consciously know it. Because we have planted many roots of bitterness, we are reaping much bad fruit. Tragically, as long as we walk this earth, we will never lose this tendency to automatically react to wounding

> **As long as we walk this earth, we will never lose this tendency to automatically react to perceived wounding with bitterness, judgment and blame.**

with bitterness, judgment and blame. This tendency is an integral part of our fallen human nature.[43]

We all judge, and we do it often. If you think you don't do it, there is one sure way to discover the truth. Ask yourself, do you do the things that you hate to do? Is there bad fruit in your life? If there is bad fruit, there are roots of bitterness in you.

Fortunately, you now have a way to clean up the mess. As often as you judge, you can forgive and be forgiven. The bad root can be pulled out as soon as it is planted.

How Can You Tell The Difference?

At first glance this may seem terribly confusing. How can you tell if the judging you have just done is good or bad? Fortunately, the Lord has provided a very simple way to tell the difference.

Suppose I live in a small town and I am thinking about going into business with a certain man. I check around and find out that this person has a reputation for being dishonest, and so I decide not to go into business with him. I have judged (discerned) as I am supposed to do.

Alternatively, suppose I live in the small town and I am thinking about going into business with a certain man. Without first checking around and discovering his reputation, I go into business with him. After the business starts I discover that he is not honest. By the time I can get myself out of the business deal it has cost me $100,000. I am now in possession of the same information (that he isn't honest) as in the first example, but you can be sure that in this situation I have done the bad type of judging. How can I tell that I have done the bad judging? Every time I think about that "jerk" I feel like strangling him. Every time I think of him I become very angry and upset. He wounded me, and I judged him for it.

---

[43] This tendency to respond to wounding with bitterness, judgment and blame is part of our fallen nature. The Bible describes this as "flesh" in some passages. However, the term "flesh" (Greek *sarx*) is a fuzzy word. It has a wide range of meanings, and in the Bible *sarx* is often used to describe other things than this tendency just mentioned above. (**See Chapter 13**, "The Bad Part Of You" for more details on this), and so I am going to avoid calling this tendency "flesh" so as to avoid confusion.

On the other hand, in the first example, I am probably not upset with the man, because I didn't judge him wrongly.   After all, he didn't wound me. I am at peace.

How can I tell whether I have judged someone in the way that I am not supposed to? I feel it. I can absolutely feel the bitterness of the bitter root that has been planted inside me.

When I realize that I have judged him in the way that I am not supposed to, I can forgive him and be forgiven by Jesus (see Chapter 5, "Forgiving Ends These Problems").   Then I no longer feel like calling him a "jerk."

A "Splinter"

We can feel the planting of a bitter root, because we have built into us a sensitivity to wounding in our heart. A parallel to this would be when we get a splinter in our finger.   We have built into us a sensitivity to physical wounding. When a splinter gets lodged in our finger, we know it is there because we feel it. When we remove the splinter, our body will know that and will tell us by a feeling of relief of the discomfort. Likewise, when we remove the bitter root, our heart will know that and will tell us (if we are listening) by a feeling of peace in place of the bitterness.

Denial

Most of the time we can tell whether we have judged another person by the feeling.   However, there are times when we will not feel bitterness towards the one who wronged us.   When a wound we have received is particularly severe, we may have built a defense to protect us from feeling the pain. For instance, a girl may have been abused by her father, and yet have no sense of her rage towards him. The pain she felt at the time was too big to live with, so she cut herself off from the feeling. We call this sort of defense mechanism "denial."   However, it will still be possible to discover there is a Bitter Root Judgment inside.   In this sort of situation, because the wounding was large, there will be bad fruit in her life that will indicate the presence of a bad root; and so she can track backwards from the bad fruit to the bad root.

Perceived Wounding

I have made the statement that we always automatically respond to
perceived wounding with bitterness, judgment, and blame. It doesn't
matter whether the other person actually, factually, wounded us.
What counts is that we feel that they did.

For instance, suppose I was abandoned by my parents when I was
a small child. This is a real wounding, and has made me sensitive to
abandonment. Then as an adult, suppose a friend of mine declines
to go to a ballgame with me, telling me he is too tired. I feel
abandoned and judge him, because it seems to me he was making an
excuse. Later I find out the friend was coming down with the flu,
and he really had wanted to go to the game with me.

There was no actual wound inflicted by my friend, but I wrongly
perceived there was, so I judged. [44] My prior wounds and
judgments make me more sensitive to how others behave around
me.

As the Lord heals these wounded areas, I will react less often,
because I will perceive less wounding less often. However, this
change should not be confused with my built in human tendency to
react with bitterness, judgment and blame. I don't react less now
because that tendency has gone away or is being healed. I react less
because I perceive wounding less often. The next time I am actually
wounded by someone, I will discover that my tendency to judge has
not gone away, because I will again find myself judging.

The sequence that occurs is as follows: My friend declines my
invitation. I perceive that I have been wounded (abandoned). This
automatically triggers my judging, which plants a root of bitterness
in my heart. I then feel abandoned, making me aware, after the fact,
that the root of bitterness has been planted inside.

---

[44] **See Endnote #4-5** for more on our tendency to respond to perceived wounds with bitterness,
judgment, and blame.

How Judgments Plant Bitter Roots In Us:

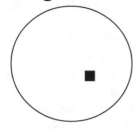

At conception we are uncluttered with darkness, except for one place (the small black square). This one dark place represents our tendency to automatically react to wounding with bitterness, judgment, and blame (part of our fallen nature).

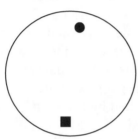

But then, as an infant, we are hungry. We cry, but nobody responds to our need. Because of the presence of the black square (our tendency to automatically react to wounding with bitterness, judgment, and blame), we judge our parents for not meeting our needs. This plants a place of darkness in us - a bitter root (the black dot).

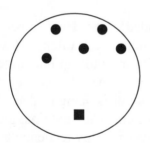

Later on, mommy and daddy have a fight, and shout hateful words at each other. We judge them for this. As life goes on, simple events like this occur by the thousands. We then have many dark areas in us.

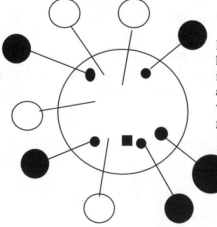

Eventually, a very unfortunate thing happens. These dark (bad) roots inside of us produce bad fruit (shown as black circles outside) in our life, while the good roots inside produce good fruit (shown as light circles).

Unfortunately, the more bad roots we have, the more bad fruit we have. This is why "judging" is so damaging to us. To make matters worse, the longer a bad root grows inside us, the bigger it gets, the more entrenched it is, and the more difficult it is to eradicate. The bigger the root, the more pervasive is the bad fruit.

It Is God's Mercy That We Feel Emotional Pain!

If we did not feel the emotional pain, we wouldn't know there is something wrong inside, and the sin would remain in us. When we die, we will go to the Great White Throne Judgment, and there all our sins will be placed before us. Scripture doesn't tell us what the negative consequences will be, but there is a strong implication that we would be better off without those sins. Since the sins that have been washed away by Jesus during our lifetime will not be there, we won't have to pay the price for them at the last judgment. Because the Lord takes the long view, including eternity, He wants to have the opportunity to forgive our sins here, in this life, before we face the Last Judgment. Of course, our unforgiven sins will not keep us out of heaven. We will still be saved, but we will suffer loss.[45]

We do not know when our life on earth will end. But as time goes by the end of our life draws nearer. It therefore becomes more and more urgent that we give our sins to Jesus. God therefore increases the pain, and our burdens get harder to carry until we get desperate enough to seek the cause. We need to forgive now so we won't have to pay later.[46]

---

[45] **1 Corinthians 3:9,13-16,** *For we are God's fellow workers; you are God's field, you are God's building . . . each one's work will become manifest; for the Day will declare it, because it will be revealed by fire; and the fire will test each one's work, of what sort it is. If anyone's work which he has built on it endures, he will receive a reward. If anyone's work is burned, he will suffer loss; but he himself will be saved, yet so as through fire. Do you not know that you are the temple of God and that the Spirit of God dwells in you?* Here "work" does not refer to "effort," but to the product. Your character is the product, the "building" (verse 9) the "temple" (verse 16). Underlining is mine.

[46] **See Endnote #4-6** for more detail on how God views our lives.

God Changes Us Into His Image

In Chapter Two I talked about the place of our will power, and the fact that in Western culture our will power has been placed upon the throne of our lives. This view is so subtle, pervasive, and automatic that it can sneak into our thinking undetected. For example, some Bible teachers try to explain that the way to walk out the Christian life is for God to strengthen our will so that we can obey. These teachers believe that our will power is the tool to bring victory. But what God intends is for us to be changed into His image. It is a miracle. When He removes a bitter root and comes to live in that place in us, obeying Him is automatic and effortless. In fact, it is so effortless that we may not even realize that we are behaving differently. The good root produces good fruit, because it can do nothing else.

Summary

We all automatically react to perceived wounding with bitterness, judgment, and blame. This flaw is a part of our fallen nature. We do this many times daily, and this is sin. Every time we do this we plant a bitter root which, in time, will bear bad fruit. The more that we are wounded, the more bitter roots we have planted, and the more we will be reaping bad things in our life. God's laws are operating against us. It is therefore important to realize that what is going wrong in our life is not because of what others did to us, but it is because of our bitter reaction to what they did. The good news

It is therefore important to realize that what is going wrong in our life is not because of what others did to us, but it is because of our bitter reaction to what they did.

is that there is a "cure" for the damage the sinning has caused. I will discuss the this in the next chapter.

Chapter 5

Forgiving Ends These Problems
Jesus Can Set You Free

Forgiveness Is Essential

We have seen that "judging" is what plants the bitter roots in our heart that causes us to have bad fruit in our lives. This is a serious condition, and we need a way to be set free from the influence of these bitter roots. Forgiving and being forgiven by God is the cure. It is the only way that the bitter root is pulled out and replaced by a good root, which is the presence of Jesus in us.

God has told us a great deal about why forgiveness is essential.

1. Forgiveness is important because God said so. Jesus is the only Judge of the universe. When we judge, we attempt to take His place. [47] God is not happy about this.

2. Forgiveness is important for us. When we judge another, we sin and this plants a bitter root in our heart. This bitter root will produce bad fruit. There is only one cure for this, and that is the blood of Jesus. He

> **Forgiveness is the only way we can be changed into the image of Jesus.**

shed His blood to take away our sins. We need His blood to wash away this sin of judging so we don't have to reap the resulting consequences that come about from the operation of God's laws. The only way to accomplish this is to forgive (from our heart) the one who wounded us, and then to be forgiven by Jesus. When He forgives us, He pays the debt we owe in the spiritual realm, and

---

[47] See **Endnote #5-1** for more about letting Jesus be the judge.

we are set free from the consequences we would otherwise have to pay for our debt.[48]   If we don't forgive (from our heart), we won't be forgiven by God (though this sin will not send us to hell).[49] If we are not forgiven by God, we will continue to do the things we hate (we will continue to experience the reaping from the operation of God's laws). There simply is no other way to be set free.[50]

Stopping the reaping from our judging takes a <u>miracle</u>. "It means that free, ethical obedience can have its origin only in miracle, quite in keeping with the view that from the fetters of flesh and sin man must be freed to obedience by the deed of God."[51]

We need a legal transaction to take place in the spiritual realm if we are to be like Jesus. Once the bitter root has been removed, and Jesus has moved into that place in our heart, good fruit begins to grow.[52]

What Does It Mean To Forgive?

There are two common obstacles that often make it difficult for us to forgive.   The first obstacle is that we misunderstand what God

---

[48]   **Galatians 1:3-4,** *Grace to you and peace from God the Father and our Lord Jesus Christ, who gave Himself for our sins, that He might deliver us from this present evil age, according to the will of our God and Father.*

   Hebrews 9:28, *so Christ was offered once to bear the sins of many.*

   1 John 2:2, *And He Himself is the propitiation for our sins, and not for ours only but also for the whole world.*

[49]   **Matthew 18:35,** *"So My heavenly Father also will do to you if each of you, from his heart, does not forgive his brother his trespasses."*

   Mark 11:25, *"And whenever you stand praying, if you have anything against anyone, forgive him, that your Father in heaven may also forgive you your trespasses."*

   Luke 6:37, *"Judge not, and you shall not be judged. Condemn not, and you shall not be condemned. Forgive, and you will be forgiven."*

   Ephesians 4:32, *And be kind to one another, tenderhearted, forgiving one another, just as God in Christ also forgave you.*

[50]   See **Endnote #5-2** for more on the great power of forgiveness.

[51]   Bultmann, <u>Theology of the New Testament</u>, Part II, p.337.

[52]   Good roots produce good fruit: "forgiveness is freedom from sin, not only from past guilt, but also from sinful behavior in the future." (Bultmann, <u>Kerygma and Myth</u>, p.107).

meant by "forgive." "Forgive" is a word that is so common among Christians that we think we know what it means. However, most of us were taught what this word means by the world around us, and so the meaning we have attached to it may not be the same as what God is referring to when He tells us to forgive.[53] Sometimes this misunderstanding gets in the way of our being able to forgive others in the process of our healing.

For instance, many of us have heard something like, "Forgive and forget." We try to do that, and we find we can't forget what the person did to us. Then we think we haven't forgiven. Or perhaps somebody has hurt us, and we may believe that forgiving means we need to again make ourselves vulnerable to that person. Then something inside us resists forgiving, because we are sure the person will wound us again. Then we find it difficult to forgive.

However, God loves you and He will not ask you to do something that is not good for you, or is dangerous or destructive to you. Once you understand what God meant when He told you to forgive, you will find it much easier to forgive from your heart. Your misunderstanding of what it means to forgive may have been keeping you in bondage.

What Forgiveness Is <u>NOT</u>

Forgiveness is **not** the following:[54]

1. It is not saying the person did not transgress or hurt us, when he or she in fact did.
2. It is not relieving the other person of their responsibility, such as making excuses for their actions. For example, "My parents couldn't help it," or "They did the best they could," or "I'd have done the same thing if I had been in their shoes."

---

[53] See Endnote #5-3 for definition of the word "forgive."

[54] Adapted from Easterday, see Bibliography.

3. It is not forgetting what the other person did. We can't forget, but the hurt can be removed from the memory, and we can be forgiven for our judging.
4. It is not trusting the other person again when he or she is still unsafe – becoming vulnerable to the person again may not be wise.
5. It is not a "feeling." Rather, forgiving is a decision. However, when forgiveness has been accomplished we will feel differently about the other person whenever we think of them.
6. It is not saying or pretending we weren't hurt and/or that we weren't angry; or ignoring the hurt feeling because we aren't supposed to be angry. Rather, we need to process our feelings, not suppress them.

What Forgiveness IS

Forgiveness is deciding not to hold the other person in debt.[55] Unforgiveness says, "You unjustly hurt me, and you owe me a debt. I will make you pay." Forgiveness says, "Even though you hurt me and owe me a debt, I am writing it off. You owe me nothing. It is not my place to make you pay, and I release you to the judgment of Jesus. He is the just Judge, and He will rightly decide the case. If there is any penalty, He will collect it."[56] Forgiveness does not say,

---

[55] Grace means: "graciousness (as gratifying) of manner or act (abstract or concrete) literally, figuratively, or spiritually; especially the divine influence upon the heart, and its reflection in the life: including gratitude" (Strong's, p.77). The second meaning of the verb is to forgive! (C. Brown, Vol 2, p.122).

It appears that when we forgive, we are connecting with (or acting like, or coming into unity with) God's nature rather than man's nature (the tendency to respond to perceived wounding with bitterness, judgment, and blame).

". . . 'dead through our trespasses, made alive together with Christ, by grace (*chariti*) you have been saved' (2:5); 'by grace . . . through faith . . . the gift of God' in opposition to 'not your own doing . . . not because of works, lest any man should boast' (2.8f)" (C.Brown, Vol 2, p.122, commenting on Ephesians 2:5-2:8ff)).

[56] **Romans 12:19,** *Beloved, do not avenge yourselves, but rather give place to wrath; for it is written, "Vengeance is Mine, I will repay" says the Lord. Therefore if your enemy hungers, feed him; if he thirsts, give him a drink; for in so doing you will heap coals of fire on his head.*

"Go get 'em, God. You make him pay."   Such a statement clearly reveals bitterness still lodged in the heart.

A Second Obstacle To Forgiving

In addition to misunderstanding what forgiveness really is, there may be a second obstacle to forgiving. We may fear that if we give up our resentment we won't be protected. We may believe that a wall of resentment will protect us. This is, of course, a lie. Holding the resentment causes us to suffer. As I will discuss in a later chapter (Chapter 8 about honoring parents), we perceive God in the same way that we perceive our parents. If they were protecting and nurturing, it will be easy for us to see God in this way. However, if they were neglectful, or unloving, or mean, or abusive, there will be a deep sense in us that all authorities are this way, including God. When our parents were this way, we had to look out for ourselves and be our own protector. Later in life we will then struggle with trusting God to be our protector. But in reality, He is the only one who can protect us.

We Are The Ones Who Suffer

If we do not forgive, we are the ones who suffer. God is a just judge, which means that no one ever gets away with anything, ever, anywhere. Not everyone believes this, but it is true. The law of God is inescapable, and whatever we sow, we will surely reap,

> *Do not be deceived, God is not mocked; for whatever a man sows, that he will also reap* (Galatians 6:7).[57]

---

[57]   Note that this is not an exception to the fact that God protects us in ways we don't know. We may be protected from reaping from some of our sins while we are here on earth, but all our unrepented sins will be placed before us at the Great White Throne judgment. We will still be saved, though we will suffer loss (1 Corinthians 3:15). Exactly what "loss" means is not explained in the Bible, but God knows. Since He loves us, He wants to protect us from this "loss." That is why He is so diligent in getting us to repent of our sins during our lifetime here on earth. He takes the long, eternal view.

    See Endnote #4-6 for more details on this.

Remove Bitter Roots Immediately!

Bitter roots are easier to eradicate if we remove them soon after they are planted. The longer they are allowed to grow, the larger the root system becomes and the more difficult they are to pull out. Gardeners understand this. When a weed first comes up in a garden, it is small and frail. It can be

Because forgiving is so important, we need to remove every obstacle that prevents us from accomplishing it, and we need to be diligent in accomplishing it.

plucked out easily. However, if one neglects the garden for some time, pulling the weeds is a big job. The roots of the weeds have then become large and entrenched, and sometimes a large hole has to be dug in order to remove them. Healing is easier if you remove a bitter root as soon as it is planted.

Another thing happens if we neglect to keep up with our "weeding." If we allow the sins to pile up, eventually they become too obvious to ignore. People who have lived in the country know what a septic tank is. It is a big cement tank buried under ground into which the wastewater from a house runs. There the waste goes through a natural process of cleansing, but some types of waste stays in the tank and gradually fills it up. Periodically it needs to be pumped out, or it overflows and makes a smelly mess. Our hearts are a bit like septic tanks. If we don't keep our own pumped out, it eventually fills up with junk, overflows and makes a mess. It is therefore important that we pump ours out every time some waste enters it. In other words, we need to forgive every time we judge so that our own "septic tank" (our heart) stays clean.

Who Do We Need To Forgive?

There are probably many people we need to forgive. Psychotherapy and Christian counseling have both tended to focus on relationships with our parents and our siblings. Without a doubt these relationships were impactful, and the roots of bitterness resulting from being wounded by them cause major problems for us.

However, the deepest hurts, the greatest emotional pain, and the most devastating fruit comes from <u>judging God</u> and <u>judging ourselves</u>. Yet it may seem strange and new to be walking through forgiveness of God and of ourselves.

Importance Of Forgiving God

Somehow it seems weird to forgive God, because He did not do anything wrong! And perhaps it is scary to think that we may have blamed Him. But I believe that all of us have judged Him in some way.

It is important to recognize that for us to have judged another does not mean that person actually wronged us. What is important is that <u>we perceive</u> that he or she has wronged us. For instance, we may feel that an individual has rejected us, and we may have become angry and judged him. Then we may find out later that the person did not reject us at all. Even though he didn't actually wrong us, <u>we still need to forgive him</u> and be forgiven. Discovering that the person had not actually rejected us will not remove the bitter root that we planted. The discovery that he did not actually reject us may make it easier to forgive, but it does not remove the bitter root that was planted when we judged them. Though we wrongly perceived the rejection, a legal transaction still occurred in the spiritual realm, and that sin needs to be paid for by Jesus, or we will surely experience the bad fruit from the bitter root.

This is the way it is with God. He did not do anything wrong, but when we judged Him, we thought He did. For instance, if as a child we were abused, it is very likely that when the abuse was happening we judged God for not protecting us. Though we may not be consciously aware of this judgment, we will reap from this bitter root until we forgive Him.

Importance Of Forgiving Yourself

It may also seem strange to recognize that you have judged yourself. How is that possible? In addition, forgiving and asking for forgiveness for judging yourself may seem very unusual and unnatural. But Paul said that God is the only one who has a right to judge you. You do not have this right.[58] I will explore this issue in more detail in Chapter 9, "There Is Buried Treasure." Here I simply want to point out that your relationship with yourself is very important. You need to repair it where it is damaged, and you need to live with yourself in a new and loving way.

I have counseled people who have been working on their Inner Healing for years and who have forgiven every person imaginable, and yet they were still suffering great emotional pain. I have found that the key for these people is that they had judged themselves and have not forgiven and been forgiven.

In fact, all the people I have ever counseled have judged themselves to some degree! I was a bit astounded when I first realized this, because none of those who taught me about prayer counseling had said anything about this (though I have since found confirmation of my realization from other writers). Self-judgment is often under-emphasized in Inner Healing.

Remember the example in the prior chapter where I cut my finger when I was cutting up carrots. When I would say to myself, "You dummy, why weren't you paying more attention to what you were doing?"

That was a self-judgment. I used to judge myself in that way very frequently. Many of us do this sort of thing to

> **First recognizing that we have judged ourselves, and then walking out the healing of it is one of the biggest keys to Inner Healing.**

ourselves regularly. You need to realize this self judging is very destructive.

When people say, "Ed, this is really weird, speaking to myself and asking myself to forgive me." To this statement I simply respond, "When you cut yourself instead of the carrot and said, 'You

---

[58] **1 Corinthians 4:3-5,** *In fact, I do not even judge myself. For I know nothing against myself, yet I am not justified by this; but He who judges me is the Lord. Therefore judge nothing before the time, until the Lord comes, who will both bring to light the hidden things of darkness and reveal the counsels of the hearts; and then each one's praise will come from God.*

dummy', who were you talking to?"   Inevitably they say, "To myself."   You see, we all speak to ourselves regularly, but it is frequently harsh and judgmental talk.   The thing that feels weird about speaking to ourselves in forgiveness is not that we are talking to ourselves, but that we are saying <u>nice</u> things.[59]

Elements For Accomplishing Forgiveness

There are certain elements involved in walking through the process of forgiving when we have judged:

1. **<u>Recognition</u>:** First, we need to recognize that we have judged (sinned). Denial and fear can often interfere with our ability to see what we have done.
2. **<u>Confession</u>:** Then we need to confess that we have sinned.
3. **<u>Repentance:</u>** This means to turn away from the sin. We need to hate the sin and want to no longer walk in that way.
4. **<u>Forgiveness</u>:** We need to make a decision to forgive, and then forgive from our heart.
5. **<u>Accept forgiveness</u>** from God. Sometimes another person needs to verbalize to us that God has forgiven us before we are able to accept this fact.
6. **<u>Ask the Lord to fill</u>** that place in our heart with His presence. We need Him to take up residence in that place that had previously contained bitterness, judgment, and blame.
7. Ask the Lord to **<u>bless</u>** the other person. If we find this difficult to do, then it is likely that forgiveness has not been fully accomplished.
8. **<u>Restitution</u>:** Sometimes we need to do something extra for the other person, to walk an extra mile. Our relationship with the Lord has already been restored through prayer, but in some situations we need to do something for the other person in order

---

[59] This conversation with myself restores the relationship I have with myself, but it doesn't stop the reaping from God's laws. So I also have to forgive and be forgiven by God

to restore our relationship with them   This is the purpose of
restitution

How To Pray

Forgiveness must come from the
heart to be effectual:

*So My heavenly Father also
will do to you if each of you,
from his heart, does not
forgive his brother his
trespasses* (Matthew 18:35).

> **It is always important
> that we forgive from our
> heart as the living Lord
> leads, rather than recite
> a rote prayer.**

Jesus always looks on the heart, not the behavior, and we can't fool
Him. Therefore it is always important that we pray as we feel led by
the living Lord, and NOT simply recite a rote prayer, as though it
were a magical formula.[60]

The Importance Of Words

Please be aware of the important position that words have in our
prayers of forgiveness. For some reason, God set up the universe in
such a way that words have power. *Then God said, "Let there be
light," and there was light* (Genesis 1:3). The words that I speak
bring my thoughts into reality. Once they are spoken, it is as though
a legal contract has been signed, or a legal event has happened, in
the spiritual realm. The words can be "bad" and bring about
difficulty (for example judging), or they can be "good" and bring
about life (for example blessing someone). Though the Bible
doesn't explain to us why words have power, it does make the fact
abundantly clear, that they do have great power.[61]

---

[60] See Endnote #5-4 for a sample prayer of forgiveness, which I have provided. Please use it only as
a guideline and not a rote prayer.

[61] See Endnote #5-5 for more scriptures on the power of words.

How To Forgive God And Yourself

Accomplishing forgiveness of God and of yourself is very similar to forgiving others who are close to us. In the case of close, important relationships, we not only want to stop the reaping from our Bitter Root Judgment, we also want to restore the relationship. If we have judged a close person, this attitude has probably affected our behavior towards them. If they are sensitive people, our new behavior has hurt them, and we need to take responsibility for our behavior and ask them to forgive us.

For example, imagine that your best friend completely forgets about your birthday. You are hurt by this, and you begin to withdraw from the relationship. Your friend can tell that you are angry, but doesn't know why. When you realize that you have judged him (or her), you need to pray as mentioned previously ("Elements Involved In Accomplishing Forgiveness").

> **In the case of close relationships, when you judge you have <u>two</u> things to do:**
> **1. Resolve the problem in the spiritual realm.**
> **2. Restore the relationship with them.**

This takes care of the <u>spiritual aspect</u> of the problem, but now you need to <u>restore your relationship</u> with him. You need to go to your friend, confess that you have judged him, and have allowed your bitterness to affect how you have treated him. Then you ask him to forgive you for withdrawing, and your friendship is restored.

<u>In a similar way</u>, when you have judged God or yourself, you likewise need to resolve the problem in the spiritual realm as well as the problem in the relationship. After all, these are the two most important relationships you have, and judgments interfere with these intimate relationships. You need these relationships to be loving, open, and intimate, or life will not go well.

For example, suppose you judge yourself when you cut yourself instead of the carrot, as in the prior example. When you realize you have done this, you confess this to the Lord, forgive yourself and are forgiven by God. Then you need to restore your relationship with yourself by speaking to yourself, confessing what you have done, and asking forgiveness. You say exactly the same things you would say to your close friend when he or she forgot your birthday.

Summary

Forgiving (and being forgiven by God) is the key to accessing God's provision for taking away our sin. It is the only door to freedom. It is the only means available for stopping the bad fruit in our lives – for us to stop doing the things that we hate. God made this provision, and it is of central importance that we understand <u>what</u> forgiveness is and <u>how</u> to accomplish it so that we can then apply this God-ordained provision for healing. Jesus came to set us free:

> *"The Spirit of the Lord is upon me, because he hath anointed me to preach the gospel to the poor; he hath sent me too heal the brokenhearted, to preach deliverance to the captives, and recovering of sight to the blind, to set at liberty them that are bruised, to preach the acceptable year of the Lord"* (Luke 4:18-19, KJV).

Chapter 6

God Is On Your Side

Knowing that my sins set in motion God's laws, and therefore every sin brings negative consequences, can make me very anxious. The power and inevitability of the operation of God's laws revealed in the following scriptures can haunt us.

> *Do not be deceived, God is not mocked; for whatever a man sows, that he will also reap* (Galatians 6:7).

> *For with what judgment you judge, you will be judged; and with the same measure you use, it will be measured back to you* (Matthew 7:2).

What happens if I don't get it right? What happens if I fail to catch every sin and have it forgiven? We may feel alone and hopeless, and may be set into striving to make sure we don't miss anything. We may then become discouraged, despondent, even desperate when we fail to catch every sin.

If the spiritual universe was simply mechanical and automatic, we would indeed be in trouble. If at this moment we were to reap the just consequences of every sin we ever committed, we would be overwhelmed. The pain and bad fruit in our lives would be unbearable.

God Is Protecting Us

Fortunately for us, God actively intervenes in this process. For His children, God holds back most of the accumulated reaping that we would otherwise experience. He loves us and does not want us overwhelmed or destroyed.

We see this easily when we think of children. For example, when children are very small, we put them in a crib with side rails. We do this to protect them from falling out of bed and getting hurt. However, there comes a time when we expect them to be able to sleep without falling out of bed.

We also provide "baby sitters" for our children when they are small. Otherwise, while we are gone they might hurt themselves, or perhaps burn the house down. We take care of them in this way because we know they are not yet ready to handle the responsibilities of looking after themselves. Eventually they will have matured enough to handle greater responsibilities, and we can then leave them alone and expect them to be responsible. In fact, they will eventually want to take care of themselves. Then we no longer should protect them to the same degree. They need to grow and practice exercising the new responsibilities while we are still available to coach them.

God protects us in a similar way. He only allows us to reap what will help us, what will motivate us to pursue our healing. He only allows us to experience what we are ready to handle, so that the experience will bring about good in our lives, rather than destruction.

The trials that you have had to bear are no more than people normally have. You can trust God not to let you be tried beyond your strength, and with any trial he will give you a way out of it and the strength to bear it (1 Corinthians 10:13, The Jerusalem Bible, underlining is mine).

Raising My Son

My son John was always a happy-go-lucky boy. He always had a lot of friends, and was very generous. However, if he had a dollar in his pocket, he spent it. After all, he knew that his parents would meet all of his financial needs, so why not? We talked to him many times about saving some money, but it never happened. We were very concerned that he would grow up to be financially irresponsible.

In the summer between his sophomore and junior year of high school we got him a good paying job with a building contractor who was putting an addition onto our house. As a growing boy, when school started in the fall, none of his old clothes would fit anymore. In the past we had always bought all his clothes. Now that he had a well paying job, he agreed that he would pay for his own new clothes that fall.

When fall came, he informed us that he needed some new clothes for school. We agreed, as his pants were three inches too short. However, over the summer he had spent all of his money, much of it on his friends. We were then faced with either bailing him out of his dilemma, or making him live with the consequences of his behavior. Since our previous words had not taught him about saving for a rainy day, we realized that he needed to experience in his life the results of his choices. So we didn't pay for new clothes.

As we all know, peer pressure is a cruel master for teenagers. When John had to go to school in clothes that were too small, each day he died a thousand deaths. Later in the fall his wrestling coach gave him an old pair of tennis shoes that he had found abandoned in a locker. John was mortified by this. What finally bailed him out of his unpleasant consequence was Christmas and clothing gifts from his grandparents. John has now become a financially responsible adult.

Were we cruel when we allowed peer pressure to impact him? Were we being unloving by allowing him to suffer for his misbehavior? Not at all. It was difficult for us to watch him suffer. We loved him, but we knew there was a lesson that he needed to learn; and it could only be learned by experience. If he didn't change his attitude towards money he would possibly suffer all of his life from financial folly. As his parents, it was our responsibility to do what was necessary to help him to grow up to be mature and responsible.

We did not create the peer pressure that made him suffer, but we did withdraw our "protection" from it. We had within our power the ability to protect him from that embarrassment by buying him some new clothes. However, it was evident that he had not yet learned to be responsible, and perhaps the only way he would become mature would be for us to withhold our "protection." It was in his best interest, even though he hated it, and he suffered. In a sense, we "used" the peer pressure, which is a cruel and merciless force, to help him to become mature and responsible.

When Christians encounter difficulties they often ask, "Why didn't God keep that from happening?" They wonder, if God is all powerful, why didn't He intervene?

Hopefully this example with my own son will help you understand how God works in our lives. He tries to gently tell us about something that we need to change. But if we don't, or can't, change our behavior, there are times that He has to allow us to suffer the consequences for what we do. Because He loves us, even though it hurts Him to watch us suffer, He is willing to endure this. He knows that we need our character changed, and that experiencing pain in our lives is sometimes the only way that we will be motivated to seek change.

God Is Raising His Children

As parents, most of us do the best we can in raising our children, but we don't do it perfectly. However, God is the perfect parent:

> *For they* (our earthly parents) *indeed for a few days chastened us as seemed best to them, but He for our profit, that we may be partakers of His holiness* (Hebrews 12:10).

God is your Father, and He is raising you like a good father raises a child. God speaks in relationship terms, because most of us have been raised in families, and many have been parents. Thus He is speaking about relationships, with which you can likely relate, because He wants you to understand experientially what your relationship with Him is like.

Those of us who are parents know how much we love our children. We also know that when they were little we were much wiser than they were, and hopefully we had their best interests at heart as we raised them. Sometimes they did not understand all the reasons why we were disciplining them as we were, and usually they were not happy with the discipline. In fact, the discipline had to be unpleasant or it would be ineffective.

We also realized that one-year-old children cannot perform as five-year-old children. Schools do not expect as much of first graders as they do of ninth graders. In the mean time, as they gradually grow, we need to do for them what they cannot do for themselves. However, it is up to us as parents to decide what they can or cannot do. Parents also need to challenge their children to help them to grow up into mature and responsible adults. If parents were to do everything for their children, they would grow up to be lazy, spoiled, self-centered, and immature. But if children are properly mentored, they grow up to be mature.

So it is with God. He is raising you for your good. He is wiser, and He has a special plan for your life. He knows what you need at any stage of your life. For example, all of you who have walked with the Lord for some time have discovered that you can't "get away with" as much as you could when you were first saved. The level of accountability for your sins has obviously increased.

Before you gave your life to Jesus, you were not God's child, and you were in rebellion against Him. At that time He let you go your own way, and you were not under His protection.[62]

You were in the world and of the world, and Satan was the one who had authority over you. However, when you responded to God's invitation and made a choice to turn your life over to Jesus,

---

[62] **Ephesians 2:11-13,** *Therefore remember that you, once Gentiles in the flesh-who are called Uncircumcision by what is called the Circumcision made in the flesh by hands-that at that time you were without Christ, being aliens from the commonwealth of Israel and strangers from the covenants of promise, having no hope and without God in the world. But now in Christ Jesus you who once were far off have been made near by the blood of Christ.*

you became God's child. At that moment reality changed for you.[63]

When you made that choice you gave Him permission to raise you as He saw best. At that time you probably didn't know the full impact of your decision. But from the moment you made Jesus your Lord, He had your permission to do whatever it took to direct you to maturity.

God Does Not Afflict You

It is important for you to know that God does not afflict you. Otherwise you might be angry at Him, and that wouldn't be good for you. God allowing you to reap some of the just consequences of your own sin is very different than God afflicting you. In the example of raising my son, if I had been the one afflicting him, I would be the one taunting him and making fun of him. I would be pointing out to all of his friends his inadequate clothing and being sure to point out his immaturity and irresponsibility. That would be an awful thing to do! Can you imagine doing that to your own child?

God specifically tells us that He won't do this to us.

Happy the man who remains steadfast under trial, for having passed that test he will receive for his prize the gift of life promised to those who love God. No one under trial or temptation should say, "I am being tempted by God"; for God is untouched by evil, and does not himself tempt anyone. Temptation arises when a man is enticed and lured away by his own lust; then lust conceives, and gives birth to sin; and sin full-grown breeds death. Do not deceive yourselves, my friends. All good giving and every perfect gift comes from above, from the Father of the lights of heaven. With him there is no variation, no

---

[63]
Romans 8:16, *The Spirit Himself bears witness with our spirit that we are children of God.*

1 Corinthians 6:19-20, *Or do you not know that your body is the temple of the Holy Spirit who is in you, whom you have from God, and you are not your own?*

Ephesians 1:13, *In Him you also trusted, after you heard the word of truth, the gospel of your salvation; in whom also, having believed, you were sealed with the Holy Spirit of promise,* *play of passing shadows. Of his set purpose, by declaring the truth, he gave us birth to be a kind of firstfruits of his creatures"* (James 1:12-18, <u>New English Bible</u>).

The above scripture touches on God's purpose in allowing trials in our lives. He says, *he gave us birth to be a kind of firstfruits of his creatures.* He also implies that this is a good thing: *All good giving and every perfect gift comes from above.* But what does this really mean?

What Is The Purpose Of Your Life?

Does your life have a purpose, or is it just a series of random events that will be over when you die? As a Christian, what does God expect of you? Does He have a plan for you? Have you ever asked yourself questions like:

- Why do bad things happen to "good" people?
- Why do I suffer?
- Why does life sometimes seem to not go my way?
- Why do my plans so often not work out?
- Will I go to hell because I sin?
- Am I pleasing God?
- Why am I not prospering?
- Why don't I feel satisfied and fulfilled?
- What is the purpose of my life?

Truly, life is frustrating and confusing when you don't know what God's plan is for you and what He wants from you.

Possible Purposes For Your Life

In reading the Bible it is possible to come up with quite a challenging list of things that Christians are supposed to do with their lives.

"The List"

We are to:

- love God.
- worship God.
- love others.
- preach the Gospel.
- bring others into the Kingdom.
- live a "good" life.
- be a good witness to the world.
- be changed into the image of God.
- resist evil.
- pray for one another.

This is an overwhelming list, and yet it isn't even exhaustive. It seems even more overwhelming when we have been striving to live up to any part of it. Most of us have tried very hard, and we have not been very successful. It may even seem impossible. The Apostle Paul experienced this same struggle.

> *For what I am doing, I do not understand. For what I will to do, that I do not practice; but what I hate, that I do. . . O wretched man that I am! Who will deliver me from this body of death? I thank God - through Jesus Christ our Lord!* (Romans 7:15, 24-25).

Paul understands our struggle, and here he is saying that Jesus can deliver us from this cycle of trying and failing, trying and failing again. But how can this happen?

Jesus Kept The Whole "List"

Jesus kept the whole "List." How did He manage to do this? He did it because it was his very nature, and therefore He did it effortlessly and perfectly. A fish swims and a bird flies. They don't have to think about it, they just do it. It is their nature. Jesus lived perfectly because he was without sin.

Then Jesus says that we are to do the same works as He did!

"Most assuredly, I say to you, he who believes in Me, the works that I do he will do also; and greater works than these he will do, because I go to My Father" (John 14:12).

How Can <u>We</u> Possibly Keep "The List?"

How can we possibly keep "The List," when we find it so difficult to keep one or two of the items? It sounds impossible. Jesus was able to keep "The List" because it was His nature. That is also the only way <u>we</u> can keep it. <u>We need a new nature</u>. We need to be changed into the image of Jesus. When have been changed, we too can keep "The List." As we are in the process of being changed into His image, we will each <u>incrementally</u> gain His nature, and we will then behave as He does, <u>step by step</u>. As each segment of our "Honeycomb" (see Chapter 3) is cleansed and inhabited by Jesus,

- **The primary thing that God wants is <u>to change us into the image of Jesus</u>. He doesn't want us to <u>act</u> like Jesus. He wants us to <u>be</u> like Jesus. When we "be" like Him, we will then "act" like Him.**
- **The good root (Jesus in us) will then produce good fruit.**

the new "good root" (Jesus) will produce "good fruit." In that specific area of our lives, our character has been transformed. [64]

Why Does God Want This For You?

We don't know all the reasons why God wants you changed into the image of Jesus, but He does reveal some of the reasons.

1. He loves you. As a result of this love, He gave His Son to make it possible for you to be set free from the just consequences of your sins. He hates sin, because it causes His children to suffer. He wants this cycle of sin and death to stop.[65]
2. You are here to be changed into the image of Jesus in order to be prepared to rule and reign with Him in eternity. You need to be like Him to be trustworthy so that you can carry out this assignment.[66]
3. He wants companions, beings that have freely chosen Him, despite the fact that in many ways it would have been easier not to choose Him.[67]

---

[64] "The kind of character development which happens in the soul is His primary interest and purpose" (Sandford, Restoring the Christian Family, p.5)

[65] **John 3:16:** *For God so loved the world that He gave His only begotten Son, that whoever believes in Him should not perish but have everlasting life.*

Romans 8:23: *For the law of the Spirit of life in Christ Jesus has made me free from the law of sin and death.*

[66] **Matthew 19:28:** *So Jesus said to them, 'Assuredly I say to you, that in the regeneration, when the Son of Man sits on the throne of His glory, you who have followed Me will also sit on twelve thrones, judging the twelve tribes of Israel.*

See Endnote #6-1 for more scriptures on God's ultimate plan for us.

[67] **Romans 8:18,** *For I consider that the sufferings of this present time are not worthy to be compared with the glory which shall be revealed in us.*

2 Timothy 2:12, *If we endure, we shall also reign with Him. If we deny Him, He also will deny us.*

Revelation 3:21, *To him who overcomes I will grant to sit with Me on My throne, as I also overcame and sat down with My Father on His throne.*

Revelation 20:4, *And I saw thrones, and they sat on them, and judgment was committed to them. And I saw the souls of those who had been beheaded for their witness to Jesus and for the word of God, who had not worshiped the beast or his image, and have not received his mark on their foreheads or on their hands. And they lived and reigned with Christ for a thousand years.*

As you can see, God made provision for you not only to go to heaven and to live with Him for eternity, but He also made provision for you in this life.

Being "Saved" Has Two Meanings.

1. The first meaning refers to the **one time event** that occurred when you made Him Lord of your life. At that moment you turned over to Him the "title deed," the ownership rights, to your life. We call this event such things as: becoming a Christian, being born again, or "justification." This event happens at the point in time when you believed in the Lord Jesus Christ and received Him into your life.[68]

From then on, you belong to God[69]. You are a member of His family[70], a child of His, and thus He has permission to do whatever He wants to in your life.

Because He loves you, whatever He does is always for your best interest.[71] He knows how to take care of those who belong to Him.

---

[68]　**Romans 10:9,** *that if you confess with your mouth the Lord Jesus and believe in your heart that God has raised Him from the dead, you will be saved.*

[69]　**1 Corinthians 6:19-20,** . . .*and you are not your own? For you were bought at a price;*

1 Corinthians 7:22-23, *Likewise he who is called while free is Christ's slave. You were bought at a price"*

[70]　**Galatians 4:3-7,** *Even so we, when we were children, were in bondage under the elements of the world. But when the fullness of the time had come, God sent forth His Son, born of a woman, born under the law, to redeem those who were under the law, that we might receive the adoption as sons. And because you are sons, God has sent forth the Spirit of His Son into your hearts, crying out, 'Abba, Father!' Therefore you are no longer a slave but a son, and if a son, then an heir of God through Christ.*

[71]　**Hebrews 12:5-12,** *And you have forgotten the exhortation which speaks to you as to sons: 'My son, do not despise the chastening of the Lord, nor be discouraged when you are rebuked by Him; for whom the Lord loves He chastens, and scourges every son whom He receives.' If you endure chastening, God deals with you as with sons; for what son is there whom a father does not chasten? But if you are without chastening, of which all have become partakers, then you are illegitimate and not sons. Furthermore, we have had human fathers who corrected us, and we paid them respect. Shall we not much more readily be in subjection to the Father of spirits and live? For they indeed for a few days chastened us as seemed best to them, but He for our profit, that we may be partakers of His holiness. Now no chastening seems to be joyful for the present, but grievous; nevertheless, afterward it yields the peaceable fruit of righteousness to those who have been trained by it.*

2. The second meaning of being "saved" refers to the **ongoing process** that then takes place in which you are being changed into His image. We call this process "sanctification," or discipleship, or growing in Godliness, or being transformed into the image of Jesus. This is a lifetime process, and is sometimes called "Inner Healing, " though this particular term does not appear in the Bible. Your sanctification is His major goal for you, and He spares no resources to bring this about. Everything else in your life is secondary to this goal.[72] You may have some other goal in life, such as happiness, or abundance, or a life without difficulties. If these other things are your goals in life, whenever you don't reach these other goals, it can be frustrating and confusing. However, it is only confusing because you don't see God's priority in that moment, because you have your eyes on the wrong goal. You may also want to read about "justification" and "sanctification" in the Glossary.

> **Your sanctification is God's major goal for you, and He spares no resources to bring this about. Everything else in your life is secondary to this goal.**

---

[72] **Hebrews 12:10,** *For they indeed for a few days chastened us as seemed best to them, but He for our profit, that we may be partakers of His holiness. Now no chastening seems to be joyful for the present, but grievous; nevertheless afterward it yields the peaceable fruit of righteousness to those who have been trained by it.*

   James 1:2-4, *My brethren, count it all joy when you fall into various trials, knowing that the testing of your faith produces patience. But let patience have its perfect work, that you may be perfect and complete, lacking nothing.*

   See Endnote #6-2 for more scriptures on God working in our hearts.

   See Endnote #6-3 for more scriptures on the process of being changed into the image of Jesus.

Recognize that the "one-time" event does not change you into the image of Jesus (being sanctified). It only puts you into a legal position for God to take you on your journey of being sanctified.[73]

God Is Very Personal With You

The events that happen in your life as a Christian are not random, or impersonal consequences of your sin, nor are they pointless. They are God's personal, loving attention to your life.

Keep in mind that the Lord's paramount goal is to change you into the image of Jesus, and everything else is secondary. Just as good parents have to allow their children to suffer difficulties if they are to mature, so God allows the trials you go through in order to bring about the transformation you need.[74]   He knows each of us

---

[73]   **Philippians 3:12,** Paul, speaking of himself (a Christian) *Not that I have already attained, or am already perfected; but I press on, that I may lay hold of that for which Christ Jesus has also laid hold of me.* (Underlining is mine).

   "The *present reality* of righteousness rests upon its having been 'revealed' by the occurring of salvation in Christ (Rom. 3:21-26; 2 Cor. 5:21; *cf* 1 Cor. 1:30). This saving occurrence, however, is the *eschatological event* by which God ended the old course of the world and introduced the new aeon. For 'when the time had fully come, God sent forth his son' (Gal. 4:4); so now 'the old has passed away' and 'the new has come' and whoever is 'in Christ' is a 'new creature' (2 Cor. 5:17). The New Covenant (2 Cor. 3:6ff.) predicted for the eschatological period by Jeremiah has taken the place of the Old Covenant." (Bultmann, Theology of the New Testament, Part II, p. 278). Note: Eschatology here refers to the end of a time or age, or the consummation of God's purpose for a particular time (Elwell p.362).

[74]   If life is going well for us, and if we then think it is because we have no sin in us, we are deluded. *There is none righteous, not one* (Romans 3:10).

   We all sin many times daily, and we have done so all of our lives; though we may be unaware of these areas of sin until the Lord shows them to us. *If we say that we have no sin, we deceive ourselves, and the truth is not in us* (1 John 1:8).

   Consequently, if Satan had free access to all areas of sin in each of us, we would be destroyed by him immediately. After all, he hates us and would miss no opportunity to oppress one of God's children. As water entering a leak in a boat, Satan would enter into us through any crack available. Since our own "boat" leaks like a sieve (lots of sin), and since Satan doesn't overwhelm and sink us immediately, there must be something else keeping him out. God's boat doesn't leak, and we are in His boat.

   Since this total destruction does not come upon us, there must be something restraining Satan. This restraint is God's protecting us in many ways, most of which we are not even aware. He knows how to protect His children. See also: Ps 23:1-6, 27:1-6, 91:1-16;Is 26:3-4, 41:10; Is 26:3-4, 41:10, 43:1-10; 2 Cor 1:10; 2 Tim 1;12 Heb 7:25; 1 Pet 4:19; Jude 24.

and <u>carefully designs each of our training programs</u> to fit us perfectly. He knows our level of maturity.[75]

This Sanctification Process Can Feel Grievous

Now no chastening seems to be joyful for the present, but grievous; nevertheless afterward it yields the peaceable fruit of righteousness to those who have been trained by it. (Hebrews 12:11).

Unfortunately, this process of being changed into His image is very difficult. If everything in our life went smoothly, we would become spoiled, self-centered, and greedy. We can see this in children who are not properly disciplined by their parents. This tendency is also illustrated in the Old Testament and the history of the nation of Israel.

- When King David began to prosper and experience a life of ease, he sinned with Bathsheba.

- King Solomon had the throne handed to him, and he always experienced a life of ease and luxury. He sinned mightily. For example, he had 700 wives and 300 concubines, *and his wives turned away his heart* (1 Kings 11:3). He also greatly oppressed the people (1 Kings 12:4).

- When God gave prosperity to the people of Israel, they strayed from God because they felt self-sufficient. They only came back to Him when threatened with destruction. This happened many times in their history. He warned them about this tendency in Deuteronomy 6:12: *"then beware, lest you forget the Lord who*

---

[75] **Hebrews 4:14-16,** *Seeing then that we have a great High Priest who has passed through the heavens, Jesus the Son of God, let us hold fast our confession. For we do not have a High Priest who cannot sympathize with our weaknesses, but was in all points tempted as we are, yet without sin. Let us therefore come boldly to the throne of grace, that we may obtain mercy and find grace to help in time of need.*

brought you out of the land of Egypt, from the house of bondage." [76]

The apostle Paul is also an example of God using Satan to bring about eventual blessing. Paul says of himself,

And lest I should be exalted above measure by the abundance of the revelations, a thorn in the flesh was given to me, a messenger of Satan to buffet me, lest I be exalted above measure. Concerning this thing I pleaded with the Lord three times that it might depart from me. And He said to me, 'My grace is sufficient for you, for My strength is made perfect in weakness'. Therefore most gladly I will rather boast of my infirmities, that the power of Christ may rest upon me (2 Corinthians 12:7-10).

Clearly, the Lord knew that Paul might become "exalted" (*huperairomai*, "to become haughty") because of the special things that he experienced, and it was clearly implied in this passage that it was within the Lord's power to remove the "thorn." But He didn't remove it, because it was in the best interest of both Paul and the cause of Christ for which Paul labored that the "thorn" remain. [77]

Therefore, each of us needs tests, trials, and discomfort to achieve God's goal for us, because these things motivate us. God undoubtedly wishes that He did not have to allow us to be afflicted and thus experience pain, but He knows He must if we are to be transformed. I am also convinced that He uses the minimum amount of pain and challenge necessary to accomplish the change, but He <u>does</u> use every bit of pressure that is necessary to accomplish His purpose.

---

[76] Also read Jeremiah, Chapter 25, Ezekiel Chapter14, and Deuteronomy Chapter 28 and Deuteronomy 6:10-12; 32:15 for more examples of Israel's waywardness.

[77] Job is another person who suffered so that his character could be changed. **See Endnote #6-4** for more details on Job's trials.

He is more interested in our character than in our being free from pain.[78]

Again, keep in mind that as Christians we are in a special relationship with God. We are now His children and we have given Him ownership of our life[79]. There will be times when we, like Paul, would rather not be experiencing the pain; but God is more interested in our character than in our comfort. Those who are not members of God's family do not have the same level of protection from evil. Since God does not "own them," He therefore does not have the same freedom to operate in their lives.

What About The Devil?

God is sovereign, and He is greater than the Devil.[80] God protects those who belong to Him. So as God's child, Satan does not have access to you unless God allows it. God sometimes even uses Satan to accomplish His purposes.

There are Christians who believe it is their job to rebuke the Devil all the time. They see a demon behind every negative thing that happens to them, and they believe it is totally up to them to stand against the Devil (in the name of Jesus, of course). It is as though they are naked and alone; and if they don't protect themselves, nobody else will. This is based upon a misunderstanding of Scripture, and this tendency may be evidence of striving, performance and a need to control. Their view is totally different than the view I am presenting.

You do need to recognize that there is an enemy and many demons. Usually, however, they have no access to you. For most

---

[78] **Hebrews 12:10-11,** *For they indeed for a few days chastened us as seemed best to them, but He for our profit, that we may be partakers of His holiness. Now no chastening seems to be joyful for the present, but grievous; nevertheless afterward it yields the peaceable fruit of righteousness to those who have been trained by it.*

[79] **1 Corinthians 6:19-20,** . . . *and you are not your own? For you were bought at a price; therefore glorify God in your body and in your spirit, which are God's.*

[80] **See Endnote #6-5** regarding the lie of *dualism,* which gives a false picture of the battle between God and Satan.

people, their problems are not demonic (see Chapter 16, "Deliverance and Inner Healing," for more details on this subject). When you gave your life to Jesus, you became His property, and He became your protector.[81]   When demons do have access, it is because God is allowing this in order to accomplish His purpose. There are, in fact, times when God's purpose is for you to practice using your authority to command demons. When Paul commanded the demon in Acts 16:16-18,[82] he first walked by the situation for many days before he acted, so he obviously did not command demons every time he saw evil. Evidently, Paul only acted when God told him to.

Random Use Of Authority Can Be Dangerous!

If you use your authority to command a demon when that is not what God does want you to do at that moment, you may find yourself getting in the way of God's plan. Or worse yet, you may find yourself in trouble and learning a hard lesson. "If God has not directly commanded you to do this kind of spiritual warfare, you are engaged in presumptive behavior. In essence, that is rebellion" (Jackson, p.38). For more on this subject, read Needless Casualties of War by John Paul Jackson.

---

[81]   2 Tim 1:12, *For this reason I also suffer these things, but I am not ashamed; for I know whom I have believed and I am convinced that He is able to guard what I have entrusted to Him until that day.*
   See Endnote #6-6 for more on God's protection.

[82]   Acts 16:16-18, 23, 30, *Now it happened, as we went to prayer, that a certain slave girl possessed with a spirit of divination met us, who bought her masters much profit by fortune-telling. This girl followed Paul and us, and cried out, saying, "These men are the servants of the Most High God, who proclaim to us the way of salvation." And this she did for many days. But Paul, greatly annoyed, turned and said to the spirit, "I command you in the name of Jesus Christ to come our of her," and he came out that very hour . . . And when they had laid many stripes on them, they threw them into prison, commanding the jailer to keep them securely . . . And he brought them out and said, "Sirs, what must I do to be saved?"*

A Change Of Attitude Results From This New Awareness

Once you realize that God is active in all the troubles you face, your whole attitude will change. Instead of fighting against what He is doing, you will tend to ask, "OK, Lord, I don't like this at all. But what are You trying to change in me through this miserable experience?" This explains a scripture that many of us have hated:

> *My brethren, count it all joy when you fall into various trials, knowing that the testing of your faith produces patience. But let patience have its perfect work, that you may be perfect and complete, lacking nothing* (James 1:2-4).

Now that you understand what God is doing in your life, this verse makes perfect sense! I used to have comfort, peace, and financial prosperity as my life's goals. At that time I thought that if I had enough faith, then my life should be smooth sailing. But it seemed to me that God would keep going by in a motorboat making waves on my placid lake.[83] At that time I would get angry whenever my life didn't go well. I used to resist what was going on, thinking it shouldn't be happening. I would either be angry with God or I would wonder what I had done wrong that had caused the problem.

---

[83]
Romans 5:3-10, *And not only that, but we also glory in tribulations, knowing that tribulation produces perseverance; and perseverance, character; and character, hope. Now hope does not disappoint, because the love of God has been poured out in our hearts by the Holy Spirit who was given to us. For when we were still without strength, in due time Christ died for the ungodly. For scarcely for a righteous man will one die; yet perhaps for a good man someone would even dare to die. But God demonstrates His own love toward us, in that while we were still sinners, Christ died for us. Much more then, having now been justified by His blood, we shall be saved from wrath through Him. For if when we were enemies we were reconciled to God through the death of His Son, much more, having been reconciled, we shall be saved by His life.* Note that here "saved" refers to the sanctification process, or transformation. (in addition to our final salvation and to the consequences of the great white throne judgment of Revelation 20:12).

Revelation 3:18-21, *"I counsel you to buy from Me gold refined in the fire, that you may be rich; and white garments, that you may be clothed, that the shame of your nakedness may not be revealed; and anoint your eyes with eye salve, that you may see. As many as I love, I rebuke and chasten. Therefore be zealous and repent. Behold, I stand at the door and knock. If anyone hears My voice and opens the door, I will come in to him and dine with him, and he with Me. To him who overcomes I will grant to sit with Me on My throne, as I also overcame and sat down with My Father on His throne."*

See Endnote #6-7 for more scriptures on how God pressures us in order to heal us.

This perspective had a tendency to put me in a performance mode by thinking that if I do right (by the power of my will, of course), things will go well in my life. If I don't do right, then things will not go well. That view is in error for a New Testament believer. This erroneous perspective eliminates God's active participation in my life. In truth, worrying and striving are not necessary. I just need to listen and obey.

Sin Has Consequences

Does the fact that God is committed to our sanctification mean it is alright to sin? After all, we may conclude, He will protect us from the consequences of our sin. But keep in mind that God is <u>actively</u> in charge of our process. If we begin to think we are so insulated from the consequences of our sin that we can sin and get away with it, God will know this and discipline us accordingly. God looks on the heart, and we can't fool Him. He is gracious to the repentant, but committed to our sanctification. If we are being casual about sin, we are not being like Jesus, and so He will go to work on correcting our misperception.

> *Moreover the law entered that the offense might abound. But where sin abounded, grace abounded much more, so that as sin reigned in death, even so grace might reign through righteousness to eternal life through Jesus Christ our Lord. What shall we say then? Shall we continue in sin that grace may abound? Certainly not! How shall we who died to sin live any longer in it?* (Romans 6:1-2).

Because God is actively in charge of our sanctification, reaping from our sin is not simply a mechanical consequence, and the consequences are not random. Sometimes He causes us to reap what we sow, because that

> **The consequences God allows are not to punish us, but to lead us to healing (to being changed into the image of Jesus).**

is what we need to pay attention to at that moment. At other times He protects us from the consequences of a sin, because that is not what He is working on in our life at that time. The consequences are not to punish us, but to lead us to healing (to being changed into the image of Jesus).

If We Resist

It is true that if we drag our feet or rebel against the lesson He is giving us, it will be harder for us. Then we will have to endure more suffering. Since He is determined to heal us, He will persist in bringing trials until we do respond. On the other hand, if we listen and obey, then the trial can end, because it has accomplished its purpose. This is one very important reason why we must understand the purpose of our trials, so that we will not fight against what God is doing, or attempt to evade his discipline.

We can do it the easy way, or the hard way.

Saul discovered this on the road to Damascus. He had been

> **God is actively in charge of our lives, and the consequences we experience from our sin are not random. They are to motivate us so as to lead us to healing**

persecuting the early church and was obviously ignoring any messages from God. God had to roll out the "big guns" to get his attention. Jesus appeared in a bright light, and Saul fell to the ground.

> *And Saul said, "Who are You, Lord?" And He said, "I am Jesus, Whom you are persecuting. It is dangerous and it turns out badly for you to keep kicking against the goad - that is, to offer vain and perilous resistance"* (Acts 9:5, Amplified Bible).

In that moment, God got Saul's attention. Saul was terrified! *Trembling and astonished he asked, Lord, what do You desire me to do?* (verse 9:6). Saul believed, and then he obeyed what Jesus told him to do.

There can, of course, also be natural consequences to things that we do in ignorance, or willfully, or because of weakness. Examples of natural consequences would be destruction to our health through smoking or over-eating, or physical injury from risky behavior. If we suffer such consequences, it may not have anything to do with God's plan for us, or His training. These consequences may simply be the natural consequences of physical laws. Even in these areas, however, God will do everything He can to warn us about the problem, and He will find a way to use these experiences as part of our process of being transformed.

God only expects us to deal with the areas of sin that He knows we are ready to work on. In other words, He has a plan for our lives, He has our lives under His control, and He only lets us pay the consequences for those sins that He wants us to deal with right now. That is part of the mystery. He has a unique and a dynamic plan for each of us, and it is ever changing as we grow. That is why a formula doesn't work.

The Christian Walk Is Not A Set Of Rules. We Have A Living God

It is important to guard against trying to reduce God to a formula. Putting Him in a box this way often happens so subtly that we are not even aware of it. For instance, when I am faced with a problem in my life, I go to the Bible to find an answer. This is good. But this quest for His guidance can go astray.

Suppose a woman is married to a non-Christian. She badly wants her husband to receive Jesus, so she "claims" Acts 16:31, spoken to the Philippian jailer: *"Believe on the Lord Jesus Christ, and you will be saved, you and your household."* But her husband remains unsaved, year after year. Many of you may have heard this scripture applied in this way.

In this same way, I once claimed a scripture at a time when my business was struggling. I had been taught that God wants us to have plenty, so I personally claimed 3 John 1:2: *Beloved, I pray that you may prosper in all things and be in health, just as your soul prospers.* Instead of improving, my business problems persisted. In fact, strange things happened to thwart my business plans. It became obvious that it was God who was getting in the way of me prospering. I was mystified, and I was angry with God because He wasn't answering my prayer as He was "supposed" to.

What went wrong? Didn't God make this promise? Wasn't I praying hard enough? Was there something wrong with my faith? Was the Devil stealing my blessing?

Yes, God did make this promise, but not necessarily to me at this moment in my life. I have since discovered an error in what I believed. I had tried to reduce God to a formula. This error is quite common among Christians. This misperception often happens so subtly that we are not even aware that we have gotten off track. The quest for guidance in my life goes astray when I take a scripture spoken to someone else in another time and take it as a promise to myself in the present. When I make this mistake, I am taking the Bible as a legalistic <u>rulebook,</u> and that particular scripture as a <u>formula.</u> When I do this, I am subtly seeing God's Word as an object, not as an expression of a living, present God.[84] I am then reducing God to a set of rules, and am subtly denying His active, living presence in my daily life.

God knew that the Philippian jailer's household would be saved, and so His word through Paul and Silas was a true, living word direct from the Living God for <u>that</u> household <u>at that time.</u> In the same way, our living God will give us the guidance we need when we need it, if we are seeking and listening.[85] His direction will be specific to us for that time in our life, will promote what is good for us, and will always be in line with His character.

There can be another hidden implication in this misuse of Scripture. I may think that if I can understand "how God does things," I can use Scripture to get what I want. One reason I fall for

---

[84] Rudolf Bultmann refers to this tendency to turn God's word into a rule-book as to "objectivize God and His actions." (Bultmann, <u>Jesus Christ and Mythology,</u> p.83).

[85] As with Paul on the road to Damascus, sometimes God will get our attention even when we are not seeking and listening. We can do it the easy way, or the hard way.

this trap is because this puts me back in control.[86] I want to be in control of my own life, because at some level I don't trust God to take care of me.

However, despite my need to control, God is the One in control of my life. I used to try to use Scripture this way, but God loved me too much to allow me to succeed in my error. He was <u>always</u> faithful to prevent me from succeeding in my attempts to use Scripture in this way. I used to get very angry with Him about it.

I now know that God frustrated me because He wanted me to know that He is a living person with a will and emotions and a good plan for my life.

He is God, He is actively in control, and I am not. And that is a very good thing!

Profoundly Different, But True!

The view I am presenting may be profoundly different than what you have believed. As a new Christian, I was greatly interested in what my new life was all about, and I wondered what I was supposed to be doing. I wanted so much to obey God. Unfortunately, I heard preaching that confused me. From one teacher I would be told that our main duty was to

> **God loved me too much to let me succeed in my delusion that I can do it myself.**

preach the Gospel. I tried that, but failed miserably. Another teacher emphasized loving God. I tried that, but knew I was doing that inadequately. At one time or another, I tried to do most of the things on "The List."[87] I wanted so much to please God, but kept falling short.

However, as time went by and I began to see what God <u>really</u> wanted from me, I experienced great relief. God knew I couldn't do

---

[86] In Martin Luther's day, the Roman Catholic Church was stuck in legalism and works. **See Endnote #6-8** to understand how Martin Luther was freed from this bondage.

[87] **See Endnote #6-9** for more details on teachings that may be confusing to us.

those things in my own strength. He knew that the only way I could obey Him was for Him to change me into the image of Jesus. I then realized how confused I had previously been.

If you have tried to obey Him and failed, this new understanding will bring great relief and will be life giving to you. When you can look at the Bible through the eyes of this new perspective, God's plan for you will make sense, and you will be able to see that His plan for you is possible to fulfill! Once you can understand what God expects, and the glorious provision that He has made so that it is possible to achieve, many otherwise confusing scriptures will no longer be confusing.

Most of this book will be devoted to showing you how you can become like Jesus, and revealing the amazing, miraculous provisions God has established through Jesus so that this transformation can happen in you.

The purpose of this book is to show you how to cooperate with God's plan for you, which is to change you into the image of Jesus.

Why It Is So Important To Know About God's Plan For Your Life

I devoted an entire chapter on the issue of God's plan for His children, because it is so highly important.

His plan for you is the very foundation for your Christian life, here on earth, and everything I have written in this book depends upon this understanding. You can either resist what He is doing, or cooperate.

- For many, the awareness that God is in charge of every aspect of their life will require a huge shift in perspective as to how they view themselves and their life as a Christian.
- This walk is not just for a sick few, but rather it is the normal life for every Christian.

- The goal of Inner Healing is not simply to remove your pain, but it has the larger goal of changing you into the image of Jesus. Pain is simply a motivator.

- Inner Healing is a new way of life, living in a new way every day for the rest of your life. You cannot go back to your old way of living or you will again be stuck.

> **Inner Healing is the very core of God's plan for your life.**

- Inner Healing is the very core of God's plan for your life. Life will only go well if you are pursuing His plan for you.

Summary

When we sin, by the operation of God's laws we set in motion negative consequences which will bring destruction in our lives. However, God loves His children and is on our side. He has the power to protect us from these consequences, and He does so. However, there are times when God steps aside and allows us to suffer these just consequences of <u>our sin</u>.

When He does allow us to suffer, it is always for our good. Though the suffering is painful for the moment, He allows it because He has a good plan for us. God wants to change us into the image of Jesus. He knows that repenting and forgiving are often difficult for us, and sometimes we need suffering and pain to motivate us to surrender to His process.

God is personally committed to this process in each of His children. He tailor makes the plan for each individual, and He personally oversees it as it

> **We can rest in the sure knowledge that our loving Father is in charge of our life.**

proceeds. Our sanctification is not a mechanical or random process, so we can rest in the sure knowledge that our loving Father is in charge.

What then shall we say to these things? If God is for us, who can be against us? He who did not spare His own Son, but delivered Him up for us all, how shall He not with Him also freely give us all things? Who shall bring a charge against God's elect? It is God who justifies. Who is he who condemns? It is Christ who died, and furthermore is also risen, who is even at the right hand of God, who also makes intercession for us. Who shall separate us from the love of Christ? Shall tribulation, or distress, or persecution or famine, or nakedness, or peril, or sword? . . . Yet in all these things we are more than conquerors through Him who loved us (Romans 8:31-35, 37).

It is a hostile world, but not a hostile God. God is on your side!

Chapter 7

Decisions That Bind Us
Inner Vows

As discussed earlier, judging is the first and primary sin that causes bad fruit in our lives. There is a second related sin which holds us in bondage, which we call an Inner Vow. It is a close cousin to judging, although it has its own features. An Inner Vow is usually present whenever there is a Bitter Root Judgment.

George, a ten-year-old boy, has a father who is a very angry man. His father's inner anger is taken out on George and his mother and his siblings. George comes to hate his father, and he judges him. So the consequences of the first sin of judging takes effect and will cause him trouble later in life. But at some point George also says to himself, "I am never going to be like my father." George has just made an Inner Vow, and this compounds and expands his future problems.

The judgment against his father is sin, and it plants a bitter root that will grow inside him and produce bad fruit in his life as a result of the operation of God's law. It is simply the way the spiritual universe works.

But he has compounded his problem by taking his life into his own hands. George decides that he will never be like his father, whom he despises. He has just entered into bondage. What will likely happen in George's adult life is that usually he will not get angry, because the Inner Vow represses his anger. But now and then he will explode in a fit of rage, and those around him will be wounded. Afterwards he will be angry with himself because he has just acted exactly the way his father did!

During those times when he is successfully repressing his anger, other people may sense the anger seething below the surface, but George will be unaware of it. After all, he has decided that being angry is bad, and he doesn't want to admit to himself that he has anger inside. In Chapter 11, "Emotions Are Your Friend," I will talk more about emotions, their nature, and how they behave.

The problem for George is that he is locked into this pattern of behavior. He hates it, but he is powerless to change it. He is again reaping from the operation of God's law, but in a slightly different way.

The Nature Of An Inner Vow

The rigid features of "always" or "never" lock us into a specific mode of behavior, in the same way that a railroad track keeps a train on a specific route.   A railroad track goes from point A to point B.   If the engineer wants to turn off somewhere in between point A and point B, he

> **An Inner Vow is a decision that we make that contains the words "always" or "never".**

is unable to do so, because the railroad track follows a specified path and doesn't go anywhere else. Similarly an Inner Vows doesn't allow for any divergence from the "path" specified by the person's declaration.

We all realize there are things in our lives that need changing, and at times we make decisions to change. We often call these decisions "New Year's Resolutions." We all laugh about them, because we have all made them and usually we can't keep them. Why are these decisions so puny while the Inner Vows are so powerful?

The difference between the New Year's Resolution and an Inner Vow is that the resolution was made with our head, whereas the Inner Vow was made with our heart. The way the Inner Vow got into our heart was that at the time we made it we were very much living from our heart. We were in a state of bitterness, and our emotions were greatly stirred. When we made an Inner Vow we were judging, and it is the power of the sin of judging that gives the Inner Vow its power.

It is important to note that many Inner Vows are not consciously spoken or even thought. This is especially true with small children. Even though they may not yet know how to talk, yet they can still make Inner Vows.

And yet there was another powerful dynamic going on when we made the Inner Vow. At that moment we were taking our life into our own hands. We decided that nobody else was going to rescue us from this awful situation, and so we were

> **When we made an Inner Vow we were judging, and it is the power of the sin of judging that gives the Inner Vow its power.**

going to have to take control of our own life.[88] Thus we judged God and we were presumptuous. In our opinion God was not fixing the situation, so we needed to do it. We presumed that we had the ability to protect ourselves with our own power. This sin is a cousin to judging.

Remember that when we judge another person we are usurping God's role, because we don't trust Him to be the just judge. In the case of an Inner Vow, when we decide to do it ourselves, we are again usurping God's role. We do

> **In the moment when we don't trust God to be our protector, we decide to take control and to be our own protector.**

this because we don't trust Him to take care of us. Right from the Garden of Eden there has been a tendency for man to want to be like God, to take His place.[89]

---

[88] See Endnote #7-1 for more about the feeling that accompanies the making of an Inner Vow.

[89] **James 4:12-16** links these two sets of sins: judging and being self-willed: *There is one Lawgiver, who is able to save and to destroy. Who are you to judge another? Come now, you who say, 'Today or tomorrow we will go to such and such a city, spend a year there, buy and sell, and make a profit'; whereas you do not know what will happen tomorrow. For what is your life? It is even a vapor that appears for a little time and then vanishes away. Instead you ought to say, 'If the Lord wills, we shall live and do this or that.' But now you boast in your arrogance. All such boasting is evil.*

See Endnote #7-2 for more details on such boasting.

The Inner Vow itself is not sin, because we have a right to make decisions. But at the time that we make an Inner Vow, we have bitterness in our heart. In that moment we don't trust God to be our protector, and we decide to take control. We decide to take God's place and to be our own protector.

When we do that, we are in sin.[90] When we sin in this way, our willpower no longer has authority over the decision that we made in our moment of bitterness. In that moment of bitterness, a bitter root was planted in our heart. A <u>spiritual event</u> occurred, writing the decision in our heart. Now that decision is no longer under the authority of our own power. God's laws are now impelling it to operate as we had decided. After this point we cannot decide to renounce it and make it stop operating. From then on it will direct our life, perhaps making us do things we no longer want to do.

Summary Of Features Of An Inner Vow

1. An Inner Vow is a decision we make that contains the words "always" or "never.

2. Therefore, an Inner Vow is rigid and locks us into specific behaviors.

3. The most powerful ones were made when we were very small.

> **Once the Inner Vow is etched in our heart, it operates unconsciously and irresistibly.**

4. They are often forgotten by our conscious mind, or were never verbalized or consciously made.

5. Often we only know that an Inner Vow is present because of the bondage in our life.

6. An Inner Vow is always connected to a Judgment. There may be several Inner Vows connected with one Judgment.

---

[90] One can now see how Inner Vows have a close relationship to Judgments. In both cases we don't trust God to do the job, so we jump in to take over, to do it ourselves.

How To Stop The Operation Of An Inner Vow

The power of an Inner Vow in our life can be broken. Since sin is what gave it power, first we need to deal with the sin. But what sin? Remember that when we made the Inner Vow we were in the process of judging. Then we committed the second sin, of being our own God – "I will do it myself."

To break the power of the Inner Vow in his life, George needs to do the following:

1. First he needs to recognize that he judged his father, forgive him from his heart, and receive forgiveness from God.
2. Then he also needs to recognize how he judged God (because He wasn't protecting him the way he thought God should) and decided to take his life into his own hands. He then needs to forgive God from his heart and receive forgiveness from God.
3. Then George can successfully renounce the Inner Vow. He would say something like this, "In the Name of Jesus, I renounce the decision that I made to never be like my father. It had been written in my heart, and Jesus, I ask You to erase it and to set me free, so that I can be free to obey You."

How does he know that he has been successful? The rigid behavior will stop. George will be able to be appropriately angry at the appropriate time, and the outbursts of rage will stop.

Again I want to emphasize that this is not a formula, or a rote prayer. The example I have presented simply lays out the principles, but we need to say the appropriate words that the Lord gives us to speak.

A Common Fear

Sometimes people are afraid to renounce their Inner Vows. Because he wants so desperately to not be like his father, George may find it difficult to renounce his Inner Vow. He is afraid that if he does so, he will become like his father. That would be intolerable (even though he currently acts like him anyway). But what actually happens when he is set free of the bondage of the Inner Vow is that he is free to feel the anger when it is present. After all, the anger was always present, but previously he wasn't free to feel it. He needs to feel it so that he can recognize that he has judged the person who currently transgressed him, and then he can process it by forgiving and being forgiven. I will speak more about this in Chapter 11 on emotions.

What About "Good" Inner Vows?

When George said "I will never be like my father," he might also have said "I will always be nice." What is wrong with this vow? Isn't it a good thing to always be nice? Sometimes we are reluctant to see that a "good" Inner Vow is a problem, but Inner vows <u>always</u> create difficulties for us. For instance, George has his car repaired and the mechanic overcharges him by $50. If George has made an Inner Vow to always be nice, it will be impossible for him to confront the mechanic, because that wouldn't be "nice." So he may rationalize his behavior: "Oh, well. It's only $50, and I know he has a family to support, so I won't say anything."   It would be appropriate to ask the mechanic politely about the overcharge, but the rigidity of the Inner Vow interferes with George's ability to do this.

George may also rationalize that it is good to be "nice," and so a "good" Inner Vow is OK. However, Jesus never told us to be "nice." Was He "nice" when he called the scribes and Pharisees *"a brood of vipers"* (Matthew 3:7), or called them *"whitewashed sepulchres"* (Matthew 23:27)?   Was He "nice" to the moneychangers when He overturned their tables in the temple? He didn't tell us to be "nice," but to be "loving," and there is a very big difference between the two. It was because of His love for His Father that He cleansed the temple.

This "good" Inner Vow that George made was based upon sin, and therefore it is not "good." We need to be free of <u>anything</u> that is based upon sin and bondage. Therefore we need to be free of all Inner Vows, including "good" ones.

"Good" inner vows compel us to establish our own righteousness, whereas Jesus came to express <u>His</u> righteousness through us. We need to be <u>free</u> to let Him do this, rather than to be locked into our own decision which may be different than what the Lord wants.

How To Know That An Inner Vow Is Present

There are two ways to identify the presence of an Inner Vow.

- **Directly.** Recognize the presence of the Inner Vow by the symptoms it produces in our life - rigid behavior that we hate.

- **Indirectly.** When we have identified a Judgment, then look for any Inner Vows that may be attached to it.

Identifying An Inner Vow Directly

Inner Vows lock us into rigid behaviors. Any time we find ourselves doing things we don't want to do and we find ourselves unable to stop the behavior, an Inner Vow is probably present. This sounds a lot like the reaping from a root of bitterness, and it should. Any time there is an Inner Vow, it is linked to a Bitter Root Judgment. They work as a unit to produce the rigid behavior. Therefore, any time we identify an Inner Vow, we need to look for the Judgment that gave rise to the Inner Vow.

Once we can identify the Judgment we can remember the event where we were wounded and we judged. Then we can likely remember the words that we uttered when we made the Inner Vow. It is also possible that we cannot consciously remember making an Inner Vow, or exactly what we said. But the rigid pattern in our life will give us a clue to what we said.

Identifying An Inner Vow Indirectly

The second way to identify the presence of an Inner Vow is to start with the judgment and track back to any Inner Vows. When we realize that we have judged another person, then look for any Inner

Vows that are connected to it. At the moment that we judge, we almost always make an Inner Vow, or several Inner Vows.

George may have made three (or more) at that moment of bitterness, such as, "I will never be like my father," "I will never get angry," and "I will always be nice."

Always keep in mind that, whenever we identify an Inner Vow, there is always a Judgment that preceded it. This is always true, because it is the Judgment that gave the vow the power to be written in our heart and to thus become an Inner Vow. On the other hand, when we identify a Judgment, there is usually, but not always, at least one Inner Vow present.

Therefore, to erase an Inner Vow we must first take away the power that wrote it on our heart - the Judgment. We do this by forgiving and being forgiven by Jesus.

Honoring Parents

There is another factor that can also cause trouble for us. The fifth commandment says to honor your father and your mother that life may go well for you. Since this is the way the spiritual world works, you need to honor them, or life will not go well for you. Clearly, George would find it very difficult to honor his father. It may be especially hard for him to do this because he doesn't really know what God is demanding of him. Perhaps he thinks this commandment is telling him that he needs to ignore all the hurt that his father inflicted on him. His misunderstanding gets in the way of his being able to honor him. But not being able to honor his father will cause bad things to happen in his life regardless of the reason why he can't honor him. Thus it is crucial to understand what God meant when he gave this commandment.

I briefly mention this commandment here to contrast it to Judgments and Inner Vows. The fifth commandment is a special operation of the laws of God, and it is distinct from Judgments and Inner Vows. Because of its importance, the next chapter is devoted to honoring our father and mother.

Summary

An Inner Vow is a mechanism that is always linked to a Bitter Root Judgment. Working together they cause us to do the things we don't want to do. When an Inner Vow is operating, it produces rigid and inflexible behavior, and our willpower is unable to overcome it. All Inner Vows, even "good" ones, need to be removed. Otherwise they will hold us in bondage; and they will obstruct our ability to obey Jesus.

Chapter 8

"That It May Go Well With You"
Honoring Parents

The Bible explains to us how the spiritual world works. A part of this description is contained in the fifth of the Ten Commandments.

The Fifth Commandment

Honor your father and your mother, as the Lord your God has commanded you, that your days may be long, and that it may be well with you in the land which the Lord your God is giving you. (Deuteronomy 5:16).[91]

If life is not going well for you, it is possible that at least a part of the difficulty is that you are not honoring your parents. Many people suffer in this exact way.

There are a few very important things to note about this commandment.

- First, it is a description of the way the spiritual world operates (see Chapter 2). If we do not honor our parents, there will be negative consequences for us as we reap from the operation of the laws of God.
- Second, there are no exceptions to this commandment mentioned anywhere in the Bible. God does not say to honor our parents only if they are "honorable.

---

[91] **Leviticus 19:3,** *Every one of you shall revere his mother and his father, and keep My Sabbaths: I am the Lord your God.*

- Third, there is a positive promise if we are able to honor our parents: *that it may be well with you.*[92] This does not mean there may not be any <u>other</u> obstacles to life going well (such as the presence of Bitter Root Judgments), but it does mean that honoring parents removes this particular barrier.

Two Extremes

There are two opposite extremes that people tend to follow in regard to this commandment. On one extreme, sons or daughters may know God's command and feel that they must "honor" their parents and submit to them, no matter how the parents treat them. They may point to the biblical admonition in the Fifth Commandment, as well as other scriptures, such as the one in the Old Testament which demands the stoning of a rebellious son.[93]

The opposite extreme is probably the most common. Here sons or daughters abandon the relationship with their parents as much as they can. If they are still living at home, they may close the parents out emotionally. If they are adults, they may choose to have as little to do with their parents as possible.

> **Not obeying the Fifth Commandment may be one of the reasons life is not going well for you.**

Both extremes bring wounding, suffering, and adverse consequences into the son or daughter's life.

---

[92]   **Ephesians 6:2-3,** "Honor your father and mother," which is the first commandment with promise: "that it may be well with you and you may live long on the earth."

[93]   **Deuteronomy 21:18-21,** *If a man has a stubborn and rebellious son who will not obey the voice of his father or the voice of his mother, and who, when they have chastened him, will not heed them, then his father and his mother shall take hold of him and bring him out to the elders of his city, to the gate of his city. And they shall say to the elders of his city, 'This son of ours is stubborn and rebellious; he will not obey our voice; he is a glutton and a drunkard.' Then all the men of his city shall stone him to death with stones; so you shall put away the evil person from among you, and all Israel shall hear and fear.*

Not Fair

For many of us, somehow it doesn't seem fair or reasonable that God expects us to honor our father and mother. We find it impossible to do so with honesty and integrity, let alone whole-heartedly. We may say, "You don't know what my parents are like." After all, how could a woman honor an alcoholic father who sexually molested her for many years? This is a valid question that should not be dismissed. Since God always looks on the heart, if you "try" to honor them, but it is done grudgingly, it won't work, and you won't be blessed. Then how do you, with honesty and integrity and without hypocrisy, truly honor dishonorable people? In fact, any person who is being authentic and honest with themselves should be asking this question.

God Is Fair

Because God is fair and is the God of truth and love, His commandment must bring life. Because of my own childhood, and the experiences of many of my clients, I struggled with this issue. Something didn't make sense to me. Certainly, what I <u>thought</u> He meant didn't fit His character. I began to speculate that maybe I didn't understand what He <u>meant</u> by "honoring." I decided to try to find out what He really meant. I was beginning to realize that when I was able to see the truth, it would fit with His character. After all, God told us about this spiritual principle so that we can be blessed.

What Did God Mean?

I spent a great deal of time investigating this question. I found the answer to be very elusive. I read every commentary and discussion of the subject that I could find, but the pieces were not coming together for me. There were lots of opinions, but none of them seemed to ring true. I was puzzled.

Just at that moment, a person died who had at one time been very close to me. This was a person who eventually hurt me a great deal, and our relationship had been almost non-existent for over 10 years.

On the plane ride on the way to her funeral, I decided to drink a toast to her. As I held the little wineglass up and toasted her, I suddenly understood what the Lord meant by "dishonoring."

I realized that while she was alive, I had been incapable of toasting her. There was deep within me a fear, a fear that if I ever thought kindly of her, we would again become close and I would again be wounded. I realized that in my heart I had "dishonored" her. [94]

I had done exactly what people do when their parents have hurt them. They are afraid to think positively about their parents, or to make any sort of positive gesture towards them. They are afraid that this will make them vulnerable to further wounding by their parents. Consequently they find themselves unable to think positively about their parents in any way. They find it difficult to think of any of the parents' positive attributes (most parents have some

> **The essence of dishonoring our parents is based on fear - fear that if we soften towards them, they will again wound us.**

positive characteristics, if the person will allow themselves to think about them) and so they cannot reach out to their parents. This is a wall they have built inside themselves for protection. Building such a wall is what it means to "dishonor" their parents. [95]

Dishonoring Differs From Judging

On the surface it may seem that dishonoring parents is an example of the more general command not to judge others. However, as we will see, there are some major differences between "judging" and "dishonoring." One of the differences has to do with whether we are

---

[94] Since she was not my parent, I had not violated the Fifth Commandment. Therefore my "dishonoring" of her, though it was real, did not have the same impact on my life as would have occurred if she had been my mother.

[95] Unfortunately, this same wall separates the person from God. See the paragraph, "How We See God" later in this chapter.

prohibited from doing it, or commanded to do it. The command not to judge only carries a prohibition. If you judge a person, you set in motion God's law against you until you forgive the person who offended you and are yourself forgiven by the Lord. If the person is not your parent, you are not obligated to enter into a close relationship with them after you have forgiven them.

On the other hand, the command to honor parents carries a positive command. An important feature of this command to honor our parents is that it is not a one time act. The Greek word used in Matthew 15:4 by Jesus (where He quotes the Fifth Commandment) makes it clear that honoring father and mother is an ongoing future requirement.[96]   This implies that in some manner you are to continue to hold them in your heart. Not only are you not to have a negative attitude, but you must have a positive attitude towards them. A grudging attitude and actions done out of duty will not suffice. Consequently, this is very problematic, and can be the source of much anxiety and difficulty which many experience in obeying the Fifth Commandment. Again, to make matters worse, God didn't say to honor parents only if they are "honorable." Your mandate to honor them is not conditioned upon their character. God simply says that you need to honor them if life is to go well for you.

Though dishonoring and judging are different, they are still linked together. If you have not judged your parents you will find it easy to honor them. On the other hand, the more harshly you have judged them, the more difficult it will be for you to honor them.

> **Dishonoring parents and judging them are different, but they are still linked together. When you find yourself unable to honor them, it is because you have judged them.**

---

[96]   In **Matthew 15:4** where Jesus speaks of honoring parents, (*"timeo"*), the Greek tense (present imperative) refers to ". . . a command to do something in the future which involves continuous or repeated action" (Zodhiates, p.1571). Consequently, honoring is not a one-time event, but rather it is an ongoing future requirement.

When you find it difficult to honor them, this is a symptom that you have judged them. While you have a root of bitterness lodged in your heart, it is probably impossible for you to turn your heart towards them. The only way that you can honor them with integrity and honesty is for your heart to be healed --- for the Bitter Root Judgments to be removed and replaced with the love of Jesus. When you have succeeded in forgiving them, honoring them becomes possible. The more Bitter Root Judgments that have been removed, the easier it will be to truly honor them.

As you work through your Bitter Root Judgments with the Lord, you will eventually reach the place of healing where you will easily find yourself concerned about their welfare, and blessing them.

Recap Of Major Features Of "Honoring" Parents

Honoring your parents relates to your **COMMITMENT** to pursue the relationship!

1. Honoring does not relate to the individual areas or specific ways where parents transgressed you and you judged them.
2. First you judged them, and then you dishonored them by abandoning them in your heart.
3. Therefore, there is no such thing as dishonorable parents, just sinful ones.
4. Since honoring parents is first an attitude of the heart, it is probably an all-or-nothing proposition: you either honor them (desire and pursue relationship) or you don't. Your heart is either turned towards them or not.
5. There are no exceptions to honoring parents listed in Scripture.
6. Therefore, the necessity to honor parents does not depend on how good or bad your parents were/are, and consequently honoring has nothing to do with what they did or your reaction to it. Of course, the details of how you can honor them, of what is possible in the relationship, will relate to how good or bad they are now.
7. Judging does have to do with what your parents did and your reactions to it, whereas honoring them is a flat mandate without

exceptions - a heart attitude. <u>This means that honoring parents is fundamentally different than judging them</u>. Of course, because the same hurtful parenting usually results in both judging and a lack of honoring on your part, judging and dishonoring are always present together.

What Does All This Mean For You?

With all I have said in mind, honoring parents is like panning for gold. Using this as an analogy, when panning for gold, <u>you are free to throw out the tailings</u> (the part that is not gold), but you are <u>not free to stop panning</u>. [97]   You cannot say, "This is such low grade ore with so little gold that I'll just stop panning." It is true that some batches of ore (one's own parents) may contain less gold than other batches (some other parents).   But gold exists in your parents if you will keep searching.   Each parent is not totally bad (though you may feel that way), but Dad or Mom also have good qualities, if you will look for them. Of course, the better your parents were, the <u>easier</u> it will be to honor them; but easy or hard, the mandate is still there.

> **You are free to throw out the "tailings," but you are not free to stop "panning" for gold.**

In panning for gold it is important to know the difference between gold and tailings if you are to accurately discern which is which. If something you need from your parents is not present, appraise it as such. You cannot get from them what they are not capable of giving. You can't change tailings into gold by wishing they were gold.

---

[97]   If you are not familiar with panning for gold, I will briefly describe it. In areas where there is gold in the ground, streambeds often will have gold and sand mixed together. In "panning" for gold, you take a shallow metal dish, put gravel and water in it, and gently tilt it back and forth. The gravel is lighter than the gold, and it will gradually spill out of the dish and leave the gold in the dish. It is a time consuming process, and it takes patience.

What This Mandate To Honor Parents <u>DOES NOT</u> Mean

Though you are required by the Lord to keep searching for the "gold" in your parents, there are misconceptions about your responsibility to honor them that need to be clarified.

Honoring parents <u>does not</u> mean:
- Letting them abuse you.
- Letting them manipulate or control you.
- Submitting to their guilt trips.
- Liking them.
- Always agreeing with them, refraining from arguing or having conflict with them.
- Submitting to their authority, or do what they tell you once you are grown.
- Needing to spend all your free time or holidays with them.
- Taking care of them while they are capable of caring for themselves.
- Having to live near them.
- Abandoning your own self-care, loving of yourself, or honoring of your own needs and emotions at all times to meet theirs.
- Neglecting to protect and defend yourself, your spouse, and your children.

What This Mandate To Honor Parents <u>DOES</u> Mean

There are certain responsibilities that you <u>do</u> have towards your parents as a part of your responsibility to honor them.

- It <u>does</u> mean that you are to be committed to panning for gold. You are to be honest about their imperfections (their wounds and bad fruit), but you must be able to give them every benefit of the doubt. You need to see them in the best light possible (as long as it is the truth). You are not free to simply abandon the relationship, as you are free to do with many other difficult, hurtful relationships. Your parents <u>are valuable to you</u> (the root meaning of the Greek word to honor),[98] even though you may not be aware of this. This special relationship with your parents is somewhat akin to marriage. You are not to "divorce" them. You are spiritually, and perhaps mysteriously, connected with them, even if you don't want this to be true. Not honoring them ("divorcing" them) hurts you. God says so. At some time in your life your parents probably did some loving things and sometimes acted in loving ways. Because children want so desperately to be loved by their parents, you need to know that these memories are cherished somewhere inside you. The more rare the good memories were, the more tightly you will probably be hanging onto those few crumbs. These good memories will be hidden somewhere in your heart. However, it may be very difficult for you to look at those memories. In fact, they may be well hidden from your conscious awareness by your defenses. But that does not eliminate their existence.

- You do need to honor them with an open heart as unto the Lord, not grudgingly or simply out of obligation. God always looks on the heart and not simply on your behavior. If you cannot do this, if your heart is still bitter, then forgiveness and repentance are not complete. This inability to have compassion for your parents is bad fruit and it means that you still have some work to do with the Lord to deal with the bad roots.

- It <u>does</u> mean, *If it is possible, as much as depends on you, live peaceably with all men* (Romans 12:18). Note *as much as depends on you*. You cannot control the other person, and are only responsible *as much as depends on you*. You are not responsible for your parents' choices or behavior. Honoring

---

[98] The Hebrew and Greek words themselves also convey the level of importance. These words carry the meaning of "heavy," "weighty," "valuable," and "costly."

See **Endnote #8-1** for more detail on the meaning of these Hebrew and Greek words.

them <u>does</u> mean that you are free to refuse to relate to them in <u>unhealthy</u> ways.

- Honoring <u>does</u> mean that while you are a child in the home you are to obey them in any way you can that is not in conflict with your relationship with Jesus and responsibilities to Him.

- Honoring <u>does</u> mean that you will care for them, if necessary, in their old age.[99] However, in the spirit of love, to simply support them financially does not seem to be an adequate or complete answer as to how to honor them. What is important is not so much what a person <u>does</u> to honor them, but rather whether <u>their heart</u> is turned towards their parents.

- Honoring <u>does</u> also mean that all the other mandates about your relationships with other people apply to your relationship with your parents. I will not elaborate on this here, because our relationships with other people is a huge subject, and it is one of the main themes of the Bible, summed up by Jesus:

Jesus said to him, "You shall love the Lord your God with all your heart, with all your soul, and with all your mind." This is the first and great commandment. And the second is like it: "You shall love your neighbor as yourself." On these two commandments hang all the Law and the Prophets. (Matthew 22:37-40).

The Nature Of Parent-Child Responsibilities Change Over Time

In evaluating your future relationship with your parents, it is important that you understand that your responsibilities towards your parents change dramatically as you grow up. Children living in

---

[99]   Deuteronomy 5:16, Matthew 15:4, and Mark 7:10.

their parents' home are a very different circumstance than adult children who have left the home, and Scripture makes clear these changing responsibilities.

For instance, sometimes Ephesians 6:1-4 can be misunderstood to mean that adult children are to continue to "obey" their parents. [100]

> *Children, obey your parents in the Lord, for this is right. 'Honor your father and mother,' which is the first commandment with promise: "that it may be will with you and you may live long on the earth;" And you, fathers, do not provoke your children to wrath, but bring them up in the training and admonition of the Lord.*

As adults, children do not owe their parents this same sort of obedience, and parents no longer have this same level of responsibility to make sure the children live Godly lives.

Family Relationships Are Always Reciprocal

Regardless of the age of the children, family relationships are always reciprocal. The relationships are never that of master and slave. For instance, though parents have a great deal of authority over their dependent children, yet their authority is counterbalanced by the command to nurture the children. This reciprocity between children and parents is expressed in Colossians 3:20-21, where the

---

[100] "In the original Ten Commandments it is addressed not so much to younger children still in the care of their parents as to older children, who are called upon to exercise a sense of responsibility for the welfare of their parents who are growing old. This seems to be its significance here in Ephesians also. " To honour one's parents implies obedience on the part of young children, but with grown-up sons and daughters it implies rather an attitude of continued respect, consideration, and care" (Mitton, p.211).

"Even after we have attained our majority, are regarded in our culture as being no longer under the authority of our parents, and are therefore no longer under obligation to 'obey' them, we still must continue to 'honour' them. Our parents occupy a unique position in our lives. If we honour them as we should, we will never neglect or forget them . . . Thus to isolate, and even symbolically to reject, one's own parents can seldom be reconciled with the command to honour them" (Stott, p.243).

See Endnote #8-2 for details on parent-child relationships, and how they change over time.

admonition to the children is counterbalanced with a responsibility to the parents:

Children, obey your parents in all things, for this is well pleasing to the Lord. Fathers, do not provoke your children, lest they become discouraged,

So the responsibility in the relationship between the child and the parents is not a one-way responsibility. Both the child and the parents have responsibilities.

"The instruction to children to obey their parents presupposes, as we have seen, the fact of parental authority. Yet when Paul outlines how parents should behave towards their children, it is not the exercise, but the restraint, of their authority which he urges upon them. The picture he paints of fathers as self-controlled, gentle, patient educators of their children is in stark contrast to the norm of his own day . . . So human fathers are to care for their families as God the Father cares for his." (Stott, p.245).

There Is Always A Way You Can Honor Parents

Several years ago I was counseling a man whose mother was a raging alcoholic. He was the result of a casual affair, and his father had never been around. When my client was still an infant, the government took him away from his mother because she was so neglectful as a mother. He spent his entire childhood in orphanages. He asked me how he could possibly "honor" his parents. Because his parents were such an extreme case of poor parenting, this was a difficult but valid question. I pointed out that he was attractive, intelligent, healthy, and very athletic. Though his parents did not purpose to give him these gifts, nevertheless he possessed them. He could honor them for these. The key point was that his heart needed to become turned towards his parents, to seek the good in them, regardless of how little "gold" he could find.

There Is No Formula

As an adult, there is no set formula as to what "honoring" means in your relationship with your parents. Some parents are very safe, and honoring them is easy and can be done in a broad range of ways. Others parents are very destructive, either to you or to your children. In such situations there may have to be severe limitations as to what is safe. It is not wise to let one's pedophile father be around one's young children. As an extreme example, if a parent is actively involved in witchcraft, <u>any</u> direct contact with them may be inappropriate. But in such a situation, you can still turn your heart towards them by praying for them. If your heart is turned towards them, you will be grieved by the bondage they are in, knowing the destruction that is going on in their lives.

Therefore, "honoring" is an individual issue, and as a result you will need to explore with the Lord what "honoring" would look like for you in your situation.

Honoring your parents is much less complex after your parents have died. The fear is gone, because you know in your heart they can't hurt you again. You only have to deal with the past.

On the other hand, while they are still alive, you have a living relationship to deal with. They may in fact wound you again. It may take courage and require ongoing forgiving for you to explore the ways that you can honor them. Finding the healthy limits of the relationship is sometimes a trial and error quest, but it is a journey you <u>must undertake</u> so that life may go well for you.

My Own Father

My father was a college professor, and was a studious, quiet, non-emotional man. He and my mother were very involved in their own careers, which they loved dearly, and my sister and I were badly neglected. I became jealous of his career and saw it as my competition for his attention. I thus judged him and any scholarly endeavors, and I decided that I didn't want to be like him.

Despite this, I somehow I managed to graduate from college (though I saw my studies as an unwelcome interruption in my social life). As soon as I graduated I left town and hardly looked back. For years I would seldom call my parents, and I virtually never thought about them. Both of them wrote several books, but I never bothered reading any of them. Clearly, I dishonored them.

Then I began my walk of Inner Healing. In the last few years of their lives I began to reconcile with them, and found my heart turning towards them. They both died in 1992, and I began my Masters Degree program in 1994. I was both curious and concerned about whether I would be blocked from entering into this "scholarly" project. I was delighted to discover that I loved graduate school, which was evidence of healing and reconciliation.

Recently I rediscovered their books, and found that I enjoyed reading them. I am now writing a book, and I am enjoying it greatly. Life goes better when we are able to honor our parents.

How We See God

How we view and relate to our parents determines how we see God. Since my parents were kindly but neglectful, I have had very little difficulty seeing God as merciful, but have had a very difficult time believing that He is proactive in my life. As a boy, I had to fend for myself. If I had any need, I had to be proactive in getting it met. For instance, when I was about 12, I wanted a bicycle of my own. I had to find a used one, and I had to come up with the money to buy it. Even for necessities, such as clothing, I had to tell them about my need, or they wouldn't even notice I had outgrown or worn out my old ones. They weren't mean spirited, just neglectful.

When I became a Christian, I saw God as being like my parents. I still had a subtle, unspoken and unconscious view that I was on my own. If I didn't initiate, God wouldn't be there.

Fortunately for me, my view was in error, and God has been diligently working to show me what He is really like. Time after time He has proven to me that He is in charge of my life, and has made it clear what a good thing that is. He initiates, and I simply follow. He is not neglectful like my parents.

The context of the Fifth Commandment links our relationship with our parents to our relationship with God.[101] This linkage is probably one of the reason why it is so important that we honor father and mother. We all need to see God as He really is.

What About Honoring Other People?

In some cultures, and in some families, there is an expectation, and even a requirement, that a person must honor other people, such as uncles and aunts. Some other persons that you may have been told to honor are grandparents, adoptive parents, uncles and aunts, other older family members, older siblings who raised you, foster parents, church leaders, teachers, and other people in authority.

Is there a requirement by God that you "honor" other people beyond father and mother? For a Christian, Scripture is the only sure guide. Father and mother are the only people for whom there is a clear mandate to honor in the way that the Fifth Commandment requires.[102] Anything beyond this is speculative. If God expected more, He would have told us clearly.

Scripture does not demand that you "honor" other people beyond your father and mother in this same way. However, it does talk about "honoring" some other classes of people, but not necessarily in the same way as in the Fifth Commandment.[103]

---

[101] The first of the two stone tablets given to Moses and Israel, containing the first Five Commandments, specified their duty to God; and the second tablet, containing the Sixth through the Tenth Commandments, specified their duties to other men. The fifth commandment (honoring father and mother) is on the first tablet, the one regarding our relationship to God, thus bringing the honoring of our parents into our duty to God (Stott, p.239).

See Endnote #8-1 for more on how our view of God is linked to our view of our parents.

[102] The Bible does also use the Greek verb *timeo* (to honor) with regard to widows (1 Timothy 5:3), all people, and the king (1 Peter 2:17). However, these others are not mentioned in the Fifth Commandment, so the honoring due these people is probably not on the same level of importance, or impact, in our lives as is the command to honor parents. We cannot with authority go beyond Scripture. If God had wanted to include these others in the Commandment, He would have done so.

[103] Perhaps one could make a case for honoring grandparents and adoptive parents in the spirit of the Fifth Commandment. But, because Scripture is not clear on this, one must be very cautious about demanding this of children. Of course, a person could always choose to honor such people, and certainly this would be pleasing to the Lord.

See Endnote #8-3 for more on honoring grandparents and adoptive parents.

Of course, the Lord does have a lot to say about the attitude you are to have in your relationships with all people, such as *love your neighbor as yourself* (Matthew 22:39).

Summary

If life is not going well for you, it is very possible that at least a part of the difficulty is that you are not honoring your parents. The Fifth Commandment is a description of spiritual reality. If you do not align your life with this spiritual truth, you suffer. The laws of God are then working to bring difficulty in your life.

The necessity to honor one's parents is an ongoing future requirement. It requires that we have our hearts turned towards them, and that we seek to have as much relationship with them as is possible in keeping with safety and healthy self-care.

It is important that we see the truth about them. Seeing their faults is not "dishonoring." However, we are not free to ignore their good attributes. We are not free to reject them in total because of their faults, but we must keep seeking to uncover and recognize what is good in them. We need to keep "panning for gold," because there is always "gold" somewhere.

"Judging" and "dishonoring" are different, but linked to each other. If we have judged our parents, it will be very difficult to truly "honor" them. If we find it difficult to "honor" them, we probably have some forgiving to do first.

> **Honoring parents is not just a nice option. It is essential if you want life to go well for you.**

There is no formula regarding what sort of relationship you can have with them. Each person's situation is different. You need to insist that any relationship with them be give-and-take, and healthy. It is important to recognize that your relationship with them as an adult is different than as a child.

When you find your heart turned towards your parents, and you are thus "honoring" them, you will have removed a major barrier to your life going well.

Chapter 9

There Is Buried Treasure
Two Places In You

"Who am I?" Haven't we all asked ourselves this question?
Philosophers throughout the ages have written on this subject, and
the conclusions are diverse. However, God knows who we really
are and what we are like. He has revealed a great deal of this in His
Word, because He wants us to know who we are. Unfortunately, the
world's philosophies have contaminated the Christian understanding
of what people are like; so even as Christians we have probably
been given a wrong picture of our nature as human beings. What is
important is what God has to say about us

What I present in this chapter is not a full or exhaustive
description of humanity. We are complex and multifaceted. I will
keep my focus narrow to demonstrate that there are other parts to
our being besides our conscious faculty. There are several parts of
us below our level of consciousness (what I will refer to as
"hidden"), including a part that is not "bad," that has a "will" of its
own, is human, and is a part of us. The model I will now present
helps me explain to you how the parts of us interact and react as we
experience life.[104]

---

[104] See Endnote #9-1 for more information about our complexity as human beings, and read Chapter
12, "The Good Part Of You" for more information about the "good" part of us.

A Diagram Of You

When the Lord created you, He created a place hidden down inside of you where he placed several attributes, such as your personal spirit, your emotions, your creativity, your curiosity, your imagination, your intuition, your masculinity or femininity, your spontaneity, your gifts, and your talents.

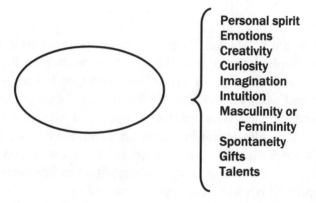

Personal spirit
Emotions
Creativity
Curiosity
Imagination
Intuition
Masculinity or
      Femininity
Spontaneity
Gifts
Talents

At this point I will not place a label on this place "inside." A label is not nearly as important as the awareness that there is a place where these attributes dwell.

There is another place the Lord created in you wherein dwells your willpower, your intellect, and your consciousness. We are consciously aware of this part of us.

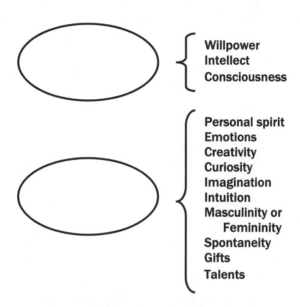

**Willpower
Intellect
Consciousness**

**Personal spirit
Emotions
Creativity
Curiosity
Imagination
Intuition
Masculinity or
          Femininity
Spontaneity
Gifts
Talents**

What Do We Call These Two Places?

The place "hidden inside" that contains your personal spirit has been given many labels by various people, including "heart," "center," "inner child," the "real self," our "true self," the "wonder child," our "inner man," etc. There are many additional terms. I have found that all of these terms are problematic, either because they are inadequate or they have become "loaded" with other

> **What we call these places is not so important as knowing what attributes dwell therein.**

meaning. For instance, "Inner Child" is a term that has been captured by New Agers and has become loaded with their meanings. I am going to choose to use the term "Treasure Inside" in this chapter, though in other places in this book I may also use the terms "heart" or "inner man," depending on which term seems most appropriate to the context. [105]

Regarding the part of us which contains our willpower, intellect, and consciousness, there are also several labels others have given to that place. Fortunately, the names for this part of us are less problematic than are the words used for our "inside" (our Treasure Inside), so I will call this conscious part our "head."[106]

---

[105] **See Endnote #9-2** for additional names for what I am calling our "Treasure Inside."

[106] Some other possible terms are, our "head," our "brain," our "outer man," or our *persona*. *Persona* is a Greek word which means "mask" (we do not reveal to the world who we really are - we hide behind a mask).

There is a third place, which is not a part of us, but which impacts us and relates to us. This place is the "World." For a small child this is predominantly his or her parents (or other primary care givers).

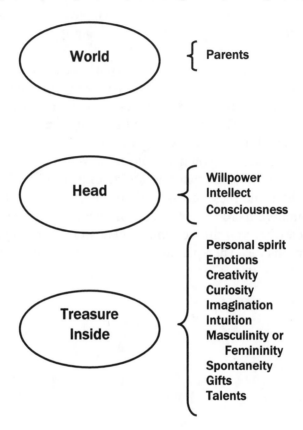

When God created us, He chose to distribute these various attributes of ours into these two different places inside of us (our Head, and our Treasure Inside) rather than mixing all the attributes together in one place. We need all the attributes that are in both places, and somehow they all need to work together. Each of the two parts of us contains valuable tools that we need in order to live our life fully.

Our childhood experiences are what form the relationship between these two parts (between our "Head," and our "Treasure Inside") and determine how all these parts are going to interrelate.

The Dynamics

You, in your conscious self (Head), receive messages from your Treasure Inside, and you also receive messages from the World (which in the early years is predominantly messages from your parents).

The messages you get from your Treasure Inside are little sensations (sometimes big sensations), awareness, and feelings. But these messages are not as overt or clear as the messages you get from the World. The messages you get from the World are overt and in your face. For instance, you get a spanking, or you fall out of bed and hurt yourself, or you get a hug from Mom.

When the message that you are getting from the Treasure Inside you is the same message as you are getting from the World (from your parents), there's no problem. In fact, the World's message then validates what you are hearing in that important language from the Treasure Inside. Then parents' messages help you to trust your inner language.

Diagram Showing Agreement Between The World And The Treasure Inside

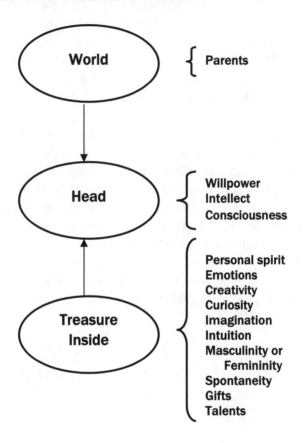

A Problem That Causes A Disconnect

But what happens when the message you get from your parents differs from the message you are getting from your Treasure Inside? For instance, a little three-year-old boy falls down and scrapes his knee. He feels pain from the Treasure Inside, and he begins to cry in response. But Dad, who is a real macho guy, says, "Don't be such a crybaby. Big boys don't cry." The little boy, who worships his father (as little boys always do) wants to please Dad, and so he represses his crying. He says to himself, "I want to be a big boy. I won't cry."

This is always the way it works. In the eyes of a child, parents and adults are godlike; and they are always right. In this example, the little boy wants his father's love and affirmation. The feeling (physical pain) coming up from his Treasure Inside is threatening to cause him not to receive Dad's love. Therefore he sees the Treasure Inside as trouble. He begins to distrust his inner language, because Dad is telling him that he shouldn't feel what he is feeling.

The little boy judges his Treasure Inside and makes an Inner Vow not to listen to it. The little boy is beginning to build a wall between his Treasure Inside and his Head (his conscious self).

Diagram Showing A Wall Forming Between The Head And The Treasure Inside

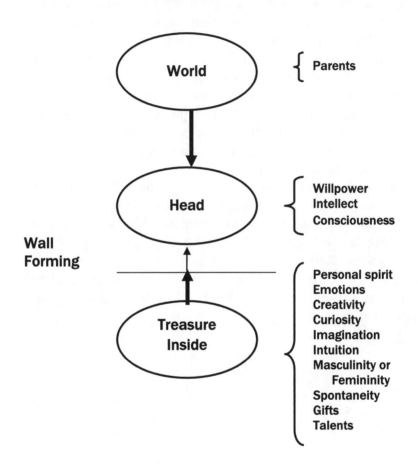

What Our Experience Should Be Like

Janet is a newborn baby. She wakes up in the middle of the night, and she is hungry. "Hungry" is a negative feeling, and when babies feel unpleasant things, they cry. Janet's mother responds, and she is a good mother. She comes into the room and is very glad to see her newborn child. She picks Janet up, and finds out that her diaper is wet. She changes the diaper, and then she sits in a rocking chair and nurses Janet. While the nursing is going on, the mother looks into Janet's eyes, plays with her hands, talks to her, and sings to her. Being a Christian mother, she openly prays for Janet. It is a wonderful bonding moment. When Janet is done nursing, her mother picks her up and gently lays her in her crib. She gives Janet a big kiss, and tiptoes out of the room.

What's going on inside Janet? Now she is no longer hungry, or wet. In addition she feels so good, because of having been close to Mama. When Janet listened to and responded to her feelings of hunger, there was a big pay off. She decides something like this (though non-verbally): "The next time I feel that uncomfortable feeling coming up from the Treasure Inside me, I'm going to pay attention and do the same thing again" (cry). Listening and responding led to good things!

Diagram Showing This Growing Willingness To Express What Comes From The Treasure Inside

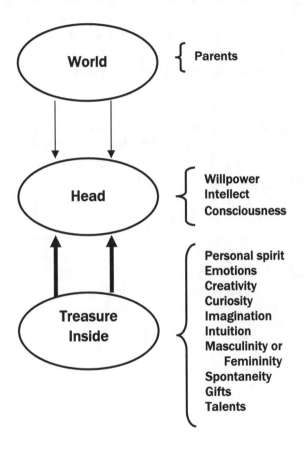

Janet's ability to hear what is going on inside her grows as a result of such affirming experience.

What Happens When We Were Not Heard

Mary is also a newborn baby. She wakes up in the middle of the night, and she too is hungry. She responds to that negative feeling by crying. But her mother is a not a good mother. Mother has her boyfriend over, and they have been drinking. The last thing she wants to do right at that moment is to take care of a crying baby. So Mary's mother, storms into Mary's room, rushes over to the crib, and screams, "I'll give you something to cry about, you little brat," and she smacks Mary on the bottom. Then Mother stomps out of the room, and slams the door.

What's going on inside Mary? Not only is she still hungry, but now she has a sore bottom. She has been traumatized, and that drowns out her hunger pangs. Responding to the uncomfortable hunger feeling by crying did not help. In fact little Mary is worse off than before she cried. So the conclusion that Mary will come to (again, not verbally) is that the hunger feeling coming up from the Treasure Inside caused trouble. When she responded to that feeling, bad things happened. Her conclusion is that what is in the Treasure Inside can be trouble. So a process of judging her Treasure Inside begins, and a desire to bury what she feels (the messages from her Treasure Inside) begins.

Diagram Showing A Loss Of Willingness To Respond To The Feelings From The Treasure Inside: The Building Of A Wall Inside.

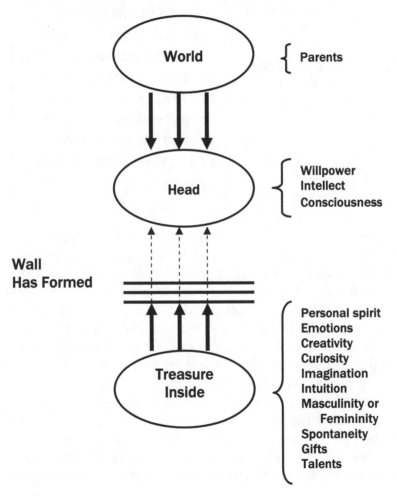

Interactions with the World happen a countless number of times to every little child as they grow up. The result of this process can lead to either growing in their ability to hear what is coming up from the Treasure Inside, or a growing tendency to repress those messages. If enough repressing goes on, if there are enough events that invalidate what is coming up from the Treasure Inside, eventually the person won't hear those inner voices anymore. They have lost the use of those valuable resources in their Treasure Inside. They have built a "heart of stone."[107]

> **If there is enough repressing going on, if there are enough events that invalidate what is coming up from their Treasure Inside, eventually they won't hear those inner voices anymore.**

The Wall

God intended for us to be whole so that we can truly be like Him. We need all of the attributes that are in both our Head and our Treasure Inside. Neither part is bad, and neither part is superfluous. Sometimes we need to analyze a situation with our intellect and then simply go and do it. Sometimes we need to listen to the messages from our Treasure Inside and act on what they tell us. However, The Wall we have built interferes with our ability to hear these internal messages. The Wall wasn't supposed to be there, and you can see from the previous diagram that when The Wall is present our access to the Treasure Inside is inhibited. In this case we have to try to live all aspects of our life from our Head, and we may not even be aware that the Treasure Inside exists. Without access to those attributes inside, we fail in some aspects of our life.

For instance, a wife may be complaining that her husband can't communicate with her. She expects him to know what is going on

---

[107] Sandford, Transformation of the Inner Man, pp.207-222.

inside her, yet she does not communicate her needs directly. Her husband is very frustrated because he is not a "mind reader." He asks himself, "How in the world am I supposed to know what she is feeling when she does not seem to know herself?"

The problem comes about because the husband is cut off from his Treasure Inside. In that place inside he <u>does</u> feel her pain and does know what is going on inside her. There <u>is</u> ongoing communication between her Treasure Inside and his Treasure Inside. However, the awareness of that information never makes it through his Wall to his conscious mind (his Head). He becomes frustrated, and his wife does not feel heard. Because of the presence of The Wall in him, the marriage is much less intimate and rewarding than God meant it to be.

It is also quite likely that the wife also has a Wall, and therefore she too may not have a clear awareness of what her own needs are.

When The Wall is built, in a sense the person has buried their humanity.

The Wall is a big problem for us, because it prevents us from being whole. We are unable to access those important gifts which are inside.

Separation From God

The living Lord communes with our personal spirit. We are designed to have a personal relationship with Him through this part of our Treasure Inside. When we can hear God's voice, we will be reliably guided by Him and prevented from sinning. We will be able to discern Satan's traps and accurately identify the deceptions of the World. Satan loses.

However, when we have shut ourselves off from our Treasure Inside, we become unaware of God's presence. We are separated from Him by The Wall, and our ability to hear Him is impaired (sometimes totally)! This is the greatest tragedy that results from the building of The Wall. I believe that building The Wall is Satan's favorite scheme, because he loves to see us cut off from God. When we are cut off from God, we have to rely on our intellect, which is ill-equipped to discern good and evil, right and wrong. Satan can then lead us into all types of error. Satan wins.

Unfortunately, history is filled with examples of people who are cut off from their Treasure Inside. Some examples are the Crusades, the Inquisition in the Middle Ages, and the Holocaust. These tragedies could not have happened if people had been able to hear the living God, because the Holy Spirit would prevent them from hurting other people in these cruel ways. The Holy Spirit was in agony over the pain being inflicted on the victims, and spoke to the hearts of those inflicting the abuse. But The Wall in these perpetrators prevented the message from getting through to the conscious faculties in their Head. They were unaware of the pain they were inflicting.

Diagram Showing How The Wall Cuts Us Off From The Living God.

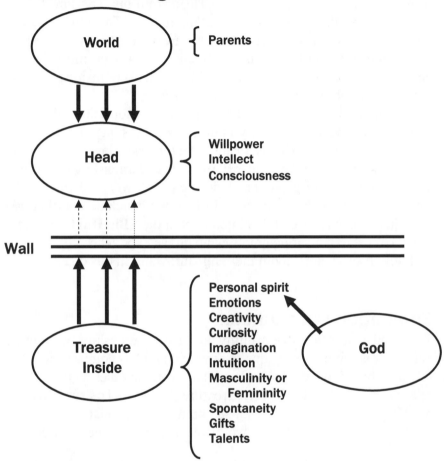

In this diagram I am not implying that our personal spirit is God. However, for Christians it is true that God does dwell in our Treasure Inside.[108] Here I am simply illustrating the fact that though God does dwell inside us and speaks to us, we may not be able to <u>consciously</u> commune with Him because The Wall gets in the way.

---

[108] **John 14:17:** *even the Spirit of truth, whom the world cannot receive, because it neither sees Him nor knows Him; but you know Him, for He dwells with you, and will be in you.*

Separation From Self

A second great tragedy that results from The Wall is a separation from ourselves, a separation of our Head from our Treasure Inside. The Treasure Inside is very important to us. The most obvious result of separation from self is that we are shut off from the benefit of all those attributes contained therein.   In fact most of our personhood, most of who we are, is in our Treasure Inside. "We are much, much more than our conscious processes."[109]

But there is a more debilitating result than not being all we are meant to be. Being cut off from ourselves causes <u>incredible internal pain</u>. Our Treasure Inside is meant to be the best friend of our Head, and suffers greatly when cut off from this relationship. The pain comes about because we have decided that who we are in the Treasure Inside isn't acceptable. In fact, we conclude that this part of us inside is bad! I call this internal pain the **"Big Hurt,"** because it is the most excruciating emotional pain we experience.[110]

I will discuss more about the "Big Hurt" later in this chapter.

Separation from Others

The Wall also affects our ability to have relationships with other people. It is the part of us that is sensitive and has compassion. It is the part of us which has relationship with another person. Real relationship is heart-to-heart (Treasure Inside-to-Treasure Inside), not Head-to-Head. There is actual communication that occurs at the heart level. Jesus could tell what was going on in peoples' hearts,

---

[109] We have tremendous assets inside us. Dr. Daniel Siegel, a medical researcher says the following: "Huge amounts of evidence support the view that the 'conscious self' is in fact a very small portion of the mind's activity . . . most of the mind is nonconscious. To put it another way, we are much, much more than our conscious processes" (Siegel, p.263). This statement is, of course, based upon scientific investigation, not Scripture. However, science and theology must converge if the science is solid; because good science only uncovers the truths about God's creation. In this case the evidence is so overwhelming that misinterpretation by scientists of this issue is unlikely.

[110] "They have come to understand that no punishment anyone might inflict on them could possibly be worse than the punishment they inflict on themselves by conspiring in their own diminishment. . . The punishment imposed on us for claiming true self can never be worse than the punishment we impose on ourselves by failing to make that claim" (Palmer, p.34).

and so can we.[111]   When we have access to this part of us, we can then feel what the other person is feeling. This sensing is called "empathy."   Our personal spirit was given to us so that we can communicate heart-to-heart in this way. However, if there is a Wall inside, our ability to consciously hear what our personal spirit is saying is impaired, or perhaps completely blocked. If completely blocked, we are forced to try to figure out what is going on in the relationship with only our head. Consequently, our relationships are shallow. We cannot feel what others feel or sense what is going on behind the personality they present to the world. It is not possible for us to have intimacy in our relationships, because intimacy is only made possible by the heart-to-heart connection.

Other people who are sensitive to their own Treasure Inside will be able to sense that they are not connecting with us. We have them locked out. Our relationships are hollow and not very rewarding to either the other people or to us.[112]

Men And Women Differ

Both men and women are wounded and react in the way I have been explaining. Both do whatever they can to stop the pain coming up from inside. However, God has so constructed men that they are more efficient at building The Wall.[113] Sometimes a man's Wall can be so impenetrable that he is totally unaware of what is going on in the Treasure Inside. Women are seldom able to accomplish this degree of shutdown. Given the same amount of wounding, women would also build a thick wall to stop the pain if they could, but they can't. They may hate themselves just as much, and they may be equally shut off from being able to live from the Treasure Inside, but they are less able to shut out the pain.

---

[111] **Matt.hew 9:4,** *But Jesus, knowing their thoughts, said ,"Why do you think evil in your hearts?"*
Luke 9:47, *And Jesus, perceiving the thought of their heart, took a little child and set him by Him.*

[112] See Endnote #9-3 for more details on how we communicate heart to heart.

[113] See Endnote #9-4 for more details on why men and women differ in this area.

Men and women <u>do not differ</u> in what is in their Treasure Inside! Both men and women have the same attributes. What has often been labeled as "your feminine side," or "women's intuition" has been so labeled because these attributes tend to be outwardly evident in women. However, the main differences between men and women are not based on what is in their Treasure Inside, but rather on the thickness of The Wall that inhibits what is in their Treasure Inside from manifesting itself outwardly. Over the ages, men have demonstrated these "feminine" gifts. For example, men are just as intuitive and artistic as women. In past history most of the well known artists, sculptors, architects, musicians, and composers were men. The gifts were obviously

> **The main differences between men and women are not based upon a difference in what is in their Treasure Inside, but on the thickness of The Wall.**

there, and in some men they managed to come out. Of course, the reason women didn't manifest those gifts publicly in the past was because until recently, they were prohibited by the culture from doing so.

How Can You Know If You Have A Wall Inside?

Are you a human being? Then you have a Wall inside. For some The Wall is like the vault at Fort Knox – nothing can get in or out. For some it is like Swiss cheese – it is solid but has holes in it. For some it is like a screen door – there is some interference, but there are more holes than blockages.

How can you know to what extent your Wall is disabling you? You can tell by the fruit demonstrated in your life. Often, if The Wall is big and thick, you may be unaware of the hurt in the Treasure Inside. You may even be unaware that something is missing. You may simply know that you are not very empathetic, or that you are not very spontaneous, or that you do not cry very easily, or that you cannot hear God's voice. Often the feedback of other people is necessary to bring to light what you cannot see. Often what you cannot see is obvious to those around you.

Since there are so many possible ways The Wall can manifest itself, I will not try to go into detail here. It is very important to realize that each person is unique. We were each created by God to be unique, and we each have our own life experiences. Consequently, there is no pat answer that fits all people. The only way to unravel this complex puzzle is in a living encounter with another person and the Lord. Only then can we identify the bad fruit and deal with The Wall. To be whole we always need to remove The Wall, and this should be the most central necessity in Inner Healing. Once The Wall is dismantled, the Lord is freed to be your Counselor, to heal you in the deepest places hidden inside you.

How Can You Remove The Wall?

The Wall is made up of Judgments and Inner Vows. The Judgments are against yourself (your Treasure Inside), and the Inner Vows are decisions to not listen to the messages that come up from the Treasure Inside. For example, the little boy who skinned his knee feels pain coming from the Treasure Inside. That Treasure Inside is compelling him to do something that Dad disapproves of (to cry), and it

> **"The Wall" is made up of Judgments and Inner Vows ....**
> **against ourselves!**

thus threatens to cause him the loss of Dad's approval. Therefore the little boy judges that place, the Treasure Inside, as being trouble. He decides "I'm not going to be a wimp. I'm going to be brave. I'm not going to listen to the pain anymore." This is an Inner Vow.

I have previously discussed how to be cleansed of Bitter Root Judgments and how to renounce Inner Vows. You deal with these Judgments against yourself and the associated Inner Vows in exactly the same way that you deal with them in relationship with other people. First you need to forgive and be forgiven in order to stop the operation of God's laws (and to take away the power that drives the Inner Vow).

Second, you need to renounce the Inner Vow. For example, "In the name of Jesus, I renounce the decision that I made to never pay attention to my emotions."[114]

Finally, you need to restore the relationship, in this case your relationship with yourself (your Treasure Inside). Your Treasure Inside is fully human and is wounded by your rejection, and yet your Treasure Inside is a part of you. [115]

You need to restore this relationship in exactly the same way as you would restore a relationship with any other person. You need to be proactive and pursue the restoration. You need to persevere, and to correct immediately any future Judgments you make against yourself. And you need to spend time in relationship with your Treasure Inside (listening, valuing, attending to, protecting, nurturing, blessing). Relationships require time spent together, and interaction.

Bear in mind that your relationship with yourself is the most important human relationship you have. Being able to have access to those attributes in the Treasure Inside depends upon you having a loving relationship with yourself. Having a Wall inside interferes with your ability to hear God, to love Him, and to love other people. Therefore, if you are at war within yourself, you cannot possibly fully and freely love others.

Loving Yourself

Removing The Wall and keeping it from being rebuilt requires you to not only tolerate your Treasure Inside, but to positively love yourself. This is not selfishness or narcissism. It is obeying Jesus' second commandment to love others as you love yourself.[116] He did

---

[114] See Endnote #5-5 regarding the power of words.

[115] This relationship is a bit of a mystery. We are "fearfully and wonderfully made" (Psalms 139:14). We are one person, and yet we are two parts. Perhaps there is a bit of a parallel with the triune God: Father, Son, and Holy Spirit who are one God and yet three persons.

[116] **Matthew 22:37-40,** *Jesus said to him, "You shall love the Lord your God with all your heart, with all your soul and with all your mind. This is the first and great commandment. And the second is like*

Footnote Continued On Next Page

not say to love others and hate yourself.[117] He said this because you were made for love, and love must start with your Treasure Inside before it can be manifested outside. God is love, and as you are changed into His image, love must permeate your being.

Loving yourself does not lead to selfishness. You become selfish when you are empty and needy inside. When you are needy, that need impels you to strive for more of what you are missing. That is the nature of any need. If the need is severe enough, you are compulsively driven to fill that empty place, even in unhealthy ways. That is when you become self-focused.

If right now I asked you for a glass of water, you would be pleased to give me one. After all, you have plenty to spare. However, if you have been wandering in the Sahara Desert for three days with no water, all you would be able to think about would be getting a drink of water. Your thirst would consume your attention, because you would soon die if you didn't get a drink. If you then found a single small glass of water, and I asked you to give it to me, it would be almost impossible for you to be big hearted and to let me have that glass of water which you so desperately need. You would be literally driven to be "selfish."

Similarly, if you lack love for your Treasure Inside, you are absolutely impelled to try to draw love out of others and out of life to fill the void. Then your need is so great, and the demand inside screams so loudly, you cannot hear others' needs. You have no reserves of love to give them. You are "selfish."

Loving is an ongoing necessity, not a one-time event. Thus you need to walk daily, moment by moment, loving yourself. This is the

---

it: You shall love your neighbor as yourself. On these two commandments hang all the Law and the Prophets."

[117] When I recognize my neediness and needs, and am diligent to fulfill my legitimate needs in legitimate ways, then inside I am satisfied, and so I have a surplus to give. I will then easily and spontaneously discover myself giving and loving. "Finally, nurture comes to us by our own cherishing of our own person. In this, we are not advocating narcissism. Rather, here is another true maxim: When we disobey the great commandment to love our neighbor *as ourselves* and cannot truly love being who we are, our spirit becomes so drained and empty, we develop ways to puff ourselves up in pride, braggadocio and in false love, to fill the vacuum. Whoever loves himself as he ought need not fear pride or selfishness. True love of oneself will overflow to others as naturally as a creek may begin to form a pond but, overfilling its banks, spill out to bless the earth beyond. We only love ourselves wrongly when we fail to love ourselves rightly" (Sandford, Healing the Wounded Spirit, p.25).

only way to continue to dismantle The Wall and to keep it from being rebuilt. When you do actively love yourself in this way, you will find it easier and easier to hear your Treasure Inside, and you will discover that you are loving God and other people. You won't be trying to do this, you will do it effortlessly. You are loving them because you have a surplus of love in your Treasure Inside. The overflow of love is good fruit from a good root.

The "Big Hurt"

When people judge themselves instead of loving themselves, they feel emotional pain. This particular sort of hurt is the most excruciating and debilitating emotional pain a person can experience. God made it to be so painful because He wants us to avoid doing this to ourselves. I call it the **"Big Hurt"** because it is so severe.   This pain of separation from ourselves, from our Treasure Inside, is so pervasive and awful that we will do anything to get rid of it.[118]

For example, suppose your best friend no longer wants to do things with you. Your friend always used to be available to go places and do things with you, but now when you ask her (or him) to come over and visit, there is always an excuse. How would that make you feel?

> **The "Big Hurt" is so enormous that it dominates our life. We will do anything to get it to go away.**

Take a moment and feel how that would make you feel.

How would you describe the feelings? Rejected, abandoned, empty, unimportant, worthless, like "dog meat?"

---

[118]   The Big Hurt is the pain that results from judgment of, and alienation from, our Treasure Inside. The pain is enormous because the offense is so great. I refer to this particular Bitter Root Judgment as "The Big Wound."

Sequence Of Events When You Judge Yourself

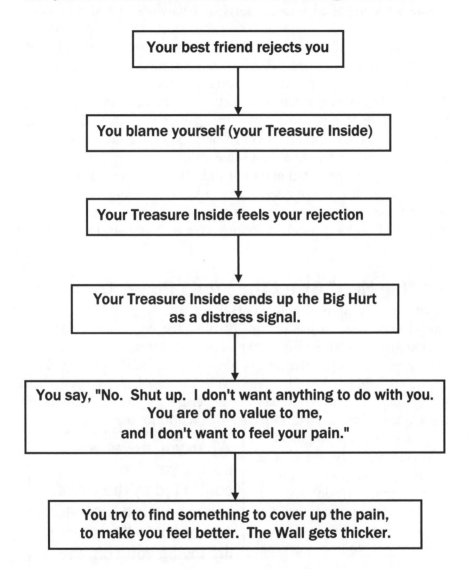

This whole sequence happens in an instant, and it is automatic. You would only be consciously aware that it has happened when you feel the Big Hurt.

Ways To Cover Up The Pain

People are compelled into all sorts of behaviors in order to keep from feeling this pain of separation.   Most addictions, codependence, and compulsive behaviors are attempts to dull this feeling.   Addictions are behaviors or substances that we discover through trial and error that seem to reduce the intensity of the Big Hurt, and thus make us feel a bit better for the moment. However, because these things only <u>cover</u> the pain rather than fixing the source of the pain (the judgment of ourselves), we must constantly indulge in them, trying to obtain some relief.

The Big Hurt then dominates our life. We fear rejection (because being rejected triggers our self-rejection). We cannot have empathy for others because our inner pain is speaking so loudly that it drowns out any such soft and subtle emotions. We are truly disabled.

The "Big Hurt" Gives The World Power Over You

When you are at war with yourself in this way, the World has control over you. It has control because the way people relate to you can trigger your self-judgment, and that brings intolerable pain. You become a people pleaser in order to avoid feeling the Big Hurt. On the other hand, when the war inside you stops, and you are then loving yourself, the World can no longer trigger the self-judgment. Then you no longer have to please the World to keep from feeling the pain of the self-judgment.

Therefore, only when it is safe <u>inside</u> you (you are loving your Treasure Inside) are you able to withstand the hurt and the evil that is in the world.

When your internal relationship is one of love and not discord, and you are determined to protect your Treasure Inside rather than

> **When you are at war inside, you are controlled by the world. When you end the war and begin to live your life loving yourself, the world loses its power over you.**

attack him or her, you are living the way God intended for you to live. And since the Lord dwells in your Treasure Inside, you can rely on Him to be your strength to keep you safe. Then you are safe from the fiery darts of the enemy. Then you have the resources to love others and to venture out into the evil world.

What About The "Bad Part?"

I have been speaking of loving yourself (your Treasure Inside), but what about the fallen nature in each human being? Since we are sinners, there is also a "bad part" inside us. However, the "bad part," which some refer to as "the flesh," is not what I have been referring to as your Treasure Inside in my diagrams. Unfortunately, many of us have seen our Treasure Inside as the "bad part," and this perception has often been reinforced both by life experiences and by some Bible teaching. I will address this issue in detail in Chapter 13, "The Bad Part Of You." I also elaborate on the "good part" in more detail in Chapter 12, "The Good Part Of You."

Much of our trouble comes from confusing the "good part" with the "bad part." We need to distinguish the difference between these two parts, and recognize that they both exist. They are not one and the same. When we have judged ourselves

> **We need to recognize that there is within us both a "bad part" and a "good part" (our Treasure Inside).**

and built The Wall, we have "thrown the baby out with the bath water." We have unwittingly thrown out the good with the bad.

Why Should You Want To Remove The Wall?

I have had numerous clients ask me why they should want to remove The Wall. After all, it keeps them from feeling emotional pain. One man in particular asked me this question, because he observed how his wife was blown about by her emotions. He, on the other hand, was able to stay cool in all situations. "Why would I want to enter her crazy world?" he asked.

This is a very important question that needs to be addressed. After all, when we have a Wall inside, we placed it there for a purpose - to protect us from pain. I told him there were several reasons why he should dismantle The Wall:

1. To have the hurts inside healed. With The Wall in place, we can't tell where our wounds are. I will talk about this in detail in Chapter 11, "Emotions Are Your Friend."
2. To have access to the resources in our Treasure Inside. Otherwise we will continue to have a very limited ability to operate in those gifts.
3. To be like Jesus. Jesus didn't have The Wall inside Him.
4. To obey Jesus. Jesus wants us to be like Him; and so when we decide that we want The Wall dismantled, we will be doing what Jesus wants us to do. Jesus will be pleased with this decision and will direct our path in this quest.[119]

For this particular man, these were convincing, as he was a man who wanted to serve and obey God. He decided to cooperate with Jesus in the process of removing The Wall.

Summary

For some reason God didn't chose to place your various gifts in one place inside you.[120] You need to become aware of the fact that there is a part of you, your Treasure Inside, over which you do not have conscious control. It is a part of you that you <u>truly need</u> in order to have intimate relationships with other people and with God. In order to have access to those attributes contained in your Treasure Inside you need to have an intimate, loving relationship with yourself. If you are presently unable to do this, there is a Wall of separation that needs to be removed. The Wall is made up of Bitter Root Judgments against yourself, and Inner Vows not to listen to that part of you. Only the blood of Jesus and the authority in His

---

[119] The Bible says, *"Be holy, for I am holy"* (1 Peter 1:16), and *Just as He chose us in Him before the foundation of the world, that we should be holy and without blame before Him in love* (Ephesians 1:4).

[120] See Endnote #9-1 for more information about our complexity as human beings.

name can remove The Wall. Removing The Wall is God's plan for you.

Key Concepts:

- **First, you are restoring a living relationship (with yourself); and**
- **Second, it is the most important human relationship you have! All your other relationships are dependent on this one.**

Chapter 10

Your Worst Trauma
Type A Trauma

Frank had a violent, alcoholic father. His father would often come home drunk and would beat his mother. Then he would come looking for Frank to beat him. When Frank was about five years old, he found a place in the back of a closet where he could hide, and his father never found him there. He felt so secure in his little hideout. It didn't get any better than this, being safe from the bad stuff going on out in the world.

But the worst thing that had happened to Frank as a child wasn't the violence – the bad things going on in his family. The most damaging thing going on in his life was the lack of the good.

We were all built for love. Love is the thing that makes us "tick," and we need lots of it to function. We were made in God's image, and God is love. Without love we are terribly wounded. In fact, research is now showing that the "lack of the good" is much more wounding than is the "bad" that happens to us.[121] When children are not copiously loved, they are fractured in the deepest places inside them. Their very foundation is destroyed.

The Lack Of The Good Is Trauma

Trauma is something that wounds us. In Christian counseling and in secular psychotherapy it was always assumed that what wounded us was the "bad things" that happened to us. This seemed logical and reasonable, because many people who struggle in life came from families where many bad things happened. It is true that when bad

---

[121] Schore, Affect Regulation and the Origin of the Self, pp85ff.

things happen to us, we <u>are</u> traumatized. These traumatic events wound us, and we need to be healed.

However, there was another type of trauma that remained hidden to counselors until recently. This trauma comes to us when we do not receive the good things that we need, and these experiences wound us <u>grievously</u>.   The "presence of bad things" has now been labeled "Type B Trauma" ("B" for bad), and the "absence of the good" has been called "Type A Trauma" ("A" for absence).[122]

Frank was totally unaware of the Type A Trauma in his life. For him, neutral (lack of abuse) was great. Not being found and beaten by dad felt as good as it can get. On the continuum below, he was satisfied with the middle (neutral) position.

Neutral   **The Bad**

He was willing to live in the middle, because he was unaware that there was more. After all, he had never experienced the good. So in reality he experienced both Type Trauma (the beatings from his father) and Type A Trauma (the absence of a loving father).   It should be noted that when Type B Trauma is present in a family, Type A Trauma is <u>also always</u> present; because a loving parent cannot be abusive to a child. So there was a whole dimension to life to which Frank was blinded. Neutral is not good enough for a child (or for an adult!). A picture of the full range of experiences is like this:

The Good   **Neutral**   **The Bad**

---

[122] Wilder, <u>The Red Dragon Cast Down</u>, p.14.

If we are to be whole, we need to experience our childhood to the extreme "good" side. So the degree of Frank's wounding was much greater than he was aware. An analogy from the physical realm may help make this clear. Before the space program we had no idea what the other side of the moon looked like, because we had never seen it. Even so scientists had an advantage over Frank, because the scientists knew that the backside of the moon existed. Not only had Frank never experienced being loved (seeing the other side of the moon), he didn't even know that one could be loved (that the backside of the moon existed). Of course, since he didn't know that part of life even existed, he had no idea of how important being loved was to him. And he was completely unaware that it had been missing!

Starvation

Another analogy might help make Frank's problem clearer. If we equate feeding a person poison with "The Bad" (Type B Trauma), and giving them good, nutritious food with "The Good," then what equates with "Neutral" below?

The Good	Neutral	The Bad
Good Food	<u>Starvation</u>	Poison

Wouldn't "Neutral" equate to lack of "The Bad" (Poison) and also lack of "The Good" (Good Food)? We call this place **<u>Starvation</u>**. Not getting any food at all (Type A Trauma) would allow us to live for awhile, certainly a lot longer than if we were being poisoned. But if the lack of Good Food went on long enough, it would also be deadly. No longer being poisoned would be a relief, but ceasing to be poisoned would not be adequate. People also need good, healthy food or they will get sick, and eventually die. "Neutral" is a bad place to be for very long.

My Childhood Story

I am a classic case of a child who experienced Type A Trauma. I came from a "good" family. My parents never fought, they almost never got angry, and they never spanked my sister or me. My father had a good job, and so we were always provided for. But as an adult I recognized a lot of bad fruit in my life. What could possibly be the root was a mystery to me. My own early experience with counseling started with a focus on uncovering the "bad" things that had happened to me. However, one day the Lord showed me what a small amount of "bad" had actually happened to me. This revelation was a bit devastating to me, and I felt like the "bad seed." Why was I so fragile that such a small amount of "bad" could be so greatly wounding?

During my counseling I became acquainted with many other people who were also in counseling, and some of them had horror stories about their lives. I could easily understand why they had problems, because they had experienced so much "bad" as they grew up. Both my counselor and I were unaware that my problems really came from neglect.

My entire childhood had been lived in the "neutral" position. Very few really bad things happened, but very few good things happened either. Though my parents were physically present, they were emotionally absent. Their emotional separation gave my sister and me a clear but subtle message that we weren't really important. After all, people give time and attention to what is important to them, and we got very little of our parents' attention.

I remember an incident when I had greatly outgrown my pants. I put them on and went to my mother to demonstrate that I needed some new ones. She looked at me, and it was almost as though she was coming out of a trance. She said, "Oh, yes. We had better buy you some," and we went and bought some. Though I had been walking around for weeks with my pants too short, she had never even noticed. Her lack of attention was not out of meanness or stinginess. She had not purposely been depriving me, but rather it was just as though I was invisible to her. I felt unimportant. That was the story of my life.

Why Is Lack Of The Good So Devastating?

The reason that the lack of the good is so devastating is that it causes us to build The Wall inside. When we experience a lack of the good, we build The Wall for two reasons.

1. We see the Treasure Inside as the source of the problem. We believe we are being ignored and not loved because there is something wrong with us. It is <u>our fault</u>.
2. We experience the pain coming up from inside us, it doesn't feel good, and we have to do something to stop feeling it.

We See The Treasure Inside As The Problem

When we are actively loved, it builds into us a sense of well being. On the other hand, when we are neglected, that builds into us a sense of inferiority. Children instinctively know that people give time to what is important to them. When parents don't actively love us, we realize there is a problem. We try everything we can to get them to fill that empty place inside us, but we never succeed. Finally we decide that the reason they are not loving us is because we aren't loveable. We decide this because that is the way little children think.[123]

> **The lack of the good is devastating because it causes us to build The Wall inside.**

So if as a child I am not loved, then the problem must be in me. I conclude that I am not loveable, and <u>I judge myself</u> (I judge the Treasure Inside).

---

[123] This way of thinking is called "egocentricity," and it is normal. Developmentally, small children's brains are not yet capable of putting themselves in another person's place. The world seems to them to revolve around them. Therefore little children think that they cause everything to happen. If daddy and mommy get a divorce, the child will often ask, "Do you think they would have stayed together if I had been a better little girl?" Little children aren't able to see that daddy and mommy have problems of their own.

We Have To Find A Way To Stop The Pain

This self-judgment is devastating to my Treasure Inside, because I was designed and intended by God to love myself. As I explained in Chapter 9, "There Is Buried Treasure," I become separated from myself, and I always feel the pain of this separation. This is the "Big Hurt," which is the worst emotional pain there is.

I would like you to again revisit the Big Hurt for a moment. This time remember an incident when you were rejected by a boyfriend or girlfriend, someone you liked a lot.

Again take a moment and feel how you felt.

That awful feeling is the feeling that little children experience when they are ignored. Imagine feeling that way all the time! That is the life experience of children whose parents don't pay attention to them. When parents never pay attention to their children they are rejecting them in a subtle way every moment of every day!

The pain is there all the time, and these children must find ways of keeping that pain at bay. They can't make their parents act differently, so they are stuck with the pain. The problem is that then the children come to believe that they themselves are the reason their parents aren't loving them. There is something wrong with them. They are "bad."

Since a child now believes that being bad is the very nature of who he or she is, there is no way to fix it. One cannot delete the source of the pain, the "bad part," because the one who is "bad" is a part of themselves. Though the child can't delete

> The "Absence Of The Good" is the most disabling trauma we can experience as a child. It causes self-rejection and The "Big Hurt" that accompanies this judgment against ourselves.

that part from which the pain arises, he or she can (and feel that they must) find a way to escape the pain. So the child separates from themselves in the only way they can, by building The Wall. Then the wound is still inside, but he or she doesn't have to feel it as intensely.

As I have said previously, this fleeing from the "Big Hurt" is what causes addictions and denial. This judgment of ourselves results in self-hatred, which is often referred to as "low self-esteem" or "shame." The definition of "shame" is <u>"I am bad."</u>

We Can't See It

The consequences of Type A Trauma are very hard for us to see in ourselves for two reasons. First of all, there was not any single event to identify, as there is with Type B Trauma. Our trauma was more like the drip-drip-drip of a leaky faucet. We are not being loved in this moment, and it hurts. We are not being loved five minutes from now, and it still hurts. We are not being loved this afternoon, and it still hurts, etc. Since our parents are incapable of giving us the love we are continually needing and craving, relief in the form of loving attention never arrives.

The second reason Type A Trauma is so hard for us to see is that we don't feel the pain anymore. The Big Hurt impelled us to shut our conscious self off from the source of the pain - our Treasure Inside. The Big Hurt was so painful that we needed to create defenses to avoid feeling

> **Living separated from myself now feels "normal" to me, so I can't see that something was wrong with my childhood.**

it. The pain was too big to live with every moment of our life. Since <u>relief</u> in the form of love never arrived, our only way to <u>avoid</u> the pain was to build The Wall inside. To the degree that we were successful in building The Wall, to that degree we became unaware that there was ever a problem! Existing with The Wall inside then feels "normal" to us, so we may not even be aware that something was wrong with our childhood.

What is "Normal?"

What is "Normal?" This is a huge question, and I will simply address it in respect to Type A Trauma. Children are adaptive and resilient. They can <u>survive</u> in all sorts of home environments, although they need a special sort of environment to <u>thrive</u>. When a childhood environment is less than optimal, a child has to find a way to get through each day. For each of us, when we were born, this was our first encounter with life on earth. We have to learn by experience. Unless our childhood is bad in the extreme, we come to see what we live as "normal." After all, we have no other benchmark or standard to compare it to. We may be aware that it wasn't pleasant, but usually we can find a way to make it tolerable. The Wall is a part of our way of adapting. Living with The Wall inside feels "normal" to us, because we cannot remember the earliest part of our life when we were still in communication with our Treasure Inside.[124]

Bonding

A major focus of current psychological research is the phenomenon called "bonding." Bonding is a connection that occurs between a caregiver, usually the mother, and a small child. Bonding begins in the womb and continues for the early years of childhood. The most crucial period is from the pre-natal time to about eighteen months.

Bonding events actually affect the physical development of a child's growing brain. Through these bonding events there are certain messages that become built into the child's brain. When bonding successfully occurs, the messages that become a part of the child are: "Someone is loving me, so I must be loveable;" "My needs are going to be met;" "Mama is here for me, and so it is safe."

When bonding does not occur, the opposite messages become built into the child's brain: "Nobody is loving me, so I must not be

---

[124] See Endnote #10-1 for more on our inability to know what is "normal."

loveable;" "My needs are not going to be met;" and "Nobody is here to protect me, so it isn't safe."

Since these messages have actually become a part of the child's brain structure, they constitute the way the child views the world. These perspectives then color all of his or her subsequent life experiences. Lack of bonding is a very deep and pervasive wound, which only the Lord can heal. And God can, because He provided a way by which the actual structure of a person's brain can be changed![125]

What We All Need

When we don't get what we need emotionally, we protect ourselves by shutting off the awareness of the "lack of the good" in our life. Since we are then oblivious to the lack of the good, we can't possibly tell you what is missing.

> **There are five good things that we all need, as a child and as an adult.**

Exactly what is the "good" that we needed but didn't get? There are five things we all needed as we grew up, and still need as adults.

1. We need eight non-sexual meaningful touches in a day. When I first read this, I thought that was ridiculous. I didn't feel like I needed that. On the other hand, if someone had asked me whether I received this, I could have easily answered, "Seldom if ever." However, I was totally unaware that I needed these touches. My denial was very effective. It was my protection from feeling the pain of not being actively loved.[126]

---

[125] See **Endnote #10-2** for more details on bonding.

[126] Regarding the power of human touch: "Experiments with rabbits fed atherosclerosis-inducing diets show that those rabbits which are held and petted by laboratory workers tend not to get atherosclerosis (hardening of the arteries). Those rabbits which are not held and petted tend to get atherosclerosis." (Whitfield, p.19). (Note: athersosclerosis is characterized by the deposit of plaque in arteries).

2. We need spoken words. Spoken words tell us that the other person knows we are present and that they desire to communicate with us. Being ignored is the opposite of this. Children would rather be loved than beaten, but they would rather be beaten than ignored. Being ignored tells us that we are not even worth the other person's time.

3. We need our parents to express high value to us. When they genuinely appreciate us and compliment us, it makes us feel good. We think that because they are interested in us, we must be worthwhile. And they are telling us specific ways in which we are worthwhile. For instance they might notice that we are good at math and will tell us something like, "You certainly have a gift with numbers. You are much better at math than I am." (Of course, the statements have to be true). The opposite of this is negative talk, such as "You are a lazy bum." These negative statements have the effect of adding to our self-judgment.

4. We need our parents to picture a special future for us. When they do this, we feel optimistic about the future, and we feel worthy of such a future. Statements like, "You are so good at math, maybe someday you can teach it." The opposite would be a statement such as, "You'll never amount to anything."

5. We need our parents to actively help us to pursue our special future, as much as it lies within their means. Even if they don't have the resources they can help us to find ways to achieve our dreams. Such actions tell us that our parents really meant it when they affirmed our gifts and talents, that they genuinely see these attributes as worthwhile, and that they see us as valuable enough for them to put forth effort on our behalf. The opposite of this would be to force us to do what they want us to do, regardless of our desires and talents. For instance, they may have a family business and want us to take it over someday. Because of their own desire they are blind to the fact that we have different talents and desires. Experiencing this tells us that

what we want, and who God made us to be, doesn't matter. Our needs are unimportant.

Behind all of these elements of blessing is one enormous theme. When parents truly give their child the blessing, it is abundantly evident that they are students of the child. They see their child as important enough to spend their time and attention and their energy focused on him or her. They understand the unique person that God created the child to be, and are delighted with who he or she is. The child knows when the parents are paying close attention to them.

This sort of awareness causes children to conclude that they must be valuable and loveable just the way they are. Their parents love them, so they must be loveable. Children are thus enabled to obey God's command to love themselves, and so life will go well for them.

Read The Blessing

These five elements I have listed are my paraphrase of what Gary Smalley and John Trent wrote in their book, The Blessing. I greatly encourage you to read their book. You will find it much easier to see your own Type A Trauma if you will prayerfully read this book.

As you read this book, take plenty of time to reflect. At the end of each chapter ask yourself if you received that particular element of the blessing. Again, as was my case, you may not have any awareness of the hurt connected with not receiving it. But you can probably answer the objective question of whether or not you received it. Be aware that to the degree that you didn't receive the blessing you were wounded with a Type A Trauma.

Though Gary Smalley and John Trent have focused their book on children, the truth is that we all need to receive these blessings throughout our whole lives. In addition, if we give these blessings to those who are important to us (spouse, children, friends), the relationship will never wither up and die. When we give another person these blessings, they shine as though all the lights have been turned on inside them, and they will always want to be around us. After all, we are giving them what they need the most – love. If we find this difficult to do, that is bad fruit, and we need to find the bad root so that we can be healed and begin to do this naturally. We can't bless ourselves or others through our own willpower, but we can as we are changed into the image of Jesus.

Summary

There are two types of trauma that we can experience as a child: the "Bad" (Type B), and the "Absence of the Good" (Type A). Of the two, we are more aware of the "Bad," but the "Absence of the Good" is actually more devastating. The absence of the Good denies us the fulfillment of our need for love. The most damaging result from this type of trauma is the destruction of our self-image and all the bad fruit stemming from judging ourselves.

Because the "Absence of the Good" is a silent killer, we are much less aware of its presence. Because of the consistent pain that neglect causes, we build The Wall to separate us from the pain. Then, since we can no longer feel the pain, we are very unlikely to know that we are hurting inside. Thus the wounds may remain, and our lives don't go well.

If we have experienced a lot of bad things as a child, this may make it difficult to realize we suffered from Type A Trauma. When a person has experienced a large amount of the "Bad," this hurt can speak so loudly that it covers up any awareness of the "Absence of the Good." But when there has been the "Bad," there has always been "Absence of the Good." Loving, healthy, sensitive parents don't do bad things to their children.

Though the "Absence of the Good" causes deep wounds in our very foundation, God's provision for us through the blood and the cross of Jesus is sufficient to heal us.

Chapter 11

Emotions Are Your Friend

Suppose you are in your car and you are in a hurry. You get stopped at a stoplight (of course, it always happens when you are in a hurry). The light finally changes to "green" and the driver in front of you does not notice it. They just sit there. What would you do? Likely, you would honk your horn. How would you feel? Wouldn't you be a bit upset? When the other car finally gets going, it is too late for you to get through the light. You then have to wait until the light turns green again. Now you are more than a little upset. How long would it take you to calm down? What would you do to calm yourself down?

We all have developed ways of dealing with our negative emotions by trial and error. We try something and it brings a bit of relief, so we add that to our repertoire as a way to deal with such unpleasant moments in the future. Still, for most of us our emotions are a bit mysterious, and we don't know what to do with them. Likely we have only been modestly successful in dealing with them.

As a child I learned to avoid my negative emotions if at all possible. This was the message that I got from living in my family, and it was the method I observed in my parents. My experience is not unusual, because our culture (and unfortunately some of the Church) say that our emotions are unreliable. Regardless of how we try to ignore them, they persist. They come and go in a seemingly mysterious way, in a way that we do not find ourselves able to adequately control. Negative emotions are a "problem" we all share.

What Are Emotions?

Are emotions simply random? Are they unpredictable? Did God make a mistake when He gave them to us? Or were they useful before Adam and Eve sinned but are now corrupted by The Fall?

Are some of them "bad?" Is it a sin to feel selfish? Is it a sin to feel jealous? Is it a sin to feel angry?

I have a burglar alarm in my home. On a couple of occasions I have accidentally set if off, and the sound the loud speaker made was ear splitting. The pain was unbearable. I had to do something right away to escape the pain. So I plugged my ears with my fingers and went to the keypad and entered the code. Then the alarm immediately stopped, so the pain stopped. But what would I do if I didn't know the code? My fingers in my ears were only mildly successful in reducing the pain, so I would have to do something else. I could leave and wait outside until the noise stopped (and the police came). Or I could find the loudspeaker and cover it over with something. That would likely not work any better than covering my ears. Better yet, I could cut the wire to the loud speaker. That would stop the noise.

The purpose of the alarm was to make known an intrusion into my house. If the alarm had been set off by a burglar instead of by me, that would be important information. If a burglar entered and I did not have an alarm, something really bad might happen. The burglar alarm was purposely designed to be impossible to ignore, because it is important that the "intrusion" stop. The neighbors and the police need to be alerted, and the intruder needs to know they have been discovered so they will stop doing their dirty work.

Our negative emotions are like that. Some of our emotions are "ear-splittingly" hurtful, because they are giving us very important information that we must not ignore. For instance, when you are in front of a group of people and you tell a joke and nobody laughs, you may feel a strong rush of shame, and your face may turn red. Or suppose a large dog rushes towards you, growling and showing its teeth. You will likely feel a large surge of fear go through you. Fortunately not all our negative emotions are that severe. God designed them to be proportional to the bad news they are giving us.

> **Your negative emotions are your friend. They are simply messages from inside warning you that there is a problem.**

You also have pleasant emotions which were given to you so that you would be attracted to whatever is making you feel good. What makes you feel good are the things that fulfill the many needs you have, such as the need for love, affirmation, sex, etc.

"Feelings" and "Emotions"

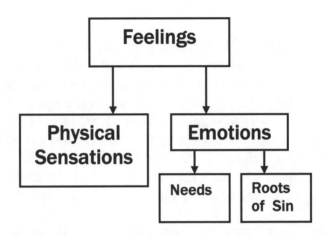

We receive various signals from our Treasure Inside to our Head. Some of these signals relate to the physical status of our body, and some of them relate to our psychological/spiritual status. When I use the term "feelings," I am including both categories. When I use the term "physical sensations" I am referring to the physical signals, and when I use the term "emotions" I am referring to the psychological/spiritual signals.

"Emotions" can be telling us about unmet psychological needs ("I need a hug"), or the presence of a root of sin, usually a Bitter Root Judgment.

"Physical sensations" and "emotions have a great deal in common, and the purpose of all of our "feelings" is to make us consciously aware of something that is going on below our level of consciousness. Most of us do not have difficulty understanding our "physical sensations (for instance I am thirsty, or my feet hurt), but our problems tend to relate to misunderstanding our "emotions." Because of the similarities between "physical sensations" and "emotions," I will often use parallels between them to clarify a point I am making about "emotions."

If God had not given your "feelings" to you, you would not have any way of knowing the status of what is going on inside of you. You would not know what your needs are, and so you would have no way of fulfilling them. If you did not feel thirst, you would not drink something, and then you would die.

Our Attempts At Bringing Peace

As a child I knew what to do when I had a physical need. When I was thirsty, I got a drink. However, I didn't know the "code" to turn off the <u>emotional</u> pain. When strong negative emotions came to me I had to find a way to reduce the pain. It was as if I started out by "plugging my ears" (I tried to ignore the message). Since that was only modestly helpful, I searched for a more effective means. I could not "leave," because the noise was in me. So eventually I "cut the wire" (I made an Inner Vow not to hear), and then the pain stopped.

Unfortunately, then the "intrusion" (the cause of the emotional pain) had not been fixed, and so the "burglar" had not been dealt with. Cutting the wire, or anything else I would do to reduce my sensitivity to my negative emotions, had bad side effects. Not hearing the alarm going off, I would not know when a "burglar" came inside and was doing his destructive work.

"Physical Sensations," since they are messages from the Treasure Inside, can illustrate the extreme consequences that can come from <u>not</u> physical pain. When I was a boy I had a friend whose father had experienced a stroke, and he had lost the feeling on one side of his body. One day my friend and his father and I were standing in their basement and we smelled something burning. It was his father's hand! He was leaning against the furnace. Since he could not feel the heat, he did not withdraw his hand, and he was badly burned. The physical pain that I feel when I touch something hot is my friend, because it motivates me to stop the pain. I quickly remove my hand from the hot surface, and thus I limit the damage to my body. Physical pain is my friend.

My emotional pain is just like that. Bad things happen when I can no longer clearly hear my negative emotions, because I have built The Wall inside. Then, when something bad would happen inside, I would not know about it. Using my metaphor, because I do not know the "burglar" is there, he is free to do his damaging work inside. I would not know about his presence until there had been so much damage that I could no longer ignore it.

Tom had daily frustrations with his boss. His boss always talked down to him and made him feel small. Tom had not had a raise in years, and yet the boss would give him so much to do that he would have to take work home at night. But Tom did not know when he was angry because he had built The Wall, and he did not feel these moments of anger. His heart was filling up with bitterness, but he was not aware of it. After he would get home from work, his wife would do some little thing that irritated him, and he would explode with anger at her. She did not just receive Tom's reaction to what she just did, but she also received the entire load that had been building up inside Tom towards his boss. It was like an avalanche. One small disturbance was the trigger, and all the "snow" that had accumulated came surging down in one deluge and buried her.

Ski areas understand avalanches. They know that if they can keep the snow from accumulating on the mountain slopes above them they can prevent an avalanche. So they regularly set off small explosive charges in the snow to bring down small snow slides that are harmless. In this way they prevent huge buildups of snow that would inevitably come down in a devastating rush.

In the same way, Tom needed to listen to, and learn to recognize, every surge of anger that he felt. Then he could pray about it immediately and avoid the "accumulation" that would otherwise eventually (and inevitably) come out as outbursts of rage. If there is not an "accumulation" inside him, when people irritate him they only receive the reaction that relates to that single transgression, not his pent up reactions to all the other accumulated hurts inside him.

We Are Needy

We are needy creatures. God made us that way. We need love, we need water, we need sleep, we need exe rcise, etc. There is nothing "selfish" about getting our legitimate needs met in a legitimate way. When our legitimate needs are not met, we are "hungry" and settle for meeting our needs in any way we can, perhaps including "illegitimate" ways, or groveling for whatever "crumbs" we can find.

For example, at this moment if I were to hand you a dirty, smelly glass of water, you would likely say, "No thank you," because you aren't that thirsty. However, if you had been wandering in the Sahara Desert for three days with no water, and then I offered you the dirty glass of water, you would eagerly snatch it from me and instantly consume it. Why? You would drink it because your need had become so great.

That is what happens when we deny our legitimate needs (or perhaps are unaware of them because we have ignored them for so long). We become so empty inside that we are driven to accept inappropriate substitutes to stop the screams coming up from inside us.

The "Code"

To appropriately end the turmoil of our negative emotions, we need to know how God intended for us to <u>eliminate</u> the pain, rather than to cover it up. He intended for us to eliminate the pain by addressing the <u>cause</u> of the pain. When we have a toothache, we can take a pain killer, or we can have the tooth fixed. When the tooth is "fixed," the pain stops.

Remember that emotional pain relates either to unmet psychological needs or to roots of sin that exist inside.

There are therefore two things we need to know about eliminating our emotional pain.

1. We need to listen to the pain rather than run from it. This way we can discover what it is telling us. When our tooth hurts, we know something is wrong with our tooth, rather than our foot.

2. Then we need to address the cause of the pain by applying the appropriate "cure." We need to have our tooth fixed by a dentist.

Unfortunately, nobody taught us how to do either of these, especially regarding the roots of sin. But it is possible to learn how do both, and therefore, it is possible to eliminate the <u>cause</u> of our emotional pain so that the pain will stop.

Understanding The Language Of Our Emotions

God gave us our "emotions," and He intended for them to be useful to us. It is therefore possible to learn this mysterious language that our Treasure Inside speaks to us. In later chapters I will go into more detail about learning this language, but here I want to point out a few important characteristics of our "emotions."

1. A negative emotion may be telling us of <u>an unmet appropriate emotional need</u>. If that need <u>is</u> met in an appropriate way, the negative emotion will go away and will likely be replaced by an emotion that feels good. We have received what we needed. For instance James, who is a little boy, needs a hug. The parent picks him up and holds him. The negative emotion will likely be replaced with a good feeling of satisfaction, which tells James he is no longer needy. Now he is ready to be put down and again explore the world.

2. A negative emotion may be telling us about a root of sin that we <u>have just planted</u> inside. These events cause us the most difficulty, and are the most mysterious to us. If unresolved, such a root will cause problems in our life (See Chapter 2 about the laws of God).

3. The emotional pain may <u>also</u> be telling us about an <u>older root</u> that we have not yet eliminated. In this case the current event has touched this old root and triggered a response from it. It is like

stubbing your toe. When you first injure it, there is pain. But until it heals, it seems as though you are constantly hitting it on something. Actually, you are probably not again hitting it hard enough to injure it further, but the toe is hyper-sensitive to pain. It is hyper-sensitive because of the previous injury. Therefore, one symptom of the presence of an old root deep inside us is when a small situation triggers a big response, a response that is out of proportion to what just happened. This is what happened to Tom in the previous example. His previous Bitter Root Judgments accumulated and eventually he exploded in anger at his wife.

4. All negative "feelings," both physical and emotional, <u>are proportional</u> to the need. The more urgent or important, the more intense is the pain. If I have a slight discomfort in my tooth, I can take my time about getting it fixed. If the pain is intense, I need to get to the dentist immediately. I can't stand to wait! That is exactly why God designed feelings this way. The intense pain tells me there is a serious problem that needs immediate treatment, and the pain motivates me to take action <u>now</u>. I find myself unable to postpone getting treatment.

5. The language of our "emotions" is not a language like English, or Spanish. It is made up of little sensations which are specific to the nature of the hurt. I will ask clients how they feel about something, for instance how their husband treats them. Often the response is something like, "I feel as though he doesn't listen to me." This is not an emotion. This is an analysis. The emotion would be something like: "I feel abandoned, unimportant, demeaned, alone." If this concept is new to you, or if you are not used to naming your feelings, **see Endnote #11-1** for a list of "feeling" words. You will find these lists useful in helping you to describe what you are feeling at a given moment.

Eliminating The Cause Of The Pain

Therefore, if there is a Bitter Root Judgment planted inside us, our negative emotions are our friend telling us about this problem. What do we do in response to the negative emotion (the "alarm" going off)? We need to key in the "code." When the cause of the alarm is sin, there is only one "code" that works. The "code" that God has provided is the provision for the washing away of our sin through the forgiveness provided by the sacrifice of Jesus. This "code" works. When we forgive and are forgiven, the negative emotion stops. It stops because the wound that the pain was warning us about has been healed. The sin has been washed away, and Jesus has come into that place in our heart. The "burglar" is now gone. Jesus' provision truly is Good News!

> **The most common source of emotional pain is the wound that sin plants in our heart.**

When I was angry with the other driver who didn't go through the green light, I had judged him. I needed to take care of that as soon as I could, immediately if possible. That way I could catch the "burglar" before he had a chance to do any damage. After I pray, if I still find myself agitated, especially if my anger is extreme and is contaminating my day, I need to look for a long buried root of sin. Perhaps I had judged my parents for never paying attention to my needs. Even worse, perhaps I judged myself as being unworthy to have my needs met by others; and therefore it is left up to me to take care of myself. Certainly, it is true that the other driver was not sensitive to my needs, and it was his behavior that touched that wound deep inside me. But it wasn't what he did that was the problem. What planted the bitter root was my reaction to what he did. Feeling the emotion gives me an opportunity to face what I did and thus to be set free from the consequences of the bitter root.

> **When we forgive and are forgiven, the negative emotion stops.**

It Is Complicated, And Yet Simple

The code to my home burglar alarm is simple, but this "code" to end my negative emotions appropriately is complex. It is complex because many of the old roots of bitterness are deeply buried and I have forgotten about them. I cannot remember many of them myself. It is therefore too complex for me to understand. But it is not too complicated for Jesus, and He will lead me in this process of finding the bitter roots and being healed. I may also need another person to walk through this with me, such as a trusted friend, or a counselor. I also need to listen to my Treasure Inside, who is telling me what is wrong inside

Ideally, teaching me how to listen to my emotion and to then pray was the job assigned to my parents. In my own childhood, my parents were as ignorant about this as I, so there was no way for them to teach me. In fact, they did the opposite of facilitating my ability to hear my Treasure Inside. They wounded me and I built The Wall, which reduced my innate ability to hear my emotions. Unfortunately, many parents are unable to mentor their children in order to help them hear what is going on in the Treasure Inside them. If this is true of you, now as an adult you need to have The Wall dismantled, and then to learn what your parents should have taught you when you were very young --- how to understand the valuable friend you have in your Treasure Inside. It is never too late.

When I first realized how shut down I had been inside, I questioned the Lord, "Why didn't I know this earlier?" I felt bitter because I had to suffer for many years before I became aware of the truth. But then I realized how blessed I was. Many people <u>never</u> learn about the "code," and they suffer for their whole life. We are blessed to know this now.

Are "Bad" Emotions Sin?

Many of us have been taught that "bad" emotions are sin. For instance we may have been taught that it is a sin to feel jealous. However, it should now be clear to you that it is <u>not</u> a sin to feel jealous. There is nothing wrong with that emotion, and so we do not need to repent of feeling jealous.   The emotion is simply the message system. There is a sin present, but <u>the sin is not the feeling</u>. There is a root of bitterness inside us (planted by a sinful reaction of judging), and we need to know about the presence of this bitter root.

- The judging was sin.
- The message (emotion) telling us this fact is <u>not</u> sin.

We <u>do</u> then need to find out what the root is and be healed of that. This may sound like hair splitting, but there is a profound difference between the <u>feeling</u> and the <u>root</u>. <u>The bitter root of sin exists, and the feeling is just the signal telling us about the root.</u> The signal is not sin, but rather it is just our faithful messenger, our helper, and our friend.

In ancient times, when a messenger brought bad news, the king had the messenger killed. Of course, the problem wasn't the messenger or the message he carried. The messenger was simply a mechanism for informing the king of what was going on elsewhere. When something bad was happening elsewhere, the news was bad. We now look at the king's response and see how ridiculous that is. And yet that is exactly what we have done if we have shut off our emotions because they are "bad."

Repressing Emotions Hurts <u>Us</u>

Repressing or trying to squash our emotions produces negative consequences in our lives. We are the ones who suffer. When we repress the negative emotions to keep from feeling the pain, we miss out on the awareness that something inside needs attention. That is what the negative emotions are telling us. If we continue to ignore them, there will be unfortunate consequences. Whatever is wrong inside will eventually come to the surface in some fashion, because the problem inside will become too large to ignore. Ulcers, insomnia, and uncontrolled outbursts of

> *Leave no negative emotion*
> *unexamined*

anger are common examples of this. When we do not allow

emotions to come "straight out" (listen to them and resolve them) as God intended, they eventually come out "sideways" and produce problems in our life.

The Paradox Of "Selfishness"

Some people believe it is "selfish" to seek to have their own needs met. They believe that it is pleasing to God for them to always give up their own needs for the benefit of others, and so they believe it is a sin to seek to get their own needs met. This belief brings about a paradox.

1. When these people thus try to always give up their own needs, they become more needy inside, and thus more focused on getting their unmet needs met. When they ignore a need, the message from their Treasure Inside gets louder and louder and eventually becomes difficult to ignore. Thus they become highly motivated to fill the need. They become more "selfish." To the degree they do succeed in denying their own need, they experience the unfortunate consequences which I have just listed ---- the emotion comes out "sideways."

2. On the other hand, when they understand that they have legitimate needs and recognize that the message coming up from their Treasure Inside is their friend, they are able to get the need met in an appropriate way. Because the need is not yet so severe that it is screaming at them for fulfillment, there is not an urgency about meeting the need. They are then still in a position to be particular as to how the need is met. They can thus succeed in having their legitimate need met in a legitimate way. When their need is met, they are no longer focused on themselves and are free to give to others. They become less "selfish."

Thus the paradox is that for those who try not to be "selfish," what seems so right (not being selfish) brings about failure. What seems so wrong (getting their own needs met) would bring about success.

This seeming paradox is fueled by their neediness. Unmet needs scream at them for fulfillment. Met needs bring about peace inside, freedom, and the ability to love others as they love themselves.

The Role Of Positive Emotions

God gave us both positive and negative emotions. So far we have been focusing on the negative ones. Remember, He made the negative ones unpleasant so we would <u>avoid</u> whatever was causing them. The positive ones are also useful. God made them pleasant so we would <u>approach</u> whatever causes them. They signal the receipt of something good for us. When children need to be held, they hold up their hands so that their parent will pick them up and fill the need. Once they have been filled with the touch of the parent, they are ready to get down and again explore the world.

Since we are needy creatures, it is important that we have a way of knowing what is good for us so we can seek it out and receive it. Feeling both positive and negative emotions is therefore meant to be our way of navigating through life.

Unfortunately, when we repress our negative feelings, we lose the good ones too. "The tragic thing about burying or smothering negative feelings is that it doesn't stop with them. The good, positive ones get clobbered at the same time." (Jacobs, p.25).

Jesus Felt His Emotions

The Bible describes Jesus as experiencing many emotions. He was sad, He wept, He was angry, and He had compassion. [127] We are

---

[127] Jesus experienced many emotions, such as:

Matthew 9:36, *but when He saw the multitudes, He was moved with compassion for them, because they were weary and scattered, like sheep having no shepherd.*

Mark 35, *So when He had looked around at them with anger, being grieved by the hardness of their hearts, He said to the man, "Stretch out your hand." And he stretched it out, and his hand was restored as whole as the other.*

Luke 19:41, *Now as He drew near, He saw the city and wept over it,*

Footnote Continued On Next Page

also instructed to experience emotions.[128] We are given permission to be angry, but we should not let it drive us into sinning. We are encouraged to be joyful. We are told that we can experience peace.

Can You Rely On Your Emotions?

It may shock you to know that your emotions are always 100% accurate. Your emotions are not <u>sometimes</u> accurate, or <u>often</u> accurate. They are <u>always</u> accurate - - - <u>in one way</u>. They <u>always</u> tell you exactly what is going on <u>inside</u> you.

Because of old wounds and the reactions that are triggered by their presence, our emotions <u>may not</u> be an accurate measure of what is going on <u>outside</u> of us. For instance, I might feel rejected by the host at a party, only to find out later he liked me! My emotion was not an accurate indicator of what was happening in my relationship with the host

> **Your emotions <u>always</u> tell you <u>exactly</u> what is going on <u>inside</u> you.**

at the party (what was happening <u>outside</u> me). Nevertheless, the feeling was giving me very important information about what was happening <u>inside</u> me. In this situation, my emotion was saying I have an old root of bitterness that was triggered when I felt rejected. I need to know this so that I can find the old root of rejection and be healed.

John 11:33; 38, *Therefore, when Jesus saw her weeping, and the Jews who came with her weeping, He groaned in the spirit and was troubled. . . Then Jesus, again groaning in Himself, came to the tomb.*

John 11:35, *Jesus wept.*

[128] In the Bible we are encouraged to experience many emotions, for example:

Matthew 5:4, *"Blessed are those who mourn, For they shall be comforted."*

Romans 12:15, *Rejoice with those who rejoice, and weep with those who weep.*

Romans 14:17, *For the kingdom of God is not food and drink, but righteousness and peace and joy in the Holy Spirit.*

Ephesians 4:26, *"Be angry, and do not sin." Do not let the sun go down on your wrath.*

Philippians 2:18, *For the same reason you also be glad and rejoice with me.*

2 Timothy 1:4, *greatly desiring to see you, being mindful of your tears, that I may be filled with joy,*

James 4:9, *Lament and mourn and weep! Let your laughter be turned to mourning and your joy to gloom.*

Whenever my emotions are not appropriate to the circumstances, this is an important clue that there is a wound inside me that needs to be taken care of. In these situations, if I blame others, or circumstances, or if I dismiss my emotions as undesirable, I rob myself of the opportunity of seeing that I have a wound inside me. Then I miss out on the opportunity of being healed. My emotion was my friend giving me important information about what was going on inside me.

Leave No Negative Emotion Unexamined

Be aware that subtle negative emotions also give you important information. The walk of constantly listening to your negative emotions should not be limited to "nuclear blasts." In fact, the majority of negative emotions that you feel will be fairly mild.

For instance, you may be a bit irritated because your wife left the top off the toothpaste tube, but you may not be so angry as to start an argument. Nevertheless, this emotion is still a signal that you judged her, and so you need to pray. Otherwise these little bitter roots will accumulate (a bundle of bitter roots will be forming in your heart), and at some point you may explode at her over something minor.

For most of us, these sorts of mild reactions happen many times a day, and we therefore need to pray many times a day. If we do this we don't have to carry the burden of those sinful reactions, because Jesus takes them. We then experience the rest that Jesus promised.

A Strange Language

If you have not been listening to what your emotions are telling you, their "language" will likely be strange to you. Our parents were supposed to teach us how to understand this language. If they didn't (and mine sure didn't, because they didn't know it themselves), and if we have been running from our emotions, we are probably not very adept at describing how we feel. Saying, "I feel like he doesn't listen to me" is not a feeling. It is a conclusion. Saying "I feel unimportant," or "I feel lonely," are descriptions of emotions. If you have difficulty describing what you are feeling, the list of negative and positive emotions in **Endnote #11-1** may help you put a name to what you are feeling. We need to learn this language so that we can understand what our emotions are telling us, and thus to benefit from the information.

Summary

Our "feelings" are special, wonderful gifts that God has given to us so that we can know the conditions that exist inside us. These messages are our helpers, and we need to listen to them.

Our "bad emotions" are not sin. They are simply the message system God gave us to alert us to when all is not well inside us, when something needs attention. We may have an unmet need, or we may have a root of bitterness inside. It is important for us to "leave no negative emotion unexamined," because our negative emotions always tell us <u>accurately</u> when there is a root of sin hidden <u>inside</u> us.

The living God has provided the way to fix all these things by washing away our sin. He also wants to walk with us in our Treasure Inside to show us what He wants to heal inside us.

Our positive emotions are also important. They are enjoyable and fun, and they will also guide us into those things that minister to us. Each

> **Leave no negative emotion unexamined.**

of us is a unique person who finds fulfillment in unique ways, and the positive emotions are the <u>signposts</u> directing us to our fulfillment. In addition, these good feelings are a <u>reward</u> for achieving cleansing from our sins, and obtaining fulfillment of our needs.

Chapter 12

The Good Part Of You
You Are Not All Bad

In the deep recesses of your being, how do you <u>feel</u> about yourself? I am not talking about your accomplishments or the image you present to the world, but how you feel deep down inside about yourself. For instance,

- Do you tend to see others as better and more capable than you?
- Do you always feel "less than" others?
- Do others seem to you to be more worthy of happiness and prosperity?
- Do you have a "poverty mentality?" (A poverty mentality is the expectation that you will never have more than the minimum necessary to live on, and that you are not worthy of more).
- Are you too easily embarrassed?
- Are you petrified to speak in front of a group?
- Do you live in fear of being rejected?
- Do you often feel like a worm?

It may surprise you to know that most of us would answer "yes" to many of these questions! Most assuredly, I was one of them.

Why would you feel this way? Is there nothing good that dwells in you? Do you therefore need to "die to self?" After all, if you are "bad," this would explain why you feel like a worm.

Who Does God Say We Are?

God doesn't agree with this view we may have of ourselves. He is very clear about this. We are made in His image.[129] You are. I am. It is not just God in us that is good (though there are also places like that). There are places in each of us that are purely "us," that are a part of who we are, that are good.[130] It is not just the Holy Spirit in us that is good. When God said, *"Let Us make man in Our image, according to Our likeness"* (Genesis 1:26), He did not say, "Let us make man to be Us." We are separate creatures from Him. We are unique, but

> **You are not a worm. You are made in the image of God, and that good part of you still exists inside you.**

made in His image. He is the pattern, but we are not Him, and He is not us.[131] This reality may be difficult for many to grasp, since there has been so much teaching and preaching about how awful we are.

His Image Did Not Leave Us When Adam And Eve Sinned

We are made in His image,[132] and His image still dwells in us.[133] Theologians do not disagree regarding the fact that the image of God

---

[129]   See Endnote #12-1 on God's image in us.

[130]   See Endnote #12-2 on uncovering the buried treasure inside you.

[131]   Some say that our spirit is the "good part," but that view does not match Scripture. **See Endnote #9-1** for more information on this issue. Also **See Endnote #12-3** on your own individuality.

[132]   Genesis 1:26-27 says the following: *Then God said, "Let us make man in our image, according to our likeness; let them have dominion over the fish of the sea"* . . . *So God created man in His own image, in the image of God He created him; male and female He created them.*

[133]   One might be tempted to say here that the image of God was in man before the fall, but after the fall, we were totally corrupted. However, Genesis 9:6, speaking after the fall, says: *Who ever sheds man's blood, by man his blood shall be shed; for in the image of God He made man.* So it is evident that the image of God still resided in man after the fall.

James 3:9 says the following, referring to the tongue: *With it we bless our God and father, and with it we curse men, who have been made in the image of God.* So, the image of God still resided in people in the time of James.

dwells in us <u>now</u>. Where there is dispute is in regard to exactly what constitutes the good part and what makes up the bad part. This dispute is not likely to be resolved until Jesus comes again, because the Scripture is not specific enough to tell us. Fortunately, we don't need to know in detail, because Jesus knows. The key point for us to realize is that <u>there is, here and now, a good part in each of us that is made in the image of God!</u>[134]

Humility And Pride

Humility is a word that is frequently misused. Often humility is viewed as recognizing what a worm I am, and how bad I am. "I am just an old sinner." But humility really means to <u>see myself the way God sees me</u>. When Jesus walked the earth He was humble, and yet He did not see Himself as a worm. He did not see Himself as less than He was, nor more than He was. He saw Himself as God the Father saw Him. He was the only begotten Son and He was God, but He was not God the Father. He did the will of the Father, not His own will (Matthew 26:39), because God the Father was preeminent.

Humility is about truth. We are not to see ourselves as more than we are, nor less than we are. Certainly, to see the truth about who we are in comparison with who God is eliminates the possibility of prideful boasting on our part. And yet, we are valuable because we are valuable to God.[135] At the same time, it is important that we find out who the unique person is that God made us to be. To

---

[134] "She did not show up as raw material to be shaped into whatever image the world might want her to take. She arrived with her own gifted form, with the shape of her own sacred soul. Biblical faith calls it the image of God in which we are all created. Thomas Merton calls it true self. Quakers call it the Inner Light, or 'that of God' in every person" (Palmer p.11).

Psalm 139:13-14: *For You have formed my inward parts; You have covered me in my mother's womb. I will praise You, for I am fearfully and wonderfully made; marvelous are Your works, and that my soul knows very well. My frame was not hidden from You, when I was made in secret, and skillfully wrought in the lowest parts of the earth.* This is hardly the description of a creature that is "all bad."

[135] **Romans 5:8:** *But God demonstrates His own love toward us, in that while we were stillt sinners, Christ died for us.* See also Ephesians 2:4, 2 Thessalonians 2:16, 1 John 4:10.

recognize our strengths that He gave us as a gift is not prideful or wrong. Pride says that we did something to earn it. Gifts by their very nature are not earned. They are freely bestowed on us and are dependent on the giver, not the receiver. So our strengths are free gifts bestowed on us, not things we manufactured or earned by our own effort.[136]   Pride is to see myself as more than I am.   See Chapter 13, "The Bad Part Of You," for more on pride.

Why Do We See Ourselves As Worms?

Let me try to explain why so many of us feel badly about ourselves. For some of us, we got constant messages from our parents that we weren't worth much. Most importantly, our parents did not give us messages that confirm the truth about our worth and our Treasure Inside - we were victims of Type A Trauma. You may remember that destroying our sense of being loveable and worthwhile is exactly what Type A Trauma does. Type A Trauma is epidemic, and to some degree it is probably universal.

Other Voices

Our siblings likely also gave us these same messages that did not confirm our worth. Since they were raised in the same home, they also suffered from Type A Trauma. In such a home there is competition for the few crumbs of The Blessing which are available in the family. Each child is trying to

The voices that wounded us are:
1. **Parents**
2. **Siblings**
3. **Our culture**
4. **The church**

---

[136] "Today I understand vocation" (what I do) "quite differently - not as a goal to be achieved but as a gift to be received. Discovering vocation does not mean scrambling toward some prize just beyond my reach but accepting the treasure of true self I already possess. Vocation does not come from a voice 'out there' calling me to become something I am not. It comes from a voice 'in here' calling me to be the person I was born to be, to fulfill the original selfhood given me at birth by God" (Palmer, p.10).

raise himself above the others, because if he can feel superior to another child, he won't feel so badly about himself at that moment.

I have an older sister who was also very wounded by Type A Trauma. She was three years older than I, was a brilliant student, and was much larger than I was. When I was growing up she would set traps for me and play tricks on me to prove how much better she was, and she used to beat me up and take my stuff. She used to make fun of me, and called me "Shrimpo," because for much of our time growing up I only came up to her shoulder. She did all of these things to make herself feel a little better about herself, and what she said and did tore me down even further. Her message just added to my already fragile self-image.

Our culture also tells us how unworthy we are. The other children are doing the same thing as our siblings – competing for the crumbs of blessing that are available. Our culture is obsessed with being Number One, and competing to be Number One is seen as a wonderful thing! Since by definition there can only be one Number One, that makes the rest of us "losers." And those who are Number One in football are probably not Number One in math, or art, or perhaps anything except athletics. Thus they too are "losers." Therefore we are all losers, and most of us feel that way about ourselves. It is a cultural sickness, and is beautifully described as such by Alfie Kohn in his book, No Contest.[137]

Interestingly, when we compare ourselves with others, the areas where we aren't as good as the others are what impact us. Ironically, when we become Number One at something, it seems hollow. The good feeling of having achieved this victory is fleeting, and we still feel badly about ourselves, because we focus on those areas where we fall short. God is clear about this: *But they, measuring themselves by themselves, and comparing themselves among themselves, are not wise* (2 Corinthians 10:12, KJV).

The Church has also tended to focus on the bad, giving us the impression that there is nothing good that dwells in us. One scripture presented in support of this is Romans 7:18: *For I know*

---

[137] Kohn, Alfie, in bibliography.

that in me (that is in my flesh) nothing good dwells.   It is in my flesh only that nothing good dwells, and these teachers assume this refers to all of my natural being.   But flesh (Greek *sarx*) is another fuzzy Greek word.   A detailed study reveals that my flesh, as referred to in this scripture, is only a part of me, not all of my being.   Read Chapter 13, "The Bad Part Of You" for more on this.   Jeremiah Chapter 17 is often raised as proof that nothing good dwells in me.   Again, we are faced with a fuzzy word, the Hebrew word *leb*.   There is significant doubt that Jeremiah is referring to our entire inner man.[138]

Further evidence we see of our own awfulness is that we are not living up to the standards laid out for us by the church.[139]   Deep inside we know we are falling short, and we feel that others are more successful as Christians. I then think, "I am surely bad."

So we believed all these voices that surrounded our formative years. Certainly, we think, they can't all be wrong. From all of this we receive our identity.   We see ourselves as bad.[140]   But these

---

[138]   **Jeremiah, Chapter 17** says in part, *The heart of man is deceitful above all things and desperately wicked; who can know it?* As I have taught earlier, we really can't specify that it's my heart where the wickedness lies. I cannot say with biblical authority exactly what part of me is deceitful and desperately wicked, because the Hebrew word here translated into English as "heart" is translated as many inner parts of me in other parts of the Old Testament. It is the translators' choice to use "heart," but there are several other options. Therefore the best I can really say in translating this verse in Jeremiah is something more like, "Somewhere deep inside of man there is a place that is deceitful above things and desperately wicked; who can know it?" Going beyond this is speculative.
     See Endnote #12-5 for more details on Jeremiah 17.
     Likewise, I can also only say that somewhere deep inside me there is a part of me that is made in the image of God. When faced with such doubt about the exact meaning of a word, we need to rely on other areas of the Word of God to clarify the meaning, if that is indeed possible. Some issues mentioned in the Bible will always remain fuzzy.
     Further evidence that Jeremiah 17 is not referring to my Treasure Inside is the destruction that occurs in my life when I see myself as all bad. Admittedly this is only indirect scriptural evidence, but it is very powerful evidence; because it is true that whenever I align myself with God's truth, blessings flow. When I align myself with a lie, curses occur. This is simply the way God's laws work.
[139]   ". . . is rooted in a deep distrust of selfhood, in the belief that the sinful self will always be 'selfish' unless corrected by external forces of virtue. It is a notion that made me feel inadequate to the task of living my own life, creating guilt about the distance between who I was and who I was supposed to be, leaving me exhausted as I labored to close the gap" (Palmer, p.10).
[140]   **See Endnote #12-4** regarding the misperception that you are all "bad."

voices are all wrong. God sees us differently, and He is always right.

How Can We See Ourselves As God Sees Us?

Many other teachers and authors have made lists of scriptures that tell us how much God loves us, how valuable we are in His sight, how we are His children, etc. They encourage us to meditate on this list, with the implication that this exercise will convince us of who we really are. While it is very important to know how God feels about us, meditating on such a list (with our head) will not change how we feel about ourselves. Those of you that have tried this know how ineffective, frustrating, and discouraging this is. In our head we know how God see us, but the messages fail to make the journey to our heart. Our feelings don't change.

Then how can you change how you feel about yourself? That is what this book is intended to show you. If you read the book and walk it out, you will begin to see yourself as God sees you, because the living God will show you. As you begin to feel His love, the lies about how bad you are will be washed away. Remember that judging yourself causes the wound which triggers the Big Hurt, and this happens because this bitter root is so contrary to how God intended for you to see yourself.

Summary

The purpose of this chapter has been to help you recognize some misconceptions about how bad you are.

There is a part of you that was corrupted by The Fall, but this corrupted part is not all of who you are. There is a part of you that is made in the image of God. It is "you," it is good, and it still

> **For you to be sanctified, all that is "you" does not have to die. You are not rotten to the core.**

exists in you. God says so in His Word. This is true whether you believe it or not.

A key part of your sanctification process (Inner Healing) is a complete change of attitude towards who you are. There is buried treasure inside you. You need to come to know that this is true before you can possibly be reconciled with yourself and have harmony inside. After all, who would want to love and be best friends with something evil?

For you to be sanctified (changed into the image of Jesus), all that is "you" does not have to die. You are not rotten to the core. God does not intend to annihilate you and replace you with Jesus. The next chapter will address the "bad part," the concept of "dying to self," and this awareness will help you sort out the "good part" from the "bad part."

Chapter 13

The Bad Part Of You
Flesh And Sin

*For I know that in me (that is, in my flesh) nothing good dwells;
for to will is present with me, but how to perform what is good I
do not find* (Romans 7:18).

This scripture makes it clear that the "bad" part of me can be termed
my "flesh." When the Bible uses the term "flesh," most of us
immediately jump to the conclusion that what is being referred to is
our entire self, and it is "bad." We think that "flesh" always causes
us to be engage in sinful behavior, such as fornication, drunkenness,
or idolatry (Galatians 5:19-21).

However, it may surprise you to know that when the Bible uses
the term "flesh," it is not always talking about a "bad" thing. For
example, when the Bible said that Jesus came in the flesh, did He
come in something that was "bad?" Since He was sinless, He
couldn't possibly be a part of something that was sinful.

*Every spirit that confesses that Jesus Christ has come in the flesh
is of God, and every spirit that does not confess that Jesus Christ
has come in the flesh is not of God.*[141] (1 John 4:2-3).

The Lord also spoke to the people of Israel and said,

---

[141] **Romans 1:3,** *Concerning His Son Jesus Christ our Lord, who was born of the seed of David
according to the flesh.*

    1 Peter 3:18, *For Christ also suffered once for sins, the just for the unjust, that He might bring us
to God, being put to death in the flesh but made alive by the Spirit.*

    1 Peter 4:1, *Therefore, since Christ suffered for us in the flesh, arm yourselves also with the same
mind, for he who has suffered in the flesh has ceased from sin.*

    2 John 1:7, *For many deceivers have gone out into the world who do not confess Jesus Christ as
coming in the flesh. This is a deceiver and an antichrist.*

Then I will give them one heart, and I will put a new spirit within them, and take the stony heart out of their flesh, and give them a heart of flesh (Ezekiel 11:19).

It is evident from the context that the "heart of flesh" that the Lord was going to give them is a good thing, not a bad thing.

When "Flesh" Is Not Bad

In fact, there are several ways that "flesh" (the Greek word *sarx*) in the Bible refers to something that is not "bad." What follows are primarily New Testament references, which were written in Greek.

1. Flesh can refer to our entire person.[142]
2. Flesh can refer to the physical part of man.
3. Flesh can refer to our creatureliness and frailty, the fact that we are finite and vulnerable.
4. Flesh can refer to something that is purely natural or external.[143]

Fuzzy Words

In our Western world we like to think our words are precise tools which we can use to understand perfectly what someone else is saying. We tend to transfer this concept to the Bible and to the languages in which it was written. With accurate definitions we can clearly understand Scripture. But often words are not so precise.

---

[142] Rudolf Bultmann adds to the variety of the meanings of *sarx*: "In fact, like *psyche* and *pneuma* . . . *sarx* can even be used to designate the person himself" (p. 233). And, "Thus, *sarx* can mean the whole sphere of that which is earthly or natural . . . Or, differently said, 'to live' or 'to walk in the flesh' means nothing else than simply 'to lead one's life as a man,' an idea which in itself does not involve any ethical or theological judgment but simply takes note of a fact; not a norm but a field or a sphere is indicated by 'in the flesh'" (Bultmann, Theology of the New Testament, Part II, pp.234, 235-236).

[143] See Endnote #13-1 for more details concerning the meaning of *sarx*.

Have you ever wondered why biologists, anthropologists, and other scientists use such long words to specify a certain species (for instance, "*saintpaulia ionantha*" for "African violet")? They do this so that when they talk with other scientists, they know <u>exactly</u> what species is being discussed. They do this because many English words have numerous meanings, some meanings of a given word being unrelated to each other.[144]

For instance, the English noun "round" has several possible meanings. When hunting, or on the firing range, it refers to one thing (a bullet). When in a bar drinking, it refers to something else (drinks for everyone). It would be a good idea if the bartender did not confuse these two meanings when you ask for a "round." Otherwise it might hurt a lot.

Many of the important concepts in the Bible are explained using fuzzy words (since that was all that was available to the writers). Then how can we understand what the author is telling us? We can gain an accurate understanding by paying attention to the "context," to what the writer is talking about at the moment. The bartender needs to recognize that the person wants to buy drinks. The manager of the firing range needs to recognize that the person wants some ammunition.

Sarx (the Greek word for "flesh") is one of those fuzzy words. It is unfortunate and confusing that the word "flesh" has such a wide range of meanings. But with careful study of the context of various passages in which the word is used, we can better understand what the writer is trying to say. We always must be on guard so that we do not apply the wrong meaning in a given context or situation.[145]

---

[144] **See Endnote #13-2** for more details on "fuzzy" words.

[145] **Also see Endnote #4-1 and Endnote #13-1** for discussions of the importance of <u>context</u> when encountering a "fuzzy" word.

The Bad Part

In the New Testament sometimes the term "flesh" does not mean something bad, but in others it <u>does</u> mean a bad thing in us. When "flesh" is referring to the "bad part," it can be referring to one of three possibilities.

When "flesh" <u>is</u> referring to the "bad part," it can be referring to one of three possibilities:

1. **Sensuality or lawlessness. Here it means a disregard for God's moral standards.**
2. **<u>Trying</u> hard to be good!**
3. **Our tendency to respond to perceived wounding with bitterness, judgment, and blame.**

It may be a surprise to you that to try to be good by your own willpower is not just futile, it is in fact sinful. The tendency to do this comes out of your "flesh" – the "bad part."[146]

The Common Denominator

Behind all three of these tendencies of the Bad Part is a common theme. All of these tendencies are based upon a "self-reliant attitude of the man who puts his trust in his own strength and in that which is

---

[146] "The sinful self-delusion that one lives out of the created world can manifest itself both in unthinking recklessness (this especially among the Gentiles) and in considered busy-ness (this especially among the Jews) - both in the ignoring or transgressing of ethical demands and in excess of zeal to fulfill them. For the sphere of 'flesh' is by no means just the life of instinct or sensual passion, but is just as much that of the moral and religious efforts of man" (Bultmann, Theology of the New Testament, Part II, p.239).

Also see Endnote #13-3 for more on the "bad part."

controllable by him."[147] There is something in us, in our "flesh," which wants to be God. This is what happened in the Garden of Eden when Satan told Eve, "*For God knows that in the day you eat of it your eyes will be opened, and you will be like God*" (Genesis 3:5), and Eve and Adam believed him and ate of the fruit. From that moment on, we humans have had the tendency to want to be our own god. That is the dynamic behind the "bad part" of each of us, which is one of the uses of the word "flesh." [148]

The Primal Sin

This desire to take God's place, to be our own god, is foundational to our difficulties in this life. This desire and drive is therefore the "Primal Sin"---the bedrock of our sinful side.

"For just this is the essence of flesh: the essence of the man who understands himself in terms of himself, who wants to secure his own existence . . . This then is sin: rebellion against God, forgetting that man is a creature, misunderstanding oneself and putting oneself in God's place" (Bultmann, Existence and Faith, p.81).

"But man misunderstands himself and puts himself in the place of God. And every man comes out of a history that is governed by this misunderstanding. He comes out of a lie; he is determined by the flesh whose power he cannot break. Were he to imagine that he could break it, he would assume that he does have himself in his own

> **For me to try to be good by my own willpower is not just futile, it is in fact sinful; and the tendency to do this comes out of my "flesh" – the "bad part."**

---

[147] Bultmann, Theology of the New Testament, Part II, p.240.

[148] See **Endnote #13-4** for more information about flesh and sin in Scripture.

power after all and would thereby repeat the primal sin" (Bultmann, Theology of the New Testament, Part I, p.83).[149]

The Wall

In Chapter 9, "There Is Buried Treasure," I referred to The Wall that separates me (my Head) from myself (my Treasure Inside). This Wall closes me off from an awareness of the living God who dwells in me. You may recall that The Wall was made up of Bitter Root Judgments and Inner Vows, both of which spring from this same bad place in me - my tendency to take God's place. When I judge, I am taking God's place as judge. When I make an Inner Vow, I am deciding to take care of myself, because I don't trust God to do

> **I need to have the blood of Jesus ever available to me, so that He can clean up the mess that I keep making inside myself.**

it. I am deciding to run my own life, because in that "bad part" of me (my flesh) I don't trust God; and I have the delusion that I can do it better.

This exact tendency has created difficulties in my own life. My parents were unavailable and not trustworthy to meet my needs. So I learned to trust only in myself, and I made a decision to do it myself. What makes this even more insidious is that our culture so highly values independence; and this ability to be self-sufficient is seen as a good thing. I certainly saw it this way.

---

[149]"The primal sin is not an inferior morality, but rather the understanding of oneself in terms of oneself and the attempt to secure one's own existence by means of what one himself establishes, by means of one's own accomplishments " (Bultmann, Existence & Faith, p.81).

"And since all pursuit, even the perverted sort, is, in intention, pursuit of life, this means seeking life where it is not - in the created world. For to deny God as Creator is to turn away from Him to the creation . . . Hence, the ultimate sin reveals itself to be the false assumption of receiving life not as the gift of the Creator but procuring it by one's own power, of living from one's self rather than from God" (Bultmann, Theology of the New Testament, Part II, p.232).

See Endnote #13-5 for more on this "primal sin" in mankind.

Also, if my parents had met my needs, I would now find it easy to trust those in charge. I would now find it easy to trust that Jesus is active in my life, and that He is looking after my needs. I would not now think I am alone in my struggles, as I often do. Fortunately, God is now at work repairing this in me!

As with so many things, we need freedom: we need to be able to act on our own behalf when this is appropriate, and to be able to be dependent when this is appropriate. When a person makes an Inner Vow, as I did ("I will always have to do it myself") we have lost freedom. Then it is very difficult to be dependent when it is appropriate. Then it feels very uncomfortable to really trust another person to meet our need. In fact, living independently is probably so automatic that we don't give it a thought. We just do it. Because of this wound in me, God has had to work very hard in getting me to trust Him and to depend on Him.

My reaction to my parents planted Bitter Roots in me. My "flesh," the "bad part" that impelled me to react as I did, is a part of my fallen nature. I will never lose the tendencies that spring from this "bad part" as long as I walk this planet. In addition, because it is a part of my very being, it operates so automatically that it has done its work before I am aware of it. Therefore, I need to have the blood of Jesus ever available to me so that He can clean up the mess that I keep making inside myself.

Don't "Throw The Baby Out With The Bathwater"

When we judge ourselves, or try to "die to self," it is because we have come to see <u>everything</u> hidden inside us as "bad." Everything seems to be in one "container." Since pain and the impulse to bad behavior come from someplace "inside," we conclude that <u>everything</u> "inside" is "bad."

However, below our level of consciousness there are at least three areas, which are symbolized by the containers in the diagram that follows (I have previously discussed each of these areas in detail in Chapters 2, 3, 4, 9, 12, and 13).

This diagram is an over-simplification of what we are like inside, presented to help you understand this particular concept. Because Scripture is not precise about it, I cannot be dogmatic about everything that is inside each of these "containers," nor that there are only three "containers" hidden inside. But I can with the backing of Scripture say that there is a good part, there is a bad part, and these two parts do not constitute all there is. I can also infer that there is a part somewhere inside that contains good roots and bad roots. We are incredibly complex inside, and the Lord is the only one who knows the whole picture. What is most important is to know that there is <u>both</u> a "bad part" and a "good part" inside us.

There Are Multiple Places Inside Us

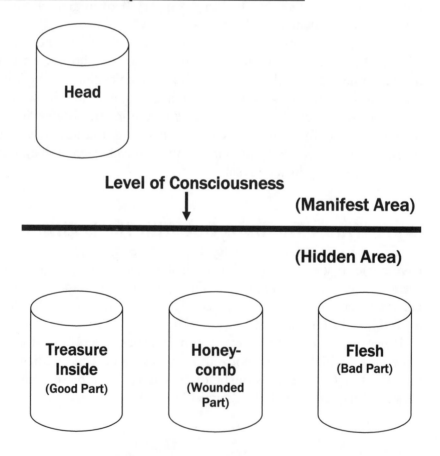

You will see a similarity between the left side of this diagram and what I talked about in Chapter 9, "There Is Buried Treasure."

When we judge ourselves, we confuse the Treasure Inside ("good part," the image of God in us) with the Flesh ("bad part") and with the Bitter Roots (the black parts in the "Honeycomb"). We think all these parts are in one container. We then condemn everything hidden inside us. We "throw the baby out with the bath water." The "good part" gets condemned along with the part(s) that are guilty.

Understanding that there are several parts hidden in us will facilitate treating each part appropriately. Our Treasure Inside and Flesh can't be changed (or "healed"). They will always be what they were from the moment God made us.

On the other hand, the "Honeycomb" (discussed Chapter 3) can be healed. It is in a sense the "battle ground" where darkness and light compete. When, because of the influence of the "flesh," we judge, a Bitter Root is planted in our Honeycomb. However, this damage can be repaired by forgiving and being forgiven by Jesus. The Bitter Root can thus be changed into a good root through the blood of Jesus. Then light wins over darkness. Then the new good root will produce good fruit.

Finally, the image of God in us needs to be affirmed and loved. Love is the "fuel" that our Treasure Inside runs on. This is why it is so devastating to judge and to hate that part. Receiving "The Blessing" (see Chapter 10) helps us develop a love for our Treasure Inside, and thus to differentiate it from the other "parts."

Where Does "Die To Self" Fit In?

There is a perspective that says that we should "die to self." This view is not uncommon in churches, and it often has deadly results. The destruction comes about through a misunderstanding of what is meant by "self." Many who advocate and teach this perspective often correctly say there is a part of us that does need to die and be reborn in the likeness of Jesus. However, the followers think this means that everything inside them is bad and needs to die.

When this misunderstanding exists, the followers are destroyed. They are destroyed because they try to kill off <u>everything</u> inside them, everything that is not under the dominion of their intellect and their will power. This misunderstanding creates a deep distrust of everything inside them, including the Treasure Inside. Thus they attempt to build The Wall in order to suppress <u>all</u> that is inside[150].

Creating An Insolvable Dilemma

To the degree that they succeed in building The Wall, they experience all the problems that The Wall creates. To the degree they do not succeed, they feel guilty and condemned. It is an insolvable dilemma, because either way they lose. They become miserable and defeated.

As I have shown, a great deal of what we struggle with is based upon a misunderstanding of what a particular word means. These misunderstandings are understandable, since so many of the theological words we use have such broad ranges of meaning. In addition, our popular culture and the New Age have redefined some words that would otherwise be useful. In order to avoid such a tragic misunderstanding, I would recommend not using the phrase "die to self." It would be much more accurate and fruitful to speak about Jesus pulling out the bitter roots and replacing them with His presence inside.[151]

Pride

Some people use the term "pride" to describe this human tendency to want to be our own God. I think this is misleading, or perhaps even dangerous, because the word "pride" is then usually understood

---

[150] ". . . is rooted in a deep distrust of selfhood, in the belief that the sinful self will always be 'selfish' unless corrected by external forces of virtue. It is a notion that made me feel inadequate to the task of living my own life, creating guilt about the distance between who I was and who I was supposed to be, leaving me exhausted as I labored to close the gap" (Palmer, p.10).
[151]   See Endnote #13-6 for more details on "die to self."

to mean "I am really something great."[152] Therefore, to eliminate "pride" means to come to the place where "I am nothing." Consequently, to label a person's flaw as "pride" is to put them on a quest to see themselves as "nothing." This aggravates the already present low esteem of self that most people have, and perhaps paradoxically brings about further wounding and destruction inside.

Such "pride" <u>is a sin</u>,[153] whereas the "bad part" I have just described is <u>our sin-nature</u>. The sin of "pride" can be repented of and washed in the blood of Jesus. [154] Then it is gone. It no longer exists as far as God is concerned. On the other hand, what I have described as the 'bad part' is not "pride." It is something much deeper, and it has nothing whatsoever to do with how we feel about ourselves. It is our <u>sin-nature</u>, and it is in every human being. There is nothing we can do to remove it. It will be present as long as we live on this earth, and it is present in people whose "self-esteem" is practically zero.

Summary

The word "flesh" in the New Testament refers to a wide range of things, many of which are not "bad." However, one use of the word "flesh" does refer to the place inside us which does not trust God, and which wants to take His place. It is out of this fallen place that most (if not all) of our tendency to sin arises. It manifests itself in disregard of God's commandments, in zeal to obey Him out of our own strength (our willpower), and in our tendency to take His place by judging.

---

[152] Webster's Dictionary defines "proud," in part, as having or displaying excessive self-esteem. "Pride" is, in part, defined as the quality or state of being proud: inordinate self-esteem.

[153] It is interesting that the term "pride" is very rare in the New Testament. It only appears three times (Strong's, p.840). Apparently the New Testament writers did not see it as a major issue to be addressed. In light of this low emphasis, it is interesting how much emphasis the Western church has been placed on the need to not be "proud." In contrast to this, sexual sins like "fornication" and "adultery" are addressed dozens of times.

[154] **Isaiah 43:25,** "*I, even I, am He who blots out your transgressions for My own sake; and I will not remember your sins.*"

     Jeremiah 31:34b, "*For I will forgive their iniquity, and their sin I will remember no more.*"

When we are children, we don't understand that we are multifaceted inside. Therefore, when we discover that we sometimes tend to be "bad," we then judge <u>everything</u> hidden inside us as "bad." We then "throw the baby out with the bathwater." This is tragic, because there is a "good" place inside us that needs to be loved. Not being able to love that "good" place brings about destruction in our lives.

When we understand the truth that we are multifaceted inside, that there are "good," "bad," and "wounded" places inside us, we are in a position to begin to successfully walk out our healing.

"And you shall know the truth, and the truth shall make you free. . . Therefore if the Son makes you free, you shall be free indeed" (John 8:32,36).

Chapter 14

Face To Face With Jesus
You Need This Experience

You are built for love. God is love. Because you are made in His image, you need love as much as you need air to breathe. It is the lack of real love that has wounded you, and it is the presence of real love that has the power to heal you.

People are imperfect in the supply of love they give us. Sometimes they give us the love we need, but sometimes love is absent, sometimes it is sporadic, and sometimes it is counterfeit. Somewhere inside, children know the difference between the real thing and the counterfeit. They can sense whether they are being filled, or drained. Real love flows from the parent to the child, fills the child with life, and the child thrives. The counterfeit flows the other way, and sucks nourishment from the child. In this case the parent is attentive, but they are attentive because they need the child to fill the parent's unmet needs. The parent draws life from the child rather than giving to the child. The child starves, and struggles, and is wounded.[155] Real love gives, counterfeit love takes.

Jesus' love is always the real thing. It is genuine. If you could experience His love, you would be filled with life from the encounter, because the flow is always from Him to you. And what if you could experience it often? Surely your cup would overflow. A goal of this

> **Meeting with the living Jesus and receiving His love will heal you in a profound way.**

---

[155] All counterfeits by their nature are meant to look like the real thing. But they always have a fatal flaw in that they are not genuine. A counterfeit $100 bill may look just like the real thing. The fatal flaw is that the bill was not issued by the government and is worthless. The fatal flaw in counterfeit love is that it is based upon the need of the parent, not the need of the child.

book is to bring you to the place where you can meet with Jesus and receive His love. His presence is life, and it heals. In the moment that you receive the love of Jesus, everything else pales.

I can rationally and intellectually understand what friendship is, and in one sense I then "know" what friendship is. However, when a friend comes to me, and I <u>experience</u> their friendship, then I <u>really</u> "know" what friendship is. It is then a "knowing" that is not just a thought, but it is a reality, an event, a "happening". It is planted in my heart, not just my head. This is also true of "knowing" God. "The incomprehensibility of God lies not in the sphere of theoretical thought but in the sphere of personal existence." (Bultmann, <u>Jesus Christ and Mythology</u>, p.43). [156]

Many times during prayer I have had clients actually come into the presence of Jesus. This experience writes on their heart the truth that God loves them. They realize they are important to Him, and in their heart is where they need to know it. When such an encounter occurs, they are changed.

One cannot be in His presence without being profoundly affected. People come out of such an encounter with a whole new awareness of who they really are, and they know in the depth of their being that Jesus loves them. They have <u>experienced</u> it. Words fail to describe this realization. When Jesus shows us anything, we <u>know</u> it is true. I suppose this is because He is Truth, and something inside us always knows this. Real love is what we have been yearning for and searching for all our life. Something inside us always knew it existed, even though we had not experienced it; and we know the real thing when we meet it.

> **You are built for love. You were wounded by a lack of love, and you receive healing when you <u>experience</u> real love. God is love, and so when you experience the presence of Jesus, you receive His love and healing occurs.**

---

[156] See **Endnote #14-1** for more on what it means to "know" Jesus.

An Impediment

If you have been unable to experience the presence of the Lord, to be able to walk and talk with Him, The Wall is in the way. The purpose of God for your life is to change you into the image of Jesus, and the most effective way to accomplish this is for you to experience His presence, to have a living encounter with Him on a regular basis. The Wall must be removed so that He can accomplish all of His work in you.

It Takes A Miracle

However, moving from your current situation to that place of intimacy with Jesus is not always easy. In fact, it requires a miracle. Or, more correctly, it may take a series of miracles. You may begin with many blockages; and as each blockade is removed, your ability to walk and talk with Him gradually becomes more and more clear. It is a process well illustrated in the scriptures.

> *So He took the blind man by the hand and led him out of the town. And when He had spit on his eyes and put His hands on him, He asked him if he saw anything. And he looked up and said, 'I see men like trees, walking.' Then He put His hands on his eyes again and made him look up. And he was restored and saw everyone clearly.* (Mark 8:23-25).

The journey to seeing Him clearly is often like this. It usually takes a sequence of healings that Jesus orchestrates. There are steps along the way from being blind to seeing clearly. Along the way you may see partially, but gradually your connection with the Lord becomes clearer. This journey would be impossible without the leading of Jesus and His healing power. Your restoration is as much a miracle as the healing of this blind man.

The complexity of your journey stems from a combination of factors:

- **Your fallen nature**
- **Your having grown up in a perverse world which is void of true love.**
- **The fact that Satan is real and his primary goal is to separate you from God.**

Things went radically wrong for all of us from the beginning, and the result is a big mess. Untangling your mess is beyond your ability. But the Lord knows the problem, and He has the cure. When you arrive at the place where you can respond to His leading, you can follow Him down the path of healing He has laid out for you. This is the path of being changed into His image.

That is why your first focus must be to come into fellowship with Him. Until you are able to experience His living presence in your life, your journey is much more difficult.[157]

To Those Who Already Hear God

There are some Christians whose wounds are such that they interfere with their relationship with themselves, but not so much with God. Thus they have a living relationship with Him, and they have an advantage over those who cannot hear God's voice. But they still need to recognize their alienation from themselves; and so they need to cooperate with the Lord as He leads them through their own healing.

---

[157] **Ephesians 3:14-21,** *For this reason I bow my knees to the Father of our Lord Jesus Christ, from whom the whole family in heaven and earth is named, that He would grant you, according to the riches of His glory, to be strengthened with might through His Spirit in the inner man, that Christ may dwell in your hearts through faith; that you, being rooted and grounded in love, may be able to comprehend with all the saints what is the width and length and depth and height – to know the love of Christ which passes knowledge; that you may be filled with all the fullness of God. Now to Him who is able to do exceedingly abundantly above all that we ask or think, according to the power that works in us, to Him be glory in the church by Christ Jesus throughout all ages, world without end. Amen.*

We Are Healed In Relationship

We, like God, are relational beings. We were wounded in relationships, and we can only be healed in relationships. A large proportion of our journey is meant to be walked out in our moment-by-moment personal relationship directly with God. And yet there is a special anointing that comes when praying with another person. I have found it to be true that our ability to experience the presence of the Lord is enhanced by the presence of others of like Christian faith. The Lord told us about this profound truth.

> *"For where two or three are gathered together in My name, I am there in the midst of them."* Matthew 18:20.

He Wants This For All Of Us

In wanting a personal, real, living relationship with the Lord, we are not begging the Lord to do something that He is reluctant to do. It was His idea. Jesus said this so eloquently.

> *"A little while, and you will not see Me; and again a little while, and you will see Me."* (John 16:17)

> *". . . that they all may be one, as You, Father, are in Me, and I in You; that they also may be one in Us, that the world may believe that You sent Me. And the glory which You gave Me I have given them, that they may be one just as We are one: I in them and You in Me; that they may be made perfect in one, and that the world may know that You have sent Me, and have loved them as You have loved Me."* (John 17:21-23).

Summary

The living presence of the Lord is where you were meant to dwell. Jesus wants it that way. And when you enter into His presence, you are changed.

If you are unable to enter His presence, The Wall is in the way. Then The Wall needs to come down.

"Father, I desire that they also whom You gave Me may be with Me where I am, that they may behold My glory which You have given Me;" (John 17:24a)

Chapter 15

A New And Living Way
How You Can Experience Jesus' Presence

Do you desire to have Jesus remove The Wall that separates you from Him and from your Treasure Inside? The first step is for you to have this desire, and to have faith that He will make it possible. Then there are some things you can do to cooperate with what He wants to do in you, ways by which you can make yourself available for Him to meet with you.

> *Therefore, brethren, having boldness to enter the Holiest by the blood of Jesus, by a new and living way which He consecrated for us, through the veil, that is, His flesh* (Hebrews 10:19-20).

Therefore, the Lord has provided a "new and living way" for this to happen. The living presence of the Lord is where you were meant to dwell, and he yearns to meet with you.

There <u>Are</u> Ways To Facilitate The Miraculous

Many of us have had spontaneous encounters with the Lord, which He alone has orchestrated. We were often ambushed by these encounters, because we weren't even seeking such an experience. In my life this has usually happened when I was in great need of a touch from Him. The greater the need, the more profound the experience.

God had a plan for Saul of Tarsus, and it was very important for Saul to get the message.[158] Saul was on his way to Damascus to persecute the Christians there. Saul was certainly not seeking a face

---

[158] Acts 9:1-19.

to face encounter with Jesus. Knowing that Saul was not very receptive at that time, the Lord appeared in such a way that Saul fell to the ground. Then the Lord spoke to Saul, and Saul the persecutor became Paul the apostle.

These more profound, spontaneous encounters happen infrequently in our lives. However, Jesus speaks to us in many other ways much more regularly. If we are listening, we may hear Him. If we aren't listening, we may miss His message. When I have a sense that He wants to tell me something, I usually go for a quiet walk and I can then receive what He is saying to me. Sometimes I am too busy and am distracted, and then I am not likely to hear when He calls. It is a bit like my cell phone. If I have my cell phone turned on, I may get a call from my friend. If I turn it off, then I won't get his call.

With my cell phone, I can turn it on and carry it with me. I am then ready if my friend calls. With Jesus, I can make preparations and listen in certain ways which can facilitate an encounter.

Jesus provided a "new and living way" for us to come into His presence.

> **Jesus provided a "new and living way" for us to come into His presence**

Therefore, brethren, having boldness to enter the Holiest by the blood of Jesus, by a new and living way which He consecrated for us, through the veil, that is, His flesh.[159]

When Jesus appears, miracles happen. When Thomas, one of the twelve disciples, experienced the presence of the risen Lord, he cried out, *"My Lord and my God!"* This encounter filled Thomas with

---

[159] **Hebrews 10:16-22,** *"This is the covenant that I will make with them after those days, says the Lord: I will put My laws into their hearts, and in their minds I will write them,' then He adds, 'Their sins and their lawless deeds I will remember no more.' Now where there is remission of these, there is no longer an offering for sin. Therefore, brethren, having boldness to enter the Holiest by the blood of Jesus, by a new and living way which He consecrated for us, through the veil, that is, His flesh, and having a High Priest over the house of God, let us draw near with a true heart in full assurance of faith, having our hearts sprinkled from an evil conscience and our bodies washed with pure water."*

faith, and he believed. [160] Though we all need to walk by faith, to believe and to persevere even when the way seems dry and hard, there are times that we all literally need to be in His presence. There are ways of counseling that are focused on coming into the actual, living presence of the Lord.

Any Believer Can Be The Prayer Partner

In the following examples there are always at least two people present, the person seeking healing and a prayer partner.   This prayer partner can be any believer, although this role is often filled by a counselor.

Listening Prayer, An Approach To Facilitate Meeting Jesus

"Listening Prayer" is an approach to experiencing the Lord that He revealed to David and Linda Olson. David was a pastor; and Linda, being a pastor's wife, was drawn into counseling through necessity. One day she was called upon to counsel a woman who was struggling greatly and was suicidal. When faced with this situation, Linda felt totally inadequate and so she cried out to the Lord for help.   God answered by speaking to the wounded woman and leading her through her healing. It was miraculous. Linda later visited a professional counselor who knew the wounded woman, and

---

[160] **John 20:24-29,** *But Thomas, called Didymus, one of the twelve was not with them when Jesus came. The other disciples therefore said to him, "We have seen the Lord." But he said to them, "Unless I see in His hands the print of the nails, and put my finger into the print of the nails, and put my hand into His side, I will not believe." And after eight days His disciples were again inside, and Thomas with them. Jesus came, the doors being shut, and stood in the midst and said, "Peace to you!" Then He said to Thomas, "Reach your finger here, and look at My hands; and reach your hand here, and put it into My side. Do not be unbelieving, but believing." And Thomas answered and said to Him "My Lord and my God!" Jesus said to him, "Thomas, because you have seen Me, you have believed. Blessed are those who have not seen and yet have believed."*

he said, "You did in one night what it would take me three years of therapy to do."[161]

This was the beginning of a ministry, and they called it "Listening Prayer." Linda said of Listening Prayer: "If we had not asked Him, I would never have known what to do – the problems were too complex. But by now, I knew my Savior wanted to heal these people, and He knew how to do it. I simply taught them how to listen to Him, and He brought them through the pain, into wholeness. But the best part, far more important than the fact that they got freedom from their emotional pain, was that each learned to have a close and lasting relationship with Jesus."[162]

The key point in this approach is that both the prayer partner and the person seeking healing sit quietly and listen. The Lord speaks directly to the person seeking healing. When the Lord speaks to an individual, the person <u>knows</u> that what has been said is the truth. Jesus knows all the problems, He knows what the person is ready to deal with, and He knows the solution. He directs the healing moments wonderfully, miraculously.[163]

Inner Child Prayer, Another Approach To Facilitate Meeting Jesus

"Listening Prayer" can facilitate a powerful time with the Lord. It provides a clear and understandable illustration of how the Lord can meet a person in prayer. There is another approach, which has several similarities to "Listening Prayer" that I have found to be most significant and productive in the counseling I do. This is "Inner Child Prayer," which was also a gift from the Lord to a counselor seeking a better way to minister. I became aware of this approach through Teresa Joy, another counselor at Elijah House (a

---

161   Olson, p.6.

162   Olson, p.7.

163   Dave and Linda Olson have written <u>Listening Prayer</u>, which is a wonderful book describing this process. It is not available in bookstores, but it can be obtained by writing to: Listening Prayer Ministries, 2624 Wind River Rd., El Cajon, CA 92019.

ministry focused on Inner Healing).[164] This counselor was seeing a client with a difficult problem, and they were in need of a special manifestation of the Lord. The Lord led her client through a miraculous encounter.

What makes this approach so useful is that it is based upon what I have been teaching thus far in this book. There is inside us an "Inner Child" (our Treasure Inside) which is locked away behind The Wall. The Wall was erected to protect the Inner Child from the World. However, The Wall, which was meant to protect, has also become a prison. It isolates the Inner Child from the hurt, but also from the Lord. The first objective of Inner Child Prayer is to help the Inner Child get to the place of trusting the Lord enough to invite Him inside The Wall. The Inner Child has been his or her own protector, but needs to come to the place of trusting the Lord Jesus to be the protector. The objective is thus to reunite the Inner Child with the Lord. Once this happens, then the Lord ministers to the Inner Child in whatever way needed.

If the person being ministered to cannot see the Lord or the Little Girl or Boy, the challenge is to pray about whatever seems to make up The Wall that is preventing her or him from seeing their Treasure Inside. As The Wall comes down, sometimes gradually, the person can begin to see what is going on inside. Sometimes this opening up

---

[164] As I have mentioned previously, the term "Inner Child" is a bit controversial, because the New Age Movement has captured it and used it. Though the Treasure Inside often manifests as a child, this is not always true. I have had clients who at different moments have gotten in touch with different parts of themselves who were of various chronological ages. Sometimes the Treasure Inside is an adult, and on the other hand sometimes a child. Some clients have even had encounters with themselves at the age of conception! The age of the one seen inside may change from one moment to the next, depending upon what memory is being worked on. But very often the deepest woundings happened in childhood, and so the person will see and connect with a child inside.

Again, the important thing to remember is not what this Treasure Inside is called, but rather to know that the Treasure Inside is a living reality. That part of the person really exists, and is profoundly human. In that place a person knows everything that has happened in their life, including many things of which the person is not now consciously aware. God meant for the person to love themselves (who God made them to be), to be in fellowship with themselves, and to be the best friend of themselves.

Also see Chapter 9, Endnote #9-2, and Appendix D, "New Age Visualization", on the New Age for more on the Inner Child.

is a gradual process, much like the blind man who first saw men as trees walking, as in Mark 8:23-25.[165]

Once people receiving ministry can see what is going on inside, sometimes they need encouragement to keep looking inside and to look around to see what is happening. After all, this is usually a new experience. In this case, a prayer partner can facilitate the process by asking the person being ministered to a few questions. The key questions that the prayer partner would ask are:

1. "Can you see the Lord?"
       If they can, the next question is, "What is He doing?"
2. "Can you see the little girl (or boy)?"
       If so, the next question is, "What is she (or he) doing?"

The most profound counseling sessions are those in which the person meets the Lord, and are simply able to walk and talk with Him. Then I, as the prayer partner, don't have to do anything or say anything. In fact, I should not say anything, but just sit quietly and take notes. When the Lord is leading the person, the healing occurs in the reality of the experience. The person being healed then knows, in the depths of his or her being, that healing has occurred. Then the fruit changes.[166]

Theophostics, A Third Approach To Facilitate Meeting Jesus

A third approach is called "Theophostic" counseling. One day, Dr. Ed Smith went to the Lord in desperation. He had been a psychologist for many years, and he had dealt with many people

---

[165] **Mark 8:23-25,** *So He took the blind man by the hand and led him out of the town. And when He had spit on his eyes and put His hands on him, He asked him if he saw anything. And he looked up and said, "I see men like trees, walking." Then He put His hands on his eyes again and made him look up. And he was restored and saw everyone clearly.* **Also see Chapter 14,** "Face To Face With Jesus."
[166] **See Appendix A, "Experiences and Testimonies"** for some more actual examples of this type of prayer.

who were suffering from Dissociative Identity Disorder (previously called Multiple Personality Disorder). Many of these people had been Satanically ritually abused, which presents a very difficult challenge. He had become frustrated because healing came to these people so slowly. One day he was to see a particular client, and he called out to the Lord for help on her behalf, and told the Lord that he needed a better way of helping her. He was frustrated and discouraged. That day the Lord showed up in a miraculous and profound way. The Lord literally appeared to the client and walked her through some deep healing.

Theophostic counseling has the following pattern. The person being ministered to listens to his or her present feelings. When a powerful negative feeling is experienced, the person seeking healing is to focus on the feeling and stir it up, instead of running from it as we are all prone to do. When the feeling becomes very strong, then the prayer partner asks the Lord to take the person back to an early time when the person felt the same way. The emotion is a royal road, past The Wall, into the heart (the Treasure Inside). The prayer partner and the person sit and wait and listen. When the Lord brings the memory to the person, he or she is to again immerse themselves in that bad experience, and to feel the intense negative feeling that is part of the memory. Then the prayer partner asks the person what the little child (the person at the time of the original event) was believing when the event was happening. The prayer partner may make some suggestions, but is careful not to push ideas upon the person. The lies that the person believed are things like: "I'm powerless;" "I will always be taken advantage of;" "Nobody will ever be there for me," etc.

For instance, if the person is a woman who was sexually abused as a child, she might believe, "I am powerless." That is very likely what she, as a child, believed when the sexual abuse was happening. In fact, at that moment it was the truth, because she was a small child, and an adult was overpowering her. At this point the prayer partner would ask her to focus on this statement. When the she focuses on the statement, if the anxiety and fear become very large, then this was a lie that she, as the child, believed. Then the prayer partner asks the Lord for the truth, and they sit and wait. The Lord

Fullness Of Life

would then speak the truth to her (not to the prayer partner). For instance, the Lord might say, "You are not powerless anymore." Because it was the Lord that spoke the truth into her heart, she knows it is true.

Then she is directed to focus again on the old memory, and the statement "I am powerless." If the fear and anxiety are gone, then the healing has occurred. If there are still strong negative feelings present, there must still be at least one "lie" still present, and the procedure is repeated. When the negative feelings are all gone, it is blatantly clear that it was the living Lord who did the healing, not the prayer partner.

Of course, my description of the process is a great simplification. Dr. Ed Smith has written and taught extensively on this approach.

The ways this approach dovetails with "Listening Prayer" and "Inner Child Prayer" are as follows:

1. Emotions can be an avenue into a person's heart.
2. The Lord is real and is present.
3. The Lord speaks directly to the person seeking healing.
4. When the person seeking healing meets the living Lord, healing takes place.

Where I have sometimes found Theophostic Counseling to be most helpful is in providing a way past The Wall, so that the person being ministered to can meet with the Treasure Inside and with the Lord.

I want to add a note of caution. I have found that it can be very useful to use a person's emotions as a possible way to circumvent their Wall, but I am not endorsing Theophostics or all that Dr. Smith teaches. I have not kept current with his ministry, but as of 1999 there were several aspects of what he taught that I did not agree with. For example, a major area of disagreement was that he did not identify sin as the bad root, and thus did no work toward repentance or forgiveness. If you would like to learn more about this approach, please contact Dr. Smith for his most recent views. [167]

The Common Thread

The three approaches that I have mentioned each have unique features, but they share common characteristics.

1. First, the person seeking healing (not the prayer partner) is the one who experiences a living encounter with the Living Lord.
2. In the encounter the person receiving the healing follows the leading of the Lord, without the direction (or perhaps the interference) of the prayer partner.
3. There is always another person present, either a counselor or another trusted friend. Truly, the presence of the Lord is most profound when we are gathered together: *"For where two or three are gathered together in My name, I am there in the midst of them"* (Matthew 18:20).
4. The Lord Jesus is the counselor. We can't make this happen or direct it. He is in charge, and He brings the healing. *"He has sent Me to heal the brokenhearted"* (Luke 4:18).

Jesus' Presence Solves The Problems

These ways of praying solve the two most difficult problems that are encountered in Inner Healing.

*   The first major problem that we encounter in Inner Healing prayer is a result of our not being able to remember our judgments and Inner Vows. The most powerful judgments and Inner Vows we make are in the first few years of life, but as an adult we cannot remember them. If we can't remember them,

---

[167] Taken from Genuine Recovery, by Dr. Ed M. Smith, (1997). Dr. Smith may be contacted at Family Care Ministries, 720 Lebanon Avenue, Campbellsville, KY, 42718.

how can we pray about them? The answer is that Jesus knows about all of them, and if we can come into His presence, He will show us what to pray about.

• The second problem is that when we forgive, we need to do so from our heart, not our head. How do we do this? How do we know for sure that what we prayed was not simply from our Head? The answer to this problem is that when Jesus leads us in the "new and living way", when we actually experience His presence, the whole event is happening in our heart. When He forgives us while we are in His presence, we know that we are forgiven.

Additional Approaches

Since these approaches are all living ways, and the Lord is in charge, there is no set technique for a person to use to arrive at a place of intimacy with the Lord. Often, as a counselor, I use a combination of these approaches, depending on how successfully the person is progressing.   For instance, if an individual has difficulty seeing past The Wall, having him or her follow a strong emotion to its source in their Treasure Inside can help get past The Wall. On the other hand, if the person has a strong Inner Vow not to feel their emotions, this approach will not work. In this situation, as soon as the person focuses on the emotion, the Inner Vow takes effect and the feeling evaporates.

> **It is important to be open to however Jesus leads. He may surprise you by meeting you in an unexpected way.**

If the person can't get in touch with his or her Treasure Inside one way, I try another. Since God is the architect of our healing process, I would expect Him to show up in any way He chooses. So it is important to be open to however Jesus leads. He may surprise you in an unexpected way, as He did with these three counselors.

Jesus Does It His Way

One striking thing to be aware of is that sometimes the Lord doesn't bring healing in exactly the way that we expect, based upon how He has taught us to pray. For instance, if you were to come into the presence of the Lord and He shows you something, Jesus might not say a word, but you know what He means. You may not actually verbalize forgiveness, and yet know forgiveness has occurred. You would simply feel a release of the bitterness hidden inside, and sense a bonding and closeness with the Lord. You then know from the encounter that Jesus loves you, has forgiven you, and has cleansed you from the sin, and yet you didn't follow the "formula."

It is very important to be aware that since we are seeking an encounter with a living Lord, and since He is the one with the plan, we must not make these approaches into formulas. We can't limit the Lord to these particular ways through which He has manifested Himself to some people in the past. We may seek Him in one way, and He may manifest Himself in another, perhaps unexpected way.

It Is True!

For those who have not experienced a living encounter with the living Lord, such as I have been describing, an encounter like this may seem impossible. Or you may believe that it is possible for others, but have trouble believing it can happen to you. Then you may become discouraged and give up. But Jesus desires to meet with each one of us. He knows that at times He is the only one who can provide the keys that we need. I know this is true, because I have met Him in this way, and I have been with many clients who have had such encounters with Him. **It is possible!**

> **Coming into the presence of Jesus is so powerful that facilitating such an experience has become my goal with every client.**

It may be encouraging for you to be able to read about the experiences of people who have had healing encounters with the

Lord in this way, and I have included several in **Appendix A, "Experiences And Testimonies."**

Coming into the presence of Jesus is so powerful that facilitating such an experience has become my goal with every client.

These Experiences Are Not "New Age"

To those with some familiarity with New Age beliefs and jargon, some of the things that I have been teaching sound very similar to New Age beliefs and practices. However, what I have presented is profoundly different than the beliefs of the New Age movement. For instance, New Agers use "visualization." Here the "teacher" paints a word picture and the "student" visualizes that picture in their own mind. For example, the teacher tells the student to visualize a door. When the "student" opens the door, the room is filled with their "heart's desire." Thereafter, that room is for the student to go to whenever they were under stress."[168]

On the other hand, in my examples, the Lord gives the "student" the picture. The key difference is that in the New Age "visualization," the "teacher" creates the picture. It is of man. In my examples, the Lord creates the picture. It is of God. In the section at the end of this chapter titled, "Additional Information For Prayer Partners," I emphasize the necessity that the "teacher" stay out of the way and let the Lord do it. If nothing happens, then nothing happens. It is of primary importance to not try to make an encounter happen.

The "new and living way" I am advocating is built on a fundamentally different foundation than is the New Age. In what I am teaching, the God of the Bible is God. In the New Age, we are all god. Everything is God. All is one.

If you would like more detailed information on the differences, read Appendix D, "New Age Visualization."

---

[168] This example is taken from an actual experience. Read the section "Visualization" in my chapter, Appendix D - "A Counterfeit."

Summary

When Jesus appears, miracles happen. There are times when all of us literally need to meet Him. Sometimes He meets with us regardless of whether we are seeking Him, but actively seeking His presence can facilitate an encounter with Him. This can best happen when we are gathered, in His Name, with another person or group. If we can't hear Him, there is simply a blockage that needs to be removed.

What Listening Prayer, Inner Child Prayer, and Theophostic Counseling all have in common are:

1. These are all related to connecting with your heart.
2. Both the prayer partner and you need to listen to the Treasure Inside. Be quiet!
3. These are all related to connecting with the living Jesus.
4. Jesus is the counselor. Nothing happens without Him.
5. The primary goal is to heal your relationship with Jesus.
6. Jesus speaks to you, not to the prayer partner.
7. It is a living <u>experience</u>.
8. When Jesus ministers to you in this way, there is never again a doubt that Jesus loves you, and that He is your healer!

If you could witness first-hand such a counseling session, then you would completely understand what I have been saying, and you would realize the power of such encounters. Unfortunately, that is not possible in a book. The next best thing is for you to be able to read about the experiences of people who have had healing encounters with the Lord in this way, and I have included several in **Appendix A, "Experiences And Testimonies."**

Our walk of healing is a diverse experience. It is something like a good marriage. A good marriage can be very rewarding. There are spectacular highs, fulfilling times of knowing we are loved. But these highs are a culmination of daily living, and are dependent upon the foundation laid in less spectacular times. Sometimes the daily relationship seems tedious, boring, mundane, routine, dry, not rewarding.   But if we handle these times with love and determination, the rewards arrive.

What I am calling a "new and living way" is a part of our walk of healing. However, the most common feature of our Christian life is our <u>daily</u> walk of listening to our Treasure Inside (and thus to the Lord who dwells there) and praying accordingly. <u>It is a whole new way of living</u>. In Chapter 16, "It Is A Journey," I will talk more about the necessity or persisting in this walk.

Additional Information For Prayer Partners

A Warning: Don't Try To Make It Happen

As a prayer partner, I must constantly be on guard not to try to orchestrate what is happening between the person seeking healing and the Lord, or between the person and their Treasure Inside.

Suppose I am trying to help someone listen to the Treasure Inside, and the one seeking healing can't hear anything from inside. There can then be a great temptation for me to try to paint a picture to get things going. We all have "a mind's eye," a place inside of us where we can picture things, like a movie screen. This is where we see dreams and daydreams, and it is where we can bring up a picture of a person we know or place where we have been. This is the place where the Lord may reveal Himself to a person as He leads them.

The temptation to paint the picture for the person is greatest if the Lord gives me a prophetic word or picture about what He wants to do. Even then I need to let the Lord be the one to show the person. For instance, if I see a picture of the Lord picking up a little child, it would be very tempting to say, "Walk over to the Lord. He wants to pick you up."

<u>Don't do this!</u>

The reason this is dangerous and is such a temptation is because New Agers have created a counterfeit of this type of counseling. This counterfeit is called "visualization." In "visualization," the counselor asks the person to be quiet, to close his or her eyes, to empty the mind, and then to focus on that screen within. Then the counselor paints a picture, saying something like this, "Picture yourself on a nice summer day sitting by a gently flowing stream. There's a field of flowers right across from you, and there's a butterfly flying from flower to flower." We all have the ability to see that picture in our mind's eye. In fact you, the reader, may have just done this as I have described the scene.

But there is a fatal flaw in visualization. It is of man. The counselor is the one who is creating the picture. See Appendix D, "New Age Visualization" for more information on visualization and the New Age.

This type of visualization is Satan's counterfeit of the real thing; and so when we enter into "visualization" we may open the door to Satan's invasion, or at least his interference. Spectacular spiritual things may happen, but they may be deceptions and create destruction. Because the temptation is so great for us to want to help, we need to be ever on guard so that we do not fall into the enemy's trap. When the person being healed is not making any progress, it is always a temptation to try to do something to get things going. However, we need to trust in the Lord instead, and to wait on Him.

It is possible for us to visualize without Satan entering in. God gave us ability to visualize. However, as with daydreaming, it is not real, but rather the visualization is a product of our own effort and imagination. And if we try to achieve healing by visualizing what we want to see, then we are in control rather than Jesus. It is not up to us to tell Jesus what to do; and if we do try to do this, we are on dangerous ground. We want only the real thing, which is the living presence of the Lord, with Him in control.

The Real Thing

Since we want only the real thing, in these types of prayer counseling it is very important that the prayer partner not suggest anything. Jesus has to be the one in charge, not man. If we are praying and listening and nothing happens, then nothing happens. If nothing happens, this is very important information. Everybody has a real, living Treasure Inside. If the person being ministered to cannot connect with that part of themselves, it is because The Wall is in the way. If there is a barrier, we need to know this so that we can work on dismantling it.

When the person is not able to connect with their heart, then both the individual and the prayer partner need to pray and listen for the Lord to give them a clue as to what judgments and Inner Vows make up this barrier. When either of them has a sense of what might be appropriate to pray, then they pray in accordance with that sense. The person may be praying very much from the head, but that is OK. If the pray is about the wrong thing, no harm is done; it's just that nothing will happen. The person cannot pray too much. But if the prayers are on target, the client will begin to sense something inside, though perhaps only dimly. For instance, the person may say, "I can see a cloud." Then the prayer partner might ask, "Lord, will you tell us about the cloud?"

Note that as a prayer partner it is OK to ask the Lord or the person questions, it just isn't OK to suggest the answers, or to direct the Lord.   There is sometimes a great temptation to suggest something, especially if the Lord has given the prayer partner a clue; but ultimately the one seeking healing needs to hear from the Lord for themselves.

In this process I am often reminded of the scripture which I previously mentioned where Jesus healed the blind man, *"I see men as trees walking."* So then the Lord touched his eyes again. Then the man was able to see clearly (Mark 8:22-25). Sometimes the process described in this scripture is very much like what we experience as The Wall is being dismantled. When The Wall comes down gradually like this, I have found this process to be incredibly faith building, because one can just watch as the prayers effectually remove The Wall, piece by piece! We then see that truly, the effectual fervent pray of a righteous man avails much (James 5:16).

A wonderful after-effect of this type of prayer is that the person's relationship with the Lord is developed. Once the person is able to come into the living presence of Jesus, there are many benefits. Not only are such seekers healed in that moment, but can now better follow the Great Counselor on a daily basis. This ongoing relationship is what Jesus has always wanted with each of us. Living in daily communion with Him is how we all were meant to live, and I believe this is the only way we can truly thrive. See Chapter 16, "It Is A Journey."

Prophetic Words

If during the counseling the Lord gives the prayer partner a prophetic word or vision, He has done this for a reason. I have found that often these words are true and accurate. They are often keys to getting things unstuck when nothing is happening. Though the word I receive is accurate, my interpretation of what the Lord has shown me is often flawed.   So when I see something – for example a dairy farm – I simply ask the person, "Does a dairy farm mean anything to you?" I once asked a lady this question, and she began to cry hysterically. The Lord used this question at that moment to show her that she had been sexually abused as a child by the hired hand at her grandparents' dairy farm. I had no idea what "dairy farm" meant to her, but the Lord did.

What is much more problematic is when I think I know what the prophetic word means. Then I have to use great discipline not to try to put my interpretation on the word from the Lord. Therefore I do need to ask the person being ministered to if it means anything to him or her, but I need to simply give what the Lord has given me, and no more. I have had many situations where I thought I knew the interpretation, but I kept my interpretation to myself. In those times when the client knew exactly what the word meant, I often discovered that my interpretation was totally wrong. Since I have a strong rule not to interpret for them, I didn't make a mess with my interpretation.   The core issue here is that the Lord can talk to the person directly, and so if what I saw was from Him, He can give the client the interpretation of what He has shown me.

This way, if the word is truly from Him, it will be just what is needed at the time. If it isn't a word from Him, the person will just say "I have no idea what a dairy farm means." Since I posed it as a question, no harm has been done; and we can just proceed. On the other hand, if we missed out on something the Lord said, it isn't buried forever. Rather, Jesus will try again to communicate, because He wants the person to understand and to be healed.

Be Humble And Careful With Your Prophetic Gift

If you are a person who considers that you have a very accurate ability to interpret what the Lord gives you, I would caution you to be very careful in exercising this gift in this situation. There are very few people who have 100% accuracy in their prophetic gifting. I have personally experienced prophets with international ministries making mistakes, sometimes huge ones! There is so much at stake, and so much damage can be done to the other person in this vulnerable situation. I would strongly suggest that you let the Lord talk to the other person instead of speaking out your interpretation. You can use what you see as a clue as to how to pray, but be very gentle. Do not say something like, "I see the Lord coming over and picking you up," even if you see that in a vision. Instead, recognize that the Lord may be showing you what He wants to do so that you can pray or ask Him questions. You can't know for sure. If the person was supposed to see this but couldn't, the fact that there is a blockage present is information that you need to know – the person isn't yet able to hear his or her Treasure Inside. Such people are not necessarily less gifted, they just have a blockage.

Chapter 16

Deliverance
And Inner Healing

To this point I have not said much about Satan and his demons and their part in our problems, except to mention how God uses Satan to accomplish His purpose in His children.[169] However, Scripture is clear that Satan and his demons are real.

Demons can in fact be present in a person who is a child of God, and the demons can be causing trouble. How can this be, since the person is "saved" and is "filled" with the Holy Spirit? Even though a believer is "filled" with the Holy Spirit, they are not like the "Honey Jar." They are like the "Honeycomb."[170] Inside the "Honeycomb" there are places that contain Jesus, but there are also places of darkness, which are parts of the heart that have not yet been "healed" (in a sense, evangelized). These places are filled with bitterness, judgment, and blame; and Jesus is not presently living in those places. If He were, there could be no darkness there, because it would have to flee. *You are of God, little children, and have overcome them, because He who is in you is greater than he who is in the world.* (1 John 4:4).

We Have Protection

It is very important to recognize that the circumstances of a child of God and an unsaved person are profoundly different. Unbelievers do not belong to God, and so God cannot intervene in their lives to the same degree as He can with those who belong to Him. Unbelievers do not have the Holy Spirit living in them, and so Satan

---

[169] See Chapter 6, "God Is On Your Side."
[170] See Chapter 3, "Remove All The Bad Roots."

has much more access to them. They are also helpless regarding getting set free from his influence. On the other hand, believers actually belong to God. God treats them as His children. Part of this New Covenant is that God protects them from evil, and part of it is that He is committed to changing them into His image. This process involves eliminating the places of darkness in them and then actually filling those places with His Spirit. If there are any demons present, or if there is any demonic influence, they are evicted as a part of this process of sanctification. See Chapters 2, 3, and 5.

How Did Demons Get There?

How did the demons get inside a person in the first place? The person sinned, and this created a dark place in a part of the "Honeycomb." The place of darkness is an invitation to Satan to spread his influence into the person, because he has a legal right to be in that dark place. If a demon is present, it is important that we know this, because it needs to be evicted.

How To Get Rid of the Demons

If demons are present, they are there because they have a legal right to be there. Therefore, the first thing to be done is to take away their legal right. That is done through Inner Healing. The sin is confessed and repented of, and Jesus washes the person clean of the sin.

The person then asks Jesus to come into that place in his or her heart and to take up residency there. Jesus then moves into that place in the "Honeycomb," and the demon has to leave; because God is stronger than demons.[171] Darkness and light cannot coexist in the same place; so that when the light comes, the darkness must flee. So then, when commanded to leave, demons must leave. When Inner

---

[171] **1 John 4:4,** *You are of God, little children, and have overcome them, because He who is in you is greater than he who is in the world.*

Healing happens first, there is generally no big fuss or mess when the demons are evicted.[172]

When Jesus dwells in that place in the person's heart, as long as the person does not again sin in the same old way and bring darkness back into that particular place, Satan and his demons have no place there. They cannot return because the place is inhabited by Jesus.

Deliverance Without Inner Healing is Dangerous

Great damage can be caused to a person if demons are commanded to leave (in the name of Jesus) without first having Inner Healing occur. Christians do have authority in His name to command demons to leave, and they must obey. If Inner Healing does not happen first, there might be a big battle, but ultimately they have to leave. In this case, since Inner Healing has not yet occurred in that place, darkness still has a legal right to be there. Eventually the demon will return, find the place still open for their occupancy, and will move back in. What is worse, this time they will bring along some of their fellow demons. Therefore, when Inner Healing does not precede deliverance, the person will end up being worse off than before. Scripture warns of this in Luke 11:20-26.[173]

---

[172] **John 8:12,** *Then Jesus spoke to them again, saying, "I am the light of the world. He who follows Me shall not walk in darkness, but have the light of life."*

2 Corinthians 4:6-7, *For it is God who commanded light to shine out of darkness who has shone in our hearts to give the light of the knowledge of the glory of God in the face of Jesus Christ. But we have this treasure in earthen vessels, that the excellence of the power may be of God and not of us.*

1 John 1:5, *This is the message which we have heard from Him and declare to you, that God is light and in Him is no darkness at all.*

[173] Jesus said in **Luke 11:20-26,** *"But if I cast out demons with the finger of God, surely the kingdom of God has come upon you. When a strong man, fully armed, guards his own place, his goods are in peace. But when a stronger than he comes upon him and overcomes him, he takes from him all his armor in which he trusted, and divides his spoils. He who is not with Me is against Me, and he who does not gather with Me scatters. When an unclean spirit goes out of a man, he goes through dry places, seeking rest; and finding none, he says, 'I will return to my house from which I came." And when he comes, he finds it swept and put in order. Then he goes and takes with him seven other spirits more wicked than himself, and they enter and dwell there; and the last state of that man is worse than the first."*

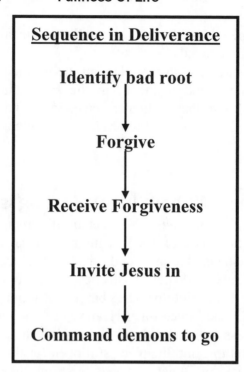

Except for the last step (Command demons to go), this diagram is simply a recap of the prior chapters of this book.

Summary

Satan and his demons are real. We need to recognize their power and to know we cannot stand against them in our own strength. However, as children of God, though we need to recognize Satan's power, we do not need to fear him. We have the most powerful ally in the universe on our side, and we belong to Him. God is fully committed to changing us into His image. He knows everything about us, including the presence of demons or the influence of darkness in us. God protects us from Satan, and in fact uses him to accomplish His purpose of sanctifying us. When we cooperate with God and walk out our process of Inner Healing, at the right time Jesus will show us the area of darkness through which Satan influences us. When we repent, forgive, and are forgiven, Jesus does the rest of the work. Satan has to flee, and Jesus moves in. Thus the focus in our Christian lives needs to be on Jesus and our own sanctification, not upon Satan.

This chapter is a very brief summary of this issue. My purpose in introducing this topic is to simply show the relationship between deliverance and Inner Healing, not to exhaustively delve into deliverance. Others have written about it more extensively. One very good book on this topic, is <u>Deliverance and Inner Healing</u> by John and Mark Sandford.

Chapter 17

It Is A Journey
Walking Out Your New Life-Inside-Out!

Inner Healing is not a one-time event. It is ongoing and dynamic. It is a totally new way of living, and it needs to be walked out daily, for the rest of your life! You must continue on your journey of Inner Healing moment by moment.

All that I have talked about in this book is irrelevant if you do not continue on the path of Inner Healing. You cannot go back to business as usual. Your old way has led you into a place of hurt and bondage, as evidenced by the presence of the bad fruit and the pain in your life. The "new and living

> **This is a totally new way of living, and it needs to be walked out daily, for the rest of your life! You must continue on your journey of Inner Healing moment by moment**

way" of Jesus leads you to healing and freedom. This journey must **revolutionize** your daily life for the rest of your days on the earth. This doesn't mean just a minor change or improvement to your old way of doing life. It is a journey, and not a destination. Your sanctification process will not be completed until you go to be with Jesus.

Moment By Moment

In your daily experience, you need to live in the moment. You are not in control, and so you do not know ahead of time when you may have need of the blood and the cross. Therefore you need always to be listening to your Treasure Inside (praying without ceasing).[174] When the Lord wants you to deal with a problem, you will know it by the negative emotion you will be feeling.

Listen Inside

Of course, if you aren't listening to your Treasure Inside, you may miss the signal. Since the Lord is actively in charge of your walk, He will indeed tell you when there is a problem. If the Lord isn't telling you of trouble (if there are no negative emotions coming up), just enjoy life. But when you feel a negative emotion, you need to pay attention. It may be an old root that the Lord is bringing up, or it may be a new root that you have just planted, or it may be both. You can only know if you are listening to the messages coming up from your Treasure Inside.

You can only succeed by living from the inside-out (Treasure Inside-to-Head).

You can't do it living from the outside-in (Head-to-Treasure Inside), as has been your old way, and which is the way the world walks. Your intellect and willpower are impotent in this area of life.

You Are Not Alone –
God Is Actively Directing Your Life

Be comforted to know that what is happening to you is not a random event, or just fate. God is actively directing your healing process, and indeed your whole life. Since you are experiencing your current struggle because God brought you to that place, He will let you

---

[174] 1 Thessalonians 5:17.

know when there is a problem inside, He will help you find it, and He will show you how to pray.[175]   When you feel a negative emotion, your first response will become, "Lord, what are you telling me right now?" Since He dwells inside you, He will speak to you through your Treasure Inside.

Your Mistakes

Do not be discouraged when you make a mistake. You <u>will</u> judge again and this will plant a new bitter root. This will continue to happen because you will never lose your tendency to automatically react to perceived wounding with bitterness, judgment, and blame. You may not be listening inside all the time, and so you will miss signals that tell you when you have done this. This sinning will happen so automatically that it will happen before you know it. Because it is so automatic you won't even know it has happened unless you are listening to your Treasure Inside.

> **This sinning will happen so automatically that it will happen before you know it.**
>
> **But you can <u>always</u> clean up the mess through His provision for sin.**

Since the Lord is committed to you, if you don't hear the first message, He will be faithful to continue to speak to you over and over, more and more loudly, until you finally hear His message. Once you see that you have again sinned, you can <u>always</u> clean up the mess through His provision for sin. It can all be fixed, no matter how badly you fail.

You can expect to miss more of the signals in the beginning, because you are not used to living this way. In addition, you may still have some barriers to hearing your Treasure Inside (The Wall

---

[175] See Endnote #17-1 for Scriptures on God leading you.

may not be all gone); and part of God's plan will be to remove this Wall. As The Wall comes down, you will find it easier and easier to hear His voice.

Because the Lord is in charge and He has the only cure, your striving will not work. You must always beware of the trap that we all so easily fall into - the trap of striving with your own willpower (and thus your own strength). Because your "fallen nature" has this strong tendency to do it yourself, you will sometimes find yourself living in that old way. However, whenever you do find yourself striving, God will show this to you, and you can be forgiven again (because it is sin).

One of the major clues that you have not been doing well in your walk is your diminished ability to hear the Lord, or hear your own Treasure Inside. He hasn't left, but rather you have allowed The Wall to be rebuilt

> **As The Wall comes down, you will find it easier and easier to hear the voice of the Lord.**

by multiple failures to "leave no negative emotion unexamined." But God is faithful, and He will not allow you to remain in that state. He will arrange events and circumstances in your life in such a way that you will again have the opportunity to be set free. You can count on Him.

Consequences Of Not Continuously Walking It Out

On the other hand, if you again start living on "automatic pilot" (your old way that is easy and comfortable and familiar to you), or you are too busy to spend the time necessary to deal with your roots as they come up, or you let anything interfere with your walk, life will not go well for you.

- You will assuredly plant <u>new roots</u> of bitterness.

- Because of your old practiced ways of seeing life, you will undoubtedly <u>re-plant</u> some of the old roots that you have previously removed (Hebrews 12:15).[176]
- You will continue to reap from the <u>old roots</u> that have yet to be revealed to you by the Lord.
- In addition, God will turn up the pressure, and He will make sure that life does not go well for you so that you will return to your walk of sanctification.   He will do this because your sanctification is the primary goal He has for your life, and it is in your best interest.

If you fall back into your old ways, especially if you are resistant to the Lord's pressure, you may be worse off than before your healing. It won't be because your earlier healing did not work.   Rather, it will be because you have destroyed the previous healing by again sinning in the same old familiar way.[177]

I have seen this consequence befall people.   A few years ago I had a client who had come from another state for an intensive week of counseling.   He had a very significant encounter with the Lord, and his life changed.   I received correspondence from his wife about how different he now was.   However, several months later I received a telephone call from him, and he said, "The healing didn't work.   I am just like I used to be."   I asked him if he had been spending time with the Lord, if he had been listening to his negative emotions and spending time with his Treasure Inside, and if he had been dealing

---

[176] **Hebrews 12:15:** *looking diligently lest anyone fall short of the grace of God; lest any root of bitterness springing up cause trouble, and by this many become defiled.*

[177] **2 Peter 2:17-22,** Peter, referring to some false teachers, *These are wells without water, clouds carried by a tempest, to whom the gloom of darkness is reserved forever. For when they speak great swelling words of emptiness, they allure through the lusts of the flesh, through licentiousness, the ones who have actually escaped from those who live in error. While they promise them liberty, they themselves are slaves of corruption; for by who a person is overcome, by him also he is brought into bondage. For if, after they have escaped the pollution of the world through the knowledge of the Lord and Savior Jesus Christ, they are again entangled in them and overcome, the latter end is worse for them than the beginning. For it would have been better for them not to have known the way of righteousness than having known it, to turn from the holy commandment delivered to them. But it has happened to them according to the true proverb: "A dog returns to his own vomit," and, "A sow, having washed, to her wallowing in the mire."*

with his bitter roots. He said, "No, I have been too busy for that."
This client had made a common mistake. He thought that his
healing was a one-time event, like having his appendix taken out.

Rewards For Continuing

If you do live in the new way, you will most assuredly be changed
from glory to glory into the image of Jesus.[178]   As your healing
proceeds, you will find more and more joy in yourself, and less and
less pain. You will find your relationship with the Lord and with
other people becoming more and more intimate and real. In short,
you will be blessed by the Lord in all your ways, because you are
obeying Him and allowing Him to truly be your Lord. Feeling good
is not a goal of your healing, but it is a reward that accompanies it.

A wonderful result of your
continued walk of healing is
that you will find yourself
behaving like Jesus in more and
more ways. The old bondages
will be falling away one by one,
and you will find yourself doing

> **Feeling good is not a goal of your healing, but it is a reward that accompanies it.**

the good that you have always wanted to do. You will find yourself
effortlessly acting in these new ways, because the new good roots
will be producing good fruit. A bird doesn't have to try to fly, and a
fish doesn't have to try to swim. They just do it, because that is their
nature. If a fish tries to fly, it will have very limited success.
Gravity never "forgets" to operate. Gravity never forgets to operate
because God made it to operate in a certain way. It doesn't have
lapses and fail to work, because it is just being what God made it to
be. When you are changed into His image in an area of your life,
you will then effortlessly operate in that new way, because God will
be making it happen. You won't have to "try."

---

[178] **2 Corinthians 3:18:** *But we all, with unveiled face, beholding as in a mirror the glory of the Lord,*
are being transformed into the same image from glory to glory, just as by the Spirit of the Lord.

Then truly your yoke will have become easy and your burden light.[179]

Persistence Is Required

Persistence is essential. When you make a mistake, it can be fixed. Jesus said,

> *"Keep on asking and it will be given you; keep on seeking and you will find; keep on knocking (reverently) and the door will be opened to you. For every one who keeps on asking receives, and he who keeps on seeking finds, and to him who keeps on knocking it will be opened"* (Matthew 7:7-8, Amplified Bible).

As the Amplified Bible here reveals, the Greek verbs in this passage denote continuous action. You will at times become discouraged, and you may wonder why the battle continues, and perhaps wonder if it is worth it.[180] At that moment it may seem too hard. But God knows this, and He will not let you be tested beyond that which you are able.[181] He also says, *And let us not grow weary while doing good, for in due season we shall reap if we do not lose heart* (Galatians 6:9). He is there with you in these battles, and He is going to use the hard times to bring forth gold in your life.

---

[179] **Matthew 11:29-30,** *Take My yoke upon you and learn from Me, for I am gentle and lowly in heart, and you will find rest for your souls. For My yoke is easy and My burden is light.*

[180] **Galatians 6:7-9,** *Do not be deceived, God is not mocked; for whatever a man sows, that he will also reap. For he who sows to his flesh will of the flesh reap corruption, but he who sows to the Spirit will of the Spirit reap everlasting life. And let us not grow weary while doing good, for in due season we shall reap if we do not lose heart.*

[181] **1 Corinthians 10:13,** *No temptation has overtaken you except such as is common to man; but God is faithful, who will not allow you to be tempted beyond what you are able, but with the temptation will also make the way of escape, that you may be able to bear it.*

Aids In Your New Journey

It is very difficult, but perhaps not impossible, to continue successfully in your walk without community. Although the center of your healing is a personal relationship between you and Jesus, that isn't the whole story. You need continued support and encouragement, and you need others to pray for you at various times in your walk of Inner Healing. God has intended for you to live in community, not in isolation; and He rewards you for doing this.[182] You also need to receive love from other people.

I am a firm advocate of the "intensive week" model of counseling (where the people receiving counseling spend five days devoted to their healing on a full time basis). I have seen major miracles, and have found it to be much more powerful than an hour or two weekly or every other week. However, there can be a major weakness in this model, if there is no follow-up. Often, after their intensive week the people go back to the city where they live, and they have no support there. They have nobody who knows about Inner Healing, and so they are isolated. This is a vulnerable and dangerous place to be, because without support it is easier to slowly slip back into their old ways without realizing it. Also, the intensive week can give people the impression, as was the case with the client I just mentioned, that their healing consists of a powerful healing time after which they can return to life as usual.

There is also a weakness in altar ministry and weekend seminars on Inner Healing when there is no future provision made for helping a person to walk out their healing journey. Without the continued walk, they can lose everything they have gained. What is worse, the person may become convinced that Inner Healing doesn't work and thus permanently give up their walk of sanctification.

Billy Graham has recognized this need that people have for ongoing help. Whenever he plans a crusade in a city, he asks local churches to mobilize and commit to following up with the people

---

[182] **Galatians 6:1-2,** *Brethren, if a man is overtaken in any trespass, you who are spiritual restore such a one in a spirit of gentleness, considering yourself lest you also be tempted. Bear one another's burdens, and so fulfill the law of Christ.*

who have just made a decision for Christ. As a result of this mentoring, the percentage of people who continue in their walk with Jesus is much higher than with most other evangelists.

The Importance Of Other People

Connecting with others who are also walking out their healing is therefore very important for you, and so I strongly encourage you to seek out resources for support. The following are some ways to access a community.

- Follow-up telephone counseling with the counselor.
- Be active in a church that has made provisions for Inner Healing.
- Establish a group of people who are on the same walk.
- Have available at least one other person (of the same sex) who is following Jesus, and who is <u>safe</u>. Even if this other individual doesn't understand Jesus' healing ways, the other person's presence will facilitate a living encounter with Jesus in the time of prayer *("For where two or three are gathered in My name, I am there in the midst of them"* Matthew 18:20).

As you begin to understand the importance of community, be sure to diligently <u>seek out</u> the resources that may be available to you. This may require you to do some persistent seeking. Depending upon where you live, finding a supportive community may be a challenge. Ask God to direct this, to bring across your path those resources He has in mind for you, because He knows your situation and is committed to you.

Don't Throw Out Your Brains

Your brains are not excess baggage. God gave them to you for a purpose. If you will remember, in Chapter 9, "There is Buried Treasure," I listed gifts, or attributes, that God has given to you to live your life. Some of these were placed in your "Treasure Inside," and some of these gifts were placed in your "Head." Your "Head" is not bad or unimportant, it just isn't God, and it isn't the only tool you have available to you. In the past we all have tended to try to rely completely on our Head and to discount our Treasure Inside. It is also an error to rely completely on your Treasure Inside and to discount your Head. You need all the gifts, as they are all "tools" that God has given you to live your life. The trick is to use the right "tool" for the right job. Your Head deals with the natural world and relies on your intellect. Your Treasure Inside deals with what is going on inside you, with relationships, and with the spiritual realm.

You need to use the correct "tool" for the job you face, or you will run into problems. A bulldozer is for moving dirt, and the Space Shuttle is for flying. If you try to fly a bulldozer by dropping it out of an aircraft, or use a Space Shuttle to move dirt (which is exactly what everybody hopes won't happen), the results are not what was hoped for. The damage or ineffectiveness of using the wrong "tool" that you possess in your own self can be just as extreme as these examples.[183]

You therefore need to listen both to your Head and your Treasure Inside (heart), recognizing what each "toolbox" is for. When dealing with an issue in the natural world, if your Treasure Inside tells you to do something that is contrary to reason, you need to be very careful and to ask the Lord for confirmation before you act contrary to your conscious reasoning. This is especially important if your decision regards an important issue with significant impact on your life. For instance, if there is something you want to buy, but you know you can't afford it, you need to proceed slowly with the decision. I have found that God is never displeased when I ask Him for confirmation regarding something I think He told me. He knows that the reason I am asking for confirmation is not because I don't want to obey Him, but rather it is because I don't always hear Him clearly. He is pleased that I want to know for sure what He is saying to me before I act.

On the other hand, in dealing with issues of the heart, if your Head tells you something contrary to what you are sensing in your Treasure Inside, you likewise need to be very careful about overriding what you are sensing from your Treasure Inside. For

---

[183] See **Endnotes #17-2 & #17-3** for more details of what can happen if we use the wrong "tool.".

example, if your son is struggling with a relationship at school, he may not tell you about it (so your head doesn't know about it). But if you can sense what is going on <u>inside</u> him (listen to your Treasure Inside), you will know he is struggling. You can then ask him if he is having a problem, and he will feel blessed because you understand him. Not only will he feel important, but then you may be able to help him deal with the problem.

Con men rely on a smooth exterior. They can easily deceive people who live in their Head. However, your Treasure Inside will sense the deceit in their heart, and will warn you. You will be getting conflicting messages from your Head and from your Treasure Inside. This is a warning to listen inside.

Of course, when your Head and your Treasure Inside are saying the same thing, this is an indication that you are probably accurately perceiving what is actually occurring.

An Aid In Listening To Your Treasure Inside

Most of us are very adept at listening to our Head. Hopefully, you are beginning to listen to the message that your Treasure Inside is telling you on a moment-by-moment basis. However, sometimes you need to know more specifically what your Treasure Inside is saying, and it would be helpful for you to have some tools to get to the bottom of what you are feeling.

To begin with, you will be new at listening to your Treasure Inside, so you need the conditions to be optimum in order for you to hear. As in any new activity there is a learning curve. However, as you practice walking in this way, it will become easier and more natural. Those who were given The Blessing[184] just naturally walk in communion with their Treasure Inside (heart). It is like breathing

---

[184] You may remember that The Blessing is the good that you needed to receive as a child, or you were wounded. See Chapter 9 if you are unclear about what I am referring to. I have borrowed the term from the title of the book, The Blessing, by Smalley and Trent.

to them, and they just do it effortlessly. That is the way it was meant to be, and the way it was before the Fall of man.

I will present a model for hearing what is going inside, which may be useful to you, as you begin this walk. As you enter into this, practice of listening inside, it is important that you realize that your heart yearns to talk to you, and for you to hear him or her. So you are not trying to get your heart to do something it is reluctant to do. Of course, keep in mind that if your Wall, or fragments of your Wall still exist, the communication will sometimes be fuzzy.

The following steps will enhance your ability to hear your heart:

1. Get quiet and comfortable. Relax. Close your eyes. Breathe deeply. If possible, be in a place with few distractions.
2. Invite the Lord to come and be with you and to lead you. Ask Him to protect you from the wiles of the enemy.
3. Ask the Lord to help you quiet your busy mind. The Eastern Orthodox Church has a prayer of the heart, and they say, "Lord, help me to fold the wings of my mind." You are not asking your mind to be comatose, but rather you are asking the Lord to help it get off the throne for a while.
4. Focus your attention on your physical heart and the area around it. I find that placing my hand on my heart helps.
5. Ask your heart your question. Attune your attention to your Treasure Inside, and thus to God who speaks there. If you seek to understand the reason for a negative feeling you recently had, ask your heart to tell you about it. Because your heart sent up the negative emotion, he or she initiated the conversation and has just been waiting for you to ask.
6. Be quiet! <u>Listen</u>. Don't try to make anything happen. If your mind begins to race, perhaps saying something like, "What a waste of time. You have a lot that you have to do," or any of its tactics to get back in control, simply go back to Step #3 again.
7. Take whatever comes up - a thought, a memory, a feeling, a scene (vision), a song, etc. Don't judge it, just accept it. Then focus on it. You may immediately know what it is telling you. If you don't, ask your heart to tell you more, and listen again.
8. When you are done, ask the Lord to help you fill your heart with appreciation. Feel the feeling. Count your blessings. Ending with a positive feeling brings you and your heart closer together.
   . . . and the peace of God, which surpasses all nderstanding, will guard your hearts and minds through Christ Jesus. Finally, brethren, whatever things are true, whatever things are noble, whatever things are just, whatever things are pure, whatever things are lovely, whatever things are of good report, if there is any virtue and if there is anything praiseworthy - meditate on these things (Philippians 4:7-8).

Do this as often as you can, so that you build rapport with your own heart - and through this, with the Lord.

Summary

If you make the mistake of thinking that your healing is a one-time event, and that you do not need to change your way of living, then you will not be successful in being healed.   You cannot go back to your old way of living and expect different results than you had before. If you do go back, you will find yourself again stuck in your old way.[185]

> **The Key:**
> **Moment by moment live the rest of your life from the inside-out.**

It will seem to you that your healing didn't work and that God failed you. However, your healing is a journey, not a destination. There is no quick fix.

> *Stand fast therefore in the liberty by which Christ has made us free, and do not be entangled again with a yoke of bondage* (Galatians 5:1).

On the other hand, if you continue, moment by moment, diligently listening to your Treasure Inside and cooperating with what the Lord is doing, you will continue to be healed and blessed by the Lord.

---

[185] See **Endnote #17-4** to see how the wrong perspective can keep us from healing.

Chapter 18

Love, An Essential Ingredient
Loving Yourself

Loving yourself is an essential part of your walk of sanctification. It is how God intended for you to live your life. It is the only way that you can live the victorious Christian life that both you and the Lord would like you to live. Through the previous chapters the act of loving yourself has been woven into the principles and scriptures. In this chapter I will bring to the forefront and summarize the concept of loving yourself.

I want to emphasize that it is of great importance that this chapter be understood in context with the rest of this book and in conjunction with everything I have said therein.

Otherwise you might misperceive what I am saying. For instance, if you only read this chapter, you might conclude that I don't think that we have a sin nature. But when you read the entire book you know that is not my position.

At War With Yourself

When you are at war with yourself, you are crippled. This war is destructive because it is not how God intended for you to live. Living at war with yourself brings destruction.

- You are a house divided against itself.

- You deny legitimate needs that you have, or you refuse to have your legitimate needs met in legitimate ways because that would be "selfish."
- These unmet needs then drive you to fill them in illegitimate ways.
- You are denied the use of the gifts God has placed in you.
- You are empty inside.
- You judge yourself and reap the consequences of this sin.
- You feel the pain of the Big Hurt which results from this alienation from yourself.
- You live in fear of the Big Hurt and are driven to find ways to avoid feeling it.
- You are in bondage to these forces and cannot live the life that God intended.
- You are the "wretched man" in Romans 7:15-24.[186]

A Truce

The war needs to come to an end. You need to make peace with yourself. You need to stop judging yourself. You need to forgive yourself and be forgiven for this. You need to begin to walk out a new life of cleaning up the messes you make whenever you judge yourself. Because you have been doing this for so long, walking in judgment of yourself has been a well-worn path. It will take time for this habitual way of living to recede. Because it is so automatic and prevalent, you will need to be vigilant. You need to listen to your Treasure Inside continually. You will feel the Big Hurt whenever you judge yourself, because your Treasure Inside will tell you about it. When you feel the Big Hurt, you will know you need to forgive and be forgiven.

---

[186] **Romans 7:15, 24-25,** *For what I am doing, I do not understand. For what I will to do, that I do not practice; but what I hate, that I do . . . O wretched man that I am! Who will deliver me from this body of death? I thank God - through Jesus Christ our Lord!*

More Than A Truce

However, ending the war is not enough. In a truce the parties have simply ceased to be actively at war. A truce does not mean the parties are friendly, and it definitely does not mean they are so positively disposed towards each other that they love each other.

So you must move beyond a truce (a lack of the bad) to loving and blessing yourself (the presence of the good). You need to begin to relate to yourself the way God relates towards you. He loves you, and you are to do the same to your Treasure Inside. If you either do not or cannot keep the second great commandment of Jesus to love yourself, life will not go well for you.

Loving Yourself Is How God Intended For You To Live

> " 'You shall love the lord your God with all your heart, with all your soul, and with all your mind." This is the first and great commandment. And the second is like it: "You shall love your neighbor as yourself." On these two commandments hang all the Law and the Prophets" (Matthew 22:37-40).

God did not say *love your neighbor and hate yourself*. He said to love your neighbor in exactly the same way that you love yourself, and to love yourself with the same kind of love that you love God (*agape*).[187] God didn't just say to love the Holy Spirit that is in you, although you are to do that too. He also said to love **yourself**! **You!**

Remember that God's commandments are simply descriptions of how the spiritual world works. If we do things that are contrary to

---

[187] When I used to read this commandment to love my neighbor as myself, I used to immediately say to myself, "Of course I love myself. God just wants me to love others that much too." However, I later realized that I treated myself terribly. I used to constantly put myself down with statements like, "You dummy. How could you be so stupid." I didn't love myself. I hated myself. I was so critical and abusive of myself that if I had treated other people in this same way, nobody would want to be within 100 yards of me. They wouldn't put up with it.

what these commandments say, we will suffer. With this in mind, it shouldn't be any surprise that life does not go well for us when we break this commandment to love ourselves. This is such a central commandment that it is one of the commandments upon which hang all the Law and the Prophets!

God created you, and He knows your frame. You are made in His image, and God is love. This is the reason why He commanded you to love yourself.

- Only when you love yourself can you love others.
- Only when you love yourself can you truly love God.
- Only when your own cup is full can you freely give to others.
- Only when you love yourself can you fellowship with God.
- Only when you love yourself can you be sanctified.
- Only when you love yourself can you live the victorious Christian life.
- Only when you love yourself and the gifts God has placed in you can you be all He intended for you to be.
- Only when you love yourself does Satan lose.

Because these are so enormously important and so central to our Christian walk, Satan has worked very diligently to cause each of us to judge ourselves and to hate ourselves, and thus cause The Wall of separation.

Giving Yourself The Blessing

Chapter 10, "Your Worst Trauma," discusses "The Blessing," which is the "good" that we all need as children and we all continue to need daily as adults, or we will be wounded. Part of living in a loving relationship with yourself is to give yourself "The Blessing"! Jesus will always do this, but you also need to. The part of you that is your Treasure

> **Part of living in a loving relationship with yourself is to give yourself "The Blessing"!**

Inside wants and needs your love. I encourage you to review that part of Chapter 9, "There Is Buried Treasure." The genuine giving of The Blessing to another person demonstrates that you care enough about them to spend time with them and to be a student of who they are. Doing this for another person says that you want to get to know them, and that you are thrilled with who God made them to be. This also needs to be your attitude towards yourself!

An Example From My Life

This idea of loving myself was absolutely foreign to me. For example, I used to see my body as a problem whenever it got in the way of my plans. When my body became tired, I would whip it to get it to do what I wanted it to do. Or if I got a side ache when I was running, I would rebuke the pain. I didn't understand that my body was simply telling me the status of what was going on inside. When there was pain, there was a problem.

Now I find myself listening to my body. When it isn't feeling good, it is not "bad." Rather, if my body is fussing, it is simply telling me that there is a problem. Now I stop and listen to it. I am its friend, not its foe, and vice versa. I sympathize with it, and seek to find out what is wrong. Then I do what I can to fix the problem. When the problem is fixed the pain stops. We (our Head and our Treasure Inside) are in this thing (life) together.[188]

Others Will Act Differently Towards You

I am sure that you have met people whom you immediately like. When this happens, you have read their heart and like what you sense. In the same way, others read your heart. When you love yourself, you will want others to meet the real you. It is as though you are saying, "Here I am. I love me. You will too." You subconsciously broadcast this, and others sense this message. On

---

[188] See Endnote 18-1 for more on trying to be what I am not, versus loving who God made me to be.

the other hand, when you hate yourself, you try to hide who you really are. You expect that if other people see who you really are, they won't like you. After all, you don't like you. You subconsciously broadcast a message that says, "Please don't get too close to me. I hate me. If you find out who I really am, you will hate me too." When other people sense these subliminal messages, they find themselves feeling about you the same way you feel about yourself. They like you, or they dislike you. They find themselves acting towards you in accordance with your feelings about yourself, even though they may not understand <u>why</u> they like you or dislike you.

Inside-Out

Therefore we are to live life **inside-out.** Most of us have been living life **outside-in.** We have only trusted our intellect and willpower, which are those parts of us of which we are

> **Living from the outside-in does not work very well.**

conscious and over which we can exert control. We <u>have distrusted what is below our level of consciousness and not subject to our purposeful control.</u> We have tried to live as though those parts in our Treasure Inside do not exist. This **outside-in** way of living has not worked very well, because God did not design us to operate that way. The truth is that the largest part of who we really are lies in our Treasure Inside, including our ability to commune with Him. God always intended for us to live **inside-out.**[189]

---

[189] See Endnote # 18-2 for another view on loving yourself by John Eldredge from his book, <u>Waking The Dead</u>.

Summary

Unfortunately, most of us have believed the lies spoken to us by the World and Satan, and have therefore harshly judged ourselves. Because we have believed these lies, we have been looking inside ourselves for things to kill, instead of for things to love to life.

We need to be collaborative with our Treasure Inside, rather than adversarial. We are in this together (us and our Treasure Inside), and we need to be friends, not enemies.

Life will only go well for you if you align yourself with God's description of spiritual reality. Loving yourself is one of the fundamental pillars upon which all of spiritual reality rests (Matthew 22:39). If you do not love yourself, destruction will be present in your life. Loving yourself is part of God's plan for you, and it is the only way that you can become all He has intended for you to be.

> **We have been looking inside ourselves for things to kill, instead of for things to love to life.**

Chapter 19

The Big Picture
A Summary

This chapter is merely a summary. Because some of what I have presented in this book is contrary to some commonly held perceptions, I could be misunderstood if this chapter is left to stand alone without you first reading the rest of the book and the biblical documentation it contains.

"We arrive in this world with birthright gifts - then we spend the first half of our lives abandoning them or letting others disabuse us of them . . . we spend the second half trying to recover and reclaim the gift we once possessed . . . What a long time it can take to become the person one has always been" (Palmer, pp. 9,12).

I could almost stop right here with this summary, because this statement by Parker Palmer so clearly displays the big picture. This reality is so very different than what most of us have believed about ourselves. For an adult Christian these statements give a clear picture of the challenges before us.

This Book Challenges Us In Several Ways:

1. **A paradigm shift: We first need to have a radical shift in how we view ourselves.** The idea that "nothing good dwells in me" is not true.[190] There is a "bad part," but there is also a "good part," which is made in the image of God. See Chapters 9, 12, & 13.

2. **Inner Healing: We need to walk with Jesus to heal the wounds resulting from the prior experiences of our life.** We also need to go to the Lord to clean up the ongoing daily messes we make (sins).

3. **Loving Ourselves: Finally, we need to live our daily life loving and blessing the "self" that God placed in us from the beginning,** which is also the part of us that is in communion with God.

What I have presented in this book is a workable roadmap for accomplishing these tasks. These comprise a life journey that has its beginning in Inner Healing, but it moves beyond that. The journey is also about being your own friend and living out of the treasure God has placed in your heart.

Inner Healing

Inner Healing is about healing the wounds that bind you and cause you so much emotional pain. This part of the process needs to happen, as it is the only way to remove the darkness planted in you by your Bitter Root Judgments, and to stop the reaping from the operation of God's laws. Jesus came and died to provide you with the way out of this darkness and bondage. When you are forgiven a sin, Jesus cleanses that area of your heart, abides there, and takes

---

[190] **Romans 7:18,** *For I know that in me (that is, in my flesh) nothing good dwells.*

upon Himself the just consequences of that sin. He actively has you on a journey to heal all of your Bitter Root Judgments.

Your Relationship With Yourself

Typically, Inner Healing has been focused upon bitterness towards other people. However, if your journey only goes this far, as it often does, you will remain crippled. The job is only half done. I have seen many people who only pursue their healing up to this point (because they don't know that there is more), and they find themselves still in bondage, and are anything but victorious in their lives.

These people have become stalled because there are still some powerful Bitter Root Judgments remaining. These judgments are against themselves. These judgments against themselves are in fact the most disabling judgments, because they have resulted in a barrier that prevents them from being whole. These judgments have caused them to bury the treasure that God placed in them for their use, and they cannot be victorious in their quest to be like Jesus without this treasure.

We have all buried our treasure to some degree. This process began from the very beginning of our lives. The world around us told us that we were unacceptable just the way we were, and we believed this lie. We thus came to see that who we really are, our Treasure Inside, is bad. Therefore we needed to hide this part of us from view and to build a more acceptable "self" to present to the world.

But God never intended for us to be cut off from our Treasure Inside. We therefore need to be healed of these judgments against ourselves so that we can be reconciled to that part of us that is made in the image of God.

Loving Yourself

The next part of your journey involves a step beyond no longer being alienated from yourself. No longer being your own enemy isn't enough. Your changed attitude towards yourself needs to be more radical than this. The change needs to be so complete that you positively love yourself and embrace who you really are. You are to see yourself as God sees you.

Therefore, being changed into the image of Jesus can only be done if you actively look for this treasure buried inside you. It is an exciting treasure hunt! God will lead you in this hunt to uncover your "birthright gifts." God placed in each of us a unique person with certain gifts and talents and abilities. This is the part of you that was created in the image of God. Only if you are unified with this part of yourself will you be able to become like Jesus. Only when you are living out of these gifts can you produce good fruit, feel joy, and fulfill your Divine design.

Eric Liddell was the 1924 Olympics gold medal winner in the 400 meter run. He was a Christian, and his sister was criticizing him for spending time preparing for the Olympics. In response he said: "I believe that God made me for a purpose: He made me fast; and when I run, I feel His pleasure. To give it up would be to hold Him in contempt. It is not just for fun. To run is to honor Him." [191]

What God Is Creating

The creature God wants to create resembles Jesus. You are His workmanship. He tells us about His plan for each of us over and over in the New Testament.[192]

To some readers, what I have been presenting may seem alien and foreign. Without a doubt these truths are weird and foreign to the lost world in which we live. But God's ways are not our ways.

"For My thoughts are not your thoughts, nor are your ways My ways," says the Lord. "For as the heavens are higher than the earth, so are My ways higher than your ways, and My thoughts than your thoughts" (Isaiah 55:8-9).

---

[191] From the movie "Chariots of Fire," 1981, Enigma Productions.

[192] See Endnote #19-1 for more evidence of how central this message is to the Gospel.

When you live life this new way, you are living as God always intended. Then God is pleased and you are blessed. Who could want more?

Keep At It

God's way works, and it is the easy yoke and light burden.

> *Come to Me, all you who labor and are heavy laden, and I will give your rest. Take My yoke upon you and learn from Me, for I am gentle and lowly in heart, and you will find rest for your souls. For My yoke is easy and My burden is light* (Matthew 11:28-30).

However, even though it is an easy yoke, there is still work to do. For instance, imagine that you have a five acre lawn to take care of. In the past you have had to mow it by hand. That would be a heavy burden, and you probably couldn't do it. Then somebody gives you a rider mower. Now mowing the lawn is easy, but you still need to do it. You still need to set time aside for it, get on the mower, and operate it. The lawn won't get mowed if you take no action.

Since your "lawn" has been neglected for years, the first cleanup will be quite a project. Then, if you mow it whenever you can see that it needs it, the job is easy.

On the other hand, if you think one "mowing" is all that was required, you will be disappointed. The grass and weeds will again grow. If you neglect to observe this and don't mow whenever the lawn needs it, your lawn will again become a shambles. This is inevitable.

Our life is like that. After the Lord has helped us clean up our years of accumulated bitter roots, if we go back to our old way (trying to do it ourselves in our own strength, or neglecting to walk in the new way), our "Honeycomb" will again become a mess. New bitter roots will be planted, because that is the very nature of our "flesh." The bitter roots will grow and produce bad fruit, because that is their nature. You will again be reaping the same pain and misery as previously. God told us about this.

But it has happened to them according to the true proverb: "A dog returns to his own vomit," and, "a sow, having washed, to her wallowing in the mire" (2 Peter 2:22).

The problem then won't be that your healing didn't work. Your difficulty will be a result of failing to walk daily with the Lord, forgiving and being forgiven.

It Is A New Way Of Life

Your sanctification process therefore does not consist of a gigantic healing from the Lord, and then a return to your old ways. It is a whole new way of living, <u>moment by moment</u>, day by day. Persistence is required.

"So I say to you, Ask and keep on asking, and it shall be given you; see, and keep on seeking, and you shall find; knock and keep on knocking, and the door shall be opened to you" (Luke 11:9).

Does this sound like a lot of work? It would be if we were alone and had to do it in our own strength. There is a hard way (living in our own strength) or an easy way (letting the Lord do it), but doing nothing is not an option. We are stuck in this world, which is a place of spiritual warfare. We can't escape from the battle zone. If we had to fight the battle alone, we would lose. Perhaps you are aware that you have been losing. Knowing our inability, the Lord came and made it possible for us to win. It is His strength and ability that will win, and He has the power and ability to protect us.

For I know who I have believed and am convinced that He is able to guard safely my deposit, entrusted to Him against that Day (2 Timothy 1:12, Berkeley).

But whenever we realize we have sinned and are therefore going to suffer, we need to repent, forgive, and be forgiven. We need to do our part. We need to get on the "rider mower."

These things I have spoken to you, that in Me you may <u>have</u> <u>peace</u>. In the world you will have tribulation; but be of good cheer. I have overcome the world (John 16:33, underlining is mine).

Rewards

Not only did God provide a way for us to clean up our messes, He also made the experience rewarding. When we apply the blood of Jesus, we experience peace and liberty. The Holy Spirit then resides in that place in our heart, having washed us clean from our sin. Consequently, in this life, in place of bitterness and suffering, we then receive a rewarding experience:

But the fruit of the Spirit is love, joy, peace, patience, kindness, goodness, faithfulness, gentleness, self-control: (Galatians 5:22-23).

Isn't this what we all want? Read the Appendix A, "Experiences And Testimonies" as an encouragement that the Lord is our healer, and He then rewards us with peace when He sets us free.

Significance Of The Book Cover Design

When we are in harmony with ourselves, and we live from the inside-out, then we have rest. The yoke is easy and our burden is light, because the gifts that flow from the image of God dwelling in us explode out into the world. We are just "being" who we are inside. God's life in us bursts forth and pours out His light and energy. It is easy because we aren't doing the good work out of our own strength, but are simply <u>allowing</u> God's power do the work.

"Let your light so shine before men, that they may see your good works and glorify your Father in heaven" (Matthew 5:16, underlining is mine).[193]

Let, not *make*, is the exhortation. We don't do it. It is done for us. The book cover design depicts this explosion of good fruit, power and light bursting forth. It seems like a paradox, to "rest" and yet shine forth. However, it is only a paradox if we think we have to work hard to make it happen.

If we are sick, we don't have to tell people. They can tell at a glance. If we are contented or happy, we don't have to tell people. It is obvious from our countenance. We don't "try" to look sick, or contented, or happy. We just are. It is effortless. What is projected forth from us is an effortless, accurate reflection of what is inside us at that moment.

Use This As A Workbook

The way that Jesus provided for us only works if you act on it. I would suggest that you use this book as an outline, as a workbook for your walk towards healing. It is most powerful when used in a group. You might consider using it in a church home group, a Bible study group, a counseling group, or just a group of your friends.

The simple format of the book lends itself to an orderly, step by step development of understanding of how God wants to transform you, and then provides a practical guide as to how to prayer about specific issues in your life.

I also use the book to prepare clients for their counseling sessions, assigning specific chapters as we progress.

In addition, the layout of the book is the format for my seminars, with small group prayer time occurring after each teaching. The

---

[193] Commenting on the meaning of "let", "The disciples of Jesus are to allow the light which they received from the heavenly Father through Jesus to shine in the world in order that they may glorify God" (Rienecker, p.12). We are to allow it, not make it happen.

teaching places the concepts in the intellect, and often triggers memories and hurts.

If the seminar ended with the teaching, no healing would result. (In the same way, your healing will not occur if you simply read the book and stop there). Prayer must occur for the blood of Jesus to be effectual. The small group prayer time provides the opportunity for people to pray for one another.

> *Confess your trespasses to one another, and pray for one another, that you may be healed. The effectual fervent prayer of a righteous man avails much* (James 5:15).

As a result of prayer, not only does healing then occur, but faith takes hold. The person knows beyond a shadow of a doubt that Jesus provides healing, because He just did! All the other members of the group are also blessed and built up, because they have witnessed the transformation. You can do this same thing in your own small group!

Don't go back to the old way.
Go forward to peace and life!

My prayer for you is that you succeed in your quest to become the person you have always been.

Appendix A

Experiences And Testimonies

I would like to thank all those who agreed to let me share their personal experiences. It is a blessing to have people willing to be transparent about the intimate struggles and victories in their own lives in order to encourage others.

This appendix is divided into two sections:
1. **Inner Child encounters with Jesus.**
2. **Other experiences and testimonies.**

Inner Child Encounters With Jesus

I again need to emphasize that in this sort of prayer, God alone is directing the imagery. It is imperative that neither the one doing the ministering nor the one being ministered to decide what will happen, or not happen. Otherwise there is a danger of opening the door so Satan and to deception. Refer to Chapter 15, "A New And Living Way," and Appendix D, "New Age Visualization" for more dialogue on this.

You will see that each person's experience is unique. The Lord ministers to a person in exactly the way they need it.

These examples are condensations of the experiences, because sometimes the experiences lasted a couple of hours.

My Experience

The first example of Inner Child Prayer is one that happened to me. Teresa Joy, one of the other counselors at Elijah House, prayed with me in this way. What happened to me was some sort of a vision, but I could tell that it was a real event that was happening. I did not orchestrate it or cause it to happen. I just waited and was available.

As I closed my eyes and listened for the Lord, in my mind's eye I saw myself in the entry of a very beautiful place. There was a curving stairway off to my right. The walls were paneled with beautiful wood, and the railings and the appointments were all of polished brass. I realized that I was supposed to walk up the stairs, so I began to do so. Although I couldn't see Him, I sensed that the Lord was walking with me on my right side. When we reached the top of the stairs, the area opened up into a concert hall.

This was also a beautiful place with polished wood and bright brass. Above and in front of me were some balconies, like those one sees in opera houses. I couldn't see anybody in them, but I sensed that I was being watched. In the center of this hall was a beautiful, shiny grand piano. I heard another person, not the Lord, tell me to sit down on the piano bench. I knew I was supposed to do that, and so I obeyed. The Lord sat next to me, on my right.

Then this same other person (who I could not see) told me to play the piano. I was distraught. I felt that I needed to do it, but I was undone: I don't know how to play the piano, and that's not something that one can fake. So I sat there, not knowing what to do. The Lord, knowing my quandary, placed His hands on the keys of the piano, and He instructed me to put my hands on top of His hands. He then played the piano beautifully!

That was the end of the vision, but I knew exactly what the Lord was healing. It was a surprise to me, because the specific issue that the Lord dealt with was not one about which I had previously been thinking. This was a new revelation.

As I grew up, my parents were very neglectful. I was left alone, to raise myself and make all of my own decisions. My parents were physically present, but not emotionally. They were not proactive in my life. I had therefore developed the view that I needed to do whatever life placed in front of me, because if I didn't do it, nobody was going to. As I grew up, I encountered challenges that I didn't handle very well. Because I was immature and ill prepared to do them, I made many mistakes and poor choices. Even though I realized I wasn't doing very well, it was just an assumption within me that I had to do whatever life placed in front of me.

In this prayer time, the Lord showed me that was not true. He showed me that there are some things that I just cannot do; and when I encounter one of these challenges, He will do it.

I came out of this experience <u>knowing</u> that what He did was real, and knowing that the message was true. I now <u>know</u> that when Jesus speaks to my heart, it is true. I know this in the depth of my being.

Experience of Matthew Manning, Founder, Lighthouse World Evangelism, Inc., Rohnert Park, California

For many years Matthew had lived a homosexual lifestyle, and he almost died of AIDS. In the process of redeeming his life, the Lord had miraculously healed him of HIV infection, which is a physical impossibility. Though the Lord had delivered him from the bondage to homosexuality prior to our counseling time, there were still basic self-esteem issues with which he struggled.

As we prayed and waited for the Lord to come, Matthew saw a strange scene. He saw Father God standing with something in the palm of His hand. At first he couldn't identify what it was, but all of a sudden, he saw it! He realized that it was <u>himself</u> that God was forming. God showed him that He created him, and He created him to be a man.

Then he saw another scene. It was the moment of his conception, and his earthly father said, "This had better be a girl!" From this vision, Matthew knew that in his spirit he had been aware when his dad uttered that statement. This meant that from the very beginning of his existence, he was convinced that he should be a girl! So his problem with his masculinity had always been with him.

At the moment that he saw God forming him in the vision, he knew God had made him to be a man, and God was happy that he was a man.   There was an enormous and powerful healing that happened inside of him; because now he knew, to the depths of his being, that he was the right sex. Through this encounter with the living God, his identity was healed.

Matthew later wrote, "Your ability to ask questions, listen, and most importantly, hear from the Holy Spirit and be guided by the

Lord Jesus Christ during each counseling session makes your ministry unique and needed in these last days. I came to you for direction and my life changed drastically. Your ability to focus me on my inner-self, a part of me that I did not know existed, brought a new dimension of healing in my life that I never knew possible!"

Experience of Rolf Numme, Wasilla, Alaska

Rolf had almost died in childbirth, and had a very difficult childhood. From his parents he received ridicule rather than support and The Blessing. He was bullied, by other children, but his parents didn't protect him.

Rolf had been a Christian for many years, and had been a very devoted believer. Yet he had suffered from bouts of depression for years, and had received many hours of counseling from a variety of practitioners. He had tried many psychotropic drugs, but he was either allergic to them, or they didn't help. And yet, after all these attempts at healing, he was still suffering desperately.

As Rolf and I listened to the Lord, Rolf saw a rickety bridge over a gorge. The gorge wasn't very wide, but it was very deep and dark inside. The Lord was standing on the other side of the gorge, beckoning for him to come across the bridge, and to not look back.

Rolf hesitated, because he was afraid. The bridge looked so fragile that he was afraid it would break if he stepped onto it. Finally, he decided to trust the Lord and to step out. As he walked across the bridge it broke, and he fell into the dark gorge.

As he lay in the darkness at the bottom of the pit, he felt so alone. "Nobody is here for me. I am always abandoned. In my time of greatest need, I will be alone."

Then he cried out to Jesus, "Where were you all these years?" All Rolf saw was a big black hole!

In that moment he realized he had a huge rage in him towards God.

"I am screaming at God", Rolf exclaimed, with amazement and some fear.

Then he said with astonishment, "He says He loves me!"

Rolf asked God to forgive him for judging Him.

He realized that he had always tried to be his own God, because he didn't trust God to be his protector.

I (Ed) sensed a darkness present. So I commanded it to leave, in the name of Jesus, and it left. It had been inhabiting this terrible, deep root of bitterness that Rolf had towards God. But now it had to go, because God had redeemed that place of bitterness in Rolf. The demonic presence no longer had a legal right to be in that place.

Then Rolf said, "Ed, I have never seen this before. For an instant I was in touch with the severity of God. You don't want to mess with this dude!"

Rolf was feeling afraid, and in awe. He said, "Lord, I want You to be my God."

The Lord gave me (Ed) the right question to ask. I asked Rolf, "Is the severity aimed towards you, or towards that evil spirit?"

Rolf was still for a moment. Suddenly he began to cry very, very hard.

After some moments he said, "You showed up. I have been waiting all these years for you to show up. And I thank you."

"You took care of the bully inside."

"You loved me that much!"

And then the Lord held him!

Rolf realized that the spirit of fear that had inhabited him came in at birth when he almost died.

This whole encounter with the Lord probably lasted no more than twenty minutes.

He felt good for the first time in his life.

The next day Rolf said, "Yesterday was the happiest day of my life."

Rolf's life was changed by this brief encounter with the Lord!

Experience of Miikka Paananen, Turku, Finland

Miikka had problems in his marriage. When he had a conflict with his wife, he felt worthless. He would contain his temper for awhile, but eventually he would explode. He hated that, but couldn't stop it. These outbursts of anger occurred frequently.

As we prayed, Miikka had several dramatic encounters with the Lord. The first thing he prayed about was trying to be his own protector.

He prayed to open the door to the Lord, and Jesus came in!

Jesus asked him "What are you afraid of?"

Miikka told Jesus, "I am always looking around for something bad to happen to me. That is why I shut the door."

Then Miikka said, "When I look at Jesus, I see I need not fear Him. He is different.

"Jesus says to me, 'I will be with you. I am not leaving you,'

I can hear Him saying, 'Yes, I am your protector. Leave it to Me. Trust Me. I will be there for you.'

I can see I don't want to come out of the womb.

There is that sense of worthlessness.

Jesus is there. He says, 'I was there to welcome you.'

He carries me out of the womb!

He is holding me, and says, 'I am not leaving you, and I am holding you.'

I can see my mother coming to see me, and then disappearing like all the others who left me.

Yeah, I can recognize I have judged myself as worthless, from the very beginning!"

Then Miikka asked Jesus to forgive him, and he apologized to his Treasure Inside for judging him as worthless. .

The next day the following happened in prayer.

Miikka saw a throne.

"Jesus is next to me, and I see there is someone sitting on that throne. And he is very angry.

Now I can see-it is my father.

Now Jesus is talking. He says to me, 'This throne is not my throne.'

Then Jesus is saying, 'Come here to see My throne.'

We are coming to a place. There are three chairs. There is a simple chair.

Jesus says, 'This is My throne.'

He says, 'This second one is for My Father. The third one is for you.'

Then Jesus says, 'Now the Father is coming!'

And I look at my Father. So safe. I don't fear to look at Him. The fear goes away

He is asking me, 'Would you like to come here and sit on My lap?'

I say, 'Yes.'. He stretches His arms, and I walk to Him, and He lifts me up to His lap.

So My Father talks to me. He is saying, 'I am your Father. This is your place. I will take care of you.'

I see the first throne. It is not God or Jesus' throne, but another throne. I can realize that I have judged my earthly father, and that I have judged God, my heavenly Father."

So Miikka prayed about his judgments on his earthly father and his heavenly Father.

Then he reconciled with his own Treasure Inside.

"Now there is peace," he said.

Miikka's Testimony Since This Experience

"Dear Ed,

Thank you for the counseling session in Helsinki in September! The days we spent together were of ultimate importance to me. We have been going through your book in our Living Waters group in Turku during this autumn. The group will continue until the end of February.

We have 5 men and 4 women and all of us are excited about the message of your book! There is a treasure buried in your book that we are eagerly digging and taking hold on. And that is the treasure of THE GOOD NEWS, THE GOSPEL to those who suffer of brokenness.

During your visit to Finland in September God put especially one verse in my heart:

Isaiah 52:7 *How beautiful on the mountains are the feet of those who bring good news, who proclaim peace, who bring good tidings, who proclaim salvation, who say to Zion, "Your God reigns!"*

I felt like you came far from behind the mountains (or sea) to Finland to bring this good news to us. And that God is preparing the same beautiful shoes for us to walk with.

God bless you.

Miikka"

Testimony of C.C., Idaho

This letter written to me is unique in that it illustrates the powerful way the Lord can manifest Himself directly to an individual, and bring His healing.

"Dear Ed,

I wanted to let you know there are wonderful things happening in our lives since we saw you last Friday.

First, there was a continuation of what God did with me while I was with you. He continued to speak to me and helped me realize I had been living my life actually believing when something bad happened or when I sinned God disappeared and I was on my own. I'm sure you can see from my Life History lots of bad things happened and I sinned badly. Oh Brother Ed, I'm so glad He was there! He never leaves His children and beauty of all, He was there before I knew He was. He chose me before the foundation of the world. And He showed me He was there in my first known dark hour.

Then He showed me He was not only there, but was active. He showed me He uses His people to protect us (you could say, "well of course", but Ed **He showed me all the people in every situation, sometimes it was even me**). The beauty of this is all the people were imperfect (imagine that..), but they did exactly what was needed, including me (He used me to protect others and myself at times). He also showed me how at least once there had been something else prepared for me (by the Devil) and even though I was sinning (by trying to meet my own need for love without God), the Lord protected me from the other thing. Actually I know this has happened more than once. Do you know what a comfort that is to me? He was in control and even though I was doing what I should not, He was loving me. **What I was missing when I sought to meet my own needs for love was NOT His presence (He never forsakes His children), but the sense of His presence. I did not feel His presence and for me that is deadly.** I think you know exactly what I mean.

Also, the Lord has done so much for me since the one visit to you, I wanted to tell you I believe one more visit with you is all I believe is necessary. However this morning, I read chapter's 10 and 11. Chapter 11 prompted another miracle Ed. I understand why I did what I did and since I have many times asked for forgiveness from God I didn't need to ask forgiveness, but I did need to see and know what the Lord Jesus had known all along and know I was forgiven. He knew I was drinking dirty water, because I was dying from thirst. He also knew I didn't know what clean water was. And He was never ashamed of me. Oh Ed, this is good, beautiful, healing news to me. I forgave myself and stopped judging myself. I am not ashamed, I understand and am thankful for a beautiful Savior who took my shame and made me clean. I thank Him also for being a righteous, just Judge (He paid the price and He is the only one who has the right to judge what He bought).

I wanted you to rejoice with me and know how God has used you and your book."

Other Experiences And Testimonies

Testimony of Wisti Rosenthal, Emmett, Idaho, and her husband Ron.

"Since I came to see you in June 2001, my life has changed drastically. I feel like I was blind before that time and that God has opened up my eyes and now I can see. I lived the first 20 years of my walk with the Lord blaming everyone else for my unhappiness I knew that intimacy with the Lord was possible for other people, but I didn't know intimacy with Him personally. He is now opening the door to that intimacy and I am experiencing a new life filled with His peace. You taught me how to get to the root of things and pray through to healing" (January 2002).

"I guess I feel like freedom in the Lord is worth any amount of money or any sacrifice. I don't think people realize how different their life can be when they are free to be intimate with the Holy Spirit.

It's about being continually filled with the Holy Spirit, filling us up, more and more. Him moving into those places in our heart that used to be dark and filled with wounding (sin). Allowing Him to completely change our thinking, our heart and everything we've ever believed about Him, ourselves and/or the Bible.

Ron has crossed some sort of threshold or something into freedom. When he called you this summer and you helped him to understand that nothing is too small to pray about (even an inanimate object), it changed something in his heart. It's been amazing to see the transformation in him into freedom.

Ron continues to grow and gain freedom. It just brings tears to my eyes whenever I think about it. I have the real Ron, finally. God's miracles are amazing.

One of the huge things that Ron and I believe is that what you're teaching is not about 'inner healing." It's the gateway to the Holy Spirit in the life of every Christian. When He resides in all of those places that used to be filled with wounding/sin, EVERYTHING changes. Scripture no longer means what it used to. You begin to see the very things Jesus was talking about. It all begins to make sense. Freedom comes and resides with you. Forgiveness is the key to EVERYTHING. We make the choice, He does the miracle in our hearts" (October 2004).

"I don't think people realize how different their life can be when they are free to be intimate with the Holy Spirit. Anyway, things are good here with the Rosenthals. Ron and I are able to work through things now and he continues to amaze me with his new ability to forgive and reconcile. WOW!

When we share our stories and our hearts with people we don't leave anything out. We are just so happy to be free and living the abundant life in Jesus that always eluded us before. The neatest thing of all is that we know this is just the beginning. The Holy Sprit has so much more love for us than we can even comprehend. We're just living the tip of the ice berg" (November 2004).

Testimony of Marilyn Rowsome, Missionary to Papua New Guinea

I was disappointed that I couldn't attend the last eight hours of instruction in Ed Kurath's seminar because of another commitment. I had already read Ed's book through so was familiar with the teaching. But I found that each time I went over it, the truth penetrated deeper into my understanding and heart.

Right at this time I was exposed to an extra large dose of rejection. As this happened, I began to notice the bad fruit emerging - negative thinking, being critical of others and getting on others, being easily irritated, but more importantly negative thinking about myself. Just when I felt like giving up saying "It doesn't work for me!" a revelation came to my heart. As I cried out "Why, Lord?" a thought dropped into my head as if from the Lord. "When you feel rejected by others, you reject yourself. When you fail to accept and love yourself, in no time the bad fruit begins to take over."

This is what I had been learning in Ed's teaching and now I could see it in myself. I quickly reread the relevant chapters of his book again. It all made such sense. For how many years had I been turning the slightest sense of rejection into rejection of myself? Oh so long! It had become a natural response. I certainly didn't need to think it through - the path down that track was well worn by 50 years of constant use. No matter how much I had filled my mind with the statements of truth about who I was in Christ, there was another louder message from my very own heart.

Recognizing the problem is the first step to healing. Then comes agreeing with God about it (confession) and desiring to live a different way. That certainly was easy because I have longed to walk in newness of life for so long! The next step is the difficult one. It involves saying sorry - something that we all find hard to do. I needed to say sorry to God for the judgments I had made. In particular the judgments I had made against myself. In straight talk this really is self-hatred. Then there were judgments against God for making me like I was. This was my sin, no one else's. And so I needed to say sorry to God and myself. Then I needed to recognize God's gracious forgiveness and embrace that with all my heart.

Yes, there were others whose actions had triggered this pathway to self-hatred in me, so I needed to forgive them too. So often they had done this unintentionally. But still it had caused me such pain and so I consciously acknowledged that pain and said "I forgive you" as one by one different instances of rejection came to my mind.

The negative emotions I was experiencing had in fact been an alarm system telling me that there was still a bitter root deep in there that had not yet been transformed and invaded by Christ. So as I listened to those emotions and tracked with God's help to the root there was healing rather than the usual condemnation. Thank you Lord that my feelings can be my friend.

I thank you, God, for this opportunity to learn through experience, to grow through real life and I look forward to more times ahead because healing is a process that you are totally committed to for me.

Marilyn Rowsome, 12 June, 2004, Papua New Guinea

Testimony of B.O, Dublin, Ireland

"In June last year I undertook a week of intensive counseling with Ed. Having struggled with depression, phobia, and shame, I am now experiencing lasting hope, freedom and peace in my heart. Through listening prayer I have experienced His forgiveness again and again."

Testimony of Ken and Donna Gift, Wailea, Hawaii

I appreciate Ed's sensitivity in allowing the Holy Spirit to reveal things to people in His way and His time. Through Ed's ministry, my life, my family, and our ministry was unjammed. We praise God for him. Inner healing was the most profound experience, outside of salvation, that either one of us have ever experienced.

Experience of Mikko Laakkonen, Helsinki, Finland

This is an example of walking out one's healing by immediately pulling out new bitter roots as they occur:

Mikko had a major tendency to judge himself. He had a great fear, the fear of "I'm, not OK" (the Big Hurt). He was afraid of his customers criticizing him, and it was very hard for him to admit he doesn't know something, because that would trigger his self-rejection.

In our counseling appointments he prayed about the root of this self-rejection. Then one evening he went to his saxophone lesson. He had forgotten that he had placed a spare reed inside the saxophone. When he began to play for his teacher, the instrument made a very strange sound. His teacher called his attention to it, and Mikko got red in the face and felt ashamed. At that instant he realized he had just judged himself. He immediately prayed about this new bitter root, and the embarrassment left completely.

When he came to his counseling appointment the next day he said, "Ed, it is so easy!"

He said that in the past he would have wrestled with the feeling of inadequacy for days. It was "easy" because he had let Jesus bear his sin of judgment.

Experience Demonstrating A Prophetic Word

Several years ago I and several other people were praying for a lady. Joanne (not her real name) was in her late thirties, and had been married once to an alcoholic man who beat her. Since then she had been in a series of relationships, all with men who were abusive to her. She wanted to be happily married, but was very discouraged.

As we prayed, I saw a picture in my mind of an old diary farm, with the cows lined up in head stocks, eating hay and being milked. I had no idea what this meant, so I asked Joanne if a dairy farm meant anything to her. She said that when she was little her grandparents had a dairy farm, and she would spend the summers there. There was a moment of silence, and suddenly Joanne began to wail and sob hysterically. The rest of us just sat in silence, having no idea of what was going on.

Finally she calmed down. She said she had suddenly recovered a memory. In it she was about seven years old, was laying under a tree, and the hired hand was sexually abusing her. The Lord knew about this and used this prophetic word to bring the memory to the surface. We prayed with her about this incident.

I didn't see Joanne again for about five years. Then one day I was visiting another very large church, and I saw her across the room. I went over and said hello.

She gave me a big hug and said, "Ed, do you remember that night?"

I told her that I certainly did.

"That night changed my life," she exclaimed.

The lesson in this is that the Lord used the picture of the dairy farm to set in motion what He had been wanting to do in her. I had no idea what the picture meant, so I just gave it as I saw it. The Lord knew, and buried inside her was the meaning. If I had tried to interpret the "picture," I would very likely have interfered with what the Lord was doing.

Appendix B
Codependence

What Is Codependence?

Codependence is a term most people have heard, but few understand. One of the reasons that most of us do not know what it means is because the term has come to be applied to a wide range of unhealthy ways of relating. It has become so broadly used that it is very difficult to define. One writer has attempted to define it simply, "A codependent person is one who has let another person's behavior affect him or her, and who is obsessed with controlling that person's behavior (Beattie, p.36).

Beattie goes on to elaborate by saying, "Whatever problem the other person has, codependency involves a habitual system of thinking, feeling, and behaving toward ourselves and others that can cause us pain. Codependent behaviors or habits are self-destructive. We frequently react to people who are destroying themselves; we react by learning to destroy ourselves. . . These behaviors can prevent us from finding peace and happiness with the most important person in our lives - ourselves (Beattie, pp. 38-39).

Speaking of codependent behaviors, she says, "Most of us started doing these things out of necessity to protect ourselves and meet our needs. We performed, felt, and thought these things to survive - emotionally, mentally, and sometimes physically.(Beattie, pp.41-42).

In one short chapter I will not attempt to cover all the ways the term "codependence" is used, and that is not my purpose in addressing the issue. There is one aspect of codependence that I want to address because it relates to a central theme of this book.

Living with a difficult person often leads us to neglect our own needs, to take all the blame, to judge ourselves, and thus to separate us from our Treasure Inside.

A Dilemma

When we confront an angry or difficult person we have two choices:

1. We can go along with what we know the other person wants (out of fear of what he or she will do or say if we don't).
2. We can stand up for ourselves and face the storm.

Most of us choose option number one, especially if the difficult person is someone with whom we must have an ongoing relationship, such as a spouse, a parent, or a co-worker. After all, we have found that it is very expensive emotionally to stand up to him or her, and we always end up losing anyway. So why not just give in and have peace. This surrendering is codependence. [194]

> **When we always give in so that the other person will not become angry, this surrendering is codependence.**

Abuse is any behavior that comes from the heart of one who disvalues the other person. [195] This is perhaps a much more broad definition than most of us are used to. Abuse is

> **If the words or attitude disempower, disrespect, or disvalue the other, then they are abusive.**

---

[194] If one person has dependency issues and leans inappropriately on the other, but the other does not buy into the game, it is "dependence". "Codependence" requires two people, one controlling and one allowing themselves to be controlled, or said another way, one dominant and one dependent. "Dependence" is singular, "codependence" is plural. The prefix "co" denotes plurality.

[195] "Verbal abuse is an issue of control, a means of holding power over another. This abuse may be overt or covert (Evans, p.13).

In comparing nurturing versus abusive relationships, Patricia Evans says: "we may take a broad view and mark the turning point or precise instance which indicates that the threshold has been crossed between common miscommunication and definite verbal abuse. This criterion is the intention of the communicator to inform or nurture the other versus the intention not to inform or nurture the other. *If the words or attitude disempower, disrespect, or devalue the other, then they are abusive*" (Evans, p.30).

"Parents need to give their children time, attention, and direction, not *use* them to fill their own need. Use is abuse" (Bradshaw, p.43).

so prevalent in this fallen world that we may think that abusive behavior is "normal." We can become so used to experiencing it that we become desensitized and accept it as a legitimate way to relate to others. As a small child, when we had not yet lost our sensitivity, we could tell the difference; but we no longer can. It now feels normal to us rather than demeaning.

A difficult person is not sensitive to the needs of others and by their heart attitude they do not validate the other's worth.

Codependence Is Destructive

Co-dependent behavior is very understandable, but it is very destructive to ourselves, to the abuser, and to the relationship.

> **Codependence is a response to abuse. For healing to occur, it is important to label the behavior of the difficult person as abuse.**

We are being destroyed, because we are being used and not blessed by the other. Remember that whenever we are wounded, we automatically react with bitterness, judgment, and blame. Therefore, every time we submit to abuse we are thus planting roots of bitterness inside ourselves. The most devastating of these roots is directed at ourselves. When we are being co-dependent, we always blame ourselves. After a conflict with the abuser, we always ask ourselves, "What did I do

> **Co-dependent behavior destroys the one being abused.**

wrong?" We are under the illusion that we are the problem (because that is the message the abuser gives). So we think that if we can just get it right, the other person will be happy and there will be peace. This judging of ourselves builds The Wall inside, and our Treasure Inside will eventually go back inside The Wall and shut the door, because we have not defended him (or her). We live in fear of the next confrontation.[196]

Such surrendering to the other person's demands is also very destructive to the abuser. Keep in mind that God's plan for <u>every</u> person, including the abuser, is to be changed into the image of Jesus. This is a difficult and painful process for all of us, and we all need life to hold us responsible for our actions if we are to see our bad fruit. When one person always gives in, the abusive person is denied the information that he or she is being inappropriate. After all, as far as the abuser can see there was no problem, because the one being abused didn't complain. The one being abused had not disagreed, so the abuser assumes everything must be fine.

Jesus spoke of the need for us to rebuke a person who sins against us.[197] If we do not do so, the person will remain in their sin, and "*it would be better*

> **Co-dependent behavior also destroys the abuser**

for him if a millstone were hung around their neck, and he were thrown into the sea!" [198] Strong words from Jesus! Jesus is saying that we will save our "brother" (or "sister") from these awful consequences if we can somehow get him to see his sin. This is exactly what our "brother" needs, although he may not welcome the correction.   Therefore, when someone abuses us, it is our

---

[196] If we grew up in an abusive home, we may not even be consciously aware that what we are receiving is abuse, because it seems "normal" to us. But our heart knows it is abuse, and The Wall is built inside. It is destructive to us even if we don't consciously realize it.

[197] **Luke 17:1-4,** *Then He said to the disciples, ,"It is impossible that no offenses should come, but woe to him through whom they do come! It would be better for him if a millstone were hung around his neck, and he were thrown into the sea, than that he would offend one of these little ones. Take heed to yourselves. If your brother sins against you, rebuke him; and if he repents, forgive him. And if he sins against you seven times in a day, and seven times in a day returns to you, saying, 'I repent,' you shall forgive him."*

James 5:19-20, *Brethren, if anyone among you wanders from the truth, and someone turns him back, let him know that he who turns a sinner from the error of his way will save a soul from death and cover a multitude of sins.* Comment: not that he is lost to God's family, but death enters his "Honeycomb," and he will reap consequences from his seed sown (his sin).

[198] **See Endnote Appendix B-1** for more on this scripture.

responsibility to tell the abuser about it so they can repent and be forgiven by the Lord.

When we become co-dependent in a relationship, over time the other person becomes less and less mature and more and more spoiled. The abuser becomes like an unruly child who is never required to be responsible for his or her actions. Children need appropriate discipline, and so do adults! The abuser is thus proceeding in the opposite direction from that which God wants him or her to go. Both the abuser and the one being abused are being destroyed rather than being healed, and the situation will not change unless it is recognized and confronted, "Repressive systems perpetuate themselves as long as they remain unrecognized" (Evans, p.9).

Co-dependent behavior is also destructive to the relationship, because it is unhealthy behavior. Instead of the relationship being one that fosters healing, it fosters destruction. As both people become worse and worse, the relationship becomes less and less healthy. The abusive behavior and the codependence rob the relationship of safety, trust, and honesty. Intimacy cannot survive in this environment. Neither person's real needs for love are being met, and so they both become more and more empty, more and more miserable, and more and more needy.

There Can Be A Third Possibility

When relating to a difficult person, in addition to the two choices I have just mentioned (of either being co-dependent or facing the storm), there is a third possible way to relate. This third choice is to serve the other person out of love and out of a desire to see the other blessed.

In my own life I have experienced both serving out of fear, and serving out of love. I was co-dependent with my first wife, who could be very difficult. I did not want to set off her anger. I would do things around the house because I didn't want her to get angry with me for not doing them.

I am remarried and I now do things around the house because I know that it will bless my wife. It is so wonderful to see her eyes light up when she sees what I have done, and she is very appreciative. I am doing the same activity that I had done in my first marriage, but now my heart's reason is very different. I don't take great credit for this change in my heart, because I am able to do this in response to my wife's giving heart. I know that if I don't do these things for her, she will willingly do them herself. There is no demand. She also does lots of thoughtful things for me.

Two Realities

We grow up in one of two realities, based upon ways of relating. One writer has labeled these two realities as "Mutuality" and "Power Over".[199] In "Mutuality," each person is important, each is valued, each one's needs are important, and each is respected and loved. When a person grows up in "Mutuality", he or she can easily have intimacy, because other people are perceived as safe. Here the power is shared.

In "Power Over," one person has the power and is in control, and the other person is powerless and is controlled. When a person grows up in "Power Over," there are only two possible roles available. You are either in control or you are being controlled. You either hold the power, or you are powerless. If you grow up in "Power Over" you are not even aware that "Mutuality" exists, because you have not experienced it. It never occurs to you that another person can be safe, and that you can therefore freely let the other have power without there being a danger of being dominated.

When a person from "Mutuality" has a relationship with a person from "Power Over," there is a problem. The person from "Mutuality" wants to share power. The person from "Power Over" interprets this reaching out as weakness, concludes this is a person that can be controlled, and proceeds to dominate the relationship. This is confusing to the person from "Mutuality," who keeps trying to establish mutuality, but this never happens.

---

[199] The Verbally Abusive Relationship, by Patricia Evans.

Can I Accomplish "Mutuality" With A Difficult Person?

Being human and fallible, I have personally found it impossible for me to be lovingly giving ("Mutuality") with a difficult and controlling person with whom I have a close relationship. Some would say it is <u>always</u> impossible (Evans, pp.28, 116); that an abusive person is always out to win, because he or she always needs to win (Evans, pp.32, 35, 127-128). When we give lovingly, the abuser views it as an opportunity to win, and so takes what we willingly give. But we can sense what is going on in the abuser, and we feel used – which is what has happened. After several of these encounters, our Treasure Inside is no longer willing to come out and love this person; and without our Treasure Inside, we cannot love.

In such a situation our only choice is to love ourselves enough to protect our Treasure Inside from the abuse. Actually, this is also the most loving thing to do for the other person, because it will cause the other to reap what he or she has sown – and hopefully recognize their abusive behavior, go to the Lord about it, and be healed. But it is sooooo hard.

What About Loving Our Enemies?

Some will point out the scriptures that tell us to turn the other cheek (Matthew 5:39), and to walk the extra mile with those who choose to use us and abuse us (Matthew 5:41), and *"But I say to you, love your enemies, bless those who curse you, do good to those who hate you, and pray for those who spitefully use you and persecute you"* (Matthew 5:44). Isn't this what we are doing when we are being nice to those who treat us badly? Many Christians who are co-dependent are under the impression this is what they are doing.

But this is <u>not</u> what they are doing. People who are being co-dependent are acting this way <u>out of fear</u>, not out of love. Note that all the above scriptures are in Matthew, Chapter 5, in which Jesus is listing things that we can't do with our willpower.[200] We are incapable of these super high standards, and we need to be changed into His image before these good fruits will flow from good roots.

Then Jesus in us will always act out of love. In a sense, Jesus is saying that then we will be <u>able</u> to walk the extra mile, or to bless those that curse us. He is <u>not</u> saying that such <u>behavior</u> is <u>always</u> the loving thing to do. Remember that Jesus didn't always act kindly towards the scribes and Pharisees. In fact He called them a brood of vipers to their face, and said they were white-washed sepulchers (Matthew 23:2-36; Luke 11:39-52). These are not co-dependent type words, but they are words of love and truth. These are things they needed to hear, and Jesus was willing to say them and face the storm that resulted. And a huge storm certainly came about, which resulted in His crucifixion!

Also remember that the Sermon on the Mount was not a rigid list of rules for us to keep. Rather they were a list of <u>good fruit</u> that will result from the only <u>good root</u>, which is Jesus living in that place in our heart. Jesus is a living person; and only if we are obeying Him, living out of His presence in us, will we know what to do, and when. Only then will we know what is the loving thing to do in a specific situation, to turn the other cheek or to confront. And only then will we be able to accomplish it from a heart of love, because we can't possibly love such difficult people on our own. We can only love them through His Spirit dwelling in us. Otherwise, if we try to do it, our behavior will be tainted with striving and impure motives.

So when we are dealing with a difficult person, it is certainly a test of whether we have been changed into Jesus' image. Such a relationship will most certainly show the bad fruit in our life, and it will give us many opportunities to forgive and be forgiven.

---

[200] See Endnotes for Chapter 2, Endnotes #2-1, 2-2, &2-3.

Summary

Co-dependent behavior is therefore destructive to both the dependent person and the forceful one, to both the one being abused and the abuser. Even though the one being abused feels all the pain, both people, and their relationship, are being destroyed. We must confront the abuser in order to love ourselves, and also to help the abuser to see their sin so they can be healed.

I have only touched lightly on this issue of codependence and abusive relationships, because it is not a major objective of this book. Cloud and Townsend deal with these issues extensively in Boundaries, as does Patricia Evans in The Verbally Abusive Relationship. I would recommend these books if you are interested in more information.

Appendix C

Communication Differences

This chapter is placed in the Appendix because it has a different character to it than does the rest of this book. Rather than emphasizing root causes in the spiritual realm, it deals with techniques for better communication. I have included it in the book because it should improve the communication between men and women in general, and husbands and wives in particular.

The issues discussed are universal communication problems that men and women have because men and women are different creatures who perceive and process life very differently and communicate differently.

A Typical Conflict

Typically, when a conflict comes up, a man relies on his head, and he wants to fix the problem. On the other hand, a woman usually just wants to be heard. For instance, a man comes home from work and his wife has had a hard day.

She says to him, "You didn't take out the garbage. You never take out the garbage."

Immediately the computer in his head begins to make calculations. He knows he usually takes out the garbage, though he did forget today.

He says, "That is not true. I take out the garbage 83% of the time."

His wife then becomes even more irritated, and says something like, "And when are you going to finish painting the back of the house?"

Now he is getting a upset himself, because now it seems as though she is determined to nag him about all of his faults, and the fight is on.

Is this sort of interchange familiar?   I think this sort of interchange between a man and his wife is as common as water is to the ocean. What has happened is that he didn't understand what she was <u>really</u> saying, and she didn't understand why he didn't understand her real need.

When she said, "You never take out the garbage," what she was <u>really</u> saying was, "Right now it <u>feels</u> to me as though you never take out the garbage." But what she verbalized was, "You never take out the garbage," because, right at the moment, it <u>did feel</u> as though he <u>never</u> took out the garbage.   The feeling was so overwhelming in that moment that it felt like reality.

Why This Difference In Perception Is Universal

There is a physiological reason why this sort of conflict is so universal between men and women. The brain structures of men and women differ. The brain is made of two hemispheres. The left hemisphere is the logical, linear thinking section, and the right hemisphere is the emotional, relational section.   These two hemispheres are connected by a bundle of nerves called the "corpus collosum." The man's corpus callosum has less nerve fibers, so his brain hemispheres are less intimately connected than are the hemispheres of the woman.

God designed each of their brains for special purposes. Historically, the man was the hunter, warrior, and protector. The woman was the nurturer and caretaker of the children. He needed to be able to shut off his emotions when facing an enemy or a tiger. She needed to be ever sensitive to her children.

With less neural pathways between the hemispheres of his brain, the man is better able to cut off and ignore the signals from his right brain. This is fine when he is facing danger, but it goes awry when the man over-uses that ability. Then he can live in his left brain, not feel his pain, and not feel what his wife is feeling. This is an abbreviated explanation of this phenomenon. **See Endnote #9-4** for a more detailed description.

Back to Our Couple

We left our couple in the middle of an argument. She was feeling emotionally overwhelmed, and he was strictly in his head. Neither could understand why the other didn't see the situation the way they themselves did.

The intense emotional reaction in the wife's right brain thus overwhelmed her, and spoke more loudly than did her left brain. If she had not been so upset to begin with, she could have heard what her left brain was saying and would have been able to be just as rational as he was about the garbage. After all, they both have a normal left hemisphere of their brain, wherein lies the ability to engage in rational, linear thinking. It is just that in that moment the wife's right brain was speaking so loudly it was drowning out her left brain.

The husband did not experience this same process, because he has been equipped by God to shut off his right brain when necessary (and sometimes when it is not actually necessary). Right in that moment was the time for him to exercise this ability. The husband has been equipped to solve the situation, the wife has not been as well equipped to do so. It is because of this equipping from God that the primary responsibility to calm down the situation rests upon the husband.

A Solution[201]

Instead of staying in his head and being analytical, if the husband were to engage his wife at an emotional level, the problem could be solved. As he listened to her heart, she would then realize that he really did want to help her resolve her upset, and that he was on board with her in it. Having been heard, then her emotions would calm, and she could settle down and be rational. All along what she really wanted was for her husband to hear her, not to "fix" the problem.

---

[201] This approach to resolving conflicts was authored by Mark Sandford of Elijah House.

So there is a method to solve such communication problems, summarized by the acronym **"HARK."**

H: "Hear" is the first step. When he realizes that she is upset, the man needs to use his God-given ability to contain his emotions. He needs to step back from his emotional response to her attack and hear her heart.

He would say something like, "Yes, I forgot to take out the garbage today, and I am sorry. It sounds as though you have had a really hard day, because usually you aren't so upset."

Then she would say something like, "It has been a horrible day. Everything has gone wrong. First, I broke my favorite dish when I was washing it. Then the dryer broke down, just when I had a huge amount of laundry to do. Then to top it off Jimmy got stung by a bee and I had to spend the entire afternoon waiting in the emergency room."

This is what she has really been wanting to tell him all along, if he had just been available to hear. Seeing the garbage cans was the last straw, and so she was letting him have the full emotional load she had been storing up all day.

A: "Acknowledge": Then he says, "If that had all happened to me, I would be an angry guy. I feel the same way when things don't go well." He is letting her know that he understands how she feels.

R: "Revisit": Now he can revisit the original conversation, but he shouldn't take this step until the situation has calmed down and he realizes his wife is ready to reconcile. Then he can speak the truth, and she can hear it. Then he might say something like, "I am sorry that I added to your load of frustration today by forgetting to put out the garbage. I do want to bless you by putting it out, and I always try to remember. I don't think I forget very often."

Now that she has been heard, her upset has calmed down. Now she can hear her left brain, and she is likely to say something like, "Yes, I know you are usually very good about taking out the garbage. I am sorry I was cross with you."

Some might recommend that he not take this step of speaking the truth for fear that she will react. However, healthy relationships are built on truth. Eventually, when the time is right, he needs to tell her that he tries to remember and usually does succeed.

K: "Kiss and make up": This is the fun part. Now they are in agreement, and the quarrel is resolved. They have both been heard.

The next time there is an argument, I would like to encourage you men to try to hold your own emotions at bay long enough to apply this approach. Here I am not advocating that you bury your emotions, but to just delay acting on them until the situation has cooled down. Then in the "Revisit" phase you can advocate for yourself if that is appropriate. You will be amazed at how many explosive situations can be resolved by this.

The Spiritual Dimension

Also keep in mind that though the conflict has been resolved between the husband and wife, there will probably be some bitter roots that were just planted. Therefore, even though the conflict has been resolved, the consequences in the spiritual realm will still need to be dealt with by each party.

In addition to the current event (and current new judgments), the reactions during the conflict may also have revealed some old bitter roots that have been hooked into. In fact, difficulties in our daily lives are often the way the Lord shows us that we have a bitter root buried in our heart. This then becomes an opportunity to advance in our healing.

Women Are Not Without Responsibility

The man does not bear all the responsibility for making a relationship work. It is when the woman is emotionally stirred that she has difficulty being logical and "reasonable." It would also be important that she take the time to express her need in a more understandable and less offensive way.[202]   In an emotional

---

[202] See 1 Peter 3:1-6.

encounter the man has been equipped by God to have the tools to restrain his emotions in order to resolve the conflict. Women can be just as logical and "reasonable" in less emotionally explosive situations, and in general they bear just as much responsibility for the relationship as does the man.

Summary

Men and women differ in how they handle a conflict. Because of the unique "equipment" that God has given to men, it is up to them to act in a way that allows the situation to be resolved in a healthy way. If the man will hold his emotions at bay for a moment and hear and acknowledge the woman's upset, then conflicts with their wives can be peacefully resolved.

Appendix D

New Age Visualization
A Counterfeit

In the prior chapter, "A New and Living Way," I presented a way of Inner Healing that might sound similar to New Age beliefs and practices.

It is important for you to understand how fundamentally different what I am advocating is from New Age thinking. When one looks at the underlying assumptions of the New Age and compares those with my perspectives, it becomes crystal clear how different they are. In line with this purpose, I will be restricting my discussion of New Age beliefs to points that are pertinent to what I have taught.[203]

Who Is God?

At their foundation, Christianity and the New Age differ on who they believe is god. Is He God, the God of Abraham, Isaac, and Jacob, or is somebody else God? To the New Age, god includes not only people, but also animals, and rocks, and trees, and "mother earth."[204]

> **The foundational difference between the New Age and Christianity is the question of who is God.**

Interestingly, the New Age, Secular Humanism,[205] Buddhism, Hinduism and many other religions are very close cousins. On the

---

[203] For a more complete discussion of the New Age, read Douglas Groothuis' book, Unmasking the New Age listed in the Bibliography.

[204] Speaking of biblical reality, "The creation is not an emanation of God; rather it is his good world made from nothing *(ex nihilo)* and upheld by his constant providence" (Groothuis, p.172)

surface they may appear to be quite different from each other; but when one delves below the surface, one can see that they are all built on the same foundation.

"All is one" is the common theme that unites all these religions. They believe that god is in everything, **and** that everything is god. Notice that I spelled "god" with a small "g."

One of the basic human weaknesses is to want to be like God, or rather to be our own god.   Again, this was the deception in the Garden of Eden when the serpent tempted Eve with the statement, *For God knows that in the day you eat of it your eyes will be opened, and* <u>*you will be like God*</u>*, knowing good and evil* (Genesis 3:5, underlining is mine).   And, of course, both she and Adam believed this deception of Satan and disobeyed God.   Presumably there was something about being like God that was attractive to them, and this tendency is a part of humanity to this very moment.

Christianity recognizes the one sovereign God, while the New Age sees man as god.   As a part of this, the New Age doesn't see man as having a sin nature, but as only needing to realize who they really are inside, and then awakening that potential.[206]   Christianity, of course, recognizes both the image of God in us, and our sin nature.   In the New Age, we are our own redeemer.[207]   In

---

[205] "The New Age and secular humanism are more like cousins than strangers . . . Our salvation, for the secular humanist comes through rational inquiry and the development of science . . . 'reason and intelligence are the most effective instruments humankind possesses' . . . The materialism of secular humanism is being usurped by the mysticism of the One. Yet both look to humanity for the answer, not to anything outside us" (Groothuis, pp. 52-53)

[206] Speaking of Carl Rogers, "For Rogers, as for many theorists within the enlightenment tradition, the inherent wisdom and goodness of the self (or any part thereof) is self-evident truth, almost a metaphysical first principle.' The revolt against the Freudian abyss and the Skinnerian machinery produced an equally unbalanced deification of the 'real self' (however that is to be found)" (Groothuis, p.83).

[207] Quoting Francis Adeney, a New Age author: " 'Once we begin to see that we are all God, that we all have the attributes of God, then I think the whole purpose of human life is to re-own the Godlikeness within us; the perfect love, the perfect wisdom, the perfect understanding, the perfect intelligence, and when we do that, we create back to that old, that essential one-ness which is consciousness' " (Groothuis, p.14).

Quoting Shirley MacLaine from her book, <u>Out on a Limb</u>: "Her 'search for identity' has led her to affirm that 'nothing is more powerful than the collective human mind.' Her central message is fourfold: first, you are all gods (although you might be ignorant of it); second, you have lived before and will live again; third, there is no death ('Perhaps our belief in death is the greatest unreality of all'); fourth, there are as many realities as there are people since we create our own reality" (Groothuis, p.15).

Christianity, Jesus is the only Redeemer, and we need Him to change us into His image.

Satan Is The God Of This World

Jesus made it very clear that there are only two sides to the cosmic war going on here on earth.

> *"He who is not with Me is against Me, and he who does not gather with Me scatters abroad"* (Matthew 12:30).

Therefore it is important to keep in mind that all of the religions that are not of the God of Abraham, Isaac, and Jacob are demonic. When we open the door to such beliefs by following some of their teachings, we invite Satan in. He can then deceive and mislead and destroy through his power, which is significant (though less than the power of God).[208] When we open the door to his power and authority, we are in great danger. This is why it is so very important to stay away from the New Age practice of "visualization." It has been presented to the psychotherapy community as a secular and scientific method, and it seems harmless. But it is not neutral. There is no such thing as "neutral." If it is not of God, it is of the world and Satan.

> **In the New age, we are our own redeemer. In Christianity, Jesus is the only Redeemer, and we need Him to change us into His image.**

---

[208] Some other non-Christian (and therefore demonic) occult practices besides the New Age, Secular Humanism, Buddhism, and Hinduism which I have mentioned previously, are Islam, Jehovah's Witness, Mormonism, the Masonic and other secret societies, The Grange, Astrology, Wicca, Hare Krishna, Yoga, Bahai, Transcendental Meditation, EST, Eckankar, Astrology, Unity, Unitarianism, Unification Church, Witchcraft, Satanism, and others. Some of these seem innocent on the surface, or are presented to us as not being religions. But they are all of Satan and rely on his power.

Specific Issues I Will Address

There are several seeming similarities between Christianity and the New Age. Some of the terms and concepts the New Age uses that on the surface seem similar to what I teach are:

1. Visualization
2. Looking inside
3. Our Inner Child
4. The idea that we can change.

1. Visualization

We experience the most profound healing when we come into the presence of Jesus. I try to bring people to the point that they can see what Jesus is doing inside them, and what their Treasure Inside is doing. Then, when Jesus does something, or says something to them, they are blessed and healed by this.

The New Age uses the term "visualization," also referred to as "guided imagery." In this process, a leader brings a person to a meditative state, and then presents a picture for the person to envision on the screen of their mind. Then they lead the person through an internal experience, sort of like a daydream.[209] This is dangerous, because it opens up the person to deception by demons.[210]

---

[209] "Guided imagery in the classroom is dangerous because it teaches children a way of dealing with problems that leaves God out of the picture." Quoting an actual experience of a pastor's son in school, 'She had them lie on the floor, close their eyes, breathe deeply, and count backward from ten. She then described a journey in which they were walking through a lovely meadow' " (Note that the teacher was describing the journey). 'They walked up the hillside and sprouted wings out their backs. They flew away to a cave; they walked into the cave and saw three doors. They opened one door and the room was filled with their 'heart's desire.' That room was to go to anytime (they were) under stress." (Martin, pp.59-60).

[210] "Guided imagery can also open us up to counterfeit christs, or 'angels of light' (cf. 2 Cor. 11:14). . . An elaborate visualization exercise could induce an altered state of consciousness quite amenable to demonic insurgents. Shakti Gawain, for instance, says that 'creative visualization' can easily introduce one to 'spirit guides,' the likes of which would be thrilled to meet us' " (Martin, p.60).

The fundamental difference between the Christian healing prayer and the New Age approach is that in Christian healing prayer it is the living Lord Jesus that leads the way. If He doesn't do anything, or the person can't see Him doing anything, nothing happens. If this is the case, either the Lord doesn't have anything to say right then; or much more likely, the person has The Wall inside that prevents the individual from the personal relationship with Jesus that is needed in order to experience His presence. It is exactly because of the dangers of crossing the line into New Age visualization that I have emphasized the importance of prayer partners keeping out of the process, of restraining themselves from suggesting anything they think should be happening.

In the New Age approach, the fatal flaw is that it is of man, not of Jesus. The leader, a human being, is leading the event.

2. Looking Inside, and
3. Our Inner Child

A second area of surface similarity relates to the existence of an inner life within us. I have taught that the core of our being, the essence of who we really are, is inside us. That portion of which we are conscious is only a small portion of our essence, and we need to be best friends with the portion of us that exists in our Treasure Inside. The part of us that we need to be best friends with is that part of us made in the image of God.

> **In Christianity, inside ourselves we encounter the image of God.**
> **In New Age belief, inside ourselves we encounter our own deity.**

But there is also a sin nature somewhere inside us, and we also have places of darkness (the Honeycomb) that desperately need to be transformed by the cleansing blood of Jesus, and then infused with His presence.[211]

The New Age also says that we need to look inside. However, they contend that when we look inside we will encounter our own deity.[212] They believe that our "inner child" is perfect, and our problem is that we have lost track of our own deity.[213]

4. The Idea That We Can Change

We do need to be changed, and that can happen. I contend that the only way we can be changed is by the blood of Jesus. We cannot do it ourselves. In fact, to think we can do so is sin. If we could change ourselves, then Jesus died in vain. The only way that there will be good fruit in our life is when He comes to live in those previously dark places. The goal of our life is

> **In Christianity, we are to be changed into the image of Jesus by His blood and cross.**
>
> **In New Age belief, we change ourselves.**

---

[211] "But as Abraham Kuyper pointed out, 'according to all sound expositors, this means only that unto the sinner are imparted the attributes of goodness and holiness, which he originally possessed in his own nature in common with the divine nature, but which was lost by sin . . . But this may not be understood as obliterating the boundary between the divine nature and the human.' Salvation is not deification; redeemed humanity should never be confused with divinity" (Groothuis, p.172).

[212] Discussing a program in a California school district: "The program includes yoga, biofeedback and guided imagery. Part of its game plan is 'to introduce the children to the Inner Self – the self that can guide them in making decisions or in knowing what is true and good' "(Groothuis, p.124).

[213] "The Christian during contemplation would never say, 'I am Christ,' but will confess with Paul: 'Not I, but Christ liveth in me' (Gal. 2:20). Our sutra (Buddhist writing) however says: 'Thou will know that *thou* art the Buddha' " (Groothuis, p.142).

to be changed into the image of Jesus from glory to glory, even by the Spirit of the Lord. However, we will always retain the fatal flaws of our fallen nature. Thus we will continue to sin and be in constant need of our Redeemer.

The New Agers agrees that we need to change, but believe we change ourselves.[214] They say that since we are god, we have within us all that is needed to bring about the change. To be changed we simply have to see who we really are inside and release that part of us. This is the heresy of works salvation and results in striving and failure.

We Need To Be Ever Vigilant

Recently I was in a large secular bookstore waiting for my wife. To kill some time I went to a section of the store marked "Religion." I picked up a book with an intriguing title and began to thumb through it. The author wrote about how in our culture we had been taught to ignore our real self that resides inside us, and we need to reconnect with that part. I was thinking, "Wow, this sounds really good." However, as I continued to thumb through the book I discovered that the author was a Buddhist and he was advocating Buddhism!

New Age thinking is all around us. Their advocates can use attractive terminology, and on the surface things may seem to make sense. However, there is always the fatal flaw of "The One" (god is in everything and everything is god), though it is often cleverly disguised and buried. It is a counterfeit, and all counterfeits are meant to look a lot like the real thing. In order to deceive people, a counterfeit $100 bill has to look an awful lot like the real thing. There are no counterfeit $40 bills, because there are no real ones; thus they would not deceive anybody.

When you think about the New Age, do not think, "How could anybody be so stupid as to believe this." I once thought this way,

---

[214] "The old lie remains intact: we are gods and need no divine authority; we control our own destiny" (Groothuis, p.129).

but on a few occasions the Lord allowed me to be deceived for a short time. I was deceived. I was blinded. [215] Satan has power. I felt the power of the principality, and I was temporarily blinded. Now I know how clever and seductive are these traps of Satan. I am sure many New Age books are intentionally written to draw in the unsuspecting.

So do not be naïve. Since Satan is the master of deceit, his clever disguises may be difficult to discern.[216] Be vigilant and test all things. Listen to the Lord in all the many ways He speaks.[217] Fortunately, you are not in this war alone. The Lord will be your guide if you will seek His wisdom, because He doesn't want you led astray.

Summary

┌───┐
The Fundamental Difference:
- **Christianity is of God.**
- **The New Age is of man (and therefore under the influence of Satan).**
└───┘

At the root level, the teaching in this book (Christianity) and the New Age are fundamentally and irrevocably different.

- Though there is agreement that there is a transcendent spiritual world, Christianity says the God of Abraham, Isaac, and Jacob is

---

[215] See Endnote #Appendix D-1 for an experience that I had in being deceived.

[216] *"For false christs and false prophets will arise and show great signs and wonders, so as to deceive, if possible, even the elect."* (Matthew 24:24).

For many deceivers have gone out into the world who do not confess Jesus Christ as coming in the flesh. This is a deceiver and an antichrist (2 John 7).

[217] Some of the ways He speaks are through His Spirit in you, the Word of God, wise counsel, testimonies of others, even circumstances. The many ways that the Lord speaks, and learning how to discern His voice, are beyond the scope of this book. There are many good books on this subject, because it is an important aspect of the Christian life.

the only God. He created all things by His word, and He sent His only begotten Son, Jesus, to redeem us. In opposition to this the New Age says that we are god; and that everything is god.

- There is an agreement that there is a reality inside us, but the view of <u>what</u> that reality consists of is totally different. Christianity says that inside, below our level of consciousness, we consist of areas that are in the image of God, and other areas that are fallen. The New Age says that inside we are god, and the "good" is already in us just waiting to be released. They deny the very existence of Satan and of evil.

- Though there is an agreement that there is a need for us to be changed, the mechanisms that produce the change are totally different. Christianity says that only Jesus can change us, and He is the only Redeemer. In fact, it is sin for us to think that we can obtain righteousness through our own strength. On the other hand, the New Age says that we change ourselves. We are our own redeemer.   "Unlike New Age philosophy, Christianity teaches that corruption, not salvation, comes from within. We need to look beyond ourselves to become better selves"[218]

---

[218] Groothuis, p.171.

Appendix E - Endnotes

Endnote for "Acknowledgements" Endnote # A-1

The Influence Of Rudolf Bultmann

Rudolf Bultmann has been an inspiration to me. He has provided me with a firm biblical foundation for a great deal of what I will be saying. Several years ago I began to read his book, Theology of the New Testament (published in 1955) which I had bought for $1.00 at a Denver Seminary book sale. I knew that he was one of the most well respected theologians of the twentieth century, but had never read any of his writings. I was so blessed as he brilliantly opened up the Word of God. I have found him to be in a class by himself in his understanding of the New Testament, and in his ability to explain seemingly complicated theological concepts.

Some theologians are suspicious of Inner Healing. It was not even mentioned in my seminary studies. At that time I was a little shaken because it seemed to me that some of the scriptural proofs written by the advocates of Inner Healing were at times a bit shallow. And though I had personally experienced some wonderful healing in my heart through Inner Healing ministry, I sometimes wondered if perhaps the critics had some good reasons for their position. After all, we need to have full assurance that what we believe and teach is based upon the truth. God makes it clear that those who teach need to be very careful. I didn't want to lead even one of His sheep astray.

I was a bit astonished to find in Bultmann's books deep proofs of the views on Inner Healing that I had been taught. I found it to be very assuring, and to some degree surprising, that Bultmann came to many of the same conclusions about the spiritual realities that God has provided for us, while approaching the Word from a very different orientation. He was neither charismatic nor was he involved in counseling, and I suspect he was not even aware that he was providing a biblical proof of what we know as Inner Healing. To me that is a very powerful witness to the truth.

Bultmann's brilliant analysis of the Word of God has dispelled all my doubts about Inner Healing (which the Bible refers to as "sanctification"). His deep insights have given me a greater appreciation for how deeply sanctification runs throughout the New Testament. It absolutely permeates the Word of God! His insights have enhanced my understanding of the scriptural foundation for Inner Healing. The Bible gives us a solid assurance that "Inner Healing" is truly provided for us.

Endnotes for Chapter 1
"Will Give You Rest"

Endnote #1-1

Salvation Is Also For This Life

According to Rudolf Bultmann, the Scripture makes it clear that "salvation" is not only for the future life but is also for this life. There grew in the Church the conception that baptism wiped away our prior sins, but now it was up to us to live a Christian life. The loss of the awareness that Jesus' sacrifice was also to empower us in this life happened very early in the Church. In fact, there is evidence in the New Testament itself of a drift into the misperception. Regarding the drift away from the true Gospel:

> "The problem of Christian living, among other problems, was present to the Church from the beginning . . . The question was whether or not this understanding would be retained – whether Christian freedom would be understood as the freedom to obey, obedience itself then being understood as the gift of grace or of the Spirit, or whether obedience would be conceived as an accomplishment and hence as the condition to be fulfilled in order to obtain salvation . . . The man who is purified from his former guilt has henceforth the chance of a new beginning but is now left to rely on his own strength to become worthy of the coming salvation by his obedience. The knowledge that the gift of grace (Paul) or of God's love (John) makes a man radically new is lost. Gone is the knowledge that a man without God's grace is a victim to the power of sin and death, that he has lost his freedom and is living in disobedience to God even if his conduct be correct, because God's law is to him a means of asserting himself before God. Vanished is the knowledge that his release from the powers that controlled him is a release to genuine obedience, but that he is never cast loose from the giving and forgiving grace of God nor left to rely upon his own strength" (Bultmann, Theology of the New Testament, Part IV, pp.203-204).

Referring to the gradual change in emphasis in Christian writing regarding the Church:

> "While the consciousness of being a non-worldly society belonging to the other world and filled with its powers does not actually get lost, it nevertheless suffers a peculiar transformation . . . Of course, that reference to the future does not get lost, but it too becomes peculiarly modified. The future salvation

toward which hope is directed comes to be seen less in the completion of the history of salvation and the transformation of the world at the dawn of the new age (as in Rom. 9-11 and 8:19-22) than in the future life of the individual beyond death . . . Correspondingly, the meaning of the sacraments comes to be seen in the fact that they mediate the powers of the future life to the individual . . . But the more the Christian's new way of life comes to be understood not as the demonstration of the new (eschatological) existence but as the condition for achieving future salvation . . . the more this reference to the future loses the meaning it had had in Paul; the dialectic relation between indicative and imperative** . . . is surrendered. Then the effect of baptism is limited to forgiveness of the sins committed in one's pre-Christian period, and the problem of sins committed after baptism arises . . . " (Bultmann, Theology of the New Testament, Vol. III, pp. 112-113).

** Note that when Bultmann refers to the "Indicative" and the "Imperative" he is referring to elements of Greek grammar. He is saying that the fact that obeying God (the "imperative" means a command) is dependent upon a work of God that has already happened in us (the "indicative" means a statement of fact).

Endnotes for Chapter 2
"Why You Are Stuck"

Endnote #2-1

We Need A Better Righteousness (Matthew 5:20-5:48)

There is a great tragedy that has gone on in much of the Church as I have experienced it. This tragedy relates to a misunderstanding of Matthew, Chapter 5. Verse 20 says, *"For I say to you, unless your righteousness exceeds the righteousness of the scribes and Pharisees, you will by no means enter the kingdom of heaven."* Then Jesus talks about a series of admonitions in the law, and then He compares those admonitions to the real truth; which has a much higher demand.

For example, verse 27 says: *"You have heard that it was said to those of old, 'You shall not commit adultery', but I say to you that whoever looks at a woman to lust for her has already committed adultery with her in his heart."*

What I was taught, and what I believed for a long time, was that Jesus was saying that I was held to a higher level of accountability than they who were under the Old Testament; because I now have Jesus in my heart.

Is this good news? Does this sound like a covenant with better promises (Hebrews 8:6)? As a matter of fact, it sounds like a bigger burden! Those who taught me to try hard were actually inadvertently admonishing me to sin!

When I was a new Christian, I worked for an aircraft manufacturing company. My desk was in a large open area with many desks, and right up in front of me was a large clock with a sweep second hand. I decided I needed a closer walk with the Lord; so told Him that every 15 minutes I would just turn my thoughts towards Him and say something like, "Hello, Lord": a very simple prayer. What happened to me over and over is that I would get busy; and then I'd look up at the clock and realize it had been two hours since I prayed that simple prayer! And it wasn't that I was offering my body to be burned, or committing to go to Africa as a missionary, or volunteering to lie on a bed of spikes. I was just going to offer up a three-second prayer, and I couldn't even do that. I felt like such a total failure. And to make things worse, the harder I tried, the more I failed.

Referring back to Matthew, Chapter 5, let me use a metaphor here. In high jumping I don't believe anybody has ever jumped over 8 feet. So let's say that the law is that high jump bar set at 8 feet. As Paul said, nobody ever kept the law. Metaphorically, they never jumped over 8 feet. So according to the view that we are now held to a higher standard, Jesus comes along and says, "I have such Good News for you. I'm going to raise the bar to 10 feet. Now see if you can jump over that!" I would submit to you that a statement like this would not be in line with Jesus' character. Therefore, something must be wrong with this interpretation of what He said.

Fortunately, this greater demand is not what Jesus is saying at all. He tells us about it in verse 48, *"Therefore you shall be perfect, just as your Father in heaven is perfect."* I had been taught, and I have read that scripture to say, "Therefore, you shall <u>behave</u> perfectly (obey these laws just listed) just as your Father in heaven is perfect." But that's not what that scripture says. It says, *"you shall <u>be</u> perfect."* The Greek word that is here translated as "be" (*esomai*) has its root in a Greek word meaning: "I exist" (*eimi*). Jesus is talking about who we <u>are</u>, not what we <u>do</u>.

This gets clearer if we go back to Matthew 5:20. There Jesus is quoted as saying, *"For I say to you, that unless your righteousness exceeds the righteousness of the scribes and Pharisees . . ."* As we talked about a little earlier, what was the righteousness of the scribes and Pharisees? It was their own <u>willpower</u>. So, what Jesus is saying is that you need a righteousness that exceeds your own <u>willpower</u>. You need a provision that will <u>change your very nature</u> so that you can <u>become</u> like Jesus, not just try to <u>act</u> like Him.

To try to keep these commandments with my willpower is not just foolish, it is sin! So those of you that are trying to be a good Christian out of your own willpower, <u>stop it</u>!

Further Commentary On Matthew 5:20-48

There exists in theological thinking five views of what these verses might mean (Hulbert, Lessons 67 and 68):

1. This is a way of salvation – the works get us into the Kingdom.
2. Penitential – these are a way that God convicts of sin.
3. Ecclesiastical – these are moral standards for believers in the Church. The Sermon on the Mount is seen as a complete compendium of the standards for a Christian's life.
4. Eschatological – this only applies in the future Kingdom age.
5. Contextually – who is the audience, and what is their need? In this view the purpose is to point out that the standards of the scribes and Pharisees fall short of the Kingom's standards. They need a righteousness that exceeds what they have been trying to do.

For several reasons, the contextual argument seems the strongest. The key point behind it is that their behavior is the **evidence**, not the **basis** of, their righteousness.

Endnote #2-2

God Does Not Strengthen Our Will

"We choose to do the right thing in situations and trust God's Spirit to give us his power, love, faith, and wisdom to do it . . . Your character is essentially the sum of your habits; it is how you *habitually* act" (Warren, p.174, 175).

These views expressed in this popular book are in direct opposition to what I am teaching, and to what the Scripture teaches. We cannot <u>choose</u> (will power), and our character is not the sum of habits, or how we habitually act. Our character is who we <u>are</u>, not what we <u>do</u>. Christ-like character comes about through a miracle of God, as He comes to abide in us in the exact area where we had previously harbored sin. Our besetting problems (Romans 7:15) are not the result of habits (the psychological realm). They are the results of the reaping from God's laws (the spiritual realm). Our will power and habits are puny in the face of the reaping.

In my experience, Mr. Warren's view sets a person to striving with their will power, because they don't know if God has strengthened their will <u>enough</u> through their prayer. When they try, they will of course still fail. They will fail because, as I have just said, God does not strengthen a person's will. But because of what Mr. Warren wrote, the person thinks they didn't pray hard enough. So they pray again, and try again. They are again defeated, over and over, which is a tragic result.

I have clients who had this exact experience when they studied <u>The Purpose Driven Life</u> and tried to apply it.

His view makes it seem like there is a "fine line" between striving (which is sin) and God strengthening our will. Being in this position is dangerous, because striving to keep the law in our own strength is sin (See Chapter 13, "The Bad Part Of You). If we try and fail, not only have we not prayed hard enough, we have just sinned. This is a very unsatisfactory place to put a person. If we pray effectually enough, (according to Mr. Warren's view), we can obey God. If we don't pray effectually enough, we actually compound our sin.

I have found that there is <u>never</u> a "fine line" between darkness and light, between evil and good, between sin and obedience. If we ever think there is, we are missing something in our understanding. There is not a "fine line" between keeping the law in our own strength (sin) and praying and having Jesus replace the bad root with a good root (which is what I propose, and what I think the scriptures say).

Endnote #2-3

The Illusion Of Our Will, Romans, Chapter 7

As I have said, one of the great tragedies in our Western culture is the elevation of our willpower and our intellect to the throne. In reality, they have become our gods, and we think that the only things that we can trust are these two faculties. The heart, and anything that we cannot consciously understand or control (such as our emotions) are seen as untrustworthy, or even perhaps bad.   But that was not how Jesus saw it, nor was it how He lived. We are immersed in Western thinking (rational, linear thinking), and this is our undoing. Mankind has always had a propensity to want to do it themselves - with their own willpower, and Western culture has become very extreme in this delusion

The Apostle Paul wrote eloquently about this dilemma in Romans, Chapter 7. This is a chapter in Scripture that used to puzzle me greatly. The one part that I understood well was the part referred to earlier in this chapter, . . . *for what I am doing I do not understand for, what I will to do, that I do not practice; but what I hate that I do. If, then, I do what I will not to do, I agree with the law that it is good; but it is no longer I who do it, but sin that dwells in me* (verse 15). This certainly lines up with my experience in life. I felt like the wretched man that Paul refers to in verse 24.

Keep in mind that the entirety of Romans, Chapter 7, is on one topic, and this fact made it even more mysterious to me. Paul says,

What shall we say? Is the law sin? Certainly not. On the contrary, I would not have known sin except through the law. For I would not have known covetousness unless the law had said, 'You shall not covet'. But sin, taking the opportunity by the commandment, produced in me all manner of evil desire. For apart from the law, sin was dead. I was alive once without the law, but when the commandment came, sin revived and I died. And the commandment which was to bring life, I found to bring death (Romans 7:7-10).

At this point I used to say, "Paul, you don't get it. You must have lived on another planet. This isn't at all how it worked for me."   Before I was saved, I sinned plenty. I didn't know what the commandments were, and I didn't care. I didn't need the law to prompt me to sin" (which is what I thought Paul was saying here).

Then one day the Lord showed me (with the help of Rudolf Bultmann) that keeping the law has to do with the <u>willpower</u>, and this was what Paul was talking about. Paul had been a Pharisee. The Pharisees were the best law keepers that ever existed. They lived in communities where they held each other accountable. You had to be an exceptional Jew to even get into the community. And yet Paul said that <u>no one</u> ever kept the law, . . . *even we have believed in Christ Jesus, that we might be justified by faith in Christ and not by the works of the law; for by the works of the law no flesh shall be justified* (Galatians 2:16).

What "tool" were the Pharisees using to try to obey God's laws? They were using their willpower. That is what Paul is referring to here. He says: *"And the commandment which was to bring life, I found to bring death. For sin, taking occasion by the commandment, deceived me and by it killed me"* (verse 10).

The Trap

This, as I now see it, definitely mirrored my experience. When I was in my early 30's, I decided to follow Jesus. When I decided that He really is who He says He is, I wanted to please Him. So what did I do? I did exactly what everybody does: I decided to obey Him.

Amazingly, this is the exact problem. This is the trap we all fall into. Does it sound strange to call this desire to obey Him a "trap?" *Because they did not seek it by faith, but as it were, by works of the law. For they stumbled at that stumbling stone* (Romans 9:32). The problem came about because I decided to obey him - with my willpower. Of course I did. I didn't know of anything else to use. I had been raised by my parents, and influenced by our culture, to think this was all that was available. But much more than this, there is something in us human beings that wants to be like God, to have control, to do it ourselves. This is why this trap is so universal. This is why we automatically decide to do it ourselves.

So, if we re-read these scriptures with the awareness that the trap of the law is our willpower, it all makes sense. Paul knew we couldn't do it. God knows we can't do it. If we could do it ourselves, we wouldn't need Jesus! *But sin, taking opportunity by the commandment, produced in me all manner of evil desire; for apart from the law, sin was dead* (Romans 7:11). What Paul is saying is that when I found out what the law required, what the command was, it automatically rose up within me to do it myself. And that was evil desire.

I believe that implantation of this tendency to rely on my own strength is one of the things that happened at The Fall in the Garden of Eden. When we determine to do it ourselves with our own willpower, we are determining to be our own God. Isn't this part of the temptation to Eve? Satan said, *." . . you will be like God, knowing good and evil"* (Genesis 3:5).

We are deluded into thinking we can do it ourselves. And I can tell you how deadly it is to "try," as Paul refers to in the next verse (Romans 7:11), *For sin, taking occasion by the commandment, deceived me and by it killed me.*

It Killed Me!

I was "killed" by this trap. As a new Christian, I wanted to obey the Lord, and so I tried very hard to keep His commands. But the harder I tried, the worse I did. I couldn't understand it, because I was trying soooo hard. "Surely there must be something wrong with me," I thought. To make things worse, nobody else seemed to be able to tell me how I could do better.

The Answer

The first part of Romans, Chapter 7, contains the answer, but it is even more mysterious, *For the woman who has a husband is bound by the law to her husband as long as he lives. But if the husband dies, she is released from the law of her husband. So then if, while her husband lives, she marries another man, she will be called an adulteress. But if her husband dies, she is free from that law, so she is no adulteress though she has married another man* (verses 2-3).

What in the world does divorce and adultery have to do with the topic of the chapter? On the surface it seems alien to the rest of Paul's thought. But here's what it means: when a person gets married, a legal transaction occurs in the spiritual realm. The two people become one; and so, if she marries another man while this covenant is still in force, she is an adulteress.

But when her husband dies, a legal transaction takes place in the spirit realm, and she's not married to him anymore. The marriage covenant is no longer in force, and so she's free to marry another man.

Verse four says, *Therefore, my brethren, you also have become dead to the law through the body of Christ, that you may be married to another, even to him who was raised from the dead, that we should bear fruit to God*. Here this entire issue of marriage and divorce is simply a metaphor that Paul is using. He is saying that we need a legal transaction to occur in the spiritual realm for us to be set free from our reaping (the things we don't want to do). The operation of the law against us was a legal transaction that occurred in the spiritual realm. We sinned, and that set the law in motion. The only legal transaction that will stop the reaping is the blood and the cross of Jesus. He needs to pay the price for our sin, so that we can be set free from the reaping in the spiritual realm. Again, keep in mind that there may still be consequences that we will have to endure in the natural world resulting from prior sins. For example, if we commit adultery and our spouse divorces us, our family is now still fractured.

In A Nutshell

Romans, Chapter 7, can then be summarized in a few sentences. "You need a legal transaction to take place in the spirit realm for you to be set free from the law of reaping (verses 1-6). You've been trying to do it with your own willpower (verses 7-13). And it doesn't work, does it (verses 14-24)! The answer is, through Jesus Christ our Lord's provision (verse 25)."

So God always knew that I couldn't keep the law. He knows that I will fail when I try to do it myself, and I am sure it grieves Him when He sees me try, and fail, and try, and fail, again and again.

The chapters in Romans which follow, as well as Paul's other epistles, are a description of how we can be victorious. My book is meant to bring out in modern English what he wrote.

For a detailed theological discussion of this issue, read Theology of the New Testament by Rudolf Bultmann, pp. 263-269.

Endnote #2-4

God's Plan and The Law

The spiritual realm has always operated in accordance with unchanging principles. Prior to God giving the Ten Commandments to Moses, people just didn't know what those principles were. Each culture created its own standards. For instance, I am aware of a tribe in Papua New Guinea who saw lying as good, and being deceitful to your enemy so you could kill him as being the highest morality. They were almost destroyed as a people, because the spiritual realm inescapably brings destruction if we lie or murder. This happens whether or not we are aware of the principles of the spiritual realm.

The Law that God gave to Moses was given so that people would know how the spiritual realm operates, for cursing or for blessing. However, then people still had to keep the Law with their own willpower. Nobody ever succeeded.

Then Jesus came and provided a way by which we could be set free from this bondage to the Law. He would pay the price for our sins, and provided a way that we could be changed into His image so that we would sin less often.

Satan immediately began to attack this law of liberty to bring people back into bondage to the Law. He knew that it was deadly for us to try to keep the Law in our own strength. The Epistles were written specifically to counteract this attempt to destroy what Jesus did to save His people. Unfortunately, shortly after the death of the Apostles the church by and large went back into bondage to legalism and has remained there for 1900 years.

God doesn't want us to remain in that bondage. He wants us to live in the "new and living way" that He provided for us in Christ Jesus.

Endnotes for Chapter 3
"Remove All The Bad Roots"

Endnote #3-1

God Will Change Us From The Inside

God makes it clear that in the New Covenant He promises to equip us to be like Him, and thus able to act like Him.

Read all of Ezekiel 11:17-20, 36:22-27, Jeremiah 31:29-34, 32:26-41, and Psalms 51:1-12 in order to see the whole story and to understand the context. I will include some small excerpts below. God says, over and over, "I will". He does not say "you must," because He knows we can't do it. He will do it in and through us.

Therefore say to the house of Israel, "This is what the Sovereign Lord says: it is not for your sake, O house of Israel, that I am going to do these things, but for the sake of my; holy name, which you have profaned among the nations where you have gone. I will show the holiness of my great name, which has been profaned among the nations, the name you have profaned among them. **Then the nations will know that I am the Lord***, declares the Sovereign Lord,* **when I show myself holy through you** *before their eyes. For I will take you out of the nations; I will gather you from all the countries and bring you back into your own land. I will sprinkle clean water on you, and you will be clean; I will cleanse you from all your impurities and from all your idols. I will give you a new heart and put a new spirit in you; I will remove from you your heart of stone and give you a heart of flesh.* **And I will put my spirit in you and move you to follow my decrees and be careful to keep my laws"***(Ezekiel 36:22-27, NIV, bold is mine).*

The last sentence is clarified by the New King James Version: **I will put My spirit within you __and cause you__ to walk in My statutes, and you will keep My judgments and do them** (Ezekiel 36:27, NKJV, underline and bold is mine).

I will take away the stony heart out of their flesh and give them a heart of flesh; **so that** *they may follow My statutes and keep My ordinances and obey them* (Ezekiel 11:19-20, Berkeley, bold is mine).

See, the days are coming, says the Lord, when I will make **a new covenant** *with the house of Israel and the house of Judah, not like the covenant that I made with their fathers . . . But this is the covenant that I will make with the house of Israel after those days, says the Lord:* **I will put my law in their inward parts***, and upon* *their hearts will I write it . . . for I will forgive their iniquity and their sin will I remember no more* (Jeremiah 31:31-34, Berkeley, bold is mine).

Endnote #3-2

Trying Hard Is Not Simply Ineffective

At first glance, it would appear that trying to stop the reaping from God's law with my willpower is simply foolish; but it is much more than this. **It is sin!** Bultmann writes:

> ". . . whether the sphere of the natural-earthly, which is also that of the transitory and perishable, is the world out of which a man thinks he derives his life and by means of which he thinks he maintains it. This self-delusion is not merely an error, but sin, because it is a turning away from the Creator, the giver of life, and a turning toward the creation – and to do that is to trust in one's self as being able to procure life by the use of the earthly and through one's own strength and accomplishment. It is in this sense, then, that 'fixing the mind on the things of flesh' is to be at war against God (Romans 8:7).
>
> The sinful self-delusion that one lives out of the created world can manifest itself both in unthinking recklessness (this especially among the Gentiles) and in considered busy-ness (this especially among Jews) – both in the ignoring or transgressing of ethical demands and in excessive zeal to fulfill them. For the sphere of 'flesh' is by no means just the life of instinct or sensual passions, but is just as much that of the moral and religious efforts of man" (Bultmann, Theology of the New Testament, Part II, p.239).

So, perhaps shockingly, when I go to a seminar and learn new tools to change my relationship with my wife, and I try real hard to change the destructive patterns going on in our relationship, I am not just engaged in futility, I am in sin! Instead, I need the blood and the cross of Jesus to change me inside, and thus change our relationship.

In The Bondage of the Will, Martin Luther wrote an entire book on the subject of the impotence of our willpower in the spiritual realm. It is somewhat tedious reading, but he makes some very powerful statements about this subject.

Endnote #3-3

A Common Misperception-Is God Telling Us To Work Hard To Be Approved?

It is easy to read many scriptures in such a way that we think they are telling us to work hard so that we will be approved by God. The book of James has many such passages, and 1 Corinthians 3:9-16 can also be so interpreted:

> *For we are God's fellow workers; you are God's field, <u>you are God's building</u>. According to the grace of God which was given to me, as a wise master builder I have laid the foundation, and another builds on it. But let each one take heed how he builds on it. For no other foundation can anyone lay than that which is laid, which is Jesus Christ. Now if anyone builds on this foundation with gold, silver, precious stones, wood, hay, straw, each one's work will become manifest; for the Day will declare it, because it will be revealed by fire; and the fire will test each one's <u>work</u>, of what sort it is. If anyone's <u>work</u> which he has built on it endures, he will receive a reward. If anyone's <u>work</u> is burned, he will suffer loss; but he himself will be saved, yet so as through fire. Do you not know that <u>you are the temple of God</u> and that the Spirit of God dwells in you?* (Underlining is mine).

Notice that when Paul uses the word "work" he is referring to the <u>structure</u> that has been built on the foundation, not the <u>effort</u>. This is clearly stated in verse 9, *you are God's building.* What could be clearer than that? What the Lord is building is His temple. As is stated in verse 16, *you are the temple of God.* <u>You are His temple</u>. Isn't that amazing? These scriptures have typically been interpreted as referring to what we <u>do</u> for God, instead of what we are to <u>become</u>. **See Chapter 6 for more detail on this.**

Endnote #3-4

"Symptom" (Fruit) Versus "Cause" (Root).

We can confuse "symptom" with "cause" in the Sermon on the Mount. We can think that God is commanding us to <u>do</u> certain things by scriptures such as:

> *"Not everyone who says to Me, 'Lord, Lord' shall enter the kingdom of heaven, but he who does the will of My Father in heaven . . . And then I will declare to them, 'I never knew you; depart from Me, you who practice lawlessness!'"* (Matthew 7:21,23).

"Now everyone who hears these sayings of Mine, and does not do them, will be like a foolish man who built his house on sand; and the rain descended, the floods came, and the winds blew and beat on that house; and it fell, and great was its fall" (Matthew 7:26).

Therefore, to him who knows to do good and does not do it, to him it is sin (James 4:17).

It sure sounds like God is commanding us to do certain things, doesn't it? And there are many, many scriptures that are worded like this.

But Jesus just finished saying that we could not do these things by our willpower (controlling or suppressing the symptom in our own strength). We can only do these things if we "be" like Jesus, as stated in Matthew 5:48 (changing the cause). So these types of scriptures are just making a statement of fact: if we are like Jesus, we will behave like Him. We can observe the condition of our heart by what we do. The only way to change what we do is to change the condition of our heart, not through our own effort.

This can be illustrated in the above three scriptures. In Matthew 7:21-23, quoted above, when we find ourselves acting like Him, and are no longer lawless (the symptom), this is evidence that we have entered the Kingdom of heaven; and we will have a righteousness that exceeds the righteousness of the scribes and Pharisees, because we have been changed into His image in that place in our heart (the cause).

In Matthew 7:25 quoted above, if the wind and rain do not wash away our house (the symptom), this is evidence that we have built our house on the Rock (the cause).

In James 4:17 quoted above, if we don't do the good that we know to do (the symptom), then this is evidence that there is sin in our heart (the cause).

The behavior, sinful or righteous, is simply outward evidence of what is inside. We have believed, and lived, as though the Christian life is from the outside-in, when in reality, it is inside-out.

1 John 2:29, in the interlinear translation by Berry, *Ye know that everyone who practices righteousness of him has been begotten.* Rienecker states the following about the tense of *has been begotten,* "perfect passive indicative (of) to bear, passive to be borne. The child exhibits the parents' character because he shares the parents' nature (Stott)" (Rienecker, p.789).

Endnote #3-5

The Title Of The Book Explained

The title of this book and Matthew 11:28-30 are probably now clearer to you. You cannot carry this burden of keeping the law by your willpower. That is a terrible burden, and is fatiguing to try to carry it yourself. Jesus wants to carry that burden for you.

> *Come to Me, all you who labor and are heavy laden, and I will give you rest.*
> *Take My yoke upon you and learn from Me, for I am gentle and lowly in heart, and you will find rest for your souls.*
> *For My yoke is easy, and My burden is light* (Matthew 11:28-30, NKJV).

The Greek words for "labor" and "heavy laden" are very revealing of the true meaning of the verses.

The Greek word translated as "labor" is *kapiao*. It means to "become weary, tired, to work hard " (Reinecker, p.34). It is in a Greek grammatical category (present participle) which "expresses continuous or repeated action (Zodhiates, p.1571). Therefore, this means that we are tired from trying hard to do what is right, over and over again.

The Greek word translated as "heavy laden" is *phartizo*. It means "to burden. The perfect tense expresses a state of weariness" (Reinecker, p.34). It is in a Greek grammatical category (perfect passive participle) which has the following characteristics. "The perfect tense looks at an action as having been completed in the past but as having existing results." The passive voice "represents the subject as receiving the action of the verb." A participle "is a verbal adjective . . . often best translated by the English participle, -ing. Example: having gone, seeing the multitude, receiving the gift" (Zodhiates, p.1570). Therefore, this word means that <u>we have had this burden placed upon us in the past, but it has ongoing consequences which is creating a state of weariness</u>.

Now you can understand why you are so weary from trying to carry this burden, and you need Jesus to carry the load for you.

Kenneth Wuest translates this beautifully:

Come here to me, all who are growing weary to the point of exhaustion, and who have been loaded with burdens and are bending beneath their weight, and I alone will cause you to cease from your labor and take away your burdens and thus refresh you with rest. Take at once my yoke upon you and learn from me, because I am meek and lowly in heart, and you will find cessation from labor and refreshment for your souls, for my yoke is mild and pleasant, and my load is light in weight (Wuest, p.28).

Endnotes for Chapter 4
"Judging Causes Problems"

Endnote #4-1

Definition Of The Words "Judge"

What Does The English Word Mean?
Webster' Dictionary defines the verb "judge" as follows:
1. to form an opinion about through careful weighing of evidence and testing of premises.
2. to sit in judgment on: TRY.
3. to determine or pronounce after inquiry and deliberation.
4. GOVERN, RULE - - used of a Hebrew tribal leader.
5. to form an estimate or evaluation of.
6. *to hold as an opinion: GUESS, THINK.*

What Does The Greek Word Mean?
"It is sometimes necessary to examine whether human behavior conforms to certain standards. Such examination, together with the ultimate assessment and, if necessary, condemnation, is expressed in the New Testament by the extensive word-group connected with '*krino*', to judge" (Brown, p. 361). *"Krino"* means (Thayer, pp.360-361):

1. to separate, put asunder, to pick out, select, choose.
2. to approve, esteem.
3. to be of opinion, deem, think.
4. to determine, resolve, decree
5. judge
   a. to pronounce an opinion concerning right and wrong.
   b. to pronounce judgment, to subject to censure (concerning and decreeing, or inflicting, penalty on one).
6. to rule, govern, to preside over with the power of giving judicial decisions.
7. to contend together, to dispute, to go to law, have a suit at law.

Interestingly then, the same Greek words are used throughout the New Testament wherever it mentions judging, whether it is "good" judging or "bad" judging; and the same English words are used to translate it, regardless of the circumstances. Therefore, to discern which meaning is intended one must consider the context. Without a doubt this has created confusion for many readers, because without the awareness of this diverse use of these words the Bible seems to be contradictory:

in one place it prohibits judging and in another place it promotes it. However, the Bible is not contradictory, and it is intended that these words are to have different meanings in different contexts.

Endnote #4-2

Judging That We <u>Are</u> Supposed To Do.

There are various words used to describe this desirable activity: examine, distinguish, decide, discriminate, determine, form an estimate, discern, esteem. There are actually three sub-categories addressed in this:

1. Naturally
2. Spiritually
3. Judicially in the Church

1. Naturally

In the natural arena, it is very important that we use our discernment and see the truth. God gave us abilities to do this, and we are to use those abilities.

> **Luke 7:43,** *Simon answered and said, "I suppose the one who he forgave more." And He said to him, "You have rightly judged."*
> **1 Corinthians 10:15,** *I speak as to wise men; judge for yourselves what I say.*
> **1 Corinthians 11:13,** *Judge among yourselves. Is it proper for a woman to pray to God with her head uncovered?*

2. Spiritually

In the spiritual realm, it is also important for us to use discernment; and the natural man is incapable of making such discernment.

> **John 7:24,** *"Do not judge according to appearance, but judge with righteous judgment."*
> **Acts 16:15,** *And when she and her household were baptized, she begged us, saying, "If you have judged me to be faithful to the Lord, come to my house and stay." And she constrained us.*
> **1 Corinthians 2:14-15,** *But the natural man does not receive the things of the Spirit of God, for they are foolishness to him; nor can he know them, because they are spiritually discerned. But he who is spiritual judges all things, yet he himself is rightly judged by no one.*
> **1 Corinthians 10:15,** *I speak as to wise men; judge for yourselves what I say.*
> **2 Corinthians 5:14,** *For the love of Christ constrains us, because we judge thus: that if One died for all, then all died;*

- Commentary on **Luke 12:56:** "Just as God is a righteous judge, so men are called upon to judge righteously (Lk 12:56); Jn 7:24) in the constant recognition that ultimately the judgment is God's (Dt. 1:17). The Christian is expected to show discrimination and judgment in moral matters, and the ability to do so is a sign of true maturity. . . " (Douglas, p.643).
- Commentary on **1 Corinthians 2:15-16:** "Probably it means something very close to 'discern' in the sense of being able to make appropriate judgments about what God is doing in the world; and the person 'without the Spirit' obviously can not do that" (Fee, p.117). "This person can 'make judgments about all things'. Such a statement of course must not be wrested from its context. It is the Spirit who 'searches all things, even the depths of God' (v. 10); therefore the person who has the Spirit can discern God's ways. . . The person lacking the Spirit can not discern what God is doing; the one with the Spirit is able to do so because of the Spirit; therefore, the one without the Spirit can not 'examine' or 'make judgments' on, the person with the Spirit." (Fee, p.118).

3. Judicially In The Church

The Church is to exercise judicial authority, and judging, in regard to those who are believers; but those outside the Church are outside their authority.

1 Corinthians 5:12-13, *For what have I to do with judging those also who are outside? Do you not judge those who are inside? But those who are outside God judges. Therefore "put away from yourselves that wicked person."* Read 1 Corinthians 5:1-6:18 for a detailed discussion of this issue.

- "To the Church God gives the grace of exercising discipline which serves to warn sinners. They that are without lack that grace so that they come at once before the judgment of God . . ." (Grosheide, p.130).

Endnote #4-3

Judging That We <u>Are Prohibited</u> From Doing.

There is a judging that we are clearly and sternly admonished <u>not</u> to do.

Matthew 7:1-2, *"Judge not, that you be not judged. For with what judgment you judge, you will be judged; and with the same measure you use, it will be measured back to you."*

Matthew 18:22-35, The parable of the ungrateful servant, ending with, *"So My heavenly Father also will do to you if each of you, from his heart, does not forgive his brother his trespasses"*

Luke 6:37, *"Judge not, and you shall not be judged. Condemn not, and you shall not be condemned. Forgive, and you will be forgiven."*

John 8:15-16, *"You judge according to the flesh; I judge no one. And yet if I do judge, My judgment is true, for I am not alone, but I am with the Father who sent Me."*

Romans 2:1, *Therefore you are inexcusable, O man, whoever you are who judge, for in whatever you judge another you condemn yourself; for you who judge practice the same things.*

Romans 14:4, *Who are you to judge another's servant? To his own master he stands or falls. Indeed, he will be made to stand, for God is able to make him stand.*

Romans 14:10-13, *But why do you judge your brother? Or why do you show contempt for your brother? For we shall all stand before the judgment seat of Christ. For it is written: 'As I live, says the Lord, Every knee shall bow to Me, and every tongue shall confess to God.' So then each of us shall give account of himself to God. Therefore let us not judge one another anymore, but rather resolve this, not to put a stumbling block or a cause to fall in our brother's way.*

1 Corinthians 4:3-5, *But with me it is a very small thing that I should be judged by you or by a human court. In fact, I do not even judge myself. For I know nothing against myself, yet I am not justified by this; but He who judges me is the Lord. Therefore judge nothing before the time, until the Lord comes, who will both bring to light the hidden things of darkness and reveal the counsels of the hearts; and then each one's praise will come from God.*

James 2:4, *have you not shown partiality among yourselves, and become judges with evil thoughts?*

James 4:11-12, *Do not speak evil of one another, brethren. He who speaks evil of a brother and judges his brother, speaks evil of the law and judges the law. But if you judge the law, you are not a doer of the law but a judge. There is one Lawgiver, who is able to save and to destroy. Who are you to judge another?*

We Can't Do It

One of the reasons we can't do it right is that we don't have all the facts or the wisdom to do it perfectly. Jesus will do it perfectly.

- Commentary on **Matthew 7:1-2:** "Judge not. The present imperative suggests that it is the habit of judging others that is condemned. Though the word judge is itself neutral as to the verdict, the sense here indicates an unfavorable judgment. Critics of others must stop short of final condemnation, for men can not judge motives, as God can." (Harrison, pp.940-941).

- Commentary on **John 8:15:** "They judge, and they can judge, only 'after the flesh'. Now it is the nature of the flesh to be weak and incomplete, so the expression draws attention to the weakness and imperfection of their judgment. It can not but be imperfect and partial."(Morris, p.440).

Another reason is that we do it with wrong motives. Jesus always loves us and has our best interest at heart. When we do this type of judging we do it with wrong, selfish, motives.

- Commentary on **James 4:12:** ". . . any slander or judgment of a brother implies. an attitude of superiority reserved solely for God, who is the omnipotent Lawgiver and Judge" (Adamson, p.177).

Yet another reason is that if we judge, it interferes with God's ability to deal with that person.

   Romans 12:19, *Beloved, do not avenge yourselves, but rather give place to wrath; for it is written, "Vengeance is Mine, I will repay," says the Lord* (Romans 12:19).

Though there are a number of reasons given why this sort of judging is prohibited, they all revolve around the fact that to condemn another is to put ourselves in God's place. It is a usurping of His place and authority. This relates to the original sin in the Garden of Eden: man's desire to be like God: "*For God knows that in the day you eat of it your eyes will be opened, and you will be like God, knowing good and evil"* (Genesis 3:5).

- Commentary on **Romans 1-3:** "All men fall under his wrath, and are without excuse (Romans 1-3). This is the reason why ultimately no man has a right to judge another." (Brown, Vol 2, p.366).
- Commentary on **Matt 7:1-2:**". . unfair or uncharitable judgments should be avoided. . . the way in which one judges others will be the way one is judged by God at the eschatological judgment . . . Judgment is God's prerogative alone" (Hagner, p.169).
- Commentary on **Luke 6:37-38:** "Judging does not refer here to the judicial decision of a constituted judge, but to the human tendency to criticize and find fault with one's neighbor." (Fitzmyer, p.641).
- Commentary on **Luke 6:37-38**:"He has in the final instance the right to judge as to the guilt or innocence of any person. . . No human being has the power or the right to this . . . He does forbid the attitude of those people who want to appoint themselves in God's place as judges over their fellow-men and to judge and condemn right and left . . . But we are never to encroach upon God's right to judge and to condemn . . . To the generous giver will be liberally given - in full in eternity, but even in measure in this life" (Geldenhuys, p.213).

There is a connection between what we are prohibited from doing and Jesus' judging

As one studies <u>our</u> judging and the eschatological (end times Great White Throne Judgment) judging <u>by Jesus</u>, it becomes apparent **THEY ARE INTIMATELY INTERTWINED.**

- "When we are judged we are chastened so that we may not be condemned along with the world (1 Cor 11:32)" (Brown, Vol 2, p.366)
- "Before God nothing is forgotten, whether deed or word. The judgment of God is the great reality of man's life (Matt. 10:28), and the only way of escaping condemnation is to be forgiven" (Brown, Vol 2, p.366). This is why it is important to forgive and be forgiven in this life.
- "However, the Christian is also given frequent warnings against the danger of passing judgment on others in a way which attempts to anticipate the final divine judgment (Mt. 7:1; Lk 6:41f; Jn 8:7; Rom 2:1; 14:4; Jas 4:1)" (Douglas, p.643).

Various commentaries on **1 Corinthians 4:1-5:**
- "Therefore, all judgment must await his coming (v.5). There was to be no pre-judgment seat judgment! . . . since the Lord alone can judge, judgment must await him. At the proper time he will perform it capably and completely, probing into the hidden things of darkness. . ." (Harrison, p.1235).
- "Scripture witnesses to a division at the final judgment between the 'righteous' and the 'wicked', the 'elect' and the 'non-elect' (Rev 20:11) . . . The divine judgment of the people of God will be a fatherly judgment. It will not be such as to place in peril the Christian's standing within the family of God" (Douglas, p.643).

Commentaries on **Romans 2:1-2:**
- "The unrepentant does not experience it (God's wrath) immediately, because God also shows him his kindness and patience. God 'also endures with much patience the vessels of wrath' (Rom 9:22). But the more the individual hardens himself and the more evil he practices, the more wrath grows. The wrath is stored up and accumulated unto the day of wrath, the day of judgment" (Schlatter, p.50).
- "The individual wants to be judge! What a lie, what arrogance! With every verdict he voices he condemns himself and eliminates every excuse . . . why is he without excuse? He judges because he knows that what is sinful ought not to happen and renders one worthy of death, and he does this while recognizing himself at the same time in every pernicious lust. . . Our own share of evil is not removed by condemning evil in others. The one who

judges is what they all are and does what they all do, thus condemning himself . . . Thus by his own action the one who judges remains inescapably bound up with the divine verdict . . . Instead of looking for truth, he is afraid of it and musters the hope of escaping it; it will affect others but not him. This correlates with his practice of judging others, without considering that he is condemning himself. (Schlatter, pp. 47, 49).

Commentary on **Matthew 7:1-2:**

- ". . . our relationship with God is inseparably linked with our relationships with our fellows. . . if we hope to escape condemnation in the day of his judgment, we must not sit in judgment on others . . . it is not that others will judge you as you judge others; but that God will judge you with severity or leniency to match the severity or leniency which you have used towards others." (Beare, pp 169, 190).

Endnote #4-4

Judging By Jesus

The end times judging of Jesus is something we all will experience: *And as it is appointed for men to die once, but after this the judgment* (Hebrews 9:27).

We suffer in this life because of our sins. It is also very clear that there is a time coming for all men to face the righteous judgment of Jesus. No one will escape, and there is no fooling Him. He sees our hearts accurately. There are actually two aspects of this final judgment. First, there will be a separating of the sheep and the goats, the saved and the lost, according to whether their name is written in the Lamb's book of life. The lost will go to eternal damnation and the saved will be with Jesus for eternity:

Matthew 25:32-34, *All the nations will be gathered before Him, and He will separate them one from another, as a shepherd divides his sheep from the goats. And He will set the sheep on His right hand; but the goats on the left. Then the King will say to those on His right hand, "Come, you blessed of My Father, inherit the kingdom prepared for you from the foundation of the world:"*

Second, at their time of judgment by Jesus, the saved will receive rewards or suffer losses, depending upon how their lives were lived.

1 Corinthians 3:11-15, *For no other foundation can anyone lay than that which is laid, which is Jesus Christ. Now if anyone builds on this foundation with gold, silver, precious stones, wood, hay, straw, each one's work will become manifest; for the Day will declare it, because it will be revealed by fire; and the fire will test each one's work, of what sort it is. If anyone's work which he has* *build on it endures, he will receive a reward. If anyone's work is burned, he will suffer loss; but he himself will be saved, yet so as through fire.*

It should also be noted that here the Bible is not talking about God judging our behavior. He judges our hearts: He looks at <u>why</u> we have done what we have done. If we have done the right things for the wrong reasons, the works are wood, hay, and straw (1 Corinthians 3:12). If our heart is right, if our character has been changed into the image of Jesus, then our behavior will be what God wants. The behavior is not the goal, it is just a way of measuring what is in our heart. Below are additional scriptures and commentaries on this subject.

Romans 14:10-13, *But why do you judge your brother? Or why do you show contempt for your brother? For we shall all stand before the judgment seat of Christ. For it is written: 'As I live, says the Lord, every knee shall bow to me, and every tongue shall confess to God.' So then each of us shall give account of himself to God. Therefore let us not judge one another anymore, but rather resolve this, not to put a stumbling block or a cause to fall in our brother's way.*
2 Timothy 4:1, *I charge you therefore before God and the Lord Jesus Christ, who will judge the living and the dead at His appearing and His kingdom:*
Hebrews 12:23, *To the general assembly and church of the firstborn who are registered in heaven, to God the Judge of all, to the spirits of just men made perfect.*
Revelation 20:11:15, *Then I saw a great white throne and Him who sat on it, from whose face the earth and the heaven fled away. And there was found no place for them. And I saw the dead, small and great, standing before God, and books were opened. And another book was opened, which is the Book of Life. And the dead were judged according to their works, by the things which were written in the books. The sea gave up the dead who were in it, and Death and Hades delivered up the dead who were in them. And they were judged, each one according to his works. Then Death and Hades were cast into the lake of fire. This is the second death. And anyone not found written in the Book of Life was cast into the lake of fire.*

Commentaries on the topic:

- "Divine judgment is both present and future reality (Rom 1:18-32)." (Elwell, p.621).
- "God's judgments are not confined to the future but are already at work in man's life in the present age (Jn 8:50; Rom 1:18, 22,24,26, 28; Rev 18:8)." (Douglas p.641).
- ". . . all men will be judged; none will be absent (2 Tim 4:1; Heb 12:23:, 1 Pet 4:5)" . . . "Christians too . . . will face a judgment" (Douglas p. 641).

- "Paul renders worthless all merely external piety because God judges what is hidden and his verdict unveils the truth (Rom 2:16, 2)" (Schlatter, p.74).

Endnote #4-5

The Tendency To Automatically React To Perceived Wounding With Bitterness, Judgment And Blame

And Its relationship To Our Inner Healing:

We will never lose the tendency to automatically react to perceived wounding with bitterness, judgment and blame. It is a part of our fallen nature. However, as we walk out our healing and remove the old bitter roots, there will be fewer things that we perceive as wounding, and so we will find ourselves judging less often. The important issue is whether we <u>perceive</u> the particular event as threatening or wounding, not whether it is in fact threatening or wounding.

Let me give an example. Suppose we have a frightening encounter with a snake at some time in our life. There is then written into the unconscious part of our self the representation of a snake being dangerous (and therefore threatening). Then suppose one day I am hiking down a trail in the woods and I see a wiggly looking thing on the trail ahead, and I immediately feel fear. It is instantaneous. My old wound has triggered this response. But I see that the "snake" does not move, so I move closer and discover that it was actually a bent stick. My prior bad experience had caused me to react instantaneously (without any conscious decision-making) to what I <u>perceived</u> as dangerous. A wiggly object had come to represent a threat. (See Siegel, Chapter 5).

My bitter roots cause me to react instantaneously to anything I <u>perceive</u> as threatening or bad. I therefore react in this way to some things that are not in fact threatening (like the stick). As I walk out my healing process and have more and more bitter roots removed, I no longer wrongly perceive danger in situations that are not in fact dangerous. Therefore I react less often with bitterness, judgment and blame. I don't react less because the "Fallen" nature in me has gotten better. I react less because I <u>perceive</u> fewer things in my daily life as threatening.

Endnote #4-6

God Takes The Long View

As one reads the scriptures and commentaries concerning judging, our present lives, and the future eschatological judgment, a very interesting truth emerges. IT IS GOD'S MERCY THAT WE SUFFER PAIN IN THIS LIFE IN THE AREAS WHERE WE SIN.

When we go to the Great White Throne Judgment in the end times, all our sins will be revealed. We will suffer loss of some sort because of them. However, if we have become aware of them while we are walking this earth, have repented of them, and had them forgiven by Jesus, they are removed. They will not exist at the Great White Throne Judgment, and we will not have to suffer loss because of them. Therefore we need to forgive and be forgiven by Jesus now so we won't have to pay later.

Psalm 103:12, *As far as the east is from the west, so far has He removed our transgressions from us.*

Isaiah 1:18, . . . *Though your sins are like scarlet, they shall be as white as snow; though they are red like crimson, they shall be as wool.*

Isaiah 43:25, *"I, even I, am He who blots out your transgressions for My own sake;"*

Jeremiah 31:34, *". . . For I will forgive their iniquity, and their sin I will remember no more."*

1 John 1:9, *If we confess our sins, He is faithful and just to forgive us our sins and to cleanse us from all unrighteousness.*

Commentaries on **1 Corinthians 4:1-5:**

- "The eschatological tension in the statements about judgment is broken neither by the emphasis in John upon its being present nor by the emphasis in Revelation upon its being future" (Brown, Vol 2, p.367).

- "Although we experience judgment initially in this life, all of us are judged ultimately after death" (Elwell, p.590).

- "No sin escapes his notice; his judgment on sins is inevitable (Rom 2:3; Heb 9:237; 10:26-27)."Elwell, p.591).

Therefore, God's actions in making us miserable now, in this life, is His work to bring us to repentance. It is a precise surgical operation, because we suffer exactly where our sin is so that we can see it and repent. He wants us to be cleansed of our sins. He knows it is better for us to suffer now for a brief time (although it often doesn't seem brief, but it is in comparison to eternity) so that we can be free of any loss we would suffer for it for eternity. Seeing this should make a great difference in how we view suffering for our sins now.

There is an additional dimension to this regarding the increase in the consequences of unrepented sin over time. John and Paula Sandford have seen:

> "The longer a judgment continues unrepented or and unconfessed, the greater increment it gains. We sow a spark and reap a forest fire, or sow to the wind and reap whirlwind. . . He moves heaven and earth to cause us to repent and confess so He can reap all our evil for us in His Son Jesus on the cross!" (Sandford, Transformation of the Inner Man, pp.239-240).

After all, the older we get the less time we have left before our death; and so the urgency for us to see our sin increases. So God makes us more and more uncomfortable so that we will wake up and repent.

Inner Healing (sanctification) is then a part of God's plan for His people: sin has consequences; but when we confess and repent, He takes the consequences from then on. Otherwise we would reap both now and in eternity.

Endnotes for Chapter 5
"Forgiving Ends These Problems"

Endnote #5-1

More On Letting Jesus Be The Judge

It is apparent that the key issue that inhibits our ability to forgive (and the reason that we judge) is: **DO WE TRUST GOD TO BE THE JUDGE?** Therefore, part of being able to forgive means that we need to trust that the person who sinned against us will be brought to justice. Our hearts have built into them a sense of justice, and so we know the person should be held accountable for what they have done. When we judge, it is a subtle admission that we don't trust God to judge them and we then take the law into our own hands. We become an illegal, self-appointed court.

However, God is a just judge: "This means that no one ever gets away with anything, ever, anywhere. But not everyone believes this. In fact, many of us are totally oblivious to the inescapable operation of law, unaware that we must pay for every misdeed" (Sandford, Restoring The Christian Family, p.128). Even though we may never know what consequences the other person will experience at the hand of God, we need to be willing to let Him work in that person's life as He chooses. We must have faith in God's faithfulness and ultimate goodness. Contrary to how we would do it, He is always correct and just, and He does it for the other person's best interest:

> *Hebrews 12:10-11, For they indeed for a few days chastened us as seemed best to them" (speaking of our earthly fathers) "but He for our profit, that we may be partakers of His holiness. Now no chastening seems to be joyful for the present, but grievous; nevertheless afterward it yields the peaceable fruit of righteousness to those who have been trained by it* (Underlining is mine).

Endnote #5-2

More On The Power Of Forgiveness –
It Takes A Miracle

We need a legal transaction to take place in the spiritual realm if we are to be like Jesus. This is what Inner Healing is all about. When we repent and forgive, Jesus comes into that place of sin, cleans it out, and takes up residence there. Then we are like Jesus in that one little area of our inner man where that bitter root had resided. Then we will behave like Jesus in that specific area, because Jesus can't do anything but act like Himself. John and Paula Sandford say that as Christian counselors, we are evangelists to the unbelieving parts of the hearts of believers (Sandford, Transformation Of The Inner Man, p.25).

So, by saying that you should stop trying to be a good Christian through the power of your own will, I am not being soft on sin, and I am not advocating passivity. Bad fruit is bad fruit, and God doesn't want the bad fruit to continue, because His children are suffering! Our behavior is simply a symptom, and not a cause or a goal. When we see bad fruit in our life, we then have two possible tools to use to stop it. We can use our willpower, or we can appropriate the blood of Jesus. If I am tempted to do something that I know is sin, and I say, "Stop it!" (I use my willpower), and it stops, it was simply a psychological event going on (an impulse, a habit, a temptation). However, if I say, "Stop it!" and it doesn't stop, then it signals to me that I have been using the wrong tool. I am then dealing with a reaping from a bitter root, and I need to use the tool that I have been given that is powerful enough to stop it: the blood and cross of Jesus. Thayer says,

For what the law could not do in that it was weak through the flesh, God did by sending His own Son in the likeness of sinful flesh, on account of sin: He condemned sin in the flesh (Romans 8:3). The Greek word here translated "condemned" (*katakrina*) means the following:

"Through His Son, Who partook of human nature but was without sin, God deprived sin (which is the ground of the *katakringa*) of it's power in human nature (looked at in the general), broke it's deadly sway (just as the condemnation and punishment of wicked men puts an end to their power to injure or do harm)" (Thayer, p.332).

When we look through the eyes of striving, we tend do see Romans 8:4-5 as admonishing us to <u>do</u> right, to try hard, . . . *that the righteous requirement of the law might be fulfilled in us who do not walk according to the flesh but according to the Spirit. For those who live according to the flesh set their minds on the things of the flesh, but those who live according to the Spirit, the things of the Spirit.*   However, when we realize what Paul is talking about in Romans, Chapters 7 and 8, we can see that he is not referring to striving, but is rather just making <u>a statement of fact</u>. He is making an observation that when we "walk" and "live" according to the flesh (by our willpower), we do not fulfill the righteous requirements of the law. That is simply what happens. But if we "walk" and "live" according to the Spirit (because we have been changed into His image through Jesus and His provision for us), the righteous requirements of the law are fulfilled. We simply walk uprightly because that is our new nature (in that area of our life).

Of course, the driver of the semi-trailer truck in my previous example in Chapter 2 had to decide to press the pedal to activate the mechanism, and likewise we have to choose to activate God's provision for the stopping of the reaping – we need to forgive so we can be forgiven. We need to choose to appropriate the blessing of the blood and the cross of Jesus.

In <u>Existence and Faith</u>, Bultmann says the following about the power of forgiveness:

> "Through forgiveness the past out of which one comes is blotted out; he comes into his now precisely out of forgiveness and therefore is free for the future" (p. 84). "The sole way of becoming free from sin is forgiveness, i.e., if man has sinned, then he is a sinner. What has happened in his past is not an individual fact that has now been left behind, but rather is present in that it qualifies him as guilty before God. Neither man nor mankind can become free from the past by their own self-will; on the contrary, they bring the past with them into every present" (p.135).

Being Made Holy

This is the only way we can be made holy. Butlmann writes, "It means that free, ethical obedience can have its origin only <u>in miracle</u> – quite in keeping with the view that from the fetters of flesh and sin man must be freed to obedience by the deed of God" (Bultmann, <u>Theology of the New Testament</u>, Part II, p.337) (underlining is mine). We couldn't ever do this on our own.

Sanctification is this process whereby we are changed into the image of Jesus. It is an ongoing procedure that God is orchestrating that will take the rest of our life to accomplish. Bultman further says,

> "The bestowal of holiness through baptism can be called 'putting on Christ'; but in addition to the indicative, 'you have put on Christ' (Galatians 3:27), we also find the imperative: 'put on the Lord Jesus Christ (Romans 13:14)" (Bultmann, <u>Theology of the New Testament</u>, Part II, p.339).

In Bultmann's statement above, he is referring to the Greek moods in each of the two separate scriptures, and the moods are different in each. The "indicative" in Greek refers to <u>a statement of fact.</u> The "imperative" refers to <u>a command</u>. So Bultmann is pointing out that there is a <u>command </u>to put on Christ (the imperative), but it is in addition to the <u>fact</u> that "you have put on Christ." In this section of his book Bultmann points out the many times in the Bible where it is clear that the imperative (the command to obey) is dependent on the indicative (the fact that we have put on Christ). We cannot obey Jesus unless we have first put on Jesus. This subtle but profound difference would only be clear to those who have a thorough knowledge of the Greek language.

> *For both He who sanctifies and those who are being sanctified are all of one, for which reason He is not ashamed to call them brethren* (Hebrews 2:11). *For by one offering He has perfected forever those who are being sanctified* (Hebrews 10:14).

God is changing us into His image one piece at a time, one bitter root at a time, one Honeycomb compartment at a time. See Chapter 6, "God Is On Your Side" for more detail on this.

So the walking out of Inner Healing is the sanctification process the Bible talks about extensively: bringing Jesus into each of the pockets of bitterness, often one little pocket at a time; having Him cleanse that place, and then asking Him to take up residence there. This is a miracle only Jesus can do. It involves both death of the old root and resurrection of the new root. Then this transformed root will bear good fruit in our life. It can then do nothing else!

By Forgiving We Put Ourselves In Position To Receive God's Grace

Grace means: "graciousness (as gratifying) of manner or act (abstract or concrete) literally, figuratively, or spiritually; especially the divine influence upon the heart, and its reflection in the life: including gratitude" (Strong's, p.77). The second meaning of the verb is to forgive! (C. Brown, Vol 2, p.122).

It appears that when we forgive, we are connecting with (or acting like, or coming into unity with) God's nature rather than man's nature (the tendency to automatically react to perceived wounding with bitterness, judgment, and blame).

". . . 'dead through our trespasses, made alive together with Christ, by grace (*chariti*) you have been saved' (2:5); 'by grace . . . through faith . . . the gift of God' in opposition to 'not your own doing . . . not because of works, lest any man should boast' (2.8f)" (C.Brown, Vol 2, p.122, commenting on Ephesians 2:5-2:8ff)).

In Theology of the New Testament, Volume II, Bultmann states:

"This 'redemption' of theirs is the 'forgiveness of sins' (Col. 1:14; cf. 2:14; Eph. 1:7; 5:26) - but not as if their life were now placed under an imperative, the fulfillment of which would be the condition for obtaining salvation, but rather thus; that with forgiveness the might of sin is broken and in their obedient conduct Life has become a present reality. Believers have died with Christ, been buried and raised with him, made alive (Col. 2:12f, 20; 3:3). Upon this indicative the imperative is founded. . . 'Put to death therefore what is earthly in you' (Col. 3:5f; cf. Eph. 4:22), and that in spite of their emancipation from the evil powers believers are charged with the duty of fighting against them (Eph. 6:10ff). The quality of being constantly menaced, which Christian living has, is clearly seen . . . The Spirit given in baptism is the guarantee of future salvation (Eph. 1:13f); but it is also the power that is bestowed in the present in the process by which one constantly becomes new (Eph. 3:16; 4:23)"(pp.176-177).

Endnote #5-3

Definition Of The Word "Forgive"

What Does The English Word Mean?

Webster's Dictionary defines "forgive" as follows:

1. to cease to feel resentment against (an offender); PARDON (one's enemies).
   (a) to give up resentment of or claim to requital for (an insult).
   (b) to grant relief from payment of (a debt).
2. To "requite" means:
   (a) to make return for: REPAY.
   (b) to make retaliation for: AVENGE
3. to make suitable return to for a benefit or service or for an injury.

Synonym: reciprocate (Webster's, p 1002).

What Do The Several Greek Words Mean?

We have seen that with the English word "judge" there is only one Greek word used for several types of judging, and we need to look at the context to tell the difference. The situation is very different the English word "forgive." In this case are several Greek words that are translated into the English word "forgive," and the various Greek words have different shades of meaning.

Aphiemi

The most commonly used Greek word that is translated as "forgive" is "aphiemi," and it occurs frequently (142 times) in the New Testament. Interestingly it is only translated "forgive" 45 times. The other 97 times it is translated as various forms of "to send forth," such as "leave," "send away,"" let alone," "forsake," "yield up," "lay aside," "remit," "put away," "give up a debt," "let go," "keep no longer." (Strong, p.17; Thayer, pp.88-89; Wigram, pp.97-98). This Greek word appears in the following scriptures:

    Matt 6:12-14, *"And forgive us our debts, as we forgive our debtors. And do not lead us into temptation, but deliver us from the evil one. For Yours is the kingdom and the power and the glory forever. Amen. For if you forgive men their trespasses your heavenly Father will also forgive you."*

    Matt 18:34-35, *"And his master was angry, and delivered him to the torturers until he should pay all that was due to him. So My heavenly Father also will do to you if each of you, from his heart, does not forgive his brother his trespasses."*

    Mark 11:25, *"And whenever you stand praying, if you have anything against anyone, forgive him, that your Father in heaven may also forgive you your trespasses."*

Luke 17:3, *"Take heed to yourselves. If your brother sins against you, rebuke him; and if he repents, forgive him."*

Charizomai

The next most commonly used Greek word is *"charizomai,"* which occurs 21 times, 10 times translated "forgive," and 8 times "freely given." The word implies to do something pleasant or agreeable, to do a favor, to show one's self to be gracious, kind, benevolent (Thayer, p.665; Wigram, pp.796-797). This Greek word appears in the following scriptures:

Ephesians 4:32, *And be kind to one another, tender-hearted, forgiving one another, just as God in Christ also forgave you.*
Colossians 3:13, *. . . bearing with one another, and forgiving one another, if anyone has a complaint against another; even as Christ forgave you, so you also must do.*

Aphesis

The third word, *"aphesis,"* occurs 17 times, but only 6 times as "forgiveness" (pardon of sins; properly, the letting them go as if they had not been committed) (Thayer, p.88). The other occurrences are: as "remission" (of their penalty) 9 times, as "deliverance" once, and as "liberty" once (Wigram, p.97). It appears in the following scripture as "forgive":

Ephesians 1:7, *In Him we have redemption through His blood, the forgiveness of sins, according to the riches of His grace.*

Apolu

Finally, the Greek word *"apolu"* occurs 67 times, but only once as "forgive." The other occurrences are as "put away" (as in divorce), "send away," "loose," "set at liberty," or "release" (Thayer, pp.65-66; Wigram, p.75). The one time it does occur as "forgive" is a very important occurrence, where Jesus says in Luke 6:37: *"Judge not, and you shall not be judged. Condemn not, and you shall not be condemned. Forgive, and you will be forgiven."* This quote is from the Sermon on the Mount.

It is interesting that the account recorded by Matthew of the same sermon (Matt 6:14) uses *"aphiemi"* instead of this word (*apolu*) to convey the idea of "forgive." Obviously the intent in both passages is to convey the identical meaning. This use of two different Greek words to convey the same meaning therefore enriches our understanding of what Jesus really meant when He spoke this.

In Classical Greek (the common usage outside the New Testament) these words tend to mean "the voluntary release of a person or thing over which one has legal or actual control;" ". . . to release from a legal bond;" ". . . also to let go unpunished, to allow in the sense of personal leniency or indulgence" (Brown, Vol. 1, pp.697-698).

The reason for going into this much detail in regard to the word "forgive," is that it is a very important concept. Words are often not precise tools, especially when one translates one language into another. One can reasonably assume that some shades of all the above meanings need to be included in our understanding of what it means to forgive. Seeing the context in which each of these words appears enhances our understanding.

In reading these verses there are three things that we can see: first, it becomes apparent that when we forgive, it means the person really <u>did</u> transgress against us, and they really <u>do owe</u> us something. The Greek word translated "debts" in Matt 6:12 ("*opheilema*") carries the idea of a legal debt, something owed (Strong, p.53). However, we are told to forgive this debt anyway, and not expect repayment.

Second, it is also apparent that we can decide to forgive, or we wouldn't be told to do so; although we need God's help to accomplish it (Sandford, <u>Restoring The Christian Family</u>, 1979, p.305).

And third, it is evident that there is a close connection between "forgiving" and "judging." In fact, it appears that **JUDGING AND FORGIVING ARE OPPOSITES**. When another person transgresses us, we have a tendency to judge them. Otherwise there would be no reason to forgive.

Endnote #5-4

Sample Prayer Of Forgiveness

I was a bit reluctant to include a sample prayer of forgiveness, because it is so easy for people to begin to use a sample verbatim when praying. It is most important that when you forgive, you are forgiving from your heart as you feel led by the Holy Spirit. So please use this prayer as simply an illustration, not a formula. Forgiveness is accomplished from the heart, not from the words.

A prayer regarding your Dad might go something like this:

"Father God, I come to You in the blessed name of Jesus.
I realize that I have judged my father, and I have inside me a root of bitterness.
I am sorry that I did this, and I don't want that awful thing in me anymore.
Dad, I forgive you for _____ (the offense).
Lord, I ask You to forgive me for this judgment of bitterness.
Forgive me for taking Your place as the judge.
I ask You to come into that place in me, remove that ugly thing from me and wash me clean with Your blood. Cleanse me in every place where that bitterness existed.

I ask You to come into that place, to fill all those places with Your presence.
Lord, I ask that You would bless my Dad.
Amen."

Endnote #5-5

The Power Of Words

For some reason, God set up the universe in such a way that words have power.
The words that I speak bring my thoughts into reality. Once they are spoken, it as
though a legal contract has been signed, or a legal event happened.

There are hundreds of examples in the Bible of the power of words. The Bible
doesn't explain to us why words have power, but it makes it abundantly clear that
words do have great power. Below are a few scriptural examples.

Genesis 1:3, Then *God said, "let there be light," and there was light.*

Genesis 13:14, And *the Lord said to Abraham, after Lot had separated from
him: "Lift up your eyes now and look from the place where you are - northward,
southward, eastward, and westward for all the land which you see I give to you
and your descendants forever."* God spoke to Abram and it was a contract.

John 1:1, *In the beginning was the Word, and the Word was with God, and the
Word was God*

John 1:14, *And the Word became flesh and dwelt among us,*

John 6:63, *The words that I speak to you are spirit, and they are life.*

Matthew 12:36, *But I say to you that for every idle word men may speak, they
will give account of it in the day of judgment.*

Romans 10:9, *that if you confess with your mouth the Lord Jesus and believe
in your heart that God has raised Him from the dead, you will be saved.*

Exodus 9:15, *So Joshua made peace with them, and made a covenant with
them to let them live; and the rulers of the congregation swore to them.* The
Gibeonites deceived Joshua and the Israelites. But despite being deceived, the
covenant spoken was honored by Joshua. It had force.

James 3:5-6, *Even so the tongue is a little member and boasts great things.
See how great a forest a little fire kindles! And the tongue is a fire, a world of
iniquity. The tongue is so set among our members that it defiles the whole body
and sets on fire the course of nature; and it is set on fire by hell.*

Endnotes for Chapter 6
"God Is On Your Side"

Endnote #6-1

Scriptures On God's Ultimate Plan For Us

Luke 22:30, ". . . *that you may eat and drink at My table in My kingdom, and sit on thrones judging the twelve tribes of Israel"*

Romans 8:29, *For whom He foreknew, He also predestinated to be conformed to the image of His Son, that He might be the firstborn among many brethren.*

1 Corinthians 15:49, *And as we have borne the image of the man of dust, we shall also bear the image of the heavenly Man.*

Ephesians 4:15, . . . *but, speaking the truth in love, may grow up in all things into Him who is the head - Christ.*

1 John 3:1-2, *Behold what manner of love the Father has bestowed on us, that we should be called children of God! Therefore the world does not know us, because it did not know Him. Beloved, now we are children of God; and it has not yet been revealed what we shall be, but we know that when He is revealed, we shall be like Him, for we shall see Him as He is.*

Revelation 5:10, *And have made us kings and priests to our God; And we shall reign on the earth.*

Revelation 20:6, *Blessed and holy is he who has part in the first resurrection. Over such the second death has no power, but they shall be priests of God and of Christ, and shall reign with him a thousand years.*

Revelation 22:5, *And there shall be no night there: They need no lamp nor light of the sun, for the Lord God gives them light. And they shall reign forever and ever.*

Endnote #6-2

Scriptures On God Working In Our Hearts

Job 2:3-6, *Then the Lord said to Satan, "Have you considered My servant, Job, that there is none like him on the earth, a blameless and upright man, one who fears God and shuns evil? And still he holds fast to his integrity, although you incited Me against him, to destroy him without cause." So Satan answered the Lord and said, "Skin for skin! Yes, all that a man has he will give for his life. But stretch out Your hand now, and touch his bone and his flesh, and he will* surely curse You to Your face!" So the Lord said to Satan, "Behold, he is in your hand, but spare his life."

Job 5:17, *Behold, happy is the man whom God corrects; therefore do not despise the chastening of the Almighty.*

Job 23:10, *"But He knows the way that I take; When He has tested me, I shall come forth as gold."*

Proverbs 3:11-12, *My son, do not despise the chastening of the Lord, nor detest His correction; for whom the Lord loves He corrects just as a father the son in whom he delights.*

1 Peter 1:6-7, *In this you greatly rejoice, though now for a little while, if need be, you have been grieved by various trials, that the genuineness of your faith, being much more precious than gold that perishes . . .*

Endnote #6-3

More Scriptures On The Process Of Being Changed Into The Image Of Jesus

Colossians 2:6-7, *As you have therefore received Christ Jesus the Lord, so walk in Him, rooted and built up in Him and established in the faith, as you have been taught, abounding in it with thanksgiving.*

Hebrews 10:16-17, *This is the covenant that I will make with them after those days, says the Lord: I will put My laws into their hearts, and in their minds I will write them," then He adds, "Their sins and their lawless deeds I will remember no more.*

James 1:2-4, *My brethren, count it all joy when you fall into various trials, knowing that the testing of your faith produces patience. But let patience have its perfect work, that you may be perfect and complete, lacking nothing.*

Endnote #6-4

Example of Job

Job is a graphic example of God using trials to change a person's heart.[219]

---

[219] **Job 1:8-12,** *The Lord said to Satan, "Have you considered My servant Job, that there is none like him on the earth, a blameless and upright man, one who fears God and shuns evil?" So Satan answered the Lord and said, "Does Job fear God for nothing? Have You not made a hedge around him, around his household, and around all that he has on every side? You have blessed the work of his hands, and his possessions have increased in the land. But now, stretch out Your hand and touch all*

Footnote Continued On Next Page

Job was proud and God used Satan to get Job's attention. God was the one who approached Satan about Job, and Satan had to get God's permission before he could attack Job. Then God set the limits as to what Satan could do. Satan then took all of Job's stuff, but Job still didn't see his sin. So then a bit later, in order to increase the pressure on Job, God approached Satan a second time, and gave him permission to attack Job's body.[220] God was so committed to Job becoming sanctified that He let Job go through some awful experiences to reach that goal. Job's friend Elihu told him the truth, that God was giving him trials to change his heart.[221] Eventually, when Job was sufficiently softened, God showed Job his sin.[222] Then Job saw his sin (pride) and repented.[223] As soon as Job repented and prayed for his friends, God ended the trials.[224] So in the end, God was successful. In just this same way God is committed to your sanctification.[225]

---

that he has, and he will surely curse You to Your face!" So the Lord said to Satan, "Behold, all that he has is in your power; only do not lay a hand on his person." Then Satan went out from the presence of the Lord.

[220] **Job 2:1-6,** *Again there was a day when the sons of God came to present themselves before the Lord, and Satan came also among them to present himself before the Lord. And the Lord said to Satan, "From where do you come?" So Satan answered the Lord and said, "From going to and fro on the earth, and from walking back and forth on it." Then the Lord said to Satan, "Have you considered My servant Job, that there is none like him on the earth, a blameless and upright man, one who fears God and shuns evil? And still he holds fast to his integrity, although you incited Me against him, to destroy him without cause." So Satan answered the Lord and said, "Skin for skin! Yes, all that a man has he will give for his life. But stretch out Your hand now, and touch his bone and his flesh, and he will surely curse You to Your face!" So the Lord said to Satan, "Behold, he is in your hand, but spare his life."*

[221] **Job 33:29-30,** *Behold, God works all these things, twice, in fact, three times with a man, to bring back his soul from the pit, that he may be enlightened with the light of life.*

[222] **Job 38:1-5,** *Then the Lord answered Job out of the whirlwind, and said; "Who is this who darkens counsel by words without knowledge? Now prepare yourself like a man, I will question you, and you shall answer Me. Where were you when I laid the foundations of the earth? Tell Me, if you have understanding. Who determined its measurements? Surely you know!"* This searing rebuke of the Lord continues from Job 38:1-41:34. There God says, referring to Himself, *He is king over all the children of pride.*

[223] **Job 42:5-6,** Job said, *"I have heard of You by the hearing of the ear, but now my eye sees You. Therefore I abhor myself and repent in dust and ashes."*

[224] **Job 42:10,** *And the Lord restored Job's losses when he prayed for his friends. Indeed the Lord gave Job twice as much as he had before.*

[225] **John 17:11,12,15,** *"Now I am no longer in the world, but these are in the world, and I come to You. Holy Father, keep through Your name those whom You have given Me, that they may be one as We are. While I was with them in the world, I kept them in Your name. Those whom You gave Me I have kept; and none of them is lost except the son of perdition, that the Scripture might be fulfilled . . . I do not pray that You should take them out of the world, but that You should keep them from the evil one"*

Philippians 1:6, *being confident of this very thing, that He who has begun a good work in you will complete it until the day of Jesus Christ.*

2 Thessalonians 3:3, *But the Lord is faithful, who will establish you and guard you from the evil one;*

Footnote Continued On Next Page

More Evidence That Job's Problem Was Sin, The Sin Of "Pride"

One of Job's friends, Elihu, who was the last to speak, spoke the truth. We can deduce this from the fact that:

> the Lord said to Eliphaz the Temanite, "My wrath is aroused against you and your two friends, for you have not spoken of Me what is right, as My servant Job has" . . . So Eliphaz the Temanite and Bildad the Shuhite and Zophar the Naamathite went and did as the Lord commanded them (Job 42:7-9).

Elihu's name is conspicuously absent from the list of those that God said did not speak the truth, so by implication Elihu did speak the truth to Job.

The other three friends gave up on Job:

> So these three men ceased answering Job, because he (Job) was righteous in his own eyes (32:1).
>
> Then the wrath of Elihu . . . was aroused against Job; his wrath was aroused because he justified himself rather than God" (32:2).
>
> "Surely you have spoken in my hearing. And I have heard the sound of your words, saying, 'I am pure, without transgression; I am innocent, and there is no iniquity in me. Yet He finds occasions against me. He counts me as His enemy; He puts my feet in the stocks. He watches all my paths'. Look, in this you are not righteous. I will answer you, for God is greater than man. Why do you contend with Him? For He does not give an accounting of any of His words. For God may speak in one way, or in another. Yet man does not perceive it. In a dream, in a vision of the night, when deep sleep falls upon men, while slumbering on their beds. Then He opens the ears of men, and seals their instruction. In order to turn man from his deed, and conceal pride from man, he keeps back his soul from the Pit, and his life from perishing by the sword" (33:8-18).
>
> "Behold, God works all these things, twice, in fact, three times with a man, to bring back his soul from the Pit. That he may be enlightened with the light of life" (33:29-30).
>
> "Do you think this is right? Do you say 'my righteousness is more than God's'?" (35:2).

---

1 Peter 1:5, . . .*who are kept by the power of God through faith for salvation ready to be revealed in the last time;*

Jude 1-2, *Jude, a servant of Jesus Christ, and brother of James, to those who are called, sanctified by God the Father, and preserved in Jesus Christ: mercy, peace, and love be multiplied to you.*

Clearly, Elihu was saying that Job was proud, that he did not see his sin, and that God was trying every way possible to get his attention in order to rescue him from the Pit.

Endnote #6-5

The Lie Of Dualism

Many religions allude to a dualism in the spiritual world, of a war between the good and the bad, between light and darkness. But this is a false picture of reality. God created all, and he sustains all. I don't know if Satan breathes, as we do. But if he does, his next breath is dependent upon the Lord. It is not an equal battle.

"**Dualism.** A theory in interpretation which explains a given situation or domain in terms of two opposing factors or principles. In general, dualisms are twofold classifications which admit of no intermediate degrees" (Elwell, p.334). In other words, dualism usually assumes a great deal of similarity between the opposing parties, and a great deal of equality in their powers and ability. But this equality is profoundly not true about God and Satan.

"Christian theology generally accepts a modified moral dualism, recognizing God as supremely good and Satan as a deteriorated creature bent everywhere upon the intrusion of evil. This, however, is not dualism in the sense of its usual definition, since Christian theology does not consider Satan to be ultimate or original, and sees him ultimately excluded from the universe" (Elwell, p.334).

Endnote #6-6

Scriptures On God's Protection

2 Corinthians 1:21-22, *Now He who establishes us with you in Christ and has anointed us is God, who also has sealed us and given us the Spirit in our hearts as a deposit.*

Ephesians 1:13, *In Him you also trusted, after you heard the word of truth, the gospel of your salvation; in whom also, having believed, you were sealed with the Holy Spirit of promise,*

Both of these scriptures refer to the fact that we are now Christ's property, and we have been sealed. "The word 'seal' means the brand or trade-mark which indicates ownership and owner's rights, and that it is in this sense that the Name serves in baptism as a 'seal'. . . Positively it puts the baptized under the protection of the

Kyrios for the future too, and secures him against demonic influences" (Bultmann, Theology of the New Testament, Part I, p.138). "*Kyrios*" is a title for Jesus. It is a Greek word meaning "supreme in authority." It is usually translated into English as "God, Lord, Master, Sir" (Strong, p.44).

Endnote #6-7

Scriptures On God's Way Of Pressuring Us

2 Corinthians 11:23-30; 12:5,7-10, *Are they ministers of Christ? - I speak as a fool - I am more: in labors more abundant, in stripes above measure, in prisons more frequently, in deaths often . . . If I must boast, I will boast in the things which concern my infirmity . . . Of such a one I will boast; yet of myself I will not boast, except in my infirmities . . . And lest I should be exalted above measure by the abundance of the revelations, a thorn in the flesh was given me, a messenger of Satan to buffet me, lest I be exalted above measure. Concerning this thing I pleaded with the Lord three times that it might depart from me. And He said to me, "My grace is sufficient for you, for My strength is made perfect in weakness." Therefore most gladly I will rather boast in my infirmities that the power of Christ may rest upon me.*

Hebrews 12:1-3, 5-11, *Therefore, we also, since we are surrounded by so great a cloud of witnesses, let us lay aside every weight, and the sin which so easily ensnares us, and let us run with endurance the race that is set before us, looking unto Jesus, the author and finisher of our faith, who for the joy that was set before Him endured the cross, despising the shame, and has sat down at the right hand of the throne of God. For consider Him who endured such hostility from sinners against Himself, lest you become weary and discouraged in your souls. . . 'My son, do not despise the chastening of the Lord, nor be discouraged when you are rebuked by Him; for whom the Lord loves He chastens, and scourges every son whom He receives.' If you endure chastening, God deals with you as with sons. Furthermore, we have had human fathers who corrected us, and we paid them respect. Shall we not much more readily be in subjection to the Father of spirits and live? For they indeed for a few days chastened us as seemed best to them, but He for our profit, that we may be partakers of His holiness. Now no chastening seems to be joyful for the present, but grievous; nevertheless, afterward it yields the peaceable fruit of righteousness to those who have been trained by it.*

1 Peter 4:12-13,17-19, *Beloved, do not think it strange concerning the fiery trial which is to try you, as though some strange thing happened to you; but rejoice to the extent that you partake of Christ's sufferings, that when His glory is revealed, you may also be glad with exceeding joy . . . For the time has come for judgment to begin at the house of God; and if it begins with us first, what will be the end of those who do not obey the gospel of God? Now, "If the righteous one is* *scarcely saved, where will the ungodly and the sinner appear?" Therefore let those who suffer according to the will of God commit their souls to Him in doing good, as to a faithful creator.*

1 Peter 5:6-11, *Therefore humble yourselves under the mighty hand of God, that He may exalt you in due time, casting all your care upon Him, for He cares for you. Be sober, be vigilant; because your adversary the devil walks about like a roaring lion, seeking whom he may devour. Resist him, steadfast in the faith, knowing that the same sufferings are experienced by your brotherhood in the world. But may the God of all grace, who called us to His eternal glory by Christ Jesus, after you have suffered a while, perfect, establish, strengthen, and settle you. To Him be the glory and the dominion forever and ever. Amen.*

Endnote #6-8

Martin Luther's Experience

"A new and revolutionary picture of God began to develop in Luther's restless soul. Finally, in 1515 while pondering St. Paul's Epistle to the Romans Luther came upon the words: 'For therein is the righteousness of God revealed from faith to faith; as it is written, The just shall live by faith' (1:17, KJV). Here was his key to spiritual certainty: 'Night and day I pondered,' Luther later recalled, 'until I saw the connection between the justice of God and the statement that 'the just shall live by his faith,' Then I grasped that the justice of God is the righteousness by which through grace and sheer mercy God justifies us through faith. Thereupon I felt myself to be reborn and to have gone through open doors into paradise.'

Luther saw it clearly now. Man is saved only by his faith in the merit of Christ's sacrifice. The cross alone can remove man's sin and save him from the grasp of the devil. Luther had come to his famous doctrine of justification by faith alone. He saw how sharply it clashed with the Roman church's doctrine of justification by faith and good works - the demonstration of faith through virtuous acts, acceptance of church dogma, and participation in church ritual" (Shelley, p.257)

Endnote #6-9

Teachings That May Confuse Us-
Why This View I Am Presenting May Be Different

Sometimes We Receive Bad Teaching

We all need to remain teachable, and yet we are to test all things. Not everything in the Bible is immediately obvious. Although the bedrock of the faith is quite clear, sincere Christians have historically differed regarding many other issues (for instance divorce or predestination). If I try hard enough to substantiate a pet belief of mine, I can "prove" almost anything from the Bible (generally by taking verses out of context). The current movement in some churches to ordain active homosexuals is one example. They have Bible verses that they use to support their position. Another example would be those who say that now that we have the Bible, we no longer need His living presence, because *But when that which is perfect has come, then that which is in part will be done away* (1 Corinthians 13:10). When we are new Christians and hear such teaching, we may believe the errors.

Some Alternative Views That Can Confuse Us

Some say that our main purpose in our life is to glorify God and to serve Him. Others say that our primary purpose is to reach the world with the Gospel. These are indeed goals, but they are not the main purpose. Serving Him out of a pure heart is rather a product of our sanctification process, not the main goal. The problem with this emphasis on serving is that it focuses on our behavior rather than on our character. It leads to striving. God did not tell us to act like Jesus, but to be like Jesus. There is a fundamental difference between these. If we are not like Jesus, but we try to act like Jesus, we are doomed to fail; because it is impossible for us to do it. On the other hand, if we become like Jesus, we will, by our new nature, act like Him. Jesus glorifies God and does His work. If we are like Him we will do likewise. Therefore, being like Jesus leads to us glorifying Him; but trying to glorify Him does not lead to being like Him.

Being changed into the image of Jesus is not a one-time event as has been taught by some. Some say that when I am saved, old things have passed away and all things have become new (2 Corinthians 5:17). They say I have become new in one step, and that I should then act that way. The problem with this view is two-fold: first, it doesn't happen that way. For example, some very well known Godly men have fallen into sexual sin. They were God's children, and His Spirit dwelled in them; and yet they sinned. Second, that isn't what the Bible teaches. This scripture is talking about my now being a part of His family (the Church), and thus being reconciled to God (see 2 Corinthians 5:18-20). This scripture does not say that I have been changed into His image. This one-time-event view does not deal with the many scriptures that describe this change as a process, which is termed sanctification

Many also view our hearts as a single unity. They say that once it has changed, it has <u>all</u> changed (the "Honey Jar"). There are also two problems with this. First, it again does not happen that way. Those who do counseling easily see that in some areas a person is like Jesus (as evidenced by the presence of good fruit in their life), and in other areas they are clearly not (as evidenced by the presence of bad fruit). Second, Scripture doesn't support this view. *For what I am doing, I do not understand. For what I will to do, that I do not practice; but what I hate, that I do* (Romans 7:15). I still sin, so it is evident that there are unbelieving places somewhere inside of me (the "Honeycomb").

Endnotes for Chapter 7
"Decisions That Bind Us"

Endnote #7-1

The Feeling That Can Accompany An Inner Vow

There is a distinctive feeling that accompanies the moment when we make a decision to take charge of our life. There is a hardness and a determination that rises up. A cartoon I saw many years ago captures this mood. There were two vultures sitting on a large cactus in the Arizona desert. Keep in mind that vultures eat dead things, so they have to wait for something to die before they can have a meal. The only other thing in this bleak landscape is a bleached-out cow skull. One vulture says to the other, "You go ahead and be patient. I'm going to kill something." That is the feeling. And what is going on in our heart at that moment is sin.

Endnote #7-2

All Such Boasting Is Evil

James 4:16 says: *But now you boast in your arrogance. All such boasting is evil.* The Greek word here translated "boast" is *kauchaomai.* It has its roots in two other words: *aucheo* (to boast) and *euchomai,* (to wish) (Strong, pp 44, 34).

Boasting

Kauchaomai has a powerful application to the sin involved in "I will do it myself." "Paul uses the words to clarify and strongly emphasize an idea which is central to his doctrine of justification. This is the teaching that man's original sin consists in glorifying himself and not giving God his due.

"Just as Paul attacks the Jewish doctrine of justification by works, so he opposes the closely related habit of human self-praise, based on fulfillment of the Law . . . The worthlessness of human boasting, when based on the law, is similarly exposed in the context of Romans 2:23. . . . They come into the category of evil, i.e. unjustified, boasting" (C. Brown, Volume 1, p.228).

Note that Romans 1:23 says: *and changed the glory of the incorruptible God into an image made like corruptible man – and birds and four-footed beasts and creeping things.*   Paul is referring to idolatry; and what we do when we think we can protect ourselves in our own strength is a form of idolatry - confidence in our own ability. We are thinking that we, rather than God, are the masters of our fate.

Remember, we have discussed the fact that keeping the law is based upon our willpower. If you re-read the above with this in mind, the meaning becomes even more clear.

Arrogance

The Greek word translated here as "arrogance" is *alazoneia*, which means braggadocio (Strong, p.9). It refers to: "an insolent and empty assurance, which trusts in its own power and resources and shamefully despises and violates divine laws and human rights . . . an impious and empty presumption which trusts in the stability of earthly things (R.V.Vaunting)" (Thayer, p.25).

Not All Boasting Is The Same

James is referring to a very different boasting than Paul refers to when he says: But of Him you are in Christ Jesus, who became for us wisdom from God – and righteousness and sanctification and redemption – that, as it is written, *"He who glories, let him glory in the Lord"* (1 Corinthians 1:30-31. The word here translated "glories" and "glory" is kauchaomai, the exact Greek word translated in James as "boasting." So it is not wrong to "boast," but we are to boast in the Lord and His provision for us, not in our own strength. Relying on our own strength is the sin, and *All such boasting is evil"* (James 4:16).

Endnotes for Chapter 8
"That It May Go Well With You"

Endnote #8-1

More On The Old Testament Command To "Honor" Parents

- "It is because parental authority is divinely delegated authority that respectful obedience to parents was invested with such great importance in the life of God's covenant people . . . Reverence for parents was thus made an integral part of reverence for God as their God . . . Hence the extremely severe penalty (death, in fact) which was to be inflicted on anyone who cursed his parents and on the 'stubborn and rebellious son' (Deuteronomy 21:18-21) who refused to obey them, defied their warning discipline and proved to be incorrigible" (Stott, p.240).

The Hebrew word translated as "honor" in Deuteronomy 5:16 is *"kabed,"* and this Hebrew word reflects the importance of the concept.

- *"Kabed* literally means 'to be heavy, weighty,' but is used almost exclusively in figurative ways, the most common being to be honorable. For a man to be 'weighty' in society is understood figuratively as his being important, respected, and honored. Greek *'time'* also includes the idea of value" (Elwell, p.531).

The Greek word *"timao"* is the word used to translate the Hebrew *"kabed"* in the above passages, and it means," . . . to prize, i.e. fix a valuation upon" (underlining is mine). It comes from another word which means "valuable," or "costly" (Strong, p.72). It also means ". . . to fix the value of something belonging to one's self" (underlining is mine). (Thayer, p.624).

Endnote # 8-2

What Does God Say About the Parent-Child Relationship?

What God means when He commands us to honor our parents depends on how God views this special relationship. Fortunately, the nature of the relationship between parents and children is well covered in the New Testament. Therefore we can discover in Scripture how God intends for these relationships to be conducted. There are a few major characteristics it is important to know about.

1. Parents have the greater responsibility in the relationship when children are young.

2. The nature of the relationship changes as children grow; and once the children are out of the home, it changes again.

3. At all stages of life the relationship is reciprocal, and each party has certain responsibilities. At no time is the relationship meant to be a one-way street.

1. Parents Have The Greater Responsibility In The Relationship When The Children Are Young

The parents have the primary responsibility in the relationship when the children are little, and this is a very heavy and complex responsibility.

> Proverbs 22:6 (Amplified) says: *Train up a child in the way he should go (and in keeping with his individual gift and bent), and when he is old he will not depart from it.*

It is often difficult for parents to put aside their own needs and to look to the needs of their children when they are getting on their nerves. It is no small feat to change how they relate to each child as the child goes through their developmental phases, and to treat each of their children as the unique individual that God made them to be.

Parents are therefore assigned by God to lovingly oversee this process of blessing the uniqueness of each individual child. Some Bible commentators have said the following:

"What children should see in their fathers is what Christ himself stands for in the conduct of life."[226]

"So human fathers are to care for their families as God the Father cares for His."[227]

"Behind this curbing of parental authority there lies the clear recognition that, although children are to obey their parents in the Lord, yet they have a life and personality of their own. They are little people in their own right. As such they are to be respected and on no account to be exploited, manipulated or crushed. 'The dominant father of the Victorian novels', writes Sir Frederick Catherwood, 'who used his own authority for his own ends is no more entitled to claim Christian authority than the rebellious son.'"[228]

2. The Nature Of The Relationship Changes Over Time

The nature of the parent-child relationship changes as a child grows. Child development research shows that a child's ability to function grows step by step from infancy on. Children are literally incapable of certain things until they reach an appropriate age. On the other hand, they <u>must</u> master certain things during a certain age period, or they will have difficulty with the next step. It will also be difficult for children to go back and master the missed skills at a later time. God designed children to develop in a sequence.

a. Young Children

When children are young, it is built into them to honor their parents. For a young child, parents are like gods who are always right. If there is anything wrong in the family, the child blames himself instead of rightly applying the blame to the parents. For instance, if parents divorce, it is typical of children to ask the question, "Do you think they would have stayed together if I were a better boy?"

As children grow, they have certain developmental tasks to accomplish. For instance, the "terrible twos" is a time when children have become aware that they are separate from the mother (and others), and their task is to gain autonomy. "The behavior of older toddlers is characterized by the phrase, 'I can do it myself'.

---

[226] Mitton, p.213.

[227] Stott, p.245.

[228] Stott, p.246.

They are less concerned with doing things their own way and more concerned with doing them on their own."[229]

b. Teen-agers

During the infamous teenage years young people develop the ability for abstract thinking (called "formal operations").[230]   Suddenly all the things their parents have told them through the years, and which they have just been doing automatically, come under question. They need to investigate for themselves to see if these things are true for them before they can truly make them their own. Sometimes parents interpret this teenage individuation process as dishonoring of parental authority. If this is how parents interpret these behaviors at this stage in the person's development, parents may wound the teenager by not cooperating with this process. Such wounding can come about by either ignoring the teen's struggles to make sense of life (which tells the teen he or she isn't important), or the parents may over discipline when the teen is only experimenting with life. ". . . experiences of parental rejection or neglect are closely linked to low self-esteem and depression."[231]

When teenagers are age-appropriately doing their developmental task (seeking to have control of their own life, and testing what they have been taught), this is not rebellion or dishonoring. They are just doing what God programmed them to do. Whereas a toddler needs to simply do what the parent says, a teenager needs to not simply do everything parents say, or risk not develop as he or she should. At this stage when individuation is occurring, honoring does not, and should not, mean rote obedience.[232] This is one of the challenges of being a parent. Parents must give the teen the maximum amount of freedom the individual can manage, and yet protect the teen from experimenting in ways that are destructive (for example teen pregnancy, drugs, etc.).

The job of parents in helping their teen to mature without giving them more freedom than they are ready for has been made more complex and difficult by the temptations in our present culture that is not Christian.

---

[229] Newman, p.263.

[230] Newman, pp.375-381.

[231] Newman, p.388.

[232] "Every child must be allowed to be himself. Wise parents recognize that not all the non-conforming responses of childhood deserve to be styled 'rebellion . . . they have to develop their independence, not because they are resistant to their parents' authority but because they need to exercise their own . . . Certainly some parents are too directive, too domineering, and thereby inhibit their children from learning to make their own decisions and so grow into maturity" (Stott, pp.247, 249).

c. Adult Children

When children become independent adults and leave the home, the parent/child relationship should change to an adult-to-adult relationship with each supporting the independence of the other. Young adults no longer owe the parents the same duties as they did when they lived in the home of their parents. As parents grow older and experience more limitations, parents may now become dependent on their adult "child."

3. The Relationship Is <u>Always</u> Reciprocal

In the New Testament, all relationships in a family are reciprocal, and there are no one-way family exhortations in the New Testament. There are responsibilities on all parties to love and care for one another.

For example, the reciprocal nature of the relationship between a husband and wife is clearly addressed in Colossians 3:18-19: *Wives submit to your own husbands, as is fitting in the Lord. Husbands love your wives and do not be bitter toward them*, and in Ephesians 5:21-33.[233] "Elsewhere, the subjection of the wife is counter-balanced by the love of the husband which becomes a reciprocal subjection (Eph. 5:21-33; Col. 3:18-21.)."[234]

Likewise, the relationship between parents and children is also reciprocal. This reciprocity between children and parents is expressed in Colossians 3:20-21, where the admonition to the children is counterbalanced with a responsibility to the parents:

Children, obey your parents in all things, for this is well pleasing to the Lord. Fathers, do not provoke your children, lest they become discouraged,

---

[233] **Ephesians 5:21-33,** *Submitting to one another in the fear of God. Wives, submit to your own husbands, as to the Lord. For the husband is head of the wife, as also Christ is head of the church; and He is the Savior of the body. Therefore, just as the church is subject to Christ, so let the wives be to their own husbands in everything. Husbands, love your wives, just as Christ also loved the church and gave Himself for it, that He might sanctify and cleanse it with the washing of water by the word, that He might present it to Himself a glorious church, not having spot or wrinkle or any such thing, but that it should be holy and without blemish. So husbands ought to love their own wives as their own bodies; he who loves his wife loves himself. For no one ever hated his own flesh, but nourishes and cherished it, just as the Lord does the church. For we are members of His body, of His flesh and His bones. "For this reason a man shall leave his father and mother and be joined to his wife, and the two shall become one flesh." This is a great mystery, but I speak concerning Christ and the church. Nevertheless let each one of you in particular so love his own wife as himself, and let the wife see that she respects her husband.*

[234] Brown, Vol 2, p.51.

Also see Ephesians 6:1-4 below.[235] So the responsibility in the relationship between the child and the parents is not a one-way responsibility. Both the child and the parents have responsibilities.

> "The instruction to children to obey their parents presupposes, as we have seen, the fact of parental authority. Yet when Paul outlines how parents should behave towards their children, it is not the exercise, but the restraint, of their authority which he urges upon them. The picture he paints of fathers as self-controlled, gentle, patient educators of their children is in stark contrast to the norm of his own day . . . So human fathers are to care for their families as God the Father cares for his." (Stott, p.245).

In the first century, the guidelines regarding family relationships, as written by Paul in the epistles to the Ephesians and the Colossians, were radically new and counter-cultural. The culture throughout the area evangelized by the Apostles was dominated by the Romans. In the Roman culture the father had <u>total authority</u> over <u>all</u> members of his family! Women were little more than property:

> ". . . Under the Roman 'patria potestas' (the father's power) the father had absolute power over his family. In the case of his children he could let them live or expose them" (to allow them to die) "at birth for any reason he chose to do so. He could sell them into slavery, or even execute them at will for any offense. This authority extended to the entire life of the son. . . ."[236]

> "The child-parent relationship is not one-sided. It is a feature of Paul's treatment of these domestic categories that the stronger have obligations to the weaker. The gospel introduced a fresh element into parental responsibility by insisting that the feelings of the child must be taken into consideration. In a society where the father's authority (patria potestas) was absolute, this represented a revolutionary concept."[237]

The relationship between a parent and a child is <u>never</u> at any time one of master and slave.

---

[235] **Ephesians 6:1-4,** *Children, obey your parents in the Lord, for this is right. 'Honor your father and mother,' which is the first commandment with promise: "that it may be will with you and you may live long on the earth;" And you, fathers, do not provoke your children to wrath, but bring them up in the training and admonition of the Lord.*

[236] Carter, p.249.

[237] Expositors, p.81.

In opposition to Roman cultural norms, "A Christian father will have a real concern for his child's happiness and welfare and in consequence will seek to see the child's point of view . . . ."[238] Otherwise the child will react: "A child has a vivid sense of justice."[239]

Therefore, the relationship between parents and a child is <u>never</u> at any time one of master and slave. The old phrase "Children are to be seen but not heard" is totally at odds with Scripture. Though parents have authority in the child's life, they also have a responsibility to the Lord to love and nurture the child for the child's best interest, not for the parents' interest. So even though the nature of the relationship between the parents and the child should change over time, and regardless of the age of the individuals and the stage in life through which they are passing, there are always responsibilities placed upon each person regarding how they relate towards the other family members.

Endnote #8-3

Honoring Grandparents And Adoptive Parents

- Please keep in mind that since Scripture is not clear about "honoring" these classes of people, what I am going to say is speculative.

- You are a direct blood descendent of your grandparents. There are special things that happen in the spirit realm between descendents and ancestors. Because of this special relationship, there is a <u>possibility</u> that God would want you to "honor" them in a way similar to parents.

- Adoptive parents are a different situation. When people adopt a child, a legal transaction occurs in the <u>natural</u> realm. But when this legal transaction takes place in the natural realm, does a legal transaction also take place in the spiritual realm, as it does when people marry? Because the relationship between a child and their primary care givers affects the child's view of God, there is a <u>possibility</u> that God would like you to "honor" adoptive parents in a way similar to parents.

---

[238] Mitton, p.212.

[239] Interpreters, p.732.

Endnotes for Chapter 9
"There Is Buried Treasure"

Endnote #9-1

Mankind Is Multifaceted

There is a commonly held view that mankind consists of three parts: body (*soma*), soul (*psyche*), and spirit (*pneuma*). One chief proponent of this view was Watchman Nee, but there have been many others. This view forces one to see the "good part" as the "spirit." After all, if "body" is bad, and "soul" is bad, then "spirit" is the only choice left. However, this three-part view is questionable in its adequacy to explain many scriptures.

> "In defining the concept *soma*, the place to begin is the naïve popular usage in which *soma* means body - as a rule, man's - which in a naïve anthropological view can be placed in contrast with the 'soul' or the 'spirit' (1 Thess. 5:23; I Cor. 5:3; 7:34)." (Bultmann, Theology of the New Testament, Part II, p.193).

> "The various possibilities of regarding man, or self, come to light in the use of the anthropological terms *soma, psyche*, and *pneuma*. Man does not consist of two parts, much less of three; nor are *psyche* and *pneuma* special faculties or principles (within the *soma*) or a mental life higher than his animal life. Rather, man is a living unity. He is a person who can become an object to himself. He is a person having a relationship to himself (*soma*). He is a person who lives in his intentionality, his pursuit of some purpose, his willing and knowing (*psyche, pneuma*). This state of living toward some goal, having some attitude, willing something and knowing something, belongs to man's very nature and in itself is neither good nor bad." (underlining is mine). (Bultmann, Theology of the New Testament, Part II, p.209).

> "Man is to be treated as a unity. His spiritual condition can not be dealt with independently of his physical and psychological condition, and vice versa . . . Man is a complex being. His nature is not reducible to a single principle" (Erickson, p.539).

Is Our "Spirit" the good part, And Our "Soul" The Bad Part?

Some say that our "spirit" is the good part of us and our "soul" is the fallen part. It would be convenient if it were that simple, but unfortunately it's not. *Pneuma* (Greek for spirit) is a "fuzzy" word with a wide range of meaning, some of which are definitely not "good," and sometimes even <u>equated</u> with *psuche* (soul). This debate over the details of the nature of man has been going on in the Church since the time of Jesus, and each side has scriptures to back up their view. This is an issue that probably cannot be settled from Scripture, because <u>all</u> of the words describing the inner parts of humanity are "fuzzy" words. "Body," "soul," "spirit," "mind," "flesh," "heart," and "life" are all words that have a wide range of meaning in Scripture, and so it is problematic to try to nail down exactly what meaning is intended in a given passage.[240] Therefore we cannot say with certainty either that the "good part" is limited to our personal spirit, or that it is not.

This uncertainty may seem like a very unsatisfactory state of affairs. Fortunately, from the standpoint of a practical walking out of our Christian life, we don't <u>need</u> to know <u>exactly</u> what word to attach to a specific function. What is important for us to know is that there is a place deep inside us that is "bad," a place that is "good," other parts that have no moral significance, and that these places are intertwined in <u>a complex unity</u> that makes up a human being.[241]

This debate is not that simple, and the only answer we can get from Scripture is that sometimes "spirit" is "good," sometimes it is "bad," and sometimes it has no moral character. Likewise for "soul."

An example which illustrates the difficulty of saying with certainty that our "spirit" is good and our "soul" is bad, is the following portion of a discussion of the Greek word *psyche* (soul).

"In Lk. 1:46 soul is used in parallel with spirit. Both have here the meaning of the whole inner man, in contrast to the outward aspect of lips and speech.

---

[240]   This uncertainty is why I have stayed away from these "fuzzy" and controversial words in defining the "good part." It is also why I have not attempted to describe every aspect of what we are like inside. For instance I have described the "Treasure Inside" by listing characteristics that are undeniably "good," and "flesh" by characteristics that are undeniably "bad." I cannot go beyond that with assurance that I am accurate. These descriptions of mine are not exhaustive and do not include every trait of a human being, nor have I attempted a detailed description of how they interact in every scenario.

Since theologians over the centuries have not been able to come into agreement about the details, I certainly am not qualified to settle the argument. Fortunately, we <u>do not</u> need to have answers to this level of detail to live our Christian life.

See Glossary for definitions for some of these words.

See Endnote #13-2 for more on "fuzzy words."

[241]   "Man does not consist of two parts, much less of three, nor are *psyche* and *pneuma* special facilities or principles (within the *soma*) or a mental life higher than his animal life. Rather, man is a living unity (Bultmann, Theology of the New Testament, p.209).

I have found that when a person believes that their personal spirit is the only "good part," it is destructive. There are clearly parts of my natural man that are not "bad," such as my awareness of my need for a drink of water. Intuitively we know this, and so the implication that everything in my "soul" is bad is very destructive, because it is not true, and our Treasure Inside knows that and is wounded by the accusation and the condemnation.

Above all, the soul is spoken of here in a sense which goes beyond the world of Greek thought. It is the seat of the religious life and of man's relationship to God" (C. Brown, Volume 3, pp.683-684).

Luke 1:46-47: *And Mary said: "My soul magnifies the Lord, and my spirit has rejoiced in God my Savior."*

Pneuma (spirit) has a wide range of meaning (Berry, p.121):
1) properly, the wind, or the air in motion
2) the human spirit
3) a temper or disposition of the soul
4) any intelligent, incorporeal being

Similarly, as defined by Thayer (pp.520-523):
1) a movement of air
2) the spirit, i.e. the vital principle by which the body is animated
3) a spirit, i.e. a simple essence, devoid of all or at least all grosser matter, and possessed of the power of knowing, desiring, deciding, and acting
4) God's power and agency
5) univ. *the disposition or influence which fills and governs the soul of any one; the efficient source of any power, affection, emotion, desire,* etc.

Pneuma is sometimes not "good":

"Thus as the heights and depths of human existence are experienced mankind's spirit is drawn to either God or the devil; it receives blessing or the subtle influences of evil and ultimate condemnation." (Elwell, p.1041).

Endnote #9-2

Names Others Have Used To Refer To That Part Of Us "Inside"

Many people have observed the presence of a part inside each of us, and have tried to define what is in there and to attach a name to that part. The names I have encountered are: Authentic Self, Center, Child Within, Core Self, Creative Child, Deepest Self, Divine Child, Essential Self, Gifted Self, Heart, Hidden Observer, Higher Self, Inner Child, Inner Child of the Past, Inner Core, Inner Guide, Inner Man, Inner Self, Internal Self-Helper, Magical Child, Natural Child, Observing Ego, Personal Spirit, Private Self, Radiant Child, Real Self, Shimmering Self, True Çenter, True Self, Unconscious Self, Unique Self, and Wonder Child: a bewildering array of possibilities. And, of course, each author has attached a description of what they think is in there.

The list of names for that part of us that is manifest outside (where I have placed Willpower, Intellect, and Consciousness) is much shorter: Adaptive Self, Conscious Self, External Self, False Self, Head, Persona (a Latin term for "actor's mask"), Personage, and Public Self.

As I have said before, what we call these parts isn't so important as to recognize that they exist, and what their functions are. Actually the controversy revolves around the inside part, not the manifest part. Most people easily accept such terms as my "head." They aren't very emotional about it. However, I have had many clients who had negative reactions to the use of some of these terms that refer to the place inside themselves, especially the term "Inner Child."

When there is this negative reaction, the term becomes an obstacle rather than an aid in the person's healing, which is unfortunate. We want to put as few roadblocks as possible in the way of the healing process.

I have thought about using several of the above terms, but have been unhappy with aspects of each one of them. Each of them falls short of conveying what I see as being in that part of us. But more importantly, these terms are loaded with other meanings which other authors and counselors have placed on them. Many of these meanings are not in harmony with who God says we are.

Coming up with a term is terribly difficult. No single term seems to be adequate to describe the enormity of this place. This place within me is fully human and alive. He is profoundly a part of me, in which God's Spirit resides; and with whom He intended for me to be in loving, intimate relationship. I presume there's no other place like it in the universe.

The term needs to be one that I will feel comfortable using in my relationship with this part of me in my daily existence with myself. On the one hand the name needs to be respectful, since he (what I am going to call my "Treasure Inside") is fearfully and wonderfully made by the Lord. He is God's handiwork, and the image of God is within him. He is changeable and multi-dimensional: sometimes he is a little child, sometimes he is incredibly wise and mature. Sometimes he needs me to hold him and cry with him, and sometimes he needs me to listen to him with great respect.

Consequently, the Lord has frustrated me in coming up with a single term, and I think He did this for a purpose. I have come to the conclusion that it is a very personal choice, and each person needs to find out what fits for them. The Hebrews knew that names were very important. When I refer to my wife as "Kay," there is a whole package of characteristics and experiences that touch me with that name.

Some people like the term "heart," because for them this is a very warm term. This term doesn't work well for me; because when I think of "heart," I see a picture of a pink piece of flesh with tubes coming out of it. I have trouble getting warm and snuggly with this picture. Sometimes people were given a nickname as a child, for example "Jimmy." As they grew up they rejected this pet name and wanted to be called by their formal name, for example "James." As they connect with their inner self, they may discover that their Treasure Inside likes to be called "Jimmy."

Therefore, for you personally, I would encourage you to discover what works for you. What you call this part of you is therefore a very personal discovery. You can even choose not to name that part; but the one thing that is not optional is to ignore the reality of that part, and to remain relationally alienated from him or her. If you continue to reject that part, you will continue to be in pain, and life will continue to be difficult. You will continue to be a house divided against yourself (Matthew 12:25).

In this book I am going to call this part my "Treasure Inside," and the outside part as my "Head." Choosing some single term is strictly for convenience. It will be more convenient in this book to have a single term to use rather than having to give a lengthy description in every reference. In picking these terms I am not campaigning for you to use them. In fact, I would discourage you from using them unless that works for you. "Treasure Inside" and "Head" are pretty neutral and rather impersonal, and I chose them specifically for that reason. Also keep in mind that this diagram is not "me" in my entirety. There is more to me, including the bad part, but I cannot yet define all the other parts of me. Likely, I never will be able to, because Scripture isn't definitive enough for this.

Endnote #9-3

Our "Treasure Inside" Communicates With Other Peoples' "Treasure Inside"

Have you ever been in a public place, like a restaurant, and you had a feeling that someone was looking at you? You turn around, and sure enough, someone was. How did you know that? Do you have eyes in the back of your head? Or were you just guessing? No, you knew it, somehow.

Interesting research is going on regarding such phenomena. In his book, The Heart's Code, Paul Pearsall reports on research being conducted at the Princeton Engineering Anomalies research program at Princeton University. The program's purpose is to pursue rigorous scientific study of the interaction of human consciousness with sensitive physical devices, systems and processes. They have proven scientifically that human beings can influence machines by consciously focusing on a desired outcome, but without touching the machine. They have also observed that two people who are bonded (for example, a married couple) jointly have a greater influence than does an individual. Though these observations are unquestionably true, nobody has the answers to what is going on, and in fact they don't know exactly what questions to ask! But there is something going on that exceeds naturalistic explanations and the limits of current theory (Pearsall, pp.44-47).

The purpose of Pearsall's book is to explore the transfer of personality characteristics from a heart donor to the heart recipient. Again, there is overwhelming evidence that heart recipients receive more from the donor than a physical heart, but the mechanism is as yet unidentified.

Because this is a new frontier, and because all the research is secular, there is no clear theory or hypothesis as to how all this relates to our personal spirit or to the spirit realm. The only solid conclusion possible at this point is that there is in fact an added dimension to human reality that has been hitherto ignored and unexplained by science, and this dimension influences how human beings relate to each other and to the world, all below the level of their consciousness.

Endnote #9-4

Why Men And Women Differ In Accessing Their "Treasure Inside"

Men and women have different brain structures. The human brain has two hemispheres, and the two hemispheres perform quite differently from each other. In a simplified description, the right hemisphere of the brain performs conceptual, sensing functions, and the left hemisphere is the center of logical, linguistic, linear processing. However, though each hemisphere has their unique way of functioning, yet the way they function separately and in unison is actually quite complex. It would be informative to look into a little more of this detail. Dr. Daniel Siegel has the following to say:

> "What we call 'thinking' often refers to the conscious verbal processing of the left hemisphere. When we are conscious of sensations and images, these may be likely to emanate from the right hemisphere. Of note is that the left hemisphere appears to be inept at reading nonverbal social or emotional cues from others. Facial recognition centers are primarily in the right hemisphere. What this suggests is that right-hemisphere 'reality', its constructed representational world, will contain the information derived from the emotional states of others. The right hemisphere's language is one of nonverbal sensations and images. In sum, the general impression of the right hemisphere as being 'more emotional' is somewhat oversimplified; it is more accurate to state that the emotional experience in the right hemisphere may be more attuned to the emotional states of others. The right hemisphere's nonverbal representations involve the essence of affect, whereas the left hemisphere may have little innate ability to construct or be conscious of such nonverbal, nonlogical view of the world." (Siegel, pp184-185).

God designed men to be the hunters and warriors, and women to be the primary caregivers. He devised a way to equip each for their necessary specialized duties by developing the male and female brains differently. Lest I be labeled as sexist, it is a fact that for thousands of years this division of tasks between husband and wife has been the necessity of life. Only in the last hundred years or so has there emerged options to live life differently.

Dr. Donald Joy describes the process by which the male brain is modified:

"During the sixteenth week of the baby's development, another major modification occurs. The structure of the brain as it develops is also dictated by the X chromosome of the mother. The brain will become a female brain if it continues as it has been until the sixteenth week. If the XY code calls for modifying the 'Adam' baby into the male option, the brain must be changed to match the body whose genitals were changed in the ninth to twelfth week.

The standard model brain which delivers in a baby girl is organized with open communication between the two hemispheres. These walnut-like halves which spread across the top half of the human head are connected by a telecommunications network called the corpus callosum. All brains contain millions of androgen-sensitive cells and fibers. These are pre-designed to dissolve and disappear on contact with male hormones. So, again, the mother's androgens are called for, as well as the hormonal production of the baby boy's testes. From the sixteenth to the twenty-sixth week a baby boy's head is literally swimming with male chemicals. The androgen sensitive cells and fibers are systematically dissolved and removed. What remains is the designer male brain. The designer male brain is modified for specialized tasks" (Joy, p.72).

In other words, the male's brain has been physically modified so that he can separate from his emotions when necessary. His logical brain (left hemisphere) is less intimately connected with his emotional states (right hemisphere) than is true of women: he has been equipped to be able to turn off his emotions. In his historical role this has allowed him to concentrate on the unpleasant task ahead of him: to kill the charging tiger, or defend his family against the enemy. When the moment is over, then he can process the experience emotionally (fall apart).

In her historical role, the woman was also equipped for her tasks: to be multi-tasked and socially sensitive. While she is cooking and sewing, she has to be aware of where the children are and what their needs are at that moment. Consequently, she has not been equipped to shut off her emotions as men can.

Difficulty arises when there is much trauma in growing up, and this gift that God gave to men is misused. When the trauma continues for long periods of time, this ability to shut off his right brain becomes generalized. Then living in the shut-down mode becomes his normal way of doing life. The activity of the right brain goes on, he just isn't aware of it. This is The Wall. Given the same level of trauma, women would do the same thing if they could, but they can't do it as efficiently. They aren't built that way.

Endnotes for Chapter 10
"Your Worst Trauma"

Endnote #10-1

What is "normal?"

It is hard for us to see ourselves and life as they really are. For us, this is how life has always been. We have never been anybody else nor lived another life, so we have no way of comparing. We have always felt this way (as long as we can remember). Therefore, to us a 'normal" or "happy" childhood may not have been all that normal or happy. Our daily life may now seem normal or happy, but it really isn't -- at least it may not be healthy. My "normal" may not be "healthy," but I don't know the difference. I may not be able to recognize "normal," because of my defenses against pain, or because I may have never experienced "normal."

I have counseled people who had significantly abusive parents, and yet they felt they had a "normal" childhood, and their parents were "loving."

Because of this, we may be the last ones to be able to see ourselves as we really are. Sensitive people who first meet us often know things about us we don't know.

Endnote #10-2

Bonding

Bonding is a phenomenon that is currently receiving much attention by researchers, and some very interesting truths are being uncovered. When a child is born, their brain is amazingly incomplete. Babies are not simply miniature adults, and there are many functions that their brains simply cannot perform. Their brains are in fact quite small, and are growing at an extremely rapid rate for the first two years after birth.

As these brain cells are created, what is their architecture? What will be their function, and how will they function together? With all animals this is primarily genetic and automatic. A horse is a horse is a horse. However, man is different. In a human baby, most of the instructions the baby brain receives regarding how to grow come from experience, and bonding is a profound part of this experience.

In a bonding moment, the baby wants to "connect" with the mother. The secular researchers say that the baby's brain needs an adult brain to model itself after. The emotional state of the mother's brain (affect) is transmitted to the child's brain, and the child's brain responds by constructing ("imprinting") its architecture to match that of the mother. The mechanism by which this happens is not defined, but I would suggest that it is a spirit-to-spirit connection that passes on the necessary information.

The quotes below are a bit difficult to follow because of their scientific basis, but they are powerful statements.

"I propose that during these eye-to-eye transactions the infant's maturing right hemisphere is 'psychobiologically attuned' (Field, 1985a) to the output of the mother's right hemisphere (Schore, p.76) ". . . the mother is *the* regulator of the functioning of the infant's developing autonomic nervous system as well. Symbiotic states are physiologically mediated by the regulation of the infant's immature and developing internal homeostatic system by the caregiver's more mature and differentiated nervous system. . . Kohut (1977) describes that as a result of the empathic merger of the child's rudimentary psyche with the maternal selfobject's highly developed psychic organization, the child experiences the feeling states of the self-object as if they were his own" (Schore, pp. 78-79). "In synchronize, mutual gaze, a state of 'mutually entrained central nervous system propensities' (Horner, 1985) involved in 'mutual regulatory system arousal' (Stern, 1983a), the infant's postnatally maturing limbic system is exposed to the maternal gleam. . . I suggest that in the psychobiologically attuned merger or fusion state in which a match occurs not between external behavioral events but between the expression of internal states (Stern), the child is stimulated into a similar state of heightened catecholaminergic-induced sympathetic arousal as the mother" (Schore, p. 80).

This is all technical jargon for "bonding." In bonding, the child has a need to "connect" with the mother (their brain needs more instructions). The mother senses this, stops all other activity, and sits facing the infant. Their eyes meet and bonding occurs. This is a joyful event to the child, and also to the mother. They continue to bond until the child no longer has the need. Then mother can go about her other business.

For the above to occur successfully, several conditions are necessary. First, the mother has to be able to sense that this is what the child wants. Second, she needs to know how important this is and to be willing to put aside the dishes or other household chores to simply sit with her child. Third, it presupposes that she is able to be in intimate relationship with another person, in this case her child. Fourth, she needs to be willing to continue the bonding moment until the child is done. This is only likely to happen with a mother who, as an infant, was able to bond successfully with her own mother. In many cases, this is not the case, and so her own children have insufficient bonding.

When bonding is occurring, there are several messages that are transmitted to the child (and imprinted on their brain). These messages are: "I am important. Mother is here for me. I must be loveable. My needs are going to be met. It is safe in the world." When the bonding does not occur, the opposite messages are imprinted on the child's brain: "I am unimportant. Mother isn't here for me. I am unlovable. My needs are not going to be met. It isn't safe in the world."

Successful bonding therefore predisposes us to love ourselves and to be optimistic by building these messages into our brain structure. Unsuccessful bonding predisposes us to see ourselves as unlovable and unimportant and to be pessimistic.

"It is a neurobiological fact that there is built into every human being, into you and into me and into our children, a neurobiological need to be in the presence of someone who is delighted to be with us, and a need to know that they're delighted to be with us. Neurobiologically, this need is called the need for joy" (Martin, p.21). "Shame is defined in the right orbital pre-frontal cortex of the brain as being all that we experience when we are in the presence of someone who is <u>not</u> glad to be with us and we know it. Shame, then, is the opposite of joy" (Martin, p.37).

The good news is that the part of the brain where the negative messages are imprinted can be changed. "The good news - the Gospel, if you will - is that God so designed the human being that the only part of the brain which retains throughout life its fetal, or original, capacity to grow and develop is the part of the brain where the joy structures are located" (Martin, p.82). So even if our brain was imprinted with the wrong messages as a child, this can be re-programmed as an adult if we are able to bond with another person. Love heals!

Endnotes for Chapter 11
"Emotions Are Your Friend"

Endnote #11-1

List Of Negative and Positive Emotions

Note that Anger is always an umbrella covering another feeling. When you feel anger you need to look underneath it to find the underlying feeling. In the list below, the feelings listed under "Angry" are the most common feelings that are underlying it. At the same time, be aware that many of the "Other Negative" emotions can also manifest themselves as anger. For healing to come one must feel what is behind the anger

Anger	Ashamed	Edgy	Insecure
Belittled	Attacked	Egotistical	Insignificant
Betrayed	Aversion	Embarrassed	Intimidated
Controlled	Baffled	Envious	Intolerant
Cross	Bewildered	Exhausted	Irritable
Disvalued	Bitter	Fiendish	Isolated
Exasperated	Blah	Foolish	Jealous
Fear	Boastful	Forlorn	Lazy
Fearful	Bored	Forgetful	Lethargic
Frustrated	Callous	Friendless	Listless
Furious	Cautious	Fussy	Lonely
Grouchy	Confused	Gloomy	Lustful
Ignored	Conniving	Gossipy	Mangy
Indignant	Contempt	Grasping	Martyred
Insecure	Cranky	Greedy	Mean
Mad	Defeated	Grieved	Mediocre
Not heard	Defensive	Grim	Melancholy
Powerless	Defiled	Half-hearted	Merciless
Threatened	Depressed	Hate	Meticulous
Unimportant	Desolate	Helpless	Miserly
	Desperate	Hesitant	Misjudged
Other	Despondent	Homesick	Misunderstood
Negative	Different	Hopeless	Morose
Abhorrence	Dirty	Hurt	Mournful
Agitated	Disappointed	Impatient	Muddled
Aggravated;	Discontented	Inadequate	Mystified
Alarmed	Disgusted	Incapable	Naked
Aloof	Dislike	Incompetent	Nauseated
Annoyed	Disdain	Indifferent	Neglected
Anxious	Domineering	Inferior	Nervous
Apathetic	Doomed	Inflexible	Obstinate
Apprehensive	Dull	Inhibited	Out of control

Out of place
Overcome
Overworked
Panicky
Paralyzed
Passive
Perplexed
Pooped
Pressured
Reluctant
Repulsed
Resentful
Resigned
Restless
Restrained

Ridiculous
Sad
Sarcastic
Scheming
Seductive
Self-conscious
Shabby
Shaky
Shy
Sick
Skeptical
Stubborn
Sulky
Suspicious
Tearful

Tempted
Tense
Terrified
Threatened
Timid
Tired
Traumatized
Troubled
Two-faced
Undone
Uncaring
Uncertain
Unconcerned
Uneasy
Un-loveable

Upset
Unglued
Unstable
Unsure
Unwanted
Uptight
Vulnerable
Weary
Wilted
Worried
Worthless

Positive Emotions

Admired
Affirmed
Alive
Ambitious
Amused
Appreciated
Approved
Astonished
Awed
Belonging
Blessed
Bold
Brave
Calm
Carefree
Cheerful
Comfortable
Compassionate
Confident
Considerate
Contented
Cooperative
Courageous
Creative
Curious
Delighted

Desire
Determined
Eager
Ecstasy
Efficient
Elated
Empowered
Encouraged
Energetic
Enjoyment
Enthusiastic
Euphoric
Excited
Expectant
Exuberant
Free
Friendly
Generous
Gentle
Glad
Gracious
Grateful
Happy
Helpful
Hopeful
Hospitable
Important

Impressed
Independent
Inspired
Interested
Irresistible
Joyful
Kind
Liked
Longing
Love
Loveable
Mellow
Merciful
Merry
Met
Open
Optimistic
Overjoyed
Patient
Peaceful
Pleasure
Reasonable
Relaxed
Romantic
Safe
Satisfaction
Secure

Self-assured
Sensible
Sensitive
Sensual
Sentimental
Serene
Serious
Soft
Sophisticated
Sure
Sympathetic
Talkative
Tender
Tenacious
Thankful
Thrilled
Tranquil
Transparent
Triumphant
Unbiased
Understanding
Understood
Validated
Valued
Vibrant
Yearning

Endnotes for Chapter 12
"The Good Part Of You"

Endnote # 12-1

You Are Made In God's Image

Psalms 8:4-5, says, *What is man that You are mindful of him, and the son of man that you visit him? For You made him a little lower than the angels, and you have crowned him with glory and honor.* I would submit to you it is unlikely that God would crown with glory and honor something that is bad.

Psalms 139:13-14, *For You have formed my inward parts; You have covered me in my mother's womb. I will praise You, for I am fearfully and wonderfully made; marvelous are your works, and that my soul knows very well.* It is evident that the psalmist is not speaking here of a bad thing.

It is very helpful and instructive to study for a moment the Hebrew words translated here into "fearfully" and "wonderfully." The Hebrew word translated here as "fearfully" (*yare*) has the following meanings: "to revere, cause to frighten" (Strong, p.52).

"To tremble; to fear, to be afraid. To revere, as one's parent. To fear God, to revere him." (Gesinius. p.364).

It is interesting to note that the Hebrew word used in this psalm is exactly the same word used in many places when the Old Testament talks about fearing God, about our attitude towards Him. Why would the psalmist use the exact word that so often talks about our attitude towards God to refer to a part of us? Could it be that he is referring to that part of us that is made in the image of God? If so, could it be that our correct attitude towards the image of God in us should be one of reverence? How many of us have this attitude towards ourselves? I can't be dogmatic about this; but if this is so, this magnifies and accentuates the awfulness of judging ourselves as bad.

The Hebrew word translated "wonderfully" (*palah*) means, "to be separated, to become distinguished, admirable (Psalm 139:14); to make distinguished, or illustrious" (Gesinius, p.675). So Psalm 139 is also saying that there is a part of me that is admirable, and illustrious. Perhaps (but only perhaps) the word "distinguished" or "separated" means that there is a part of us that is different from other parts of creation.

One authority says, "The Bible does not indicate exactly what the image of God in mankind is" (Youngblood, p.593).

After concluding that the image of God does in fact exist in people, Millard Erickson says the following, speaking of the debate over the exact nature of this image: "The existence of a wide diversity of interpretations is an indication that there are no direct statements in Scripture to resolve the issue" (Erickson, p.512). However, he indicates there is general agreement among theologians on the following (Erickson, p.513):

- The image of God is universal within the human race.
- The image of God has not been lost as a result of sin or specifically the fall.
- There is no indication that the image is present in one person to a greater degree than in another.
- The image is something in the very nature of man, in the way in which he was made.
- The image refers to the elements in the makeup of a man, which enable the fulfillment of his destiny.

This issue of the image of God in man has been hotly debated for over 2000 years. No serious theologian I'm aware of denies the presence of the image of God in mankind. The debate and the differences all revolve around trying to define in detail what that image is. I believe all these attempts are destined to failure and frustration, because the Bible simply does not give us the full details. When we use information outside the Bible, we need to be less dogmatic and more careful about our conclusions. Nevertheless, it is legitimate to look at other evidence, as long as it does not contradict Scripture.

Other Evidence Of The Image Of God In Us

Do we have observable evidence that we can see in peoples' lives of the existence of good in them?   We will only be truly successful and happy in a career if it is in line with who we have been created to be. There is also a strong move in many churches to help people discover what their spiritual gifts are. Many churches have discovered that people flourish, and God's work moves forward with greatest vigor, when people are living and ministering in their own spiritual gifting. Willow Creek Community Church in Illinois is one ministry that has developed a system of testing and identifying Christians' spiritual gifts, and those churches which are using this approach are having very exciting results.

- Is it bad to be musically gifted?
- Is it bad to have artistic talent?
- Is it bad to have a brilliant ability to analyze?
- Is it bad to have organizational gifts?
- Is it bad to be good with numbers?

I think we would all agree that these are good things, not bad things.   We all know how difficult it is to try to do some of the things that we are not gifted to do. It is a great blessing that God has given a variety of gifts, because there are a variety of tasks to be done. Here I am using the term "gifts" to describe both natural gifts and spiritual gifts, because they are usually intimately connected.

> "God, the creator, made us in His image. We are here to help Him continue to build the Kingdom. For this purpose God gave us gifts, dependable strengths, each of us with a unique pattern of strengths. So each is uniquely equipped to contribute, and together we provide team effort, that is, constantly adding good to His kingdom" (Haldane, p.A-19).

It is interesting to speculate that if each of us has a piece of God, and like puzzle parts, they differ; when we are all put together, the aggregate is the full image of God – the completed puzzle (the Body of Christ).

Based upon my own experience, I believe that a major part of the image of God in us is the bottom circle in my diagram (my "Treasure Inside") in Chapter 9, "There Is Buried Treasure."   There I listed our personal spirit, emotions, creativity, curiosity, imagination, intuition, masculinity or femininity, spontaneity, gifts, and talents as being in that place. There are undoubtedly more treasures in that good place, but I mention these to illustrate the type of attributes that live there.

Endnote #12-2

Recovering Your Buried Treasure

Being changed into the image of Jesus is simply uncovering who you really are. You were created in the image of God; but because of a sinful world and the part of you that is sinful, the image of God in you became buried. As the bitter roots are healed and The Wall comes down, you again become who you are, who God made you to be and always intended you to be. Being changed into His image does not mean that your uniqueness becomes obliterated. You do not become a non-person.

Parker Palmer expresses this view of the "good part" as follows:
- "She did not show up as raw material to be shaped into whatever image the world might want her to take. She arrived with her own gifted form, with the shape of her own sacred soul" (p.11).
- "We arrive in this world with birthright gifts - then we spend the first half of our lives abandoning them or letting others disabuse us of them . . . we spend the second half trying to recover and reclaim the gift we once possessed" (p.12).
- "What a long time it can take to become the person one has always been!" (p.9).

- "Self-care is never a selfish act - it is simply good stewardship of the only gift I have, the gift I was put on earth to offer to others" (p.30).
- "She decided, 'I will no longer act on the outside in a way that contradicts the truth that I hold deeply on the inside. I will no longer act as if I were less than the whole person I know myself inwardly to be" (p.33).
- "God asks us only to honor our created nature, which means our limits as well as potentials" (p.50).
- "This is the God who, when asked by Moses for a name, responded, 'I am who I Am' (Exodus 3:14), an answer that has less to do with the moral rules for which Moses made God famous than with elemental 'isness' and selfhood. If, as I believe, we are all made in God's image, we could all give the same answer when asked who we are: 'I Am who I Am,' One dwells with God by being faithful to one's nature. One crosses God by trying to be something one is not. Reality-including one's own-is divine, to be not defied but honored" (p.51).
- ". . . it often takes the eyes of others to help us see. Our strongest gifts are usually those we are barely aware of possessing. They are a part of our God-given nature, with us from the moment we drew first breath, and we are no more conscious of having them than we are of breathing" (p.52).

Your life is about being who you <u>are</u>, not who you think you <u>should be</u>!

Endnote #12-3

You Are Not "Erased" As Jesus Fills You

Commenting on 1 Corinthians10:16:
- "The cup of blessing which we bless, is it not the communion of the blood of Christ? The bread which we break, is it not the communion of the body of Christ?". . . "Similarly, *koinonia* in 1 Cor 10:16 means 'participation' in the body and blood of Christ and thus union with the exalted Christ. This fellowship with Christ comes about through the creative intervention of God. It happens through the transformation of man to the very roots of his being. It is birth into a new existence, and can be expressed by the contrast of life and death. This new existence is not a divinization in the sense of mysticism and the mystery religions, but incorporation in Jesus' death, burial, resurrection, and glory. <u>It is not the elimination or fusion of personality but a new relationship based on the forgiveness of sins"</u> (C. Brown, Vol 1, p.643, underlining is mine).

- *Koinonia* (translated as "communion" above, meant "union with." "This fellowship with Christ comes about through the creative intervention of God. It happens through the transformation of man to the very roots of his being"

(C. Brown, Vol 1, p.643). In 1 John 1:3,6,7, *koinonia* refers to "A new relationship based on the forgiveness of sins (C. Brown, p.643).

Endnote 12-4

Am I All Bad?

Sometimes the messages that "I am all bad" are a bit subtle. One author says:

> "The word 'healing' seems to imply that something got broken, so we fix it. In our carnal minds formed in the world, healing may yet mean 'to restore something formerly good to working order again' – like a good car with some hidden flaw which creates a malfunction until a mechanic discovers and fixes it. That's fine. Good things need to be mended. But that analogy can not be applied to the human soul. . . But no structure in our carnal nature is to be patched up; every part is to be slain and reborn. . . The inner being is not good, that it should be restored" (Sandford, <u>Transformation of the Inner Man</u>, p.19-20).

I think the author would likely defend this statement by saying the good part, the part created in the image of God, is my spirit. But there are clearly parts of my natural man that are not "bad," such as my awareness of my need for a drink of water. Intuitively we know this, and so the implication that everything in my soul is bad is very destructive; because it is not true, and our Treasure Inside knows that and is wounded by the accusation and the condemnation.

Seeing myself as made up of three parts (body, soul, and spirit) can easily lead to this mistake. If I am made of three parts, and I have to decide which one is "bad," "soul" gets the nod. But it isn't that simple (Note that in the three part view of man the Greek word *soma* = body, *psyche* = soul, and *pneuma* = spirit).

> "Likewise, the wish (1 Thess. 5:23) that 'your spirit and soul and body may be kept sound and blameless' evidently means only that the readers may be kept sound, each in his entirety. So far as form is concerned, this is a trichotomous scheme of anthropology. . . nothing more is to be gathered from this passage than that Paul can also speak of a *pneuma* that is human. In this use, *pneuma* can mean the (whole) person and take the place of a personal pronoun (I, or me) just as soma and *psyche* can" (Bultmann, <u>Theology of the New Testament</u>, Part II, p.206).

> "Man does not consist of two parts, much less of three; nor are *psyche* and *pneuma* special faculties or principles (within the *soma*) of a mental life higher than his animal life. Rather, man is a living unity. He is a person who can become an object to himself. He is a person having a relationship to himself (*soma*)" (Bultmann, <u>Theology of the New Testament</u>, Part II, p.209).

We are dealing with three more fuzzy Greek words (*soma, psyche*, and *pneuma*). These words are not the precise tools that our Western mind desires, and their meaning varies depending on the context. In other words, it isn't that simple. In the face of such ambiguity it is important to not go beyond what is clear. Again, we can say that there is a part of me that is made in the image of God (good), and there is a part that is fallen (bad). To go beyond that is problematic, and perhaps dangerous.

See Endnote #9-1 for more details on this debate.

Endnote #12-5

More On Jeremiah 17

The Hebrew word *leb* in Jeremiah 17:9, which is commonly translated into the English word "heart," actually has a great variety of meanings in the Old Testament. According to The Brown-Driver-Briggs Hebrew and English Lexicon, the Hebrew word *leb* has the following range of meanings (Brown, F et al, pp. 524-525):

1. in the midst of the sea
2. the inner man, soul
3. the mind, knowledge, memory
4. inclination, resolutions and determinations of the will
5. conscience
6. moral character
7. the man himself
8. seat of appetites
9. seat of the emotions and passions
10. seat of courage
11. seat or organ of mental acts

According to Strong's Exhaustive Concordance of the Bible (Strong's #3820) , *leb* means (Strong, p58):

> "the heart; also used (fig.) very widely for the feelings, the will and even the intellect; likewise for the centre of anything."

Seeing this variety of meanings for the word, it becomes evident that it was the translators' choice to translate *leb* into the English "heart;" but as one can see there are many other possibilities that seem to include virtually any part of a human being. Which meaning was Jeremiah's intent in this passage? Nobody knows but God and Jeremiah. So we need to not be dogmatic about our choice. Probably the best we can say is "somewhere deep inside there is a part of man that is deceitful."

Endnotes for Chapter 13
"The Bad Part Of You"

Endnote #13-1

The Several Possible Meanings Of *Sarx* (flesh)

Following are further details on these four aspects of the flesh (C. Brown, Volume I, pp.678-680):

"Since the meaning of *sarx* varies radically from context to context, several distinct points must be made about the hermeneutics of this term."

"1. In some contexts, especially in the Old Testament, *sarx* calls attention to man's *creatureliness and frailty*; to the fact that he is fragile, fallible, and vulnerable. Thus 'all flesh is grass, and its glory is like the flower of the grass. The grass withers, the flower fades (Isa. 40:6-8; cf. 1 Pet 1:24). However promising and flourishing it appears at first sight, it holds out no certain promise of being able to withstand pressures which are brought against it."

"2. In other contexts *sarx* is used quite simply to denote the *physical* part of man, and does not offer an evaluation of man as a whole. 'Infirmity of the flesh' (Gal. 4:13) is physical illness; and flesh in 1 Cor. 15:39 means the physical substance appropriate to a given physical environment. The NT asserts the importance of the physical as over and against ideas which later developed in gnosticism. (a) Especially in Johannine thought this relates to the incarnation: 'the word became flesh' (Jn. 1:14; cf. 6:51-56);"

"3. To assess a truth or a phenomena "in accordance with the flesh (*kata sarka*, or *kata en sarka*) is to reach a verdict on the basis of purely *human, external, or natural considerations* . . . It is an assessment which leaves spiritual dimensions out of the account. Thus Paul admits that very few of the Corinthian congregation are wise in the 'ordinary' sense of the term (1 Cor. 1:26). Jesus warns the Pharisees that they are almost certain to misunderstand him, because they judge his testimony in purely human terms alone (Jn. 8:15)."

4. A quite different use of *sarx* appears in the major theological passages in Paul such as Romans 8:5-8, which concludes, 'those who are in the flesh can not please God.' In this passage the mental outlook of the flesh (*to phronema tes sarkos*) is hostile to God. 'Flesh' here evaluates man as a sinner before God. The outlook of the flesh is *the outlook oriented towards the self, that which pursues its own ends in self-sufficient independence of God.* (a) It is most striking, as R. Bultmann and R. Jewett have rightly pointed out, that Paul explicitly speaks of the 'fleshly' outlook in connection with the law and

circumcision. The fleshly mind in Gal. above implies 'shifting one's boasting from the cross of Christ (Gal. 6:14) to the circumcised flesh (6:13) (R. Jewett, op. Cit., 95). It represents the desire to secure one's righteousness independently of God's grace in Christ by means of the law. Thus in Jewett's words, '*sarx* for Paul is not rooted in sensuality but rather in religious rebellion in the form of self-righteousness' (p.114). As Bultmann expresses it, flesh represents 'trust in oneself as being able to procure life . . . through one's own strength and accomplishment" (C. Brown, Volume 1, pp.678-680).

Endnote #13-2

Fuzzy Words

Scientists create very specific names for the objects they study. They do this because most English words are not precise enough. Scientists need to know exactly what is the object under discussion. For example, a few of the humanoid creatures that have been identified have been given the following names:

Some humanoid creatures:
- Homo habilus (lived about 2 million years ago)
- Ardipithecus ramidus (5.8 million years ago)
- Orrorin tugenesis (6 million years ago)
- Sahelanthropus tchadensis (7 million years ago)

Scientists aren't just trying to make it difficult for the rest of us who aren't as well educated in their specialty. Rather, they need to create precise words as tools of their trade.

Our English words are not this precise. If you look in a dictionary for almost any English word, you will see some range of meaning. In some cases, the range is huge. For example, a common English word that is familiar to Christians is "mind." This is a noun, which is defined as follows by Webster's Ninth New Collegiate Dictionary (1983):

1. RECOLLECTION, MEMORY
2. A. the element or complex of elements in an individual that feels, perceives, thinks, wills, and especially reasons.
   B. the conscious mental events and capabilities in an organism.
   C. the organized conscious and unconscious capabilities in an organism
3. INTENTION, DESIRE.
4. The normal or healthy condition of the mental faculties
5. OPINION, VIEW
6. DISPOSITION, MOOD

A.   a person or group embodying mental qualities
B.   intellectual ability
7. Christian Science: GOD
8. A conscious substratum or factor in the universe

Now, do you know exactly what people mean when they refer to your mind? Of course you don't. The word has too broad a range of meaning for you to know which meaning is intended, until you understand the context in which it is being used.

Unfortunately, most words in both English and Greek have a significant range of meanings. They are therefore inexact tools for conveying what the writer intends, and we always need to be aware of this problem. To make it worse, since these are familiar words, we often think we know what a word means, or the word may be loaded with emotional meaning for us.

. The problem is compounded further when one attempts to translate Greek into English. For example, Strong's Exhaustive Concordance lists 13 Greek words that are translated into the English word "mind." Samples of the meanings of these words are:

- Deep thought
- Sane (of sound mind)
- Recollect
- Predisposition
- Intellect
- Have a sentiment
- To remind
- Spirit
- Modesty
- Suggest to memory
- Cognition
- Passion
- The feelings

Because of this wide range of meaning, when you read the word "mind" in an English translation of the Bible, you don't know very much about what the writer is saying unless you research which Greek word he was using. Even then you need to consider the context in which he was using the word to understand what he really meant.

Endnote #13-3

More Information On The Sinful Side

"As a modifier of verbs the phrase" ('according to the flesh') "has an altogether different meaning: It stamps an existence or an attitude not as natural-human, but as sinful" (Bultmann, Theology of the New Testament, Part II, p.237).

"That is to say, we do not have here, as it might seem, a mythological concept, as if 'flesh' were conceived as a demonic being. Neither do we have a physiological concept, as if 'flesh' here meant sensuality. Rather, the sinful has its origin in 'flesh' in this respect: that that conduct or attitude that directs itself according to 'flesh', taking 'flesh' for its norm, is sinful - as the cited sentence, Romans 8:5, clearly says: 'existence in the flesh' realizes itself in 'setting the mind on the things of the flesh' (RSV)" (Bultmann, Theology of the New Testament, Part II, p.238).

Please note that this term "setting the mind" is a translation of the Greek "*phroneo*," which means "an attitude."

"But the crucial question is whether 'in the flesh' only denotes the stage and the possibilities for a man's life or the determinative norm for it - whether a man's life 'in the flesh' is also life 'according to the flesh' - or, again, whether the sphere of the natural - earthly, which is also that of the transitory and perishable, is the world out of which a man thinks he derives his life and by means of which he thinks he maintains it. This self-delusion is not merely an error, but sin, because it is a turning away from the Creator, the giver of life, and a turning toward the creation - and to do that is to trust in one's self as being able to procure life by the use of the earthly and through one's own strength and accomplishments" (Bultmann, Theology of the New Testament, Part II, p.239).

Endnote #13-4

More Information On Flesh And Sin In Scripture

To try hard to please God using our willpower is not just futile, it is sin!

"To the category of conduct 'according to the flesh' belongs above all zealous fulfillment of the Torah; it does so because the man supposes he can thereby achieve righteousness before God by his own strength . . . This passage" (Philippians 3:3-7) "makes it especially clear that the attitude which orients itself by 'flesh', living out of 'flesh', is the self-reliant attitude of the man who puts his trust in his own strength and in that which is controllable by him" (Bultmann, Theology of the New Testament, Part II, p.240).

In fact, Bultmann points out that we can be <u>slaves</u> to the flesh. Bad roots produce bad fruit. When we transgress God's laws we sow a seed in the spirit realm, and we shall surely reap.

"That the worldly man is full of fear is indicated by Paul's reminder to the believers, 'For you did not receive the spirit of slavery to fall back into fear' (Romans 8:15). The period before faith, that is, was under the sway of fear. This sentence also shows that it was a period of 'slavery'. And that holds true not only insofar as both Judaism and paganism are under slavery to the 'elemental spirits of the universe,' which for the Jews are represented by the Torah, for the Gentiles by 'beings that by nature are no gods' (Galatians 4:1-10), but it especially holds true insofar as 'life after the flesh' leads into slavery to 'flesh' and 'sin.' Both he who 'desires' and he who is 'anxious with care,' both he who 'boasts' and he who 'relies upon' something, in reality makes himself dependent upon that which he supposes he can control . . . 'You are not your own; you were bought with a price' (1 Corinthians 6:20), that brings to light the whole paradox that he who apparently belongs to himself and has himself at his own disposal is a slave . . . it is, nevertheless, clear that this language stamps flesh and sin as powers to which man has fallen victim and against which he is powerless" (Bultmann, Theology of the New Testament, Part II, pp.243-245).

"If, now, the demand of the 'commandment' is this 'you shall not desire', its intent is to snatch man out of his self-reliant pursuit of life, his will to rule over himself. When it is further said that by this very demand, sin has awakened, that rests upon a conviction that man fundamentally strives in the wrong direction. The life that the Torah offers him (v. 10: 'for life')" (Romans 7:10) "he wants to attain himself, by his own power" (Bultmann, Theology of the New Testament, Part II, p.250).

We determine to do it with our own willpower. Here Bultmann is referring to Romans 7:10: *And the commandment, which was to bring life, I found to bring death.* As I have previously written, it is the perverse reaction that we naturally leap into from our fallen nature. When we realize God's demands, we automatically set out to obey Him – and by this we sin; because we set out to obey Him in our own strength.

If we could control our own life, Christ died in vain!

Endnote #13-5

The Primal Sin

In <u>Existence & Faith,</u> Rudolf Bultmann calls this tendency to "do it ourselves," or to be in control as the "Primal Sin." It is the tendency to want to be like God, which was Satan's sin and Adam and Eve's sin in the Garden of Eden (Genesis 3:5). Bultmann says,

> "The primal sin is not an inferior morality, but rather the understanding of oneself in terms of oneself and the attempt to secure one's own existence by means of what one himself establishes, by means of one's own accomplishments " (Bultmann, <u>Existence & Faith</u>, p.81).

> "There is no difference between security based on good works and security built on objectifying knowledge. The man who desires to believe in God must know that he has nothing at his own disposal on which to build this faith, that he is, so to speak, in a vacuum. . . man before God has always empty hands" (Bultmann, <u>Jesus Christ and Mythology</u>, p.84).

Note that "objectifying knowledge" is the attempt to create formulas or a rulebook by which we can figure out how God "works."

This drive to seek security by good works, or by objectifying God, is based upon the need to be in control. If we can figure out how God "works," then we can work the system for our own benefit.

> "For just this is the essence of flesh: the essence of the man who understands himself in terms of himself, who wants to secure his own existence. . . This then is sin: rebellion against God, forgetting that man is a creature, misunderstanding oneself and putting oneself in God's place" (Bultmann, <u>Existence & Faith</u>, p.81).

> "But man misunderstands himself and puts himself in the place of God. And every man comes out of a history that is governed by this misunderstanding. He comes out of a lie; he is determined by the flesh whose power he can not break. Were he to imagine that he could break it, he would assume that he does have himself in his own power after all and would thereby repeat the primal sin" (Bultmann, <u>Existence and Faith</u>, p.83).

Endnote #13-6

Where Does "Die to Self" Fit In?

There is a perspective that says that we should "die to self." Unfortunately, this view produces deadly results! As I have mentioned, there are some who teach this that don't really mean that everything inside a person has to die, but their listeners often hear something different. On the other hand, there are those who teach "die to self" who really do mean that everything inside a person has to die. This teaching typically says that it is "godly" to ignore your own needs and to <u>always</u> put them aside in order to serve others. You may have heard of the priority of living advocated by some:

First God.
Second, others.
Then you.

In fact, to want your legitimate needs met is labeled as "selfish." This perspective is often taught by those who have an extreme desire to "be good," and to serve the Lord. They then present "dying to self" as living radically for the Lord, of being totally sold out to Him.

Because it is taught with such zeal for the Lord, it may sound very good. However, those who have attempted to follow this teaching have found it to be destructive to them, and it truly is. There are good, solid, biblical reasons why it is destructive.

1. **First** of all, this teaching sets us to strive with our own will power to deny and bury our own needs and desires. To try to do it in our own power is sin, so such teaching is actually encouraging us to sin. Sin always brings destruction. In this case, one of the side effects is to make us feel like the wretched man of Romans 7:24, as we try so hard, but fail over and over again to accomplish this "dying." *O wretched man that I am! Who will deliver me from this body of death?* We are miserable because we are constantly aware of our "selfish" feelings. We can't seem to be able to purge them.

2. **Second**, the Bible does not tell us to <u>always</u> put aside our own needs. In fact, to strive to follow the Lord in this way is actually discouraged. Self-chastisement is not what God has called us to, **Colossians 2:23,** *These things indeed have an appearance of wisdom in self-imposed religion, false humility, and neglect of the body, but are of no value against the indulgence of the flesh.* When we do lay down our life for others, it must be out of love, not self abasement, **Romans 15:1-2,** *We then who are strong ought to bear with the scruples of the weak, and not to please ourselves. Let each of us please his neighbor for his good, leading to edification.* The Bible tells us to put others' needs on the <u>same</u> level as our own, not above them. **Philippians 2:4,** *Let each of you look out not <u>only</u> for his own interests, but <u>also</u> for the*

interests of others. (Underlining is mine).

3. **Third**, this teaching causes us to judge as "bad" what God created and called "good." "Die to self" is typically based upon a misperception of who we are, upon the idea that Romans 7:18 says *there is nothing good that dwells in me.* But this scripture makes it clear that "nothing good" dwells in only a part of me, and here Paul calls that part "my flesh." **Romans 7:18,** *For I know that in me (that is in my flesh) nothing good dwells.* As I have explained in Chapter 12, there is a part of me that is made in God's image. That part is a part of "me," and it is good. The problem is that "die to self" does not differentiate between the part of me that is "good" and the part that is "bad," and so "die to self" results in throwing out the good part along with the bad part. The bad part of me does have to "die," but <u>the good part has to be loved</u> to fullness of life. Otherwise I suffer.

4. **Finally**, trying to "die to self" <u>always</u> backfires and sets us up to be more "selfish," not less. Ignoring our legitimate needs is like saying to a person who is thirsty, "Ignore your thirst." If the person tries to ignore it, they don't become less thirsty; they become more and more thirsty. Eventually they will do almost anything, even "bad" things, to get a drink of water. That is the way it works with all of our many needs. We are needy creatures, because God made us that way. If our legitimate needs are not met in a legitimate way, then the need will grow and grow, and eventually we will be willing to accept inappropriate substitutes in order to quench our thirst. The unfortunate consequences that result are things such as affairs, promiscuity, lying, inability to empathize with another person, and bragging (and many more). These "selfish" behaviors are emotions "coming out sideways." So admonishing a Christian to "die to self" will <u>always</u> backfire! Read Chapter 11 on emotions for more details.

As mentioned above, Philippians 2:4 <u>does</u> say that we need to <u>also</u> look out for the interests of others. If we try to keep this command (or any other of God's commands) with our own willpower, we are actually sinning, and we will fail in our attempt. If we find ourselves having difficulty loving others, we need to see this as bad fruit and look for the bad root. We can only keep the laws of God if the desirable behavior is good fruit out of the good root, and the good root is Jesus living in that part of our heart.

Endnotes for Chapter 14
"Face To Face With Jesus"

Endnote #14-1

We Really "Know" Through Encounter

"God's Word is not a mystery to my understanding. On the contrary, I can not truly believe in the Word without understanding it. But to understand does not mean to explain rationally. I can understand, for example, what friendship, love and faithfulness mean, precisely by genuinely understanding. I know that the friendship, love and faithfulness which I personally enjoy are a mystery which I can not but thankfully receive. For I perceive them neither by my rational thinking, nor by psychological, nor by anthropological analysis but only in open readiness to personal encounters. In this readiness I can understand them in a certain way already before I am given them because my personal existence needs them. Then I understand them in searching for them, in asking for them. Nevertheless, the fact itself that my yearning is fulfilled, that a friend comes to me, remains a mystery (Bultmann, Jesus Christ and Mythology, pp. 43-44, underlining is mine).

Endnotes for Chapter 15
"A New And Living Way"

Endnotes: See Appendix A, "Experiences And Testimonies" for examples of Inner Child Prayer.

Endnotes for Chapter 16
"Deliverance And Inner Healing"
No Endnotes

Endnotes for Chapter 17
"It Is A Journey"

Endnote #17-1

God Leads You!
Though the following scriptures are usually used to indicate the leading of the Holy Spirit in general, they ring profoundly true regarding God's leading in your healing process.

> **Romans 8:26-32,** *Likewise the Spirit also helps in our weaknesses. For we do not know what we should pray for as we ought, but the Spirit Himself makes intercession for us with groanings which cannot be uttered. Now He who searches the hearts knows what the mind of the Spirit is, because He makes intercession for the saints according to the will of God. And we know that all things work together for good to those who love God, to those who are the called according to His purpose. For whom He foreknew, He also predestined to be conformed to the image of His Son, that He might be the firstborn among many brethren. Moreover whom He predestined, these He*

also called; whom He called, these He also justified; and whom He justified, these He also glorified. What then shall we say to these things? If God is for us, who can be against us? He who did not spare His own Son, but delivered Him up for us all, how shall He not with Him also freely give us all things? (Underlining is mine).

Endnote #17-2

We Need All Our "Tools"

There are two extremes that are traps for Christians. On one hand we ignore our Treasure Inside, and on the other we ignore our Head. Our culture ignores the Treasure Inside (heart) and only values the Head. Some of the difficulties that result from this are:

- Tendency to make heartless decisions.
- Inability to have intimate relationships or to be close to others.
- Inability to hear others' hearts and to be empathetic
- Not to have an awakened conscience.
- Inability to commune with the Living God.

Many seminaries have fallen into this extreme and see the Scriptures as something to be studied (like one would study physics), but not experienced. Some people have fled to this approach to life as a result of abuse of spiritual gifts in the church, or because of overly emotional parents who were unpredictable or irrational.

On the other hand, some Christians have come to the conclusion that it is not very "spiritual" to use logic and reason; and so they ignore their head. These people elevate the prophetic and the "word" they believe that they receive from God to such a place that it must be believed even if it is obviously unwise or imprudent. After all, God said it! But did He? Some Christian groups go so far as to ignore education and job experience as a necessary basis for doing a particular job, or performing a function in a church or ministry. Consequently many Christians are relegated to the bottom rungs of the economic ladder, because they are not qualified for well-paying jobs; and by ignoring prudent business principles many Christian churches and organizations are ill managed and ineffective.

Endnote #17-3

I Ignored My "Head"

I personally fell into the error of ignoring my head. In 1985 I was in a small church where the view was that everything that happened had a spiritual basis. I had been in the medical insurance business for years, and at this time my business began to deteriorate. My church friends and I sought the Lord: was I in sin? Was I not praying enough? Was I not contributing enough to the church? Was the Lord teaching me something? My office was located in a very spiritually dark part of Boulder, Colorado, so we wondered if it was an attack of the enemy. However, nothing we prayed about helped.

Finally, in 1993 the Lord told me to sell my business and to go to seminary to become a Christian counselor. When the Lord told me this, I knew positively that He had said this to me. Despite the decline in my industry, I found a ready buyer (a bit of a miracle). Two years later the man who had bought my business sold it to a large national company, and a year later the national company closed its doors!

What had started in 1985 was a "megatrend," a huge national change going on in the group health insurance business. All group medical insurance was beginning to be consolidated in gigantic HMO's (which is now the group insurance landscape), and small operations like mine were too small to compete. It was like Wal-Mart coming into a community and putting many of the local small businesses out of business.

But I had been blind to what was happening in the natural because my church's theology said that it was a spiritual problem. Had I opened my natural eyes in 1985 and studied the business environment, I would have discovered this "megatrend" going on, and I could have sold my business eight years earlier than I did-for much more money.

My closed-minded focus on the spiritual (my heart) and ignoring the natural (my head) cost me dearly. It was not the enemy, and it was not because I was in sin. And the Lord was the one who had to rescue me (by telling me to sell my business to become a counselor). Amazingly, I didn't figure out what had really been going on until 1996 when the national company closed the business down!

Endnote # 17-4

The Wrong Perspective Can Keep Us From Healing

There are some misperceptions about our Christian life that can prevent our receiving what Jesus has provided for us. Unfortunately, these misperceptions are very common among Christians and churches.

It has been my experience that Twelve Step groups are much safer places than are many churches. The Twelve Step groups are safer because the people in these groups see themselves differently. They know they are broken, that they are powerless to change their own life, and that they are in a process of walking out their new life.

In an Alcoholics Anonymous meeting, when a person wants to speak, the first thing they say is, "I am George Smith, and I am an alcoholic." These admissions eliminate the need to try to look good. Because others at the meeting freely admit their weakness and impotence, everybody there accepts and freely admits their own frailty. Since admitting of their struggles and failures is acceptable, the other people there are ready to reach out to them and help them.

Unfortunately, as Christians, we often feel the need to look like a good Christian. We fear that if we admit our shortcomings we will not be seen as "spiritual" and will not be accepted.

The following chart compares some Misperceptions with Reality.

Misperception	Reality
Living Our Own Life	Praying Without Ceasing
Get healed to get rid of the pain	Walk continuously in dependence on the Lord (This is why our healing is usually a long process, not a one-time bolt of lightning from the Lord).
Perspective (an illusion) that if I get rid of my wounds, I will be OK	Realization that I sin continuously, and I need the Lord's provision continuously - and always will (I have the nature to automatically react to every perceived wounding with bitterness, judgment, and blame).
I have the need to be accepted by others.	I have the need to be accepted by the Lord.
I want to prove that I am spiritual through a good life (look good, look "spiritual").	I admit my situation - that I sin a lot and need the Lord continually
Look Good	Be Real

Endnotes for Chapter 18
"Love, An Essential Ingredient"

Endnote #18-1

Trying To Be Something I Was Not

For many years I tried to be "balanced," focusing on developing those areas I wasn't so good at. I didn't realize I was trying to be something I am not rather than being who God made me to be.

I do need to develop some levels of functionality in areas I am not so good at. For example, my wife is not good at math, but she needs some level of skill in it to balance her checkbook, etc. But my emphasis should have been on honoring those gifts God gave me. He gave them to me for a purpose. When I deny them, I am saying God made a mistake.

Receiving "The Blessing" causes me to love who I am, rather than who I want to be. It is OK to say, "I am not very good at math," if that is true. It is likewise OK to say, " I am good at math" if that is a strength God gave me. Such recognition is not pride. It is the truth. It is a gift from God, and I did not do anything to earn it. I received it out of the generosity of God.

Endnote #18-2

We Have A Treasure Inside

'"Above all else, guard your heart' (Prov. 4:23). We usually hear this with a sense of 'keep an eye on that heart of yours,' in the way you'd warn a deputy watching over some dangerous outlaw, or a bad dog the neighbors let run. 'Don't let him out of your sight.' Having so long believed our hearts are evil, we assume the warning is to keep us out of trouble. So we lock up our hearts and throw away the key, and then try to get on with our living. But that isn't the spirit of the command at all. It doesn't say guard your heart because it's a criminal; it say guard your heart because it is the wellspring of your life, because it is a *treasure*, because everything else depends on it. . . *Above all else?* Good grief - we don't even do it once in a while. . . We live completely backward. 'All else' is above our hearts. Ill wager that caring for your heart isn't even a category you think in. . . But God intends that we treat our hearts as the treasures of the kingdom, ransomed at tremendous cost, as if they really do matter, and matter deeply" (Eldredge, pp.207-208).

Endnotes for Chapter 19
"The Big Picture"

Endnote #19-1

This Message Is Central To The Gospel!

This message of our transformation into the image of Jesus is central to the Gospel. It is not just a "feel good" appendage that we can dismiss as a nice option for those who are really hurting. In fact, this message absolutely permeates the New Testament, and it seeps out of every pore. Once one understands the message, it leaps off the page, especially in the writings of Paul and John. Try it and see. I will give you another example below.

The importance of this message is why Satan worked early and hard to kill it. The Epistles were written precisely to counteract Satan's attempts to rob people of the provisions that Jesus made for us. However, Jesus' provision for us is foolishness to man:

> **1 Corinthians 2:14,** *But the natural man does not receive the things of the Spirit of God, for they are foolishness to him; nor can he know them, because they are spiritually discerned.*

And this provision is bigger and more important than we realize:

> **1 Corinthians 2:9,** *Eye has not seen, nor ear heard, nor have entered into the heart of man the things which God has prepared for those who love Him.*

His provision for us to be changed into His image is an integral part of the entire message about Jesus, both about who He was and now still is, and about what He came to do and what He still does now.

This provision is a vital part of these truths, and without this provision we are defeated in this life. Without this truth, the impact of Jesus on our lives is gutted and only has relevance in saving us from hell. Being saved from hell is no small thing, but it is only a part of the message. He also has made provision for us while we walk on this earth.

And yet, the provision for being changed into His image while we walk this earth also impacts what will happen to us when we go into eternity. If we are not changed into His image during this life, we will be saved, but we will suffer loss.

This message is clearly spelled out in 1 Corinthians 3:9-17:

> 9.   *For we are God's fellow workers; you are God's field, **you are God's building**.*

10.   *According to the grace of God which was given to me, as a wise master builder I have laid the foundation, and another builds on it. But let each one take heed how he builds on it.*

11.   *For no other foundation can anyone lay than that which is laid, which is Jesus Christ.*

12.   *Now if anyone builds on this foundation with gold, silver, precious stones, wood, hay straw,*

13.   *each one's **work** will become manifest, for the Day will declare it, because it will be revealed by fire; and the fire will test each one's **work**, of what sort it is.*

14.   *If anyone's **work** which he has built on it endures, he will receive a reward.*

15.   *If anyone's **work** is burned, he will suffer loss; but **he himself** will be saved, yet so as through fire.*

16.   *Do you not know that **you are the temple** of God, and that the Spirit of God dwells in you?*

17.   *If anyone defiles the temple of God, God will destroy him. For the temple of God is holy, **which temple you are**." (boldface and underlining are mine).*

The "work" Paul is referring to is the <u>structure</u> that is being built, not the <u>effort</u> to build it, as has often been the interpretation. What is this "structure?" **You** are the building he is building. **You** are the structure. **You** are the temple.

* *You are God's building* (verse 9).
* *which temple you are* (verse 16).

Jesus doesn't want you to suffer loss as you enter eternity. The only way that can be possible is that you have been transformed into His image in this life, so that your "building" is gold, silver, and precious stones, not wood, hay and straw. He loves you so much that He came and died for you so that you can be eternally blessed.

Endnotes for Appendix A
"Experiences & Testimonies"

No Endnotes

Endnotes for Appendix B
"Codependence"

Endnote #Appendix B-1

It Would Be Better That A Millstone . . .

Then He said to the disciples, "It is impossible that no offenses should come, but woe to him through whom they do come! It would be better for him if a millstone were hung abound his neck, and he were thrown into the sea, than that he should offend one of these little ones. Take heed to yourselves. If your brother sins against you, rebuke him; and if he repents, forgive him. And if he sins against you seven times in a day, and seven times in a day returns to you saying, 'I repent', you shall forgive him." (Matthew 17:1-4).

In this scripture Jesus is saying that it would be better for the one who sins against you that he would have a millstone hung around his neck and be thrown into the sea than to have sinned against you. If he dos this to you, you need to call it to his attention (rebuke him) so that he can repent and not have to pay the consequences of his action that the laws of God will exact from him. If you do not point it out to him, that what he did was not OK, he may not even realize he has sinned. Even if he doesn't realize that he has sinned, the laws of God have been set in motion and he will suffer. You rescue him from these consequences by pointing it out to him. This is why the Lord instructs us, *rebuke him*.

Endnotes for Appendix C
"Communication Differences"

No Endnotes

Endnotes for Appendix D
"New Age Visualization"

Endnote #D-1

I Was Deceived

Several years ago, while I was unmarried, I encountered a woman who was a nationally known author and an old neighbor. She pursued a friendship, and I went along with it. I began to sense something unique about her. For instance, I discovered that when I was around her, I was able to more clearly see my own wounds and issues. I shared this with her. She laughed and said that many people had shared that same observation with her.

One evening she was doing a book signing for her most recent book, and she invited me to come with her. Afterwards we went to dinner with a number of her friends. When we arrived at the restaurant my spirit was troubled, but I ignored the warning. After all, she and her friends were very accepting of me.

I experienced several such incidents when with her when my spirit was troubled, but I ignored them all. I was fascinated with something in her. I was drawn by some sort of power she had. Then one day I was having dinner with her and several of her friends. She pulled out a magazine in which she was the featured writer. Her picture was on the front cover. The name of the magazine was, "New Age." At that moment it was as though the Lord had hit me between the eyes with a club. It was now so obvious that it made me laugh. The Lord's prior subtle warnings hadn't worked, so He finally spoke in a way that I could not ignore. I immediately cut myself off from this woman and her group.

After it was over I asked the Lord what this experience was about. I sensed that He allowed me to go down this path for awhile so that I would experience the power that does exist in the New Age Movement. I needed to experience this so that I would not be cocky, thinking "How could anybody be so dumb as to get sucked into such a weird, ungodly belief." Now I <u>knew</u> how a person could get sucked in. There is power in the New Age Movement, and it is fascinating. The New Age has drawing power and the ability to cloud our discernment. *For false christs and false prophets will arise and show great signs and wonders, so as to deceive, if possible, even the elect* (Matthew 24:24).

Fortunately, the Lord was in charge of my life, was using that experience to equip me, and rescued me in time. I suspect that if I had not gotten the message that last night, He would have done something really huge to get me out of danger. It is a lot less painful to hear the subtle message rather than to wait until God gets really firm.

Appendix F
Glossary

The definitions in this glossary are of necessity short, and are therefore not complete expositions on the words. Some of these terms are so vast that they have had many complete books written about them. My intent is to give a definition that is limited to the context in which I use the term in this book. On the other hand, I have purposely avoided short one-sentence definitions, because I have found that these abbreviated definitions often fail to adequately convey the concept and can lead to misunderstanding.

I have not attempted to define all the theological words in the Bible, but rather simply those that are related to the subject of this book and which may cause confusion if not defined. Here the English word is followed by the Greek word in Italics and the Strong's Concordance number in parenthesis, and then my definition.

I have also included a few terms that I have coined, or that are commonly used in Inner Healing. I would also refer you to the Index for other subjects.

Addiction: A compulsion to use any substance, behavior, or relationship which makes me feel a little better about myself. I am compelled to indulge in the addiction because it relieves the pain of the Big Hurt, if only for a moment. An addiction has its root in separation from self, because that is what causes the Big Hurt. The only cure for an addiction is healing the relationship with myself. In addition, there can sometimes also be a physical component to an addiction to a substance, such as alcohol or a drug.

Big Hurt: See Chapter 9.

Big Wound: See Chapter 9.

Blood of Jesus (Also see "Cross of Christ" below): In the Old Testament, "The Bible makes it clear that the satisfaction or payment for human sins was made by the death of a specified animal substitute: 'For the life of the flesh is in the blood, and I have given it to you upon the altar to make atonement for your souls; for it is the blood that makes atonement for the soul' (Lev. 17:11). In the New Testament, this Old Testament idea of sacrifice is applied to Christ's blood. References to the 'blood of Christ' always mean the sacrificial death of Jesus on the cross. References to the blood of Christ were made by Paul (Rom. 3:25); Peter (1 Pet. 1:19); John (Rev. 1:5) and the author of Hebrews (Heb. 9:14). Although all have sinned, 'we have redemption through His blood, the forgiveness of sins: (Eph. 1:7)" (Youngblood, p. 221).

And by Him to reconcile all things to Himself, by Him, whether things on earth or things in heaven, having made peace through the blood of His cross (Colossians 1:20).

"Thus Col. 1:20 refers to 'the blood of his cross.' Little blood was shed in crucifixion, so that must mean simply his death. . . References to the blood are a vivid way of saying that we owe our salvation to the death of Christ" (Elwell, p.163).

Body: *soma* (4983);

"In defining the concept *soma*, the place to begin is the naïve popular usage in which *soma* means body-as a rule, man's-which in a naïve anthropological view can be placed in contrast with the "soul" or the "spirit" (1 Thess. 5:23; 1 Cor. 5:3; 7:34). The body has its members, which comprise a unity within it (Rom. 12:4-8; 1 Cor. 12:12-26). . . it is clear that the *soma* is not a something that outwardly clings to a man's real self (to his soul, for instance), but belongs to its very essence, so that we can say man does not have a *soma*; he is *soma*, for in not a few cases soma can be translated simply "I". . . The *soma* is man himself, while *sarx*" (the flesh) "is a power that lays claim to him and determines him"(Bultmann, Theology of the New Testament, Part II, pp.193-201).

Context: In studying the Bible, it is of primary importance always to pay attention to the context. The context is the overall subject that the author is discussing in the current passage, as well as how this passage fits into the current paragraph, as well as how this paragraph fits into the current book of the Bible. There is a saying that "A text without a context is a pretext." A pretext is an attempt to make a scripture say what we want it to say, regardless of what the biblical writer intended. An extreme example of taking words out of context would be a ransom note made up out of words cut out of a newspaper and pasted onto a sheet of paper. The newspaper said those exact "words," but not with that meaning.

Cross of Christ (Also see "Blood of Jesus" above): "The blood and the cross" are terms that we commonly encounter. In Inner Healing, I have often heard the admonition to "Take it to the cross," and frankly, for a long time I didn't know what that meant. It means to appropriate for ourselves the whole provision that Jesus made for us through his incarnation, his death, his resurrection, his place at God's right hand, and all that means to us now. Therefore this admonition to "Take it to the cross" refers to appropriating the legal transaction that Jesus made possible (Chapters 2 through 8).

"It is 'by the blood of his cross' that God has made peace, in reconciling 'all things to himself ' (Col. 1:20ff.). This reconciliation is at once personal and cosmic. It comes because Christ has set aside the bond which stood against us with its legal demands, 'nailing it to the cross' (Col. 2:14).

Further, the cross is the symbol of our union with Christ, not simply in virtue of our following his example, but in virtue of what he has done for us and in us. In his substitutionary death for us on the cross, we died 'in him' (cf. 2 Cor. 5:14), and 'our old man is crucified with him,' that by his indwelling Spirit we might walk in newness of life (Rom. 6:4ff.; Gal. 2:20; 5:24ff.; 6:14), abiding 'in him'" (Douglas, p. 254).

"Thus the cross symbolizes the glory of the Christian gospel (1 Cor. 1:17); the fact that through this offensive means of death (1 Cor. 1:23; Gal. 5:11), the debt of sin against us was 'nailed to the cross' (Col. 2:14), and we, having 'been crucified with Christ' (Gal. 2:20), have been freed from sin and death and made alive to God (Rom. 6:6-11)" (Youngblood, p.315).

Faith: *pistis* (4902). This is a complex word, difficult to define in a few words. This concept is more properly dealt with as the subject of an entire book. However, I will try to give a basic flavor to this word: Faith is, "persuasion, i.e. credence; morally, conviction . . . especially reliance upon Christ for salvation" (Strong, p.58).

". . . for Paul, 'faith' is precisely the waiver of any accomplishment whatever and thereby is radical obedience . . . obedience which waives righteousness of one's own. . . 'Faith', which arises from 'what is heard' (Rom. 10:17), consequently contains a knowing. . . Ultimately 'faith' and 'knowledge' are identical as a new understanding of one's self. . . 'the surpassing worth of knowing Christ Jesus' (Phil. 3:4-10) . . . That is the reason why 'grace' as well as 'faith' can likewise be named as the opposite of 'works' to designate the basis for rightwising;" (making us righteous) "for 'faith' is what it is only with reference to the 'grace' which is actively present in the word" (Bultmann, <u>Theology of the New Testament</u>, Part II, pp.314-324).

Flesh: *sarx* (4561). This word has a wide range of meanings. It can simply mean my natural body, or the whole sphere of that which is earthly or natural, neither of which involve any ethical or theological judgment. It can also mean an existence or an attitude not as natural-human, but as sinful (Bultmann, <u>Theology of the New Testament</u>, Part II, pp. 232-238). See my Chapter 13, "The Bad Part Of You," for more details. Because of this range of meaning, we need to be aware of the context to determine the specific meaning in a given passage.

Glorified, glorify: *doxazo* (1392). "from 1391 (doxa), to render (or esteem) glorious (in a wide application" (Strong, p. 24).

> ". . . refers to the recognition belonging to a person, honor, renown. . . When we read in Rom. 3:23 that some come short of or lacked the glory of God, it means they are not what God intended them to be. . . *Doxa* embraces all which is excellent in the divine nature . . . More specifically, *doxa* means not the outward glorious appearance, attracting attention to the person or thing itself, but that glory shown from within reflecting in the appearance which attracts attention" (Zodhiates, p.1684).

Moreover whom He predestined, these He also called; whom He called, these He also justified; and whom He justified, these He also glorified (Romans 8:30). Therefore, when we have been changed into His image in an area of our heart, then we show forth His glory in that place. The bad root has been replaced by a good root, and then there is good fruit.

Grace: *charis* (5485). "graciousness (as gratifying) of manner or act (abstract or concrete) literally, figuratively, or spiritually: especially the divine influence upon the heart, and its reflection in the life; including gratitude (Strong. p.77)." 'by grace . . . through faith. . . the gift of God' in opposition to 'not your own doing . . . not because of works, lest any man should boast' (Ephesians 2:8f)" (C. Brown, Vol. 2, p.122). Grace is the active intervention of God into people, events, etc. "Justification by works of the law" (will power) "and justification by divine grace appropriated in man's faith exclude each other" (Bultmann, Theology of the New Testament, Part II, p.263) (Romans 6:14; Ephesians 2:8-9).

Humility, humble: *tapeinoo* (5013). "to make low, bring low" (Thayer, p.614). Mankind wants to be God, and to be "humbled" means to be put in our proper place. However, this does not mean to see oneself as a worm or as totally unimportant. Rather it means to see ourselves the way God sees us: He is the Creator, and we are the creature; and yet we are valuable because we are made in His image, because He loves us, and because we are valuable to Him. See Chapter 12, "The Good Part Of You," for more details.

Inner Healing: See "Sanctification."

Justify, justified: *dikaloo* (1344). "to render (i.e. show or regard as) just or innocent"(Strong p.23). It is an <u>act</u> by which a person is declared righteous.   Even though we are guilty of a sin, through the blood of Jesus we are acquitted. He pays the price and the sin is washed away, so we no longer have to pay the price for the just consequences of our sin. We are declared to be righteous.

> "If man's death has its cause in the fact that man in his striving to live out of his own resources loses his self, life arises out of surrendering one's self to God, thereby gaining one's self. . . Strictly speaking, righteousness is the condition for receiving salvation or 'life' . . . is not something a person has as his own; rather it is something he has in the verdict of the 'forum'" (=law court)". . . to which he is accountable. He has it in the opinion adjudicated to him by another" (in this case, God) (Bultmann, <u>Theology of the New Testament</u>, Part II, pp. 270-272).

Being justified freely by His grace through the redemption that is in Christ Jesus (Romans 4:24).

Justification differs from sanctification (see below). Justification is the washing away of the sin by the blood of Jesus, whereas sanctification is the subsequent infilling of the Holy Spirit into that area of our heart once it has been cleansed.

Know, Knowledge:

There are two families of words translated into English as "know" or "knowledge".

1. Ginosko (1097): usually to know experientially, as contrasted to *eido* (1492); usually to know intuitively.
2. Oida (1492), to perceive, know intuitively as contrasted with *ginosko* (1097)" (Zodhiates, pp. 1675,1675),

Clearly, it is important for us to find out which of these Greek words is being translated into the English words "know" or "knowledge" in a given passage, because these two Greek words have significantly different meanings. *Ginosko* takes place in our "Head", and *oida* takes place in our "Treasure Inside." There is a real danger in our culture to jump to the conclusion that "knowing" always relates to conscious learning in our intellect (our "Head"), and this is not always what the Greek is saying.

Mind, to mind, minded: Unfortunately, the English word "mind" is used to translate more than a dozen different Greek words, with meanings that range from "deep thought," to "soul," to "recollect," to "predisposition," to "intellect," to "have a sentiment," to "be mentally disposed," to "spirit," to "memory," to "cognition." Because of this wide range of meaning, when we read the English word "mind" in an English translation of the New Testament, at that point we don't know much. In order to understand what the writer is saying, we need to find out what Greek word is in the original text, and then find the meaning of this Greek word. We will also need to look at the context to determine the proper meaning.

For our culture, since we so honor the conscious "mind," there is a great danger that we will assume that "mind" is always referring to our "Head." As you can see, the biblical author may actually be saying something very different than this.

Peace: The Greek word *eirene* is the word translated into "peace". It means "peace, rest, in contrast with strife," and "denotes a state of untroubled, undisturbed well-being . . . Used together with *eleos* (1656), mercy for the consequences of sin, and also with *charis* (5405), grace, which affects the character of the person. Peace as a Messianic blessing is that state . . . wherein the derangement and distress of life caused by sin are removed. Hence the message of salvation is called the Gospel of peace" (Zodhiates p.1686)

Pride: Needing to see myself as more than I am (or think I am), or differently than how God sees me. It has its roots in separation from self and therefore a need to fill the empty place inside that craves love (the Treasure Inside). Pride comes from a place of woundedness. See Chapters 12, and 13 for more details.

Repent, repentance: *metanoeo* (3340): "to think differently or afterwards, i.e. reconsider" (Strong, p.17). "to change one's mind" (Thayer, p.405). "In a religious sense implying pious sorrow for unbelief and sin and a turning from them unto God and the gospel of Christ . . . Jesus draws a picture of the true penitent person. Such is assured of the forgiveness of the Father whose love has anticipated his return and gone out to seek and save" (Zodhiates, p.969, 970). Since repentance means to make a decision to go another way, we cannot do this for another person, but only for ourselves. Daniel did not "repent" for Israel. He confessed their sin and asked for mercy and forgiveness (Daniel 9:4-19).

Righteous, righteousness: *dikaios* (1342): equitable (in character or act); by implication, innocent, holy" (Strong, p.23). It is the state of one who has been justified.

"Righteousness is a present reality. . . Therefore, the righteousness which God adjudicates to man (the man of faith) is not 'sinlessness' in the sense of ethical perfection, but is 'sinlessness' in the sense that God does not 'count' man's sin against him (2 Cor. 5:19)" (Bultmann, Theology of the New Testament, Part II, p. 276). There can be a misunderstanding "that 'righteousness' denotes the ethical quality of a man, whereas in truth it means his relation to God" (Bultmann, Theology of the New Testament, Part II, p. 277). "Righteousness, then, can not be won by human effort, nor does any human accomplishment establish a claim to it; it is sheer gift. . . 'Righteousness', then, has its origin in God's grace - i.e. in His act of grace accomplished in Christ" (Bultmann, Theology of the New Testament, Part II, pp.281-284).

But to him who does not work but believes on Him who justifies the ungodly, his faith is accounted for righteousness (Romans 4:5).

Sanctify, sanctification: hagiazo (37) & hagiasmos (38). "to make holy, i.e. purify or consecrate" (Strong, p.7).

". . . means not only the activity of the Holy Spirit to set man apart unto salvation but also enabling him to be holy even as God is holy. It is not only the transfer of a sinner into the ranks of the redeemed but the change in the character of the redeemed sinner to be holy even as God is" (Zodhiates, p.1657).

In other words this is the process by which we are changed into the image of Jesus, one area of our heart at a time. This is what happens in Inner Healing, and Inner Healing is simply another word for Sanctification. It is the topic of this book! Also see "justification" above.

Sin: *hamartia* (266)): to miss the mark (and so not share in the prize) (Strong, p.10).". . . everything opposed to God . . . In 1 Jn, sin is seen as the opposite of love (agape)" (C. Brown, pp579, 582).

"The power of sin operates not only in the fact that it completely dominates the man who has become its victim, but also in the fact that it forces all men without exception into slavery;" (Bultmann, <u>Theology of the New Testament</u>, Part II, p.249).

In my words, sin is a behavior that sets God's laws in motion bringing destruction (death) into our life. That is why God warns us of these actions in His Word, and why God hates sin - it destroys His children.

Sin-nature: *anomia* (458): "illegality, i.e. violation of law or (gen.) wickedness" Strong, p.12). It is usually translated as **"iniquity"** in English. Whereas sin is a <u>behavior (what we do)</u>, our sin-nature is our <u>fallen nature (a part of who we are)</u>. This fallen nature is the tendency or propensity in us that impels us to sin . It is the tendency in us that I discuss in Chapters 4, "Judging Causes Problems," and Chapter 13, "The Bad Part Of You." We will never lose this tendency (our sin nature) as long as we are on this earth, because it is a part of fallen mankind.

Soul: *psyche* (5590): It is difficult to separate the meanings of *soma* (body), *psyche* (soul) and *pneuma* (spirit), as they are sometimes used interchangeably, and yet sometimes they refer to different aspects of mankind. However, it is important to recognize that:

> "Man does not consist of two parts, much less of three; nor are *psyche* and *pneuma* special faculties or principles (within the *soma*) of a mental life higher than his animal life. Rather, man is a living unity." Further, "The term *psyche* (soul), so often used with *soma* to designate man in his entirety, occurs relatively seldom in Paul. . . Paul uses *psyche* altogether in the sense current in the Old Testament-Jewish tradition; viz. to designate human life, or rather to denote man as a living being" (Bultmann, <u>Theology of the New Testament</u>, Part II, p.203-204).

Spirit: *pneuma* (4151) (spirit with a small "s"): This is a term that would require an entire book to describe, so my description here will of necessity be incomplete. The secular Greek word means,

> "A movement of air; the spirit, i.e. the vital principle by which the body is animated; a spirit, i.e. a simple essence, devoid of all or at least all grosser matter, and possessed of the power of knowing, desiring, deciding, and acting; God's power and agency; the disposition or influence which fills and governs the soul of any one; the efficient source of any power, affection, emotion, desire, etc." (Thayer, pp.520-523).

Pneuma is not necessarily used in all these ways in the New Testament. Also see "Body" (*soma)* and "Soul" (*psyche)* in this glossary.

> "In this use, *pneuma* can mean the person and take the place of a personal pronoun just as *soma* and *psyche* can. . . When Paul speaks of the *pneuma* of man he does not mean some higher principle within him or some special intellectual or spiritual faculty of his, but simply his self, and the only question is whether the self is regarded in some particular respect when it is called *pneuma*. . . Just as in the Old Testament (soul, life, self) and (spirit) are to a large extent synonymous, Paul, too, can use *pneuma* in a sense similar to that of *psyche*. . . In Rom. 8:16 the divine *pneuma* which Christians have received (v. 15) is expressly distinguished from 'our *pneuma*'."(Butlmann, Theology of the New Testament, Part II, p.206).

Treasure Inside: The image of God in you. See Chapter 9.

Understand, understanding, understood: This English word is used to translate more than a dozen different Greek words, with a wide range of meaning. Some of these Greek words refer to attributes in our "Head", and some in the "Treasure Inside." In other words, the understanding can be cognitive and conscious, or it can be intuitive or experiential and unconscious. Therefore, when we read the English word "understand" in an

English translation of the New Testament, we don't know much. We need to look at the specific Greek word used and the context to determine the proper meaning. The same danger exists as with the word "mind" mentioned above.

World: "World" is used in the New Testament to translate two different Greek words, *kosmos* and *aion*. The English word "world" therefore can have a range of meanings, such as the planet earth; the material world; the populated world; mankind as a whole; society as alienated from God and under the sway of Satan; and the complex of ideas and ideals which govern men who belong to the world in this ethical sense.

In my usage in Chapter 9, I am referring to everything in the natural world outside the individual, especially parents, siblings, peers, and the culture.

Appendix G
Bibliography

Adamson, James B. (1976). The Epistle of James. Grand Rapids, MI: Wm. B. Eerdmans Publishing Company.

Anonymous World Services, Inc., (1976). Alcoholics Anonymous. New York, NY: Alcoholics

Amplified Bible (1965). Grand Rapids, MI: Zondervan Bible Publishers.

Anderson, Neil T. (1990). Victory Over The Darkness. Ventura, CA: Regal Books.

Beare, Francis Wright (1981). The Gospel According to Matthew. New York, NY: Harper & Row, Publishers.

Beattie, Melody (1992). Codependent No More & Beyond Codependency. New York, NY: MJF Books.

Berkeley Version In Modern English, (1959). Grand Rapids, MI: Zondervan Publishing House.

Berry, George R. (1981). Interlinear Greek-English New Testament. Grand Rapids, MI: Baker Book House.

Bradshaw, John (1990). Homecoming. New York, NY: Bantam Books.

Brown, Colin, General Editor (1986). The New International Dictionary of New Testament Theology, 4 Vols. Grand Rapids, MI: Zondervan Publishing House.

Brown, F., Driver, S., and Briggs, C. (2001; rpt.). The Brown Driver-Briggs Hebrew and English Lexicon. Peabody, MA: Hendrickson Publishers, Inc.

Bultmann, Rudolf (1966). Existence & Faith, Shorter Writings of Rudolf Bultmann. New York, NY: The World Publishing Company.

Bultmann, Rudolf (1958). Jesus Christ and Mythology. New York, NY: Charles Scribner's Sons.

Bultmann, Rudolf (1961). Kergyma and Myth. New York, NY: Harper & Row, Publishers.

Bultmann, Rudolf (1955). Theology of the New Testament, Parts I-!V. New York, NY: Charles Scribner's Sons.

Carter, Charles W. (1977). The Wesleyan Bible Commentary, Volume Five. Grand Rapids, MI: Baker Book House.

Cloud, Dr. Henry and Townsend, Dr. John (1992). Boundaries. Grand Rapids, MI: Zondervan Publishing House.

Curtis, Brent and Eldredge, John (1997). The Sacred Romance. Nashville, TN: Thomas Nelson Publishers.

Dossey, L. (1985) . Beyond Illness: Discovering the Experience of Health. Boulder, Colorado: Shambhala.

Douglas, J. D. (1982). New Bible Dictionary, Second Edition. Wheaton, IL: Inter-Varsity Press, Inc.

Easterday, Douglas (1990).   Brochure, Restoration through Forgiveness. Lindale, TX: Last Day Ministries

Eldgedge, John. (2003). Waking The Dead. Nashville, TN: Thomas Nelson, Inc.

Elijah House, Inc. (1997).   Training for the Ministry of Prayer Counseling, Section I. Post Falls, ID: Elijah House, Inc.

Elwell, Walter A. (1984). Evangelical Dictionary of Theology.   Grand Rapids, MI: Baker Book House.

Erickson, Millard J. (1985). Christian Theology.   Grand Rapids, MI: Baker Book House.

Evans, Patricia (1992).   The Verbally Abusive Relationship.   Holbrook, MA: Adams Media Corporation.

Expositor's Bible Commentary. (1978).   Grand Rapids, MI: Zondervan Publishing House.

Fee, Gordon D. (1987). The First Epistle to the Corinthians.   Grand Rapids, MI: Wm. B. Eerdmans Publishing Company.

Fitzmyer, Joseph A. (1981). The Anchor Bible, The Gospel According To Luke (I-IX). Garden City, NY: Doubleday & Company, Inc.

Goldhuys, Norval (1979). Commentary on the Gospel of Luke.   Grand Rapids, MI: Wm. B. Eerdmans Publishing Company.

Groothuis, Douglas R. (1986). Unmasking the New Age.   Downer5s Grove, IL: Intervarsity Press.

Grosheide, F. W. (1953). Commentary on the First Epistle to the Corinthians. Grand Rapids, MI: Wm. B. Eerdmans Publishing Company.

Hagner, Donald A. (1993).   World Biblical Commentary, Volume 33A, Matthew 1-13. Dallas, TX: Word Books, Publisher.

Haldane, Bernard and Haldane, Jean (1997). Gifts. Dependable Strengths for Your Future. Seattle, WA: Bernard Haldane.

Harrison, Everett F., Editor. (1962). The Wycliffe Bible Commentary.   Chicago, IL: Moody Press.

Hulbert, Terry C. (1989).   "Gospels/Life of Christ: (Audio Tape Series).   Grand Rapids, MI: Institute of Theological Studies, Division of Outreach, Inc.

Interpreter's Bible, Volume X. (1953).   New York, NY: Abingdon Press.

Jackson, John Paul (1999).   Needless Casualties of War.   Fort Worth, TX: Streams Publications.

Jacobs, Joan, (1976). Feelings. Wheaton, IL: Tyndale House Publishers, Inc.

Jerusalem Bible, The; Alexander Jones, General Editor (1969). Garden City, NY: Doubleday & Company, Inc.

Joy, Donald M., Ph.D. (1985).   Bonding.   Nappanee, IN: Evangel Publishing House.

Keener, Craig S. (1993).   The IVP Bible Background Commentary, New Testament. Downers Grove, IL: InterVarsity Press.

Kohn, Alfie (1980). No Contest. Boston, MA: Houghton Mifflin Company.

Luther, Martin, (2003 rpt.). The Bondage Of The Will.   Translated by Packer, J.I. and Johnston, O.R. . Grand Rapids, MI: Fleming H. Revell.

Martin, Sandra (1998). The Joy Component. Duncanville, TX: Sandra Martin.

Martin, Walter, (1989). The New Age Cult. Minneapolis, MN: Bethany House Publishers.

Miller, Alice (1988). The Untouched Key. New York, NY: Doubleday.

Missildine, W. Hugh, M.D. (1963). Your Inner Child of the Past. New York, NY: Pocket Books.

Mitton, C. Leslie (1976).   New Century Bible, Volume On Ephesians. Greenwood, SC: The Attic Press, Inc.

Morris, Leon (1971). The Gospel According To John. Grand Rapids, MI: Wm. B. Eerdmans Publishing Co.

Morrisset, Robert (Undated). "Forgiveness". Unpublished outline. Post Falls, ID: Elijah House.

Morrisset, Robert (1996). "What is Forgiveness?". Unpublished brochure. Post Falls, ID: Elijah House.

Morrisset, Robert (1995). "A Common Misunderstanding". Elijah House News. Post Falls, ID: Elijah House.

New English Bible (1961): Oxford University Press.

New King James Version of the Holy Bible. (1983). Nashville, TN: Thomas Nelson Publishers.

Newman, Barbara M. & Philip R. (1991).   Development Through Life. A Psychosocial Approach.   Pacific Grove, CA: Brooks Cole Publishing Company.

Olson, Dave & Linda (1997). Listening Prayer. San Diego, CA: Dave & Linda Olson.

Palmer, Parker J. (2000). Let Your Life Speak. San Francisco, CA: Jossey-Bass.

Payne, Leanne (1991). Restoring the Christian Soul. Grand Rapids, MI: Baker Books.

Pearsall, Paul, PhD (1998).   The Heart's Code.   New York, NY: Broadway Books.

Rienecker, Fritz (1980).   Linguistic Key to the Greek New Testament.   Grand Rapids, MI: Zondervan Publishing House.

Sandford, John and Sandford, Paula (1979).   Restoring The Christian Family. Plainfield, NJ: Logos International.

Sandford, John and Sandford, Paula (1982).   The Transformation of the Inner Man. South Plainfield, NY: Bridge Publishing, Inc.

Sandford, John and Sandford, Paula (1985). Healing the Wounded Spirit. South Plainfield, N.J: Bridge Publishing, Inc.

Sandford, John and Sandford, Paula (1991). Basic Counseling School Manual. Seminar presented at the Basic Counseling School, Hinton, Alberta, Canada.

Sandford, John and Sandford, Mark. (1992). Deliverance And Inner Healing. Grand Rapids, MI: Fleming H. Revell.

Schlatter, Adolph (1995). Romans, The Righteousness of God. Peabody, MA: Hendrickson Publishers.

Schnoebelen, William (1991). Masonry, Beyond The Light. Chino, CA: Chick Publications.

Schonfield, Hugh J. (1985). The Original New Testament. New York, NY: Harper & Row.

Schore, Alan N. (1994). Affect Regulation and the Origin of the Self: The Neurobiology of Emotional Development. Hillsdale, NJ: Lawrence Erlbaum Associates, Publishers.

Seamands, David A. (1991). Healing for Damaged Emotions. Wheaton, IL: Victor Books.

Shelley, Bruce L. (1981). Church History In Plain Language. Dallas, TX; Word Publishing.

Siegel, Daniel J. (1999). The Developing Mind. New York, NY: The Guilford Press.

Smalley, Gary and Trent, John, PhD. (1986). The Blessing. New York, NY: Pocket Books.

Strong, James, LL.D., S.T.D. (1990). The New Strong's Exhaustive Concordance of the Bible. Nashville, TN: Thomas Nelson Publishers.

Stott, John R. W. (1979). The Message of Ephesians. Downers Grove, IL: Inter-Varsity Press.

Thayer, Joseph H., D.D. (1977). A Greek-English Lexicon of the New Testament. Grand Rapids, MI: Baker Book House.

Tregelles, Samuel P. LL.D. (1979). Gesenius' Hebrew and Chaldee Lexicon to the Old Testament Scriptures. Grand Rapids, MI: Baker Book House.

Wand, J.W.C., D.D. (1946). The New Testament Letters. London, UK: Oxford University Press

Warren, Rick. (2002). The Purpose Driven Life. Grand Rapids, MI: Zondervan.

Webster's Ninth New Collegiate Dictionary. (1983).   Springfield, MA: Merriam-Webster Inc., Publishers.

Whitfield, Charles L., M.D. (1987). Healing the Child Within. Deerfield Beach, FL: Health Communications, Inc.

Wigram, George V. (1979). The Englishman's Greek Concordance. Grand Rapids, MI: Baker Book House.

Wilder, E. James, PhD., et al. (1999). Living From The Heart Jesus Gave You. Van Nuys, CA: Shepherd's House, Inc.

Wilder, E James, PhD., (1999). The Red Dragon Cast Down. Grand Rapids, MI: Chosen Books.

Wuest, Kenneth S., (1980). The New Testament, An Expanded Translation. Grand Rapids, MI: William B. Eerdmans Publishing Company.

Youngblood, Ronald F., General Editor (1995). Nelson's New Illustrated Bible Dictionary. Nashville, TN: Thomas Nelson Publishers.

Zodhiates, Spiros, ThD. (1992). The Complete Wordstudy Dictionary, New Testament. Chattanooga, TN: AMG Publishers

Zodhiates, Spiros, ThD. (1986).   The Hebrew-Greek Key Study Bible. Chattanooga, TN: AMG Publishers.

Appendix H - Indices

Subject Index

Scripture Index

About The Author

In 1985, Edward Kurath found himself in a personal crisis. Through the ministry of others, the Lord used these struggles to bring healing and thus changed the course of his life.

He sold his insurance business of 22 years and enrolled in the counseling program at Denver Seminary. Following this, he spent four years as a staff counselor with Elijah House, a prayer counseling ministry located in Post Falls, Idaho.

He now has his own international counseling and teaching ministry. He is a Licensed Professional Counselor and a Licensed Marriage and Family Therapist.

He and his wife Kay live in Post Falls, Idaho. They have four children and eight grand children.

Kay is a career/life coach. Her approach leads people to discover their Divine Design so they can align their lives with God's purpose.

(Photo by Aundrea Harrell, Makawao, Hawaii)

Contact Information:

Book Orders:

- Online: www. divinelydesigned.com
            or
            Online bookstores, such as Amazon.com

- By Phone: (208) 755-9206

- Mail: Divinely Designed
             PO Box 999
             Post Falls, ID 83877, USA

- Your local bookstore

Counseling and Seminars

- Online: www. divinelydesigned.com

- E-mail: edkurath @divinelydesigned.com

- Phone: (208) 755-9206